HEARTS AND MINES

HEARTS AND MINES
The US Empire's Culture Industry

Tanner Mirrlees

UBCPress · Vancouver · Toronto

© UBC Press 2016

All rights reserved. No part of this publication may be reproduced, stored in a retrieval system, or transmitted, in any form or by any means, without prior written permission of the publisher, or, in Canada, in the case of photocopying or other reprographic copying, a licence from Access Copyright, www.accesscopyright.ca.

24 23 22 21 20 19 18 17 16   5 4 3 2 1

Printed in Canada on FSC-certified ancient-forest-free paper (100% post-consumer recycled) that is processed chlorine- and acid-free.

Library and Archives Canada Cataloguing in Publication

Mirrlees, Tanner, author
Hearts and mines : the US empire's culture industry / Tanner Mirrlees.

Includes bibliographical references and index.
Issued in print and electronic formats.
ISBN 978-0-7748-3014-0 (bound). – ISBN 978-0-7748-3015-7 (pbk.)
ISBN 978-0-7748-3016-4 (pdf). – ISBN 978-0-7748-3017-1 (epub)

1. Cultural industries – United States.   2. Mass media – Social aspects – United States.   3. Mass media – Economic aspects – United States.   4. Mass media – Political aspects – United States.   5. National security – Social aspects – United States.   6. National security – Economic aspects – United States.   7. National security – Political aspects – United States.   8. Civilization – American influences.   9. Imperialism.   I. Title.

P94.65.U6M57 2016   302.230973   C2015-905080-4
                                                  C2015-905081-2

Canadä

UBC Press gratefully acknowledges the financial support for our publishing program of the Government of Canada (through the Canada Book Fund), the Canada Council for the Arts, and the British Columbia Arts Council.

This book has been published with the help of a grant from the Canadian Federation for the Humanities and Social Sciences, through the Awards to Scholarly Publications Program, using funds provided by the Social Sciences and Humanities Research Council of Canada.

UBC Press
The University of British Columbia
2029 West Mall
Vancouver, BC V6T 1Z2
www.ubcpress.ca

Contents

Preface: The Personal Is Geopolitical / vii

Acknowledgments / xvii

Introduction: The US Empire's Culture Industry, circa 2012 / 3

1 The US Empire and the Culture Industry / 30

2 Public Diplomacy and Selling the American Way to the World / 64

3 The US Culture Industry: Still Number One / 103

4 The DOD–News Media Complex / 131

5 The DOD-Hollywood Complex / 163

6 The DOD–Digital Games Complex / 201

Conclusion: US Empire, Cultural Imperialism, and
Cultural Policy, at Large / 236

References / 259

Index / 299

Preface
The Personal Is Geopolitical

I grew up in a small town called Port Colborne, twenty-five minutes down a highway from the US-Canadian Peace Bridge. When I was a high school student, I worked as a dishwasher and cook at various local restaurants, often serving American lakefront cottage owners and tourists in the summer season. In my leisure time, I consumed more American cultural products than I did those "made in Canada," ritually watching Hollywood movies and TV shows. Each year, I visited family in the United States, shopping and going to the movies in Buffalo, New York, and Ocean City, New Jersey.

When I was a teenager, I was vaguely aware of Canadian nationalist worries about the presumed "threat" of Americanization, but my frequent trips to the United States and avid consumption of US cultural goods made the United States seem part of my whole way of life. On the whole, I harboured few critical feelings about America. And like many people all over the world, my general sense of America was largely derived from the media representations I was exposed to. I assumed that the US Air Force was like the one Tom Cruise piloted for in *Top Gun*; most American teenagers, I imagined, were indistinguishable from those blond, zit-free folks appearing in *Beverly Hills 90210*. Moreover, from action and war movies I gleaned that the US government was good, securing the world against the bad threatening Others; TV shows taught me that America was a vast and expansive middle-class society with few social antagonisms. The developing picture of America in my head, as painted by American entertainment, was enlarged when, in

1996, I got a job as a shift manager at Blockbuster Video. I remember feeling excited to be part of this company's "cast," and I relished the free movie, TV show, and video game rentals I got in exchange for upselling Coca-Cola and buttery microwave popcorn.

At this time in my life, I thought I would work at Blockbuster or some other service sector job, marry my high school girlfriend, and settle down to a middle-class life. For at least three generations, that's exactly what many working-class people in my hometown set out to do and thought they did. But that wasn't really an option for me, because the economic base of my community had shrunk, making fewer standard-waged jobs available. Plant closures due to offshoring, the decimation of unions and "good jobs," and the growth of part-time and low-waged retail jobs were facts of life for me and other teenagers. INCO and the Maple Leaf Mill, once a bastion of job security for many workers in the post–Second World War period (including my grandfather and uncle), now employed few workers. As a result, fewer young people, like me, followed their parents' work-life trajectories. Without good-paying jobs, people in my town spent less on everything, including video rentals. Facing a decline in profits, Blockbuster Video closed up shop, putting me out of a job.

Soon after, I searched around for a university degree program to enroll in, because that was what adults were saying young people would have to do if they wanted to "climb the ladder," from alienating, low-skilled, blue-collar jobs (that were mostly gone anyway) and toward what, at the time, many hoped would be meaningful and high-skilled, white-collar careers in the much hyped New Economy. After one year at a community college that aimed to prepare me to create graphics for marketing firms, I became the first in my family to enroll in university. I attended the School of English and Theatre Studies at the University of Guelph between 1997 and 2001.

In the week of the September 11, 2001, attacks, when al-Qaeda agents hijacked and flew commercial airplanes into New York City's World Trade Center, I started my Master of Arts degree in the same program. For that entire week, like so many around the world, I watched the 24/7 news media replay videos of airplanes exploding into the towers and the towers smoking and then falling. Stunned journalists kept asking: "Why do they hate us?" Though Canada was not attacked, TV's power to visually conjoin the United States and Canada made the terror feel close to home; suddenly, once distant discussions about US strategic interests were ever-present, in bars, in daily newspapers, on the radio, and on TV. When TV

Preface

brought 9/11 and the Bush administration's declaration of a global War on Terror to Canada, I wanted some time and space to read, think, talk, and learn more about what was going on – to dialogue with others. I wanted to exchange ideas about why the attack had happened, gain a deeper sense of what the causes of terrorism were, and contemplate what the best response might be. I wanted people all over the world to do the same. As a liberal-minded student, I felt that public deliberation in the United States, Canada, and elsewhere about these matters was not only needed but also the best means to responsive policy and global understanding. Public deliberation about terrorism, its causes, and the most effective way of stopping it, however, proved difficult.

On September 20, 2001, George W. Bush appeared on American and global TV to declare a new struggle between the United States and "Terror." He told citizens around the world, "Either you are with us, or you are with the terrorists." Through TV, Bush told me, along with citizens in every country watching his speech, that if we didn't choose to give unwavering and absolute support to US foreign policy, we would be considered a threat to the nation. Bush's speech attempted to impose closure on the space for public deliberation about war, a space that should always remain open in a democracy, given war's immense consequences. But there seemed to be no time for this, as Bush imposed his dominant idea on the public about what the US national security interest was and was not, what the United States should and must do, and who America's friends and enemies were. This upset me. US foreign policy was being determined by the executive branch in the name of the people, without giving the people a chance to deliberate about it. I bristled at this unilateralism and felt myself become increasingly critical of US foreign policy and the US Empire itself.

A genuine choice is never forced, but the US president seemed to be telling citizens they had to make a choice between two options he had already chosen: support the nation in its global War on Terror or be framed as a supporter of Osama bin Laden's global jihad. I didn't identify with either option and thus rejected both. Looking for a path between them, I sought out alternative sources of information that might help me develop a more multidimensional view of what was going on. In independent bookstores and on alternative or left news websites, I gathered information that assured me the world system was more complex than Bush's TV address had made it seem. I picked up *9-11* by Noam Chomsky (2001), a collection of short interviews with Chomsky that posed provocative questions that weren't being asked elsewhere. Was the invasion of Afghanistan the most effective way of reducing terrorism? Was it true that the United States had in the past terrorized civilians to achieve its interests? Was the primary cause of growing antipathy toward the United States not the country's "way of life" but the foreign policy decisions that often supported the interests of transnational companies at the expense of democracy?

These questions led me to more articles, books, and websites, which emboldened my sense that the media representations of America I had grown up with concealed a more complex and ugly reality. I self-reflexively came to see the image of America – which I had carried around in my head for most of my life – as a by-product of media representation, not of knowledge. With the goal of better understanding the world, I moved to Toronto in September 2002 to enter a new PhD program: the Joint Program in Communication and Culture at York University and Ryerson University. There, I enrolled in courses on theories of the new imperialism and the politics of culture offered by historical materialists like Aijaz Ahmad, Scott Forsyth, Colin Mooers, Leo Panitch, and Ellen Meiksins Wood. These scholars were kind, generous, and wise; they helped me develop a deeper knowledge of the US Empire and emboldened my conviction that the kind of world system it aimed to promote and police needed to be changed, and for the better. From my perspective, the future did not look bright as the social problems of class inequality and poverty, racial and sexual oppression, human-caused climate change and ecological calamity, cultural discord, ethnocentrism, and xenophobia persisted and were worsened by the US-led War on Terror.

In the time between 9/11 and the commencement of my studies as a PhD student, the United States put Iraq in its crosshairs, and I was deeply afraid of a new world war. Bush said Saddam Hussein was in cahoots with Osama bin Laden (and was responsible for 9/11) and that he possessed weapons of mass destruction (WMDs) and intended to use them against the United States. He said that Iraqis wanted the United States to liberate them. To protest this dubious pretext for war, I joined the Toronto Coalition to Stop the War, and in solidarity with millions of people in nearly every major city around the world, I marched and sang in opposition to war and in support of a better world. I believed that if millions of people all over the planet united behind the peace activists, we could stop the US government from waging a pre-emptive war against an autocratic state and basically defenceless people. After the February 15, 2003, global peace demonstrations rocked the planet and inspired *New York Times* journalist Patrick Tyler to claim there were two twenty-first-century superpowers, the United States and global public opinion, I believed that in the new global media age, the empire might bend to the multitude's will. But I was wrong. The first ever global pre-emptive expression of anti-war solidarity did not stop the war. People all over the world were united, but they were defeated.

On the morning of March 20, 2003, the United States invaded Iraq. Its "Shock and Awe" campaign, or the aerial bombardment of Baghdad for nearly two full days, was a global media event and a highly rated TV spectacle. As millions of people around the world sat in front of their TV sets, eyes fixed on bombs falling and exploding on Baghdad, perhaps oblivious to the civilians killed, the global peace movement continued to rally. With a number of diverse social movements, I participated in a one-day peace festival in Toronto called "One Big No" at Nathan Phillips Square on April 12, 2003. Radio personalities from the CBC, Canadian musical acts like the Cowboy Junkies, The Lowest of the Low, Danny Michel, The Rheostatics, and DJS, plus clowns, stilt-walkers, jugglers, poets, puppeteers, and installation artists, with thousands of Torontonians, joined the peace movement to oppose the war. At this event, activists, academics, and artists expressed their solidarity with the American and global peace movement, fostered new pacifist networks for consciousness raising, and peacefully and creatively conveyed their dissent, surrounded by police.

Yet, apart from this public intervention, the world felt far less friendly, for the Iraq war was a polarizing event that stoked partisan flames. As the US occupation proceeded throughout 2003 and into 2004, my pacifist politics and criticisms of the news media's framing of war were met with resentment, astonishment, and rejection by friends, family members, and even strangers. My late dad and some of my old high school acquaintances who did not share my privilege of a university education called me a "terrorist sympathizer." Some conservative-minded family members thought I was "crazy" and believed I had been brainwashed by the "cultural Marxist elites" who were supposedly running Canadian universities. I also took my protest to the Internet, where on chat forums and in the comments sections of online magazines like *Mother Jones*, I got into spirited arguments with war boosters, who were quick to demonize me. Angry face-to-face and virtual responses to my pacifist position suggested to me that some citizens had internalized the US Empire's policy ideas as their own. Why was this so? How did dominant ideas about America and US foreign policy get generalized as "common sense"? What had compelled so many people to internalize and reproduce a particular idea about the world that was not of their own making and not even supported by the states in which they lived?

The culture industry (the means of producing, distributing, and exhibiting cultural commodities) and the circulation of popular imagery of and stories about America and US war policy provided some clues. Contrary to the laissez-faire myth of a deep antagonism between the US government and the culture industry, the US government seemed to have enlisted media companies and cultural products in a large-scale campaign to package, promote, and sell America and US war policy to the world. Between the 2002 US invasion of Afghanistan and 2003 invasion of Iraq, *Rebuilding Afghanistan*, made by the US Office of Public Diplomacy and Public Affairs, was rebroadcasted by private and public TV networks in at least twenty-five countries, from India to Mexico. Hundreds of US journalists were vetted by and embedded with the military's PR corps, and Colin Powell and Donald Rumsfeld appeared on TV news networks citing Judith Miller's *New York Times* story about Iraq's possession of WMDs to sell the pre-emptive war in Iraq to a skeptical public. Hollywood films like *Tears of the Sun* (2003)—shaped in part by the US Navy's entertainment liaison officer Bob Andersen—framed US military intervention as motivated by humanitarian goodness, while on Fox TV, *24*'s Jack Bauer raced against a ticking terrorist time bomb, assassinating and torturing foes to secure America and the world. Meanwhile, Leo Burnett, an advertising agency, cashed in on a multi-million-dollar public relations contract with the US Army to tell young Americans they could improve themselves by serving in its "Army of One" in Iraq. The video game industry piggy-backed on this program of military-led moral uplift, rolling out Second World War nostalgia games like *Medal of Honor: Rising Sun* (2003) to immerse players in a first-person simulation of the "good war" against Nazism, while *Desert Storm II: Back to Baghdad* was sold and played at the same time as the actual siege of Baghdad occurred. Soon after, the United States Patent and Trademark Office received almost thirty trademark applications from firms looking to capitalize on the exclusive use of the "Shock and Awe" phrase for War on Terror–branded commodities like baby toys, bowling balls, energy drinks, and condoms.

Throughout the 1990s, some globalization theorists declared that the world system of territorial nation-states, national culture industries, and national media-cultures had been eclipsed by a new one of cross-border flows of capital, people, technology, media, and ideas. Yet, the US territorial state's post-9/11 decision to wage a unilateral war of choice to impose its societal model in Iraq and beyond, and the US culture industry's manufacture of nationalistic cultural products complicated globalization theory. The world system was clearly still one in which the power of the US territorial state, culture industry, and national identity persisted. These circumstances moved me away from globalization theory toward emerging political-economic and historical research on the US Empire and capitalist imperialism. David Harvey's (2003) *The New Imperialism* and Leo Panitch and Sam Gindin's (2004) path-breaking article "Global Capitalism and American Empire" were hot off the press, and these works offered compelling models for understanding the dynamics of the US Empire and imperialism, past and present. Debates about the determinations, form, and effects of the US Empire intrigued me, as did the prospect of examining how and why the culture industry supported the US Empire.

What is the US Empire? Why did so many people in the Unites States and elsewhere seem to consent to and look favourably on American foreign policies, personnel, and practices, no matter how dubious or controversial? How does the US government attempt to move the "hearts and minds" of citizens inside and outside of its own territorial borders toward its own strategic interests through the culture industry and its products? Why does a culture industry that is not owned or controlled by the US government produce so many cultural products that support official policy? What is the precise nature of the relationship between the US government and the culture industry: one of conflict or symbiosis? How do US state and culture industry relationships support the production and flow of cultural commodities that glorify the US Empire's policy, personnel, and practices?

These political questions grew out of my desire to understand and stop the most contentious and calamitous US foreign policy decision of the early twenty-first century and ended up becoming key research questions for my PhD dissertation, "The State of Cultural Imperialism," which I wrote between 2003 and 2007. Soon after completing my PhD, I set out to publish a book version of my dissertation with UBC Press. I would have liked to have completed this book many years ago, but what one aspires to do is not always what one is able to do, especially in these precarious times. As I continued to revise this book, I read outside of my comfort zone and integrated new material, both theoretical and empirical. This was a humbling experience that expanded my understanding of the US Empire's culture industry; conceptual and normative political positions I took for granted as a PhD student seemed less obvious to me and needed further qualification. My knowledge about the US Empire's culture industry also deepened between 2008 and 2012 as I taught numerous upper-year courses on topics like foreign policy, state theory, global media, development communication, cultural imperialism, and public diplomacy at three different universities, where student questions helped me hone my position.

Also, I almost abandoned this project when Barack Obama was elected president of the United States in 2008. My naïve hope that Obama would and could fundamentally change the direction of the US Empire tempered my critique. I regret that I was wrong. For a short time, though, the Obama presidential win seemed to revivify the United States' global clout and roll back the international creep of anti-Americanism. Yet, this "Obama effect" dissipated when it became apparent that his administration was continuing the War on Terror. A little more than two years after Obama's re-election campaign video "Ending the War in Iraq: A Promise Kept" crossed channels, American F/A-18 fighter jets were striking ISIS in Iraq, and hundreds of US military advisors were being deployed there. As Obama's two-term presidency nears its end, it pushes the Trans-Pacific Partnership trade deal in East Asia while the US DOD and State Department "pivot" toward this region to contain a rising China. The US Empire expands, globalizing capitalism and warring against multiplying enemies, across territorial boundaries, with no foreseeable end in sight.

The consequences of the twenty-first-century geopolitical economy of the US Empire are well documented: trillions in public wealth spent on breaking and failing to rebuild foreign nation-states; overstretched and eroded domestic state capacity for provisioning public goods to its own citizens; and the undermining of the democratic ideals at home, which are supposedly secured with drone strikes, surveillance, and even torture abroad. As the world system undoubtedly undergoes significant changes, these trends are accompanied by projections, both fearful and celebratory, of the decline and fall of the US Empire.

For the short term, the United States remains the world system's only empire, as America's economic might, military preponderance, and culture industry are without rival. This book offers an introduction to the geopolitical economy of the US Empire's culture industry and the state and corporate sources of an imperial commodity culture. It focuses on the past and present geopolitical-economic underpinnings of US government strategies to promote "America" to the world, and US media–corporate efforts to circulate cultural commodities to consumers in transnational markets. By doing so, it sheds light on the joint US government and media-corporate initiatives, policies, and practices that substantively shape the content of many seemingly autonomous cultural commodities into a means of trying to influence how people all over the world perceive America. This book's study of the state and corporate organizations that shape what people read, watch, and hear forwards critical knowledge about the US Empire's culture industry; it also works to de-fetishize this empire's army of cultural commodities, which war against the democratic prospect of people forming reasoned opinions about the role of the US government in world affairs and having these opinions as a guide to their own destiny.

Acknowledgments

This work could not have been completed without the time, knowledge, and energy of many people and organizations.

By way of acknowledgment, this book has been published with the help of a grant from the Federation for the Humanities and Social Sciences, through the Awards to Scholarly Publications Program, using funds provided by the Social Sciences and Humanities Research Council of Canada.

I am grateful to the many instructors and professors I met while shifting between jobs at the University of Guelph-Humber, Ryerson University, and York University for being kind and supportive.

Thank you to my many wonderful colleagues at the University of Ontario Institute of Technology, whom I am fortunate to work with and learn from: Shahid Alvi, Nawal Ammar, Scott Aquanno, Rachel Ariss, Andrea Braithwaite, Carla Cesaroni, Aziz Douai, Gary Genosko, Rob Halpin, Alyson King, Tim MacNeill, Thomas McMorrow, Jonathan Obar, Isabel Pedersen, Barb Perry, Tess Pierce, Phil Shon, Andrea Slane, and Arshia Zaidi.

Cheers to Scott Forsyth, David McNally, John McCullough, Barbara Crow, and Paul Boin, who made my PhD defence a wonderful experience and who long after that continued to encourage me.

A big thank you to Greg Albo, Sam Gindin, Leo Panitch, Bryan Evans, Pance Stojkovski, and others for giving me a formative socialist-project education that continues to be meaningful.

Thanks also to Robin Andersen, Enda Brophy, Nicole Cohen, Greig de Peuter, Greg Elmer, Matt Flisfeder, Mark Hayward, Kirsten Kozolanka, Ganaele Langlois, Pat Mazepa, Alan Sears, Sarah Sharma, Mitu Sengupta, David Skinner, John Shields, Dwayne Winseck, and others for being so generous. I have learned much from you and your many contributions to knowledge.

I am indebted to Shane Gunster, Richard Maxwell, and David Grondin, as well as one anonymous reader, for substantive reviews and immensely helpful revisions suggestions. The knowledge they shared with me throughout the review process shaped and strengthened this work in significant ways.

I express sincere gratitude to my judicious, wise, and extraordinarily patient editor at UBC Press, Emily Andrew, who supported the most rigorous and beneficial peer review process I've ever known, plus many excellent and memorable conversations over lunch together at L'Espresso Bar Mercurio. My appreciation extends to UBC Press editor Megan Brand, who helped fine-tune my writing, and to Laraine Coates, who helped my book reach readers.

My affection goes out to my dear friends Nick M., Mark S., Ian R., and Greg K., who motivated me to continue working on this project each time I put it on the shelf. I am especially grateful to my great pal Joe K.-K. for sharing his immense knowledge of left history, film, and TV, over pints.

I would like to thank my family (C.M., J.M., M.E., A.S., U.B., U.R., S.K., E.K., M.K.) for being so supportive of and patient with me over the many years it took to complete this work. Lauren: thank you for being you (talented, creative, brilliant, meticulous, hilarious, cat-loving) and especially for being my best friend for the past decade.

Finally, I would like to dedicate this work to Colin Mooers, my PhD mentor and friend, who for the past twelve years has been wonderfully supportive and inspiring in too many ways to list. Had it not been for Colin and our critical dialogues at Il Gatto Nero about historical materialism and the worldly conditions that it aims to understand and change, for the better, this book would not be.

HEARTS AND MINES

Introduction
The US Empire's Culture Industry, circa 2012

In 2012, the US market for cultural goods was the world's largest, and the US culture industry – or the US-based media companies that produce, sell, distribute, and exhibit cultural commodities – was the world's most prosperous and powerful (Bond 2013; PricewaterhouseCoopers 2013).

The Walt Disney Company, Time Warner, News Corporation, Comcast-NBCUniversal, Viacom, and other mega US-based media companies straddled the globe, doing business across national markets, polities, and cultures. CNN, the biggest twenty-four-hour TV news channel in the world, outreached its rival networks BBC World News, Al Jazeera, Sky News, and Euronews and edged out smaller competitors to become the "undisputed #1 news brand in Africa" (CNN 2012). The reign of Hollywood over world cinema continued to be undisputed as well, with the six major studios raking in 62.7 percent of the global box office (Hoad 2013) and making inroads into China, which that year surpassed Japan as the world's largest film market next to the United States. As Hollywood blockbusters like *The Avengers*, *Skyfall*, and *The Dark Knight Rises* pervaded world theatres, American TV shows beamed across borders to be scheduled by TV networks spread over four continents. The CBS TV series *CSI: Crime Scene Investigation* captured the attention of more than 63 million viewers in 2012 and was the year's most watched TV show (Mail Today Reporter 2012). The top two bestselling video games in the world gaming market of 2012 for the Xbox 360, the PlayStation 3, the Wii U, and the personal computer were *Call of Duty: Black Ops*

II and *Madden NFL 13*, both produced by US-based game companies (Tassi 2013). As of May 2012, the ten most Internet-pirated films of all time were Hollywood-owned as well, with *Transformers*, *Inception*, *The Hangover*, and *Star Trek* being downloaded millions of times from torrent sites, along with HBO's globally watched *Game of Thrones*, which was reportedly the year's most pirated TV show (Lewis 2013).

The US culture industry's global economic power and the near omnipresence of American cultural commodities – news programs, motion pictures, TV shows, video games, and interactive digital content – are facts. While capitalism (the profit-oriented production of commodities for sale using the waged and unwaged labour power of workers and privately owned technology) drives the US culture industry's growth, the US national security state has come to rely on and harnesses this industry's cultural commodities as instruments of hegemony, or pro-American consent-building, particularly regarding issues of national security and war. In a period typified by a world economic slump, growing anti-imperial sentiment, and burgeoning media markets in the BRICS bursting with clashing ideas and images, the US state is ramping up campaigns to make America and US foreign policy attractive all over the world. In this context, US media corporations are aiding the government's efforts by mobilizing the labour of cultural workers to manufacture and project positive images of American power to readers, listeners, and viewers.

In 2012, US-based Capitol Records' teen idol Katy Perry hooked up with the US Marines to make the MTV-ready music video for her hit song "Part of Me." In this video, Perry catches a cheating boyfriend but instead of getting angry at him gets taken by a military recruitment ad that tells her "All Women Are Created Equal, Then Some Become Marines." To spite her boyfriend and cope with heartbreak, Perry joins the Marines, cuts her hair, camo-paints her face, and endures basic training at the Marine Corps Base Camp Pendleton alongside actual US Marines, who dance, march, train, sing, and fight along to her song. Following the production of "Part of Me," Perry said shooting the video turned her into a "wannabe Marine" and made her "so educated on people in the service," whom she has "always respected" as "the heart of America" (Warner 2012).

In the same year the US Marines enlisted Perry's pop image to help it brand itself as a women-friendly establishment and portray military service as a righteous path to women's liberation, Warner Bros. Pictures, a Hollywood giant, prepared to release *Man of Steel* (2013). This blockbuster film casts the classic DC Comics character Superman alongside the men and women of Team Edwards Air Force Base and the air force's multi-billion-dollar stealth jet, the F-35 Joint Strike Fighter. Superman and the F-35 fly over Smallville together, at the speed of light, securing it from alien evil. "It was a great choice," said Mark Scoon, an executive at Warner Bros. "Our experience at Edwards has been beyond phenomenal, no matter how you look at it – from the bottom up, or top down. There has been an extraordinary [amount of] cooperation across the board" (Mowry 2012).

While *Man of Steel* travelled the globe, taking in $25.8 million from China's box office in one weekend alone, NBC was broadcasting a reality show called *Stars Earn Stripes*. Produced by reality TV mogul Mark Burnett and hosted by retired military general Wesley Clark, the show pairs B-list actors like Dean Cain (Superman on *Lois and Clark: The New Adventures of Superman*), Eve Torres (a WWE Divas champion), and Todd Palin (husband of Sarah Palin and snowmobile race champ) with US Navy SEALs, Marines, and Green Berets to complete military training challenges in competitions to win money for various charities. NBC's website described the show "as an action-packed competition show that pays homage to the men and women who serve in the US Armed Forces and our first-responder services" (NBC 2012). In response to criticisms that it cheapened war by turning it into a hokey sports competition, US Navy Corpsman Talon Smith candidly quipped: "Entertainment is how America will receive information" (Yahr 2012).

Yet, in 2012, many Americans were not passively receiving information about the military from TV; instead, it came from the interactive entertainment market, wherein "console wars" between companies like Sony, Microsoft, and Nintendo raged and millions of people paid for digital software to virtually "play kill" as soldiers in "dirty wars." *Medal of Honor: Warfighter*, for example, was marketed by Electronic Arts (EA) in 2012 as "an aggressive, gritty, and authentic experience that puts gamers in the boots of today's most precise and disciplined warrior." In the virtual boots of elite Tier 1 operators, players travel from Pakistan to the Philippines to Somalia, Madrid, Yemen, and elsewhere, battling al-Qaeda. According to EA, the game was "written by active US Tier 1 Operators while deployed overseas and inspired by real world threats." Seven US Navy SEALs worked as EA consultants on this virtual war commodity, and one of them was even a bona fide member of SEAL Team Six, which killed Osama bin Laden (Martin 2012). To let players browse, buy, and try the guns they virtually shoot in the game, *Medal of Honor*'s website promotionally linked to the retail sites of major US weapons manufacturers (Meier and Martin 2012). And in major cities across the United States, massive billboards for *Call of Duty: Black Ops II* loomed over pedestrians and urged them to virtually enlist in war: "There is a soldier in all of us."

As video games enlisted citizens as soldiers in virtual and virtuous versions of a US-led global War on Terrorism, the Silicon Valley companies that run much of the Internet and World Wide Web, virtual worlds (*Second Life*, developed by Linden Lab), social media platforms (Facebook and Twitter), and video-sharing websites (YouTube) were hosting pages, feeds, and channels for Department of Defense (DOD) and State Department PR events. In the massive online world of *Second Life*, the army created two islands with the purpose of encouraging young people to join the military. The first island was a "welcome centre" information kiosk through which you could contact a recruiter, while its "experience hub," the second island, helped avatars to have "virtual military experiences like jumping out of airplanes, and rappelling off of towers and using a weapon" (Shachtman 2008). If avatars performed these army activities well, the DOD awarded them with points toward Linden dollars, which they could then spend on virtual army T-shirts and ball caps.

While the US Army was busy virtually recruiting followers, the United States Agency for International Development was, with the help of private contractors, running ZunZuneo on the actual island of Cuba. This "Cuban Twitter" aimed to give Cubans a platform for interactive communications uninfluenced by their state – but influenced by the US state's public diplomacy 2.0 campaign. After pulling subscribers into this social media network with apolitical soccer updates, popular music clips, and weather forecasts, ZunZuneo's operators planned to flood user accounts with messages aimed at galvanizing "smart mobs" to ignite a "Cuban Spring" against the communist state (AP 2014).

In 2012, the US government was making use of the culture industry's new media platforms to conduct interactive information operations and customized public diplomacy campaigns, but it also continued its long-standing practice of promoting its policy, personnel, and practices through the older media of print, radio, and TV news broadcasting. Across the fifty states, more than 14,000 private newspapers, radio stations, and TV networks carried feel-good "news releases" about the activities of American soldiers, sailors, airmen, marines, and civilians, all compliments of the DOD's Joint Hometown News Service (JHNS). From its bases – Fort Meade, Maryland, and Norfolk, Virginia – the public affairs staff of the news service generated about 500,000 glowing stories that year, like holiday greetings from global military bases, family homecoming celebrations, college graduation ceremonies, and tear-jerking soldier-dog reunifications (ACC Public Affairs 2013). Profit-seeking news companies passed this DOD-produced free content on to their readers, listeners, and viewers through their outlets, but without letting their audiences know that the DOD's Joint Hometown News Service was the originating source (AP 2009). While the DOD was flooding the local news with camouflaged soldier-generated content, the Broadcasting Board of Governors (BBG), a US federal government public diplomacy agency responsible for managing a network of broadcasting firms, was promoting America around the globe. The BBG's Voice of America, Radio Free Europe/Radio Liberty, Radio and TV Martí, Radio Free Asia, and the Middle East Broadcasting Networks (Alhurra TV, Radio Sawa, and Afia Darfur) transmitted content intended to "inform, engage and connect people around the world" with America, reaching more than 175 million people per week (BBG 2012).

Clearly, 2012 was a busy year for US state-employed public affairs specialists who, with help from media corporations and their cultural workers, shaped music videos, films, TV shows, news stories, video games, virtual enclaves, and tweets to be sold in markets as a persuasive means of selling the US Empire to the world.

The Topic and Premises

This book is about the US Empire's culture industry, a concept I employ to name a contradictory convergence of the interests of the US national security state and US-based media companies. The US Empire's culture industry flags a geopolitical-economic nexus of the government (striving to promote itself and engineer public consent to dominant ideas about America and US foreign policy around the world) and US-based yet globalized media corporations (seeking to make money by producing and selling cultural commodities to consumers in world markets). Although the US state and media corporations are different kinds of organizations that pursue distinct interests (the former, national security and the latter, profit-maximization), this book focuses on showing how they often work together to manufacture and sell commodified imagery and messages of America at home and abroad. The geopolitical interests of the US state and the capitalist goals of US media corporations do not always march in lockstep, and at times they conflict, yet the US Empire's culture industry points to a more collusive relationship between these two organizations than is often recognized.

Through chapter-by-chapter analyses of the past and present-day partnerships and alliances between the US national security state – the

Department of State and the Department of Defense in particular – and US media corporations, this book explores how and why the US state facilitates and legitimizes the profit interests of these corporations and, in addition to operating its own publicity agencies, also contracts, subsidizes, works with, and gives them economic incentives to make commercial TV shows, films, news stories, video games, and web content that aim to win people's consent to the US Empire. This book covers articulations of the US government and US-based globalized media corporations and concentrates on the consolidation of tenuous state-corporate media complexes that manufacture cultural commodities to make money and manage public opinion. By documenting the mutually reinforcing interests of the US state and media corporations, two institutions not commonly associated with one another and whose connections are not always apparent, this book forwards a critique of the US Empire's culture industry.

Hearts and Mines also offers a generalist introduction to the US Empire's culture industry using a popular writing style and numerous relevant examples that ground key concepts and support theoretical claims. It documents key sectors of the US Empire's culture industry – public relations, TV and print news, Hollywood, and video games – to show the US state and media companies working together to produce cultural commodities that aim to make the US Empire a normal part of life. While there are significant books that deal with single topics such as the US Empire (Cox and Stokes 2012; Panitch and Leys 2004; Panitch and Gindin 2012; Harvey 2003, 2005; C. Johnson 2004; Wood 2003); US foreign policy, public opinion, and the news (Herman and Chomsky 1988; Rutherford 2004; Taylor 1997); the global media and culture industries (Fitzgerald 2012; Flew 2007; Herman and McChesney 1997; Scott 2005; Sparks 2007b; Thussu 2006; Tunstall 2008; Winseck and Jin 2011); international political communications, public diplomacy, and propaganda (Cull 2008; Dizard 2004; Snow 2003; Taylor 1997); digital war games (Halter 2006; Huntemann and Payne 2010); and popular militainment (Andersen 2006; Boggs and Pollard 2007; Dittmer 2010; Der Derian 2001; Jenkins 2012; Stahl 2010), this book brings these and other related topics together into one volume and aims for a synthesis.

Each chapter in this book intervenes in a specific area of inquiry relevant to the past and present geopolitical economy of the US Empire's culture industry to document the source organizations that own, produce, distribute, and exhibit imperial cultural commodities that sustain the empire as a way of life. Through qualitative analysis and interpretation of US state and corporate source material (policy documents, official reports, and transcripts) and secondary material (news articles, widely available public data, and related scholarship), *Hearts and Mines* explains how symbiotic geopolitical and economic relationships between the US state and media corporations drive the production and flow of US imperial commodity culture, and it addresses the consequences of this unity.

The book's first premise is that the United States is an empire, which is a significant point of contention among scholars. At the end of the Cold War, Tomlinson (1991) said that "globalizing modernity" heralded the end of the US Empire and the rise of "a different configuration of global power" that supports the "interconnection," "interdependency," and "integration" of all areas in the world system but is not directed by an imperial state or set of states. Tomlinson's notion that "globalization" is "a far less coherent or culturally directed process" than imperialism, which was "a purposeful project" or "the intended spread of a social system from one center of power across the globe" (175), was echoed by other prominent scholars in the 1990s (Appadurai 1997). At the turn of the millennium, Hardt and Negri (2000) declared that the twentieth-century imperialist convergence of the geopolitics of territorial states and the economics of national corporations had been superseded by a new post-statist type of sovereignty – a deterritorialized, bio-political, and transnational global capitalist empire. For these theorists, "the United States does not, and indeed, no nation-state can today, form the center of an imperialist project" (xiv). The end of the US Empire in theory extends to the outright disavowal of it in American presidential rhetoric. In a 2013 speech to the United Nations, for example, President Obama described the government's unique willingness to "use all elements" of "power, including military force," to secure its "core interests in the region[s]" of the Middle East and North Africa. He said the United States "must remain engaged" there for the sake of America's "security" and for the world's, which "is better for it." Obama spoke of the central and directive role of the United States in spreading liberal capitalism across the globe, saying "America is exceptional" because it has "shown a willingness through the sacrifice of blood and treasure to stand up not only for our own narrow self-interests, but for the interests of all." Yet, Obama maintains, "The notion of [an] American empire may be useful propaganda, but it isn't borne out by America's current policy or public opinion" (White House 2013).

Chapter 1, "The US Empire and the Culture Industry," argues that the US Empire is not passé or an anti-American "propaganda" term; it is current and actually exists. How, then, is the United States an empire? What is its historically specific form and style of rule? What instruments of power does it possess? What drives its expansion? Who rules the US Empire? What ideas and beliefs justify it? Is it in decline? And why and how is the culture industry significant to the US Empire? Chapter 1 answers these questions with its broad overview of the US Empire and the culture industry.

The book's second premise is that the US culture industry's global expansion is driven by transterritorial capitalist goals, backed by the geopolitical power of the US territorial nation-state. The exploration in this book of the intertwining of culture industry economics and state geopolitics poses a counterpoint to those who perceive the global pervasiveness of American cultural commodities as an effect of "free markets." Recall, for example, former CEO of Time Warner J. Richard Munro's (1990) claim that "no soldier or representative of our government is in the business of being an enforcer of Hollywood." "When people buy 'Hollywood'," continues Munro, "they do so freely ... because they want the best value for the best price" and because American cultural products "are as good [as] or better than those produced by any other country." Munro sees American cultural products as getting pulled from the United States across borders by sovereign consumers, who demand that Hollywood give them the films, TV shows, and music videos they want, when they want them. Dutifully, reflectively, and reactively, US-based globalizing media corporations do just that, spreading their commercial content across TV, theatre, and mobile screens everywhere – to make consumers happy.

A more complex market-centric explanation of the US culture industry's global dominance moves beyond this neoliberal ideal of the sovereign consumer and contemplates the competitive advantage of US media companies vis-à-vis the following: emerging media rivals in less powerful countries; the vertically and horizontally integrated ownership structures that incorporate and raise barriers to entry for smaller firms; oligopolistic market control strategies, block booking, and flexibly selling cheap; huge production and marketing budgets that underpin "high quality" products and channel transnational attention toward them; globally or universally resonant texts, which companies design to appeal to people all over the world; and large and wealthy English-speaking markets of consumers that are culturally similar to the United States (Rauschenberger 2003).

The focus on the capitalist determinations of the culture industry's power is important but ultimately one-sided, for capitalist logics alone cannot explain the US culture industry's global dominance. This undialectical economistic explanation ignores politics – namely, the role of the US state in "enforcing" the culture industry's business interests in the United States and across borders as benefactor, buyer, and booster of its commodity flow. The free market explanation also downplays how the culture industry and the US state may align to bring about changes in other countries. As Dean Garfield, a former executive vice president and chief strategic officer of the Motion Picture Association of America (MPAA), says, "Our industry" is "a powerful force of public diplomacy" and "effectual in advocating for and enabling economic change *more than* ideological change"(USC Annenberg 2009). To show how the US state buttresses the culture industry's economic interests and demonstrate how the culture industry helps the state to bring about economic *and* ideological changes around the world, Chapters 2 and 3 highlight the state organizations, policies, and practices that supported the historical growth and current global dominance of the culture industry.

Chapter 2, "Public Diplomacy and Selling the American Way to the World," focuses on the PR apparatus for promoting the American Way to the world from the First World War to the post-9/11 global War on Terror. What are the key junctures, institutions, and policies in the history of US public diplomacy? How did public diplomacy agencies work with media firms to promote America and expand markets for their products? What strategies did they use to do so? Chapter 3, "The US Culture Industry: Still Number One," highlights the capitalistic and state strategies that support the twenty-first-century global prosperity of the US culture industry. How does this industry expand into other countries? What strategies do US media corporations employ to integrate non-US culture industries into their chains and networks of power? What political strategies does the US state use to support the culture industry? Against the notion that the sun has set on US global media dominance, this chapter highlights the continued top position of the US culture industry in the world market and government support for it.

The book's third premise is that the US Empire's growth is tied to war – preparing for war, waging it, and glorifying it – and focuses on how the permanent war effort is routinely supported by the US state and media companies, which manufacture cultural products that aim to engineer public consent to militarism. Andrew Bacevich (2005, 2) observes how, in the post-9/11 period, US culture was increasingly "militarized," with American national identity and well-being defined and expressed "in terms of military preparedness" and "military action." Patriotism is thus reduced to unquestioning support for military policy, personnel, and practices; state coercion is the first solution to each global problem; and American global military dominance is absolutely necessary in a world divided between a righteous and benign Us and an evil and threatening Them. "If war is to be opposed," says Judith Butler (2010, ix), "we have to understand how popular assent to war is cultivated and maintained." What, then, are the organizational sources of the militarization of American culture that make ongoing war look and feel so good?

In 1969, Herbert I. Schiller (1969) pointed to a "military-industrial-communications complex"; in 1970, Senator J. William Fulbright (1970) scrutinized a "Pentagon Propaganda machine"; and in the late 1990s, the postmodern international relations scholar James Der Derian (2001) focused on the "military-industrial-media-entertainment network." These complexes and networks expressed an alliance of the US military and media firms and their joint manufacture of popular films, TV shows, media events, exhibits, and more, intended to persuade civilians to identify their interests with militarism. However, the notion that the military and news companies, film and TV studios, and video game firms actively collaborate to push militarizing commercial images and messages on the public is controversial, even for some political economists of communication. Herman and Chomsky's (1988) "propaganda model" (PM), for example, conceptualizes symbiotic interactions between state and media-corporate elites when describing the roles of "sourcing" (concentrated elite attempts to source media companies with content so as to set the media agenda and frame) and "flack" (organized elite efforts to denounce dissident voices that don't align with the status quo) as "filters" that, though exogenous to the culture industry, nonetheless shape its output. But the PM, though still analytically useful, discounts the ways that military and corporate organizations may *routinely* work together to *intentionally* make cultural products with the goal of moving public opinion toward the status quo and making money. Herman and Chomsky claim consensus-building media output sometimes "arise[s] at least in part from knowing joint action, sometimes by government request or pressure," but then go on to say that "these are the exceptional cases" and that the market is "the main mechanism through which the PM does its work" (cited in A. Mullen 2009, 17).

This book contends that "knowing joint action" by US military and culture industry elites is really not that "exceptional" because military public affairs officers and corporate image-makers frequently team up to manufacture cultural products for ends that serve military PR goals and capitalism's bottom line. Chapters 4, 5, and 6 focus on how the DOD and media corporations, Hollywood studios, and video game developers come together to make militarized cultural commodities that sell war as a way of life as well as sell in markets. By documenting the organizations, policies, and practices that bring the US military and media firms together, these chapters show how joint state and corporate actions to make war consensus-building cultural products are quite common in the history of the US Empire. Chapter 4, "The DOD-News Media Complex," centres on how the DOD's PR arm and news media corporations converge to produce a steady flow of commodified war propaganda. Chapter 5, "The DOD-Hollywood Complex," focuses on how the DOD and Hollywood studios co-produce blockbuster films that glorify state violence and discourage anti-war storytelling. Chapter 6, "The DOD-Digital Games Complex," examines a mutually beneficial relationship between the DOD and video-game companies and shows how central war simulation games have become to the DOD's preparation for, promotion and waging of, and recovery from war. These chapters explain the existence of war media commodities with regard to their sources of production and illuminate the complexes that shape, script, produce, package, and promulgate them.

The book's study of the intertwining of the US state and media companies and the ways these organizations collaboratively shape media and cultural products that carry images of and messages about America to influence opinion and behaviour raises questions about the nature of US society, the US media system, and cultural policy. Does the US Empire's culture industry support or undermine the country's democratic ideals? What do the workings of this industry suggest about the characteristics of the American media system? And how might the existence of the US Empire's culture industry complicate the notion that the US state does not do cultural policy? The Conclusion, "US Empire, Cultural Imperialism, and Cultural Policy, at Large," addresses these questions.

Method: A Geopolitical Economy of the Culture Industry

This book's study of the US Empire's culture industry is guided by the political economy of communications method, which is often (though not always) defined by four significant tenets: holism, historicism, moralism, and praxis (Wasko, Murdock, and Sousa 2011, 2). In what follows, I discuss how this book mobilizes this method and complements it with a geopolitical focus.

Holistic

This book's political economy approach is *holistic* in that, instead of "treating 'the economy' as a bounded domain, it focuses on the relations between economic practices and social and political organizations" (Wasko, Murdock, and Sousa 2011, 2). McChesney (2008, 12) says the political economy of communication method links "the media and communications systems to how both economic and political systems work, and how social power is exercised, in society." It focuses on how capitalism (the profit motive, competition, supply and demand) and the state (policy, law, and regulation) influence and shape the structure, conduct, and output of the culture industry. Through structural and institutional analysis of the relationships between profit-seeking media firms and government agencies, policies, laws, and regulations, political economists illuminate the "power relations that mutually constitute the production, distribution, and consumption of resources, including communication [and cultural] resources" (Mosco 2009, 24). This book recognizes that the US culture industry is owned by market-oriented media companies, but it holistically focuses how US media corporations link and connect to the state and how their economic goals intersect with and are often buttressed by the US state's geopolitical aims. By focusing on the active role played by the US state as a supporter of the culture industry and shaper of the cultural products it sells, this book's political economy approach highlights how geopolitical power intersects with and influences the culture industry's capitalist logics and cultural output. *Hearts and Mines* thus attends to the mutually reinforcing power interests and structural alliances between the government and its culture industry, two institutions not commonly associated with one another and whose connections are not always apparent. The holistic study of the constitutive role of the state and the culture industry is of growing importance to communication historians (Allen and Stamm 2014), and state media, communication, and cultural policies have long been a significant focus in the critical political economy of communication tradition (Freedman 2008, 2014; McChesney 2004, 2008).

Historical
In addition to being holistic, this book is historically grounded. Political economists recognize the importance of trying to understand what's new but say the fixation only on "what's going on now" at the expense of "what came before" is a problem, especially in *presentist* capitalist societies where many have difficulty connecting the past to the present to a number of possible futures. McChesney (2014a, 17) claims: "Our job is to understand the present and put it in historical perspective," and this book's political-economic approach does so by contemplating what's new about the US Empire's

culture industry in the early twenty-first century but with an eye to the past. Much of this book focuses on the US Empire's culture industry in the first decade of this century, but it also addresses important continuities with the past that tend to be obscured by those who say we are living in radically new times. In 2011, Hillary Clinton declared that the United States was in a new global "information war" for "minds and attitudes" (Tharoor 2011). Noting the rise of competitors to US ideological influence, such as Al Jazeera, Russia Television, and user-generated digital media, Clinton said the United States must get back "in the game" of doing "what we do best" (Tharoor 2011). By that, Clinton meant working with media firms to engineer the consent of publics all over the world to elite constructions of America. Yet this book argues that the US state never exited the global "game" of working with media firms to make products that aim to sell the US Empire. By contextualizing twenty-first-century developments with respect to the *longue durée* of the US Empire, it shows how state-culture industry complexes are not a distinguishing feature of the post-9/11 period but rather extend back to the early twentieth century – the First World War, to be exact.

Moralism
This book's political economy approach is also concerned with moral and ethical questions surrounding the essence of a good society and the normative role of cultural production in it. What is a good society, a secure one? A deeply democratic and socially just one? What ends should culture fulfill? Profit? Propaganda? Education? Public deliberation? This book's approach places the ends and means of the US Empire's culture industry into the moral and ethical spheres so as to turn them into objects of judgment, but without falling into the trap of strategic thinking, which represents a good society as a more secure one, as though security is naturally an inevitable perquisite for or corollary of a good society. This book takes issue with the notions that a more "secure" society is necessarily a better one and that culture's normative role in society is to secure capitalist profits and state power. Fascist Germany was obsessed with securitizing culture, and so too was the Soviet Union. But these were undemocratic and unjust societies. The United States is not a dictatorship or autocratic country, but the state's national security goal has justified many undemocratic and unjust means for achieving it, such as the violation of civil liberties, the erosion of governmental accountability, transparency blackouts, clandestine operations and assassinations, human rights abuses, and insidious forms of propaganda,

censorship, and surveillance (Blum 2004; J. Risen 2014). Cultural products that affirm these means of security afflict the republic. For political economists, a good society is a deeply democratic and socially just one in which cultural products inform, inspire, and educate citizens to deliberate about the most substantial and consequential issues of the day while fostering rituals that cement human bonds of empathy, understanding, and solidarity. This book's judgment of the US Empire's culture industry is guided by the belief that the United States and its means of producing and distributing cultural goods do not have to be the way they are and by the hope that they could be much better – that is, in ways that are more democratic and socially just.

Praxis
The moral and ethical concerns of the political economy approach "place its practitioners under an obligation to follow the logic of their [critical] analysis into practical action for change" (Wasko, Murdock, and Sousa 2011, 2). Praxis is the idea that academics ought to try to understand the world and change it in some way for the better. While administrative researchers often seek to understand and change things on behalf of the powerful, critical researchers question the assumptions, goals, and actions of the powerful. Putting the lie to the conservative populist view of academics as being out of touch with reality or eggheads in some free-floating ivory tower, many founding US communications studies scholars – Carl Hovland, Paul Lazarsfeld, Harold Lasswell, Wilbur Schramm – conducted "administrative" research in support of the US Empire (Hardt 1988), or, as Lasswell (1970) later put it, the "institutions of war and oligarchy." During the First World War, they applied their knowledge to research on psychological warfare to enhance the US military's capacity for waging it (McDowell 2003). Throughout the Cold War, the CIA and DOD played a significant role in financially underwriting communication studies as a "science of coercion" to incubate new tools for managing the minds of target publics at home and abroad (Simpson 1994). Indeed, the US state funded academic research "in areas that could overtly (propaganda studies) or covertly (development communication studies) promote American (anti-Soviet) campaigns" (Bah 2008, 186). In the post–Cold War era, strategic think tank researchers like David Rothkopf (1997, 1) wrote articles such as "In Praise of Cultural Imperialism?," which advise the US government to join forces with American media corporations to "win the battle of the world's information flows, dominating the airwaves as Great Britain once ruled the seas." In the global War on Terrorism, liberal theorists

of "soft power" exalted the US culture industry as an instrument of geopolitical power. Nye (2004) called on the US State Department and the DOD to join forces with Hollywood, news media corporations, and PR firms to attract people to US values, identity, and foreign policy. Like Nye, Fraser (2003, 13) asserts that, though US military "hard" power should be used by the state to force others to do what it wants in certain circumstances, "American leadership in the world must [also] depend on the assertion of soft power – namely, the global appeal of American lifestyles, culture, forms of distraction, norms, and values." Fraser (266) says, "American soft power (movies, television, pop music, fast food) promotes values and beliefs that, while contentious, are ultimately good for the world." Moreover, he argues that "America's weapons of mass distraction are not only necessary for global stability, but also should be built up and deployed more assertively throughout the world." There is clearly a long line of administrative-minded scholars who put their minds to work for the US Empire, and many continue to align their research with its goals. This book's *critical* political economy research, however, forwards the idea that the status quo of US Empire ought to be changed and can be changed.

Theoretical Antecedents: Herbert I. Schiller, Redux

The topic of the US Empire and the culture industry has long been important to many leading political economy of communications scholars, from all over the world (Boyd-Barrett 1977, 1998; Dorfman and Mattelart 1975; Downing 2011; Herman and McChesney 1997; Innis 1950, 2007; Jin 2007, 2011, 2013; Mattelart 2002; McChesney 2004, 2014a; Murdock 2006a, 2006b; Sparks 2007b, 2012; Smythe 1981; Thussu 2006; Tunstall 2008; Winseck and Pike 2007). This book, however, treads in the footsteps of Herbert I. Schiller, the world's premier critic of the US Empire and communications. Schiller passed away on January 29, 2000, a little less than a year before the 9/11 terrorist attack. Apart from one special *Television and New Media* journal issue called *Remembering Herbert I. Schiller* (Maxwell 2001), a superb stand-alone, book-length examination of Schiller's work and relevance (Maxwell 2003), and a favourable review essay (Murdock 2006b), research that explicitly supports and extends Schiller's work is hard to come by. In what follows, I refine Schiller's conceptual positions and describe this book's affinity with them.

First, Schiller (1969, 9) conceptualized the United States as a unique post-colonial empire in a world system. Following the Second World War, the world system's centre of economic and geopolitical gravity shifted from the territorial colonial-imperial powers of old Europe (Great Britain, France, Germany) to the United States, which emerged as a new kind of empire without formal territorial colonies. The old colonial empires directly ruled over their territories, but the United States was an empire that strove to rule markets indirectly in a world system comprised of outwardly sovereign states (H.I. Schiller 1992, 48–49). Unlike the colonial powers of a previous era, the United States did not pursue the direct domination of territories, economies, and polities, but rather sought to build and police a world system of states that shared its core features: the capitalist mode of production, the liberal democratic state form, and the consumerist "way of life." While some post-9/11 authors portrayed the US Empire as a new, twenty-first-century formation driven by a neoconservative elite (i.e., the Project for the New American Century), in the late 1960s, Schiller (1969) had already observed how US military power was being deployed around the world "to extract privilege and prevent social change that might limit that privilege." For Schiller, imperialism – in its colonial and post-colonial forms – was a fact of a world system that had "existed for hundreds of years"; what he analyzed was "the transformation of that system – in its realignments of power centres, its changed sources of exploitation, and its modern mode of organization and control" (9). In this book, I share with Schiller a sense that the United States is an empire, that imperialism is a fact of world history that still needs to be critically analyzed, and that US foreign policy largely supports capitalism and American and transnational corporate interests. In Chapter 1, I synthesize significant research on the US Empire and highlight how the culture industry economically, geopolitically, and ideologically supports this empire.

Second, Schiller (1973) conceptualized the United States as a class-divided society ruled by a power elite – society is divided between financial and industrial owners of the means of production ("the owners") and people who must sell their labour in exchange for a wage ("the workers"). By explaining how capitalism tore US society asunder and the role of the US state in cementing the power of corporate elites, Schiller challenged the liberal pluralist theory of the US state-society relationship in mainstream US political science, which represented the government as a neutral mediator of clashes between different interest groups. Schiller (10) said that "government, and the national government in particular, remains the centrepiece of the neutrality myth" that represented its constituent parts – Congress, the judiciary, and the presidency – as "beyond the reach of special interests" and committed to "serving everyone impartially and disinterestedly." For Schiller, the notion that the US government is "socially neutral" masked how the interests of corporate elites were almost always privileged by the state against the interests of the working poor, labour unions, progressives, and socialists. Schiller bemoaned that deliberative and representative democratic processes were "continually pressured and often captured by commercial lobbies and interests" and warned citizens of the "quickening migration of key decisions from public committees to company boardrooms" (quoted in Murdock 2006b, 210). He observed how a "small group of corporate and governmental decision-makers" (3) made the most consequential policy decisions for everyone else. Schiller's concerns about how capitalism makes a class society and corrupts democracy continue to be relevant. At present, 1 percent of the world's population controls about 40 percent of the world's total wealth; the eighty-five richest people in the world control more wealth than the nearly 3.5 billion people who make up the poorest half of the population; the 400 richest Americans own more assets than the poorest 150 million combined; the top 1 percent of US households controls about 23 percent of the nation's total income; and the average US chief executive officer is paid approximately 330 times more than the average US worker and 774 times as much as a minimum-wage worker (Cassidy 2014; Piketty 2014; Reich 2010; Stiglitz 2011). Worldwide, over 200 million people are unemployed; wages are at an all-time low while profits are at an all-time high; and more than 3 billion people live on less than USD$2.50 a day (Common Dreams 2012). In this book, I share Schiller's lasting and entirely relevant critique of capitalism's consequences and incompatibility with substantive equality and democracy in both the economic and the political spheres. Today, major governmental decisions, policies, and regulations are advanced by executive-level elites without much public input and largely on behalf of the wealthy few and corporate special interests (Domhoff 2013; Gilens 2012; Gilens and Page 2014; Nichols and McChesney 2013).

Third, Schiller conceptualized US cultural imperialism as part and product of the US Empire. Schiller (1976, 9) defined cultural imperialism as "the sum processes by which a society is brought into the modern world system and how its dominating stratum is attracted, pressured, forced, and sometimes bribed into shaping social institutions to correspond to, or even promote, the values and structures of the dominating centres of the system." Sparks (2007b, 212) claims that there "is a degree of uncertainty in Schiller's definition as to whether the process [of cultural imperialism] is one of seduction or coercion." While Schiller (1976, 16) did talk about cultural imperialism as coercion, he also said that the United States integrated other societies "with the mutual consent, even solicitation of the indigenous rulers" who strove to "eagerly to push their people and their nations into the world capitalist economy." Schiller (17) argued that, though the global expansion of capitalism, the liberal state form, and the consumerist way of life in the post–Second World War era was pushed by the state, "the cultural and ideological homogenization of the world" by this system was being pursued by the US elites in conjunction with a "strong, collaborative role of the ruling groups" in the other states. He stated that, because cultural imperialism relies on invitation or consent, not just direct force, "it may be inappropriate to describe the contemporary mechanics of cultural control as the outcome of 'invasion,' though I, too, have used this term in the past" (196). Schiller thus conceptualized cultural imperialism as various persuasive and coercive practices employed by the US state and corporate sector to promote and universalize a dominant culture or "way of life" (i.e., the capitalist mode of production, political and juridical norms, language, customs, and ideas) in other countries with the goal of influencing them and without reciprocation by the countries it aimed to change. Schiller's definition of cultural imperialism covers both coercive and persuasive means and actions, not only one or the other. It closely resembles the concept of hegemony in international political economy (R.W. Cox 1993; Gill 1993; Harvey 2003). Dominant states such as the US struggle on behalf of the dominant social class for hegemony (or dominance) in the world system and attempt to attract, integrate, and incorporate subordinate others; they combine tools of persuasion and coercion and even brute force to elicit or compel consent. In this book, I employ the above broad and qualified concept of US cultural imperialism.

Schiller (1992, 51) conceptualized US cultural imperialism as relying heavily on the mechanisms of economic power (transnational corporations) and military power (a "military-industrial complex") but also saw it as being supported by US media and communications corporations. Schiller (1991, 51) said the "American imperial structure" depended on "a marriage of economics and electronics, which substitutes in part, although not entirely, for the earlier 'blood and iron' foundations of more primitive conquerors." Schiller (1969, 80) claimed that "each new electronic development widens the perimeter of American influence, and the indivisibility of military and commercial activity operates to promote even greater expansion," and he boldly declared that "American power, expressed industrially, militarily and culturally has become the most potent force on earth and communications have become a decisive element in the extension of United States world power" (206–7). Schiller (1976, 30) conceptualized US media and communications corporations as agents of the sum processes of US cultural imperialism. He observed how US media corporations entered other countries and integrated them by establishing technological infrastructures for US financial investment and commodity production, distribution, exhibition, and marketing and said that these companies' media products ideologically reinforced this process by transmitting, "in their imagery and messages, the beliefs and perspectives that create and reinforce their audiences attachments to the way things are in the system overall." Schiller also said that as media corporations travelled across borders in pursuit of profit, they carried with them an entire "infrastructure of socialization" – capitalist production modes, liberal democratic ideals, a consumerist ethos, and so on (9). In effect, media corporations materially and ideologically supported the universalization of the United States' capitalist and consumerist model and contested particular societal models that did not conform to the US model's dominance. In Schiller's theory, media corporations are not independently cultural or media imperialists; rather, they support and are supported by the geopolitics of the US state. Sparks (2007a, 214) clarifies: "Media companies profit from the political and military successes of imperialist states with which they are associated," but "they do not act as imperialists in their own right" (216). Like both Schiller and Sparks (2007a), I conceptualize US media corporations and their commercial products as part of the "sum processes" of US cultural imperialism.

Fourth, Schiller conceptualized the US Empire as running a permanent PR campaign. In the early twentieth century, Walter Lippmann (1922) and Edward Bernays (1923, 1928) argued that participatory democracy was impossible in the United States, because citizens did not possess the time, intellect, or interest that would enable them to intelligently deliberate about and shape public policy decisions. They said that enlightened elites were best able to figure out what the national interest was and should use the media to "manufacture" or "engineer" public consent to that interest. Lippmann offered an elitist theory of public opinion in democracy; Bernays developed a PR industry that maximized profit by trying to control it on behalf of power elites. Throughout the twentieth century, the more that non-elite publics tried to participate in democracy, the more that state and corporate efforts aimed at managing public opinion with PR became routinized. As a consequence of elite efforts to "take the risk out of democracy" (Carey 1995) with PR, the West's "mass democracies" became "market democracies in political as well as economic terms; or, to be more exact ... marketplaces of democracy" (Rutherford 2000, 268). Throughout the twentieth century, US corporate efforts to get large numbers of consumers to buy commodities mixed and blurred with state efforts to channel the citizenry's opinion toward official policy (Retort 2004, 9). Public participation in major policy decisions is now basically "limited to the response of people as consumers and spectators" and "to the [policy] commodities and sights on offer" (Rutherford 2000, 275). Schiller (1973) bemoaned the United States' marketized democracy and the US state's and corporate sector's use of PR to sell policy and peddle public opinion in ways that undermined the deliberative potential of citizens and the prospect of democracy. For Schiller, state PR aimed to manage public opinion about the US Empire at home and bolster its attractiveness and deflect criticisms with "public diplomacy" abroad. Schiller (1991, 124) observed the growth of a vast "complex" of state-run PR agencies that targeted publics around the world with campaigns designed to influence perceptions of America and US foreign policy, saying "public diplomacy" aimed to get "a grip on the minds of foreign audiences so that the foreign policies of the United States ... are admired, or at least, accepted and tolerated" (H.I. Schiller 1976, 20). Apart from these brief comments, Schiller did not elaborate on the nature of public diplomacy, and this state- and corporate-PR practice has been neglected in studies of cultural imperialism (Maxwell 2003, 124; Taylor 1997, 80). Chapter 2 historicizes the US state's and corporate sector's use of public diplomacy to sell the American Way to the world so as to change it.

Fifth, Schiller conceptualized US-based media conglomerates as the world's most powerful producers, distributors, and exhibitors of cultural goods. He examined how corporations first took control of the US communications system – telecommunications, film, the news, radio, and TV broadcasting – to create a cartel-like oligopoly and then incorporated cultural "spheres of activity that historically have been public and non-commercial," such as art galleries, museums, and libraries (1984, 28). Having gained control of the US communications and cultural spheres, American conglomerates expanded their operations abroad, integrating non-US cultural industries and media systems into their globe-spanning networks and chains. Schiller was the first critical scholar to observe the global growth and power of the US culture industries following the Second World War, noticing how "Hollywood was already a dominant force in world film" and how "American jazz and popular music" had established a global lingua franca. Schiller (1991, 1) recognized the rise of non-US culture industries in the post–Cold War era and "seismic shifts in the balance of world power" yet maintained that "the American media-cultural sphere remains intact, if not more secure than ever." He said that the effects of the American culture industry's global dominance were unequal, asymmetrical, and imbalanced media ownership and trade relationships between the United States and other countries; the displacement of public broadcasting by the US private model; and the transformation of the media into a mechanism for delivering people's attention to advertisements. Schiller (1976, 24–25) focused on the role of the US state in boosting and cementing the US culture industry's global power with "the free-flow of information doctrine." This doctrine espoused a free media as the centrepiece of a free society and assumed that without "private ownership of a newspaper, radio or television station, or other medium ... there is no freedom." On behalf of the US culture industry, the state promoted the free flow doctrine around the world while opposing countervailing "state efforts to safeguard national film, television, and publishing industries" (1992, 23). While US foreign policy-makers portrayed the sovereign right of non-US states to protect and promote their cultural scenes as a "denial of freedom" (1991, 23), Schiller said their main goal was to secure the freedom of the US culture industry to sell its goods wherever it liked. In Chapter 3, I show how the global market power of US media corporations, the asymmetries in media ownership and trade, and US state support for US culture industry dominance persist.

Sixth, Schiller (1991, 75) conceptualized the US Empire as one at permanent war. He echoed former president Dwight Eisenhower's concern about the development of the US Empire's "military-industrial complex" (MIC), meaning the interlocking of the DOD, corporations, and American universities (76), and stated that each of these organizations had a material interest in maintaining or increasing public expenditure on national security and war. In the absence of a lasting enemy threat, Congress would be less inclined to annually allocate billions of dollars to the DOD to secure the nation. Permanent peace would cut into the profit margins of the US arms corporations that produced and sold weapons to the DOD and the civilian firms and universities that relied on DOD contracts. The DOD allocated immense public funds to private sector research and development projects, spinning out and calling "forth innovations in information and communications technology (ICT)" like computer electronics, artificial intelligence, satellites, and the Internet (D. Schiller 2008b, 126). The DOD was also one of the biggest consumers of the militarized ICTs produced and sold by the corporate recipients of its subsidies. Herbert Schiller shared with Eisenhower a fear of the MIC's "acquisition of unwarranted influence," worried that the MIC's conflation of military, industrial, and intellectual power would "endanger" American "democratic processes," and wanted the "councils of Government" and "an alert and knowledgeable citizenry" to guard against the MIC's corruption of the republic. But Schiller (1991, 95) was skeptical that citizens could become properly knowledgeable about the MIC, because the media that were supposed to keep the public informed about it had significant links to the DOD: the "same forces that have produced the military-industrial complex in American society-at-large have accounted for the rise of a powerful sub-sector, but by no means miniature, complex in communications." As mentioned earlier, Schiller called this sub-sector a "military-industrial-communications complex": an "institutional edifice of communications, electronics, and/or cultural industries" that links and connects the DOD and media corporate power (Maxwell 2003, 32). Schiller (1991) documented how the DOD "channeled enormous R&D funds from its astronomical budget into work on new information technologies" (5), supported communication industry growth as an "enormous guaranteed market" for corporate media goods and services (95), operated its own communications network (121), and outsourced propaganda jobs to advertising and PR firms, which, reliant on "heavy taxpayer support," took in "more than 200 million a year" to "bestow legitimacy and respectability to the entire military program" (121–22). Schiller (1992, 1) also scrutinized the DOD's expansion of its own PR agencies and these agencies' efforts to manage public perceptions of war by sourcing the news media. DOD PR agents shaped the news agenda by holding press conferences, releasing briefings to journalists, organizing media events, and dispatching their own persuaders to the news media (H.I. Schiller 1973). The result was pro-military and pro-war cultural output. In Chapters 4, 5, and 6, I update and extend Schiller's account of the military-industrial-communications complex. In a period in which "military spending is hardwired into really existing capitalism" (McChesney 2014a, 24), the complex continues to be a helpful concept for "dissecting the interlocking interests of corporate and military communications bureaucracies" (Maxwell 2003, 32) and highlighting the organizational sources of militainment products.

Seventh, Schiller (1976, 6) conceptualized cultural products – news, advertisements, TV shows, and films – as expressive carriers of US capitalist-consumer, military, and exceptionalist ideologies. Schiller (1973, 81–94) said the United States' "recreational-entertainment products of the Madison Avenue-Hollywood work and image factories" and "all the familiar forms of popular culture" were not escapist fluff; many were conveyer belts for the US Empire's dominant ideas. Schiller (1976, 106) did not, however, contend that "all cultural products in an advanced capitalist society are single-mindedly fashioned to impose an ideology favorable to the system's dominators" but instead said the cultural industry takes "into account the social realities of the time" when manufacturing commodities designed to resonate with audiences by touching on "some of the potentially explosive issues of the day" and "incorporating the contradictions of the social setting." Schiller also highlighted how the US culture industry customized cultural products to better connect with the cultural-linguistic particulars of audiences beyond the United States, but he noted that, overall, "the content and style of the programming, however adapted to local conditions, bear the ideological imprint of the main centers of the capitalist world economy" (10). In the early 1990s, Schiller (1991, 15) observed how American "cultural styles and techniques" had become "trans-nationalized" to serve "the ideological and marketing ends of capital, wherever its origin." A shift from the production of a distinctly American commodity culture toward a new "transnational corporate culture" that expressed a "heavy flavor of US media know-how, derived from long experience with [US] marketing and entertainment skills and practices," had occurred (15). The US culture industry has mastered transnational cultural product design strategies (i.e., blockbuster films, global TV formats, and glocalized brands), yet Chapters 2, 4, 5, and 6 show how the complexes shape media and cultural products that continue to carry geopolitical content in support of the US Empire. While international relations scholars, cultural studies scholars, and critical geography scholars offer deft readings of the textual intersections between the fictional geopolitical content of media products and the actual geopolitics of the US national security state (Carpenter 2007; Dittmer 2010; Dodds 2008; Grondin 2014) to show how the US Empire is imagined culturally, Schiller's approach helps to identify the US state and corporate source organizations that control the means of producing, distributing, and exhibiting such products.

Eighth, Schiller conceptualized resistance to the US Empire and had confidence in people's ability to understand and transform the dominant material conditions of the world in which they lived. Schiller understood that, while people are born into inequitable social conditions they do not choose, they nonetheless possess the agency to make society into something other than what it is. Schiller said the US Empire posed a major barrier to participatory democracy, social justice, and lasting peace, but he did not see it as irresistible (H.I. Schiller 1973, 191; 1984, 123). While state-corporate media complexes tried to control public opinion, people could resist this process by developing a "critical consciousness" (1976, 96–99). Given Schiller's nuanced understanding of the interplay of structure and human agency, it is surprising that the most pervasive and dubious criticism of his work is that it fails to account for agency and resistance to media ideology (see Roach 1997 for a summary). Schiller (1976, 155; 1989, 149) did not dispute the fact that people actively interpret media messages in various ways but thought that this was not an adequate strategy for resisting the US Empire. Schiller located resistance to the US Empire not in the interpretive activities of viewers but in internationalist solidarity movements that mobilized resources, built capacities, and struggled to transform the world (1976, 80, 92). For Schiller, resistance to the US Empire took diverse forms: the macro-political tactic of democratizing communications policy and the micro-political tactic of new-media activism. Schiller tirelessly fought to democratize US and global communications policy within and against the US state (and around the world) (Maxwell 2003). As a public intellectual and new-media activist, Schiller wrote numerous articles for progressive magazines like *The Nation*, collaborated on the Paper Tiger Video collective's TV show called *Herb Schiller Reads the* New York Times and supported the resistance of an "untold number of individuals and groups outside the mainstream working with tape recorders, cameras, video recorders, film, music, print, radio, graphics and public art forms" (1976, 189). Prefiguring the present-day excitement surrounding participatory media production by about forty years, Schiller (1973, 189) said that "The involvement of many people in the media, on their own initiative and out of their own desire to communicate, is ultimately the strongest defence any society has against information control and mind management." Although I share Schiller's humanist position, this book focuses on how the structures of the US Empire's culture industry aim to influence how people think and behave, not the ways people actively react to and possibly resist these efforts. So, while I am very interested in how people in various contexts oppose, interpret, co-opt, transform, and remix the products of the US Empire's culture industry, this is not the book's focus. The Conclusion, however, does highlight some salient lines of opposition to the US Empire's culture industry.

Beyond Cultural Imperialism? Hold the Press!

This foregrounding of Schiller's work aligns with recent returns to and reconsiderations of cultural imperialism theory in global media and communication studies (Jin 2007; Nordenstreng 2013; Sparks 2012).

From the early 1980s to the present day, numerous scholars have moved beyond cultural imperialism theory with innovative and empirically grounded studies of cross-border media power relationships and processes (see Mirrlees 2013a for a summary). At best, this new generation of globalization scholars problematized cultural imperialism theory's rigid centre-periphery model of the world system (Appadurai 1997) with dynamic studies of non-US media capitals, culture industries, culturally proximate audiences, and cultural goods (Curtin 2003; Keane 2006; Straubhaar 1991); showed how sovereign territorial states have not fallen to global markets but exist and use cultural policy tools to protect and promote their culture industries (and national cultures) against US media power (Grant and Wood 2004); disputed the notion that media traffic moves in only one way, from the United States to the rest, by exploring two-way and multidirectional media flows (Thussu 2007); debunked caricatures of the audience as manipulated and victimized with ethnographic studies of the ways viewers actually interpret, identify with, and derive pleasure from American entertainment (Ang 1985; Liebes and Katz 1990); challenged singular and essentialist notions of "national culture" by examining cultural hybridity (Kraidy 2005; Morris 2002); and deconstructed a sometimes patronizing "discourse of domination" that risked reproducing what it aimed to oppose (Tomlinson 1991). At worst, some scholars seemed to celebrate "the production, trading and consumption of media artifacts without any serious attempt to locate these within structures of differential wealth and power" (Sparks 2012) and encouraged readers to embrace "an affirmative, 'everything for the best' view of globalization" that was out of touch with "radical history, economics and political studies" (Curran 2002, 182). By the turn of the twenty-first century, globalization was "the most popular and influential way of thinking about the world, and the world of media and communication in particular" (Sparks 2007a, 190). As a result, cultural imperialism became a "far less fashionable a critical position in academic circles" (Tomlinson 1999, 79) and was often challenged by scholars who said it failed to reflect "the complexity of intercultural relations" (Kraidy 2005, 4).

Cultural imperialism theory came of age in the early 1970s – the height of the Non-Aligned Movement's struggle for a New World Information and Communication Order – and much has changed since then. But what has been downplayed, or at least minimized, in the paradigmatic switch from cultural imperialism to new studies of post-imperial globalization is attention to the continuity of the US Empire and the ways that the culture industry still links with and supports it. Dan Schiller (2008a, 99) says that, as scholars moved beyond cultural imperialism, "inequalities resulting from US corporate-state dominance over the international political economy of communications – and struggles to remedy this by developing redistributive policies – were conjured out of the academic mind" and that this was a strange intellectual development, because "transnational companies, almost entirely based in developed market economies controlled virtually every major communications industry segment," and "in communications policy, as elsewhere, the US government continued to throw its weight around the world without regard for local preferences." In this context, globalization theory downplayed the continued power of the US Empire. Brennan (2003, 202) contends that globalization theory's idea that history has arrived at "a world beyond nationalism that is both post-colonial and post-imperialist ... should more properly be seen as the US empire's particular national mythology" (202). Bourdieu and Wacquant (1999, 41–42) go so far as to claim that globalization is an effect of US cultural imperialism or the ability of the United States to universalize its particular interests: "the strongly polysemic notion of globalization ... has the effect, if not the function, of submerging the effects of imperialism in cultural ecumenism or economic fatalism and making transnational relationships of power appear as a neutral necessity."

It is a mistake to reduce all theories of globalization to distractions from or apologias for the US Empire and cultural imperialism, but the displacement of studies of the US Empire and cultural imperialism by globalization is no less problematic. So while many scholars set out to dissect the deficiencies of Schiller's cultural imperialism hypothesis, this book gives further evidential weight to what *is* still sufficient in it and supports recent attempts to revise and extend it for new times. Sparks (2012, 294) is critical of Schiller but nonetheless says "it is possible to advance a viable and coherent concept of cultural imperialism" by analyzing "the ways in which state power and cultural power are intertwined in the production and circulation of cultural artifacts." This book's study of how the US national security state and media corporations co-create imperial cultural products aims to do so. Nordenstreng (2013, 354), another esteemed global communications scholar says "imperialism in general and media imperialism in particular occupy intellectually a vital place in international media studies." This book concurs.

Overall, this book offers a critical geopolitical economy of communication study of the US Empire's culture industry; the US state's use of PR at home and "public diplomacy" abroad to sell America and permanent war to the world; the past and present configurations of the military-industrial-communications complex; the intertwining of cultural commodities with exceptionalist and militaristic ideologies; and the state and corporate shaping and use of new interactive media to achieve strategic goals. As mentioned earlier, the conflicts between an empire and a republic, corporate power and democracy, propaganda and public opinion that Schiller's work addressed have not been transcended by new times (or new theories). They continue to be some of the most important issues of our age.

1

The US Empire and the Culture Industry

At a 2002 address to the US military academy at West Point, New York, then president George W. Bush declared, "America has no empire to extend or utopia to establish. We wish for others only what we wish for ourselves: safety from violence, the rewards of liberty, and the hope for a better life." In a June 4, 2009, televised speech to the Muslims of the world, President Barack Obama said something similar: "Just as Muslims do not fit a crude stereotype, America is not the crude stereotype of a self-interested empire." Across the Republican/Democratic divide, borders, and time periods, Bush's and Obama's speeches are united by their denial of the US Empire, and with them stand numerous twentieth-century US politicians and foreign policy-makers who have long described US economic, military, and cultural expansion as "non-imperialistic."

The denial of the US Empire by politicians carries over to academia as a theme in American historiography (W.A. Williams 1955, 1980; Schroeder 2003) and in the liberal study of international relations, where Nye (2004), who is well aware of the extraordinary economic, military, and cultural might of the United States, insists that "Empire is not the narrative we need to help us understand and cope with the global information age of the twenty-first century" (139). Appellations like "liberal hegemon," "sole superpower," or "world leader" are perhaps more congenial to US soft power. Beyond the realm of political rhetoric and academia, a large number of Americans seem hesitant to contemplate the reality of their empire as well.

Writing for the popular website Salon.com, David Sirota (2011a) grapples with the significant question: "Why can't we [Americans] say 'empire'?"

It is possible that Americans have a hard time acknowledging the US Empire because the idea feels un-American to the core. After all, the American Republic emerged as result of a violent revolutionary struggle against an empire, and the United States does not these days fit the profile of an old colonial empire. The United States does not exercise centralized political control over other territories but instead seems to support territorial state formation (sometimes after toppling existing states). It does not seek to establish formal colonial outposts and often promotes the rights of people to democratically govern themselves (so long as the other's sovereignty aligns with its interests). It does not directly impose symbols of its own way of life on other nations to destroy them but exists in a world system in which outwardly different national symbolisms flourish (and tries to universalize "brand America").

Set against the routinized denial of the idea of an empire, how surprising it was when, following 9/11, arguments for the US Empire were all the rage among strategic think tanks and establishment intellectuals. For much of the twentieth century, the US Empire was "made plausible and attractive in part by the insistence that it is not imperialistic" (Innis 1995), but after 9/11, the US Empire was being insisted on by numerous intellectuals as something absolutely necessary for the promotion and protection of America and a world order of neoliberal states and capitalist economies. In a 2001 *Weekly Standard* piece entitled "The Case for American Empire," for example, Max Boot (27) said the 9/11 "attack was a result of insufficient American involvement and ambition" and that to prevent future attacks, the United States would need to be "more expansive in our goals and more assertive in their implementation." In a *Foreign Affairs* article called "The Reluctant Imperialist," Sebastian Mallaby (2002) argued that the United States must embrace its "reluctantly imperial" role in the world, especially when dealing with failed states that harbour "terrorists, drug smugglers and other international criminals." Niall Ferguson (2005) averred that the US Empire exists and should use its colossal military power to enforce the free movement of goods, capital, and labour. In a much-cited *New York Times* piece called "American Empire: The Burden," Michael Ignatieff (2003) concurred: "The 21st century [American] imperium is a new invention in the annals of political science, an Empire lite, a global hegemony whose grace notes are free markets, human rights and democracy, enforced by the most awesome military power the world has ever known." Ignatieff argued that the United States must spread its democratic and capitalist values and shape the internal affairs of other countries using diplomacy and short-term military interventions. In the more recent piece for *The Atlantic* called "In Defense of Empire," Robert D. Kaplan (2014) says the United States is the only entity on the planet capable of providing and maintaining "global order" in the face of mounting anarchy because "US air and sea dominance preserves the peace" and "protects democracies" from "being overrun by enemies."

Ethnocentric and problematic as these apologias for the US Empire are (Mooers 2006), they breathe new life into a concept that has too long been relegated to the margins of public discourse and shirked by mainstream international relations scholars (Barkawi and Laffey 2002). Despite America's proclivity to deny its empire and the fact of its anti-colonial tradition, the post-9/11 raft of pleas for a US Empire brought to the fore of academic debate and public discourse a hard truth: the United States really is a unique kind of empire. While a few scholars and many anti-war activists read the US Empire as a distinctly post-9/11 phenomenon stemming from the unilateral foreign policy of the Bush II administration and the Project for a New American Century (Dorrien 2004; Halper and Clarke 2004), historians and political economists threw into relief the much longer and expansive history of the US Empire (Bacevich 2004, 2005; Harvey 2003, 2005; C. Johnson 2004; Panitch and Gindin 2012) to show that the United States did not become an empire the day George W. Bush took the White House, and it did not stop being one when Obama won his place there (Scahill 2013; Turse 2012).

At present, the United States is not in the main an empire in the way that European colonial empires once were, but just because it does not now fit the profile of empires of old does not mean that it is not an empire. Empires have taken many different forms, and there is a need to be "sensitive to the historical particularity of different" empires, "their unique structures of political rule, their specific modes of social reproduction and their correspondingly singular forms of cultural self-understanding" (Colás 2008, 3). That said, empires commonly tend to be expansionist, pursue a certain kind of "order," are hierarchically organized, and claim to be culturally unique (9). With this in mind, this chapter describes the US Empire's historically particular form and style of rule, tools of hegemony, economic and geopolitical expansion, hierarchical decision-making structure, and imperial culture ideology. By doing so, this chapter shows the United States as a unique empire – formally, through territorial annexations; informally, through its expansionist attempt to build and superintend a world system of proxy or client territorial states aligned and integrated with it; and culturally, with its exceptionalist credo of being fundamentally different from and superior to all other nation-states and thus fit to rule the world. After describing the key facets of the US Empire, the chapter intervenes in the current debate surrounding the question of the US Empire's decline and then closes with a synoptic overview of the culture industry's importance to the US Empire. Overall, the chapter presents a holistic account of the historical and geopolitical-economic dimensions of the US Empire and its culture industry.

The US Empire, Capitalist Imperialism, and Hegemony

The modern history of capitalism and the Westphalian interstate system is part and product of the rise and fall of different types of empires, some colonial, others post-colonial, but all of which have *expanded* their polities, economies, and cultures in pursuit of their interests. Harvey (2003, 27) conceptualizes the engine of an empire's expansion as a "contradictory fusion" of two power logics – the geopolitics of a territorial state and the economics of capitalist accumulation. He describes "capitalist imperialism" as a fusion of the geopolitics of a territorial state (the political, diplomatic, and military strategies of a state as it struggles to assert its interests and achieve its goals vis-à-vis other states) with the economics of capitalist accumulation (the commodification, production, trade, investment, and exploitative practices of corporations as they competitively seek to maximize profitability in markets). The territorial logics of the state and the deterritorializing logics of corporations do not always intertwine in functional ways and may even "tug against each other, sometimes to the point of outright antagonism" (28), but capitalist imperialism refers to how the geopolitical goals of a territorial state are shaped and supportive of, though not determined, by the transterritorial search of corporations for new sources of labour to exploit, resources to control, and markets to sell to. According to Harvey, "the State is the political entity ... that is best able to orchestrate these processes" (32).

When it is applied to the US Empire, I take Harvey's concept of capitalist imperialism to describe the processes and means by which the US territorial state facilitates and legitimizes the business interests of large and small-scale American corporations as they compete to control the resources and markets of other territories. Bluntly, the US Empire's expansion is driven by transterritorial capitalist goals backed by territorial state power. American capitalist imperialism points to how the government supports the interests of US-based globalizing corporations, legally, diplomatically, and, if necessary, through the use of military force, in the territories in which they aim to operate (R.W. Cox 2012). It signals a synergistic relationship between the US state and American firms – that is, the intertwining of the geopolitical goals of the government and the economic priorities of American globalizing corporations. American corporations, for example, lean on the US state to make the world safe for their prosperity, and the state often does so in pursuit of its own "national interest." The state serves capitalist interests, not just because of the power that business lobby groups wield over foreign policy, but also because the growth of American capitalism is a source of GDP (an index of the "national interest") and tax revenue (which it depends on to sustain itself). For the US government, it would seem that what's good for American business is equivalent to what's good for America: the American capitalist interest in ruling world markets seems tantamount to the American security interest in a world system of rival states and capitals.

In pursuit of its interests, the US Empire has combined territorial and non-territorial styles of rule. Since the earliest days of the Republic, the state has employed internal and then external colonization to expand its frontiers and widen the space for capital accumulation (M. Cox 2004). Eliga Gould (2012) argues that, when delegates to the Continental Congress of July 4, 1776, declared the United States' right "to assume among the powers of the earth, the separate and equal station to which the Laws of Nature and of Nature's God entitle them," they asserted the US's place among the European colonial powers and its ambition to colonize people and territory not yet conquered by them.

Following the American Revolution, the newly formed US state engaged in "internal colonization," dispossessing and destroying many Indian nations (Wolfe 2006). Rationalized by Manifest Destiny – the belief that Americans were a special people divinely ordained by God to expand across the North American continent, from the Atlantic seaboard to the Pacific Ocean – the US state widened its frontier westward, purchasing Louisiana in 1803, annexing Texas in 1845, acquiring Oregon from Britain in 1846, and seizing the rest of the western landmass and California after the 1848 Mexican war. The US Empire also expanded through "external colonization" or the annexation of foreign territories. On the verge of the Spanish-American War of 1898, the United States integrated Hawaii as a naval base and way station to the Philippines, and after defeating the Spanish Empire, it took temporary control of Cuba and established long-standing territorial authority over Puerto Rico, Guam, and the Philippine islands (Ninkovich 2001; LaFeber 1975). The United States also occupied the Dominican Republic between 1916 and 1924 and exerted near total sovereignty over Haiti between 1915 and 1942 (Renda 2001).

In the eighteenth and nineteenth centuries, the US Empire's style of rule was clearly territorial, and though it annexed a few territories in the early twentieth century and still possesses many military outposts beyond its own borders today (C. Johnson 2004), since the mid-twentieth century, the United States has actively distinguished its style of rule from European colonial empires to become history's first full-fledged post-colonial empire (Bacevich 2004; M. Cox 2004; W.A. Williams 1955; Young 2001; Steinmetz 2005). Following the conquest of the Philippines and up until the Second World War, US politicians, businesses, and citizens contemplated the pros and cons of further territorial colonial expansion (Ninkovich 2001, 200). Worried that a colonial empire would undermine the Republican ideal, raise taxes to finance foreign wars and garrisons, and result in unwanted cultural mixing, US foreign policy strategists eventually decided it would be more prudent to pursue a new kind of empire, without colonies. During the Second World War, territorial colonialism was rejected: "The age of imperialism is ended," declared Under Secretary of State Sumner Welles in 1942 (cited in Ninkovich 2001, 234). The United States' post-colonial empire would enable its corporations to rule world markets yet relieve the state of the burdensome costs and responsibilities of colonial administration (Young 2001). Territorial colonialism involved one state's "seizure of sovereignty from locals and the formation of a separate colonial state apparatus" (Steinmetz 2005, 344) to rule them, but the US Empire strove to develop a world system of sovereign and "modern" territorial states (Young 2001) allied to and integrated with its geopolitical economy (Panitch and Gindin 2004, 2012). From 1945 to the present day, the US Empire's expansion has been driven by the interest of building and policing a world system of states that embrace free trade and capitalism, sometimes democracy, and, atypically, social justice.

At present, the US Empire is by no means stable or coherent, because there are numerous non-integrated states and opponents that are able to assert and pursue policies that do not always make Washington happy. The US Empire seeks to build and rebuild its *hegemony* in an antagonistic world system in which territorial states have sovereignty and assert different and often conflicting interests. What, then, is hegemony? In the neo-Gramscian field of international political economy, hegemony generally refers to the efforts of one dominant state (on behest or on behalf of its ruling strata) to get other states and publics in the world system to do what it wants them to do, using instruments of coercion and persuasion or a combination of the two: it may use threats, bribes, punishments, or outright warfare, or it may persuade another state to do what it wants by projecting itself as a moral authority or leader to be followed. In the former strategy, the state liquidates and directly dominates rivals or opponents; in the latter, the state goes to great lengths to elicit the consent of others, to attract and co-opt them (Harvey 2003). Nye's (2009) liberal concept of "smart power" says something similar about power in world affairs (sans social class power); it advises and encourages US foreign policy elites to balance hard power strategies (making others do what you want by coercing them) with soft power strategies (getting others to want what you want by attracting and co-opting them) in their struggle to "lead" the world. The US state has, often with the support of corporations and private groups, used tools of coercion and consent to get other states and publics to do what it wants and to want what it wants and to internalize institutions, policies, ideas, values, and practices that align with its vision of world order.

The US Empire claims the monopoly of the legitimate use of coercive force within its territorial borders and sometimes beyond them, declaring and waging war; recruiting, housing, training, and deploying soldiers; allocating public wealth to firms for the research and development of weapons technology; and initiating and coordinating gargantuan public relations campaigns to justify its largesse. The US Empire *coercively* encircles the globe with bases, monitors populations via a planetary surveillance apparatus, attacks computer networks, imposes sanctions on recalcitrant others, threatens rivals, exploits shocks to push structural adjustment policies, conducts black operations, assassinates enemies, tries to topple whole regimes, and wages total wars (Blum 2004; Chomsky 2002; Klein 2007; Parenti 2004; Scahill 2013; Turse 2012). From the Second World War to the present day, the US Empire has expanded in a permanent state of war, conducting overt and covert coercive operations in China (1945–46, 1950–53), Korea (1950–53), Iran (1953), Guatemala (1954, 1967–69), Indonesia (1958), Cuba (1959–60), Vietnam (1961–73), the Belgian Congo (1964), Laos (1964–73),

Peru (1965), Cambodia (1969–70), Chile (1973), Nicaragua and El Salvador (the 1980s), Beirut (1982–84), Grenada (1983), Libya (1986, 2011), Panama (1989), Iraq (1991–99, 2004–12), Somalia (1992–93), Bosnia (1995), Serbia (1999), Sudan (1998), Syria (2012–), Yemen (2015–), Yugoslavia (1999), Afghanistan (2001–), Venezuela (2002), Haiti (1994–95, 2004), Iran (2005–), Pakistan (2008–), and Ukraine (2012–). Furthermore, the United States' wars to protect and promote freedom and democracy have frequently been undertaken at the expense of these ideals (Blum 2004; Klein 2007; LaFeber 1999; Pecency 1999). The government has supported, directly and indirectly, the growth of capitalist autocracies in many countries and at democracy's peril: Argentina (to 1983), Chile (to 1998), China (at present), Cuba (to 1959), Guatemala (to 1985), Egypt (at present), Iran (to 1979), Nicaragua (to 1979), the Philippines (to 1986), Portugal (to 1968), and Saudi Arabia (at present). To spread capitalism, the US state has dismantled popular movements (e.g., the Sandinistas), attempted to assassinate Communist leaders (e.g., Fidel Castro), and supported coups against democratically elected governments (e.g., the Unidad Popular government) when these threatened the presumed property rights, markets, or resource bases of American multinational corporations (Blum 2004; Klein 2007; LaFeber 1999; Parenti 2004; Pecency 1999; Perkins 2009).

The US Empire has also employed *persuasive* strategies to achieve its goals, building and integrating allied nation-states, educating foreign business leaders and the heads of neoliberal parties, provisioning military security to protectorates, delivering development aid in return for compliance with structural adjustments and contracts to US firms, establishing dollar dependencies, launching pro-American PR campaigns, spreading supermarkets and ideals of consumer sovereignty, and seducing publics with Hollywood films, MTV broadcasts, and brand-name promises. In sum, the US Empire uses both coercion and persuasion simultaneously to build and rebuild its preferred world order (de Grazia 2005; Cull 2008; Dizard 2004; Fraser 2003; Harvey 2003; Lundestad 1998; Nye 2004; Perkins 2009; Panitch and Gindin 2012; Snow 2003).

The concept of US imperial hegemony in no way posits the US Empire as some omniscient or omnipresent entity, which, God-like, controls everything that is happening all over the world, all the time: ongoing conflicts between the United States and China, Russia, Iran, and other countries highlight the relative autonomy of non-US states to pursue interests that irritate and affront the US Empire. Furthermore, the states allied to or integrated with the US Empire are not hopeless and helpless dependents. The business and political elites of many of the US Empire's numerous "allies by invitation" (Lundestad 1998) across the Americas, Europe, and elsewhere often chose to integrate with the US Empire as a way to meet their own hegemonic national interests and goals. Contemplating the consensual underpinnings of integration, Cox (2003, 22) says, "While many [states] may resent the metropolitan centre, most are conscious of the fact that the benefits of living under the American imperium normally outweigh the disadvantages." Although the power relationship between the US and other states is asymmetrical and imbalanced, the United States does not directly control or formally dominate its subordinates. The US Empire's integrated ally states are relatively autonomous marginal competitors and major collaborators; they do not always already do what the United States tries to compel or cajole them to do.

In addition, many states in the world system are not integrated into the US Empire. A Pentagon strategist and US military professor, for example, says these states are not part of the US Empire's "functioning core" of integrated states and economies but rather part of a "Non-integrating Gap" that must be closed (T.P. Barnett 2004). Because there is never any guarantee that the US Empire will have the integrative effects it intends, the US state and corporations go to great lengths to continually build up and rebuild its hegemony, proactively and reactively, willfully targeting non-integrating opponents (e.g., a small group of terrorists) and prospective rivals (e.g., a large bloc of states). When a state or bloc of states rejects the US Empire's universalizing vision of world order and tries to rally others behind a counter-hegemonic particularism of their own making, the US Empire tries to contain, deter, or crush the movement. It might, for example, put its military boot down on recalcitrant groups and "rogue states" or give compliant others new incentives to keep obeying. So, while US imperial hegemony places limits on the ideas and actions of others (integrated or not), counter-hegemonic struggles by state and non-state actors are always possible, even probable.

The US Empire's Pursuit of World Capitalist Order

Between 1890 and 1945, US capitalist expansionism was supported by the US state's foreign policy of "liberal developmentalism" (Rosenberg 1982). This policy was driven by the idealistic notion that other states could and inevitably would follow the United States' liberal capitalist developmental trajectory, that the global spread of capitalist industry and consumerism would be good for all, and that the cross-border flow of trade, investment, and media would unite the world in peace. During this period, the US state promoted liberal developmentalism and went to great lengths to "protect private enterprise and to stimulate and regulate American participation in international economic and cultural exchange" (Rosenberg 1982, 7). The United States' first capitalist imperialist foray was in China. In 1898, US President William McKinley proposed an open-door policy that would grant all nation-states access to China, while US Secretary of State John Milton Hay negotiated an agreement with other Western powers to guarantee "equal and impartial trade with all parts of the Chinese Empire," all the while preserving "Chinese territorial and administrative" capacity (W.A. Williams 1955).

During the First World War, the central powers of Germany, Austria-Hungary, and the Ottoman Empire waged war against the allied powers of the United States, Russia, France, Italy, and England, and US President Woodrow Wilson presented his famous "Fourteen Points" speech to build support for the spread of capitalist openness and democracy (Rosenberg 1982). On January 8, 1918, Wilson promoted the goal of universalizing free trade, democratic state forms, and national self-determination to the world. To persuade Congress and states about the virtue of a League of Nations (the forerunner to the United Nations), Wilson claimed that this particular US national interest was inseparable from the world's interest, but Congress refused to support it, as did much of the international community.

The Monroe Doctrine of 1823 had made some headway in turning Latin America into the United States' first post-colonial sphere of economic and geopolitical influence, and President Franklin Roosevelt's Good Neighbour policy of 1933 enabled US companies – like the United Fruit Company – to continue their expansion there. On the verge of the Second World War and facing Nazi Germany's incursions in a region the United States had long regarded as its backyard, the United States turned Latin America into a full-fledged workshop for fine-tuning its post-colonial strategy of rule. Greg Grandin (2006, 23) states, "The United States had apprenticed itself as a fledgling empire in Latin America, investing capital, establishing control over crucial raw materials and transit routes, gaining military expertise, and rehearsing many of the ideas that to this day justify American power in the world."

Over the course of the Second World War, the colonial empires of Europe began to crumble, and the world system's centre of gravity shifted from Great Britain to the United States. In 1942, US Secretary of State Cordell Hull asserted the United States' stewardship role over the emerging post-colonial world system, arguing that the movement "towards a new system of international relations in trade and other economic affairs will devolve largely on the United States because of our great economic strength" and that "[we] should assume this leadership and the responsibility that goes with it, primarily for the reasons of pure national self-interest" (cited in Stokes, 2005, 221). As the chief architect of this new post–Second World War world system, the United States built the General Agreement on Tariffs and Trade, the International Monetary Fund (IMF), and the International Bank for Reconstruction and Development (which later become the World Bank), NATO, and the UN. These structures and institutions formed the foundations of *Pax Americana* (LaFeber 1994). In the aftermath of the Second World War, the United States was an economic juggernaut, home to the most powerful industrial and financial corporations, holder of the world's reserve currency, and the repository of the biggest share of gold. It was also a military behemoth, with a gigantic national security bureaucracy and military-industrial complex.

From 1945 to 1991, the United States and Soviet Empires battled for world supremacy, each super-state struggling to universalize and integrate others into its own particular economic model, political form, and culture ideology. Citing a hostile expansionist Soviet Union, the 1950 NSC-68 (National Security Council Paper, titled "United States Objectives and Programs for National Security") top-secret report outlined the general objective of US foreign policy during the Cold War: to actively extend and defend US-approved capitalist developments and to defeat the Soviet Union and all associated socialist developments. The NSC-68 claimed that the United States' "overall policy at the present time" is "designed to foster a world environment in which the American system can survive and flourish." The strategy of containing Soviet expansion was thus coupled with one that sought to "open up the world politically, culturally, and above all, economically" to US interests (Bacevich 2004, 4). In pursuit of its two-pronged goal, the United States expanded its sphere of economic and military influence wider and wider, smashing barriers to corporate expansion, waging wars in numerous countries, and integrating many enemies and allies (Bacevich 2004). Throughout the Cold War, the US state "played an exceptional role in the creation of a fully global capitalism and in coordinating its management, as well as restructuring other states to these ends" (Panitch and Gindin 2012, 2). In the 1950s, for example, the US state used the Marshall Plan to rebuild Western Europe and Japan along US lines, and in the 1960s, it employed the Act for International Development to push post-colonial states to drive capitalist modernization down the fast lane to development and pull them away from the Soviet Union (Latham 2000). While the Non-Aligned Movement sought to steer an independent path between United States and Soviet Empires, the US state promoted capitalist "development" as the only legitimate one, while framing alternatives as threatening, even illegitimate. At the Cold War's end, the United States and the Soviet Union had fought "hot" proxy wars across Southeast Asia, Africa, the Middle East, and Latin America, killing millions of people and contributing to the abjection and immiseration of millions more (Lucas 2007).

The Berlin Wall fell in 1989, and the Soviet Union collapsed in 1991, enabling the US Empire to open up new spaces for capitalist accumulation and democracy promotion. Francis Fukuyuma (1991) interpreted this new post-Soviet world system as the utopian endpoint of history that all prior civilizations had been moving toward. The demise of "actually existing socialism" was read as a victory of the United States' free-market model over rationally planned economies, of liberal democratic state forms over autocratic ones, and a globalizing consumerist way of living – carried by satellite TV, entertainment, and ads for brands – over Hollywood's much-loathed cultural-nationalist enclaves. Yet, in the same year that Fukuyama celebrated the end of history, the US state assembled a coalition of nearly 1 million soldiers, about 2,000 fighter aircraft, a little more than 3,000 tanks, and about eight aircraft carriers, two battleships, twenty cruisers, twenty destroyers, and five submarines, and then waged war on Iraq to punish Saddam Hussein for invading Kuwait and getting too close to Saudi Arabia – a key US oil supplier.

In addition to having the most powerful military, the United States had the largest economy in the world and it used its military might and incredible economic clout throughout the 1990s to build neoliberal states, boost global corporate profit interests, and push free trade with help from the IMF, the World Trade Organization, and the World Bank (Gowan 1997). Observing the continuity of US foreign policy, Michael Cox (1995, 5) said, "The underlying aim of the US to create an environment in which democratic capitalism can flourish in a world in which the US still remains the dominant actor, has not significantly altered." On behalf of corporate interests, the US state and its Anglo-European allies used their "unipolar" moment to plan and lead a purposeful project to build and integrate neoliberal states deeper into the circuitry of global capitalism (Bacevich 2004, 102). Thomas Friedman's (1999) "Manifesto for a Fast World" urged US foreign policy-makers to maintain the United States' exceptional role as world super-cop and made the Washington Consensus palatable for public consumption: "[T]he hidden hand of the market will never work without a hidden fist" wrote Friedman. "The hidden fist that keeps the world safe for Silicon Valley's technologies is called the United States Army, Air Force, Navy and Marine Corps." By the mid-1990s, many states had adopted "a new constitutionalism for disciplinary neo-liberalism" (Panitch 1996, 87), while social democracy wailed and waned. The restructuring of non-US states, however, was achieved through alliance building among American and transnational elites that shared a mutual class interest in the neoliberal project (Harvey 2005).

Following the 9/11 terrorist attacks, the Bush administration declared a global "War on Terror" against rogue states and networks of Islamists that use violence to achieve political objectives. The "Bush Doctrine" espoused the following foreign policy prescriptions. First, it moved away from a policy of containing threats to US national security and toward a policy of eliminating threats anywhere in the world. Second, it eschewed the ideal of multilateral power sharing, diplomacy, and decision-making and pushed unilateral US interventionism in the affairs of other sovereign states that failed to align with the United States' vision of world order. Third, it extolled the maintenance of "full spectrum dominance," or a permanent US military advantage over all rival states and groups (Halper and Clarke 2004). At the same time, the Bush Doctrine aimed to spread capitalism and liberal democracy around the world, continuing the US Empire's long-standing project of global material and moral uplift. The post-9/11 *National Security Strategy*, for example, universalized US liberal capitalist developments and rejected alternative developmental paths, stating that there is one "single model for national success: Freedom, democracy, and free enterprise" (iv). In the years following 9/11, the Bush administration disavowed the Anti-Ballistic Missile Treaty, rejected the Kyoto Protocol and the Biological Weapons Convention, backpedalled from the Mine Ban Treaty and the Comprehensive Nuclear-Test-Ban Treaty, opposed the International Criminal Court, and portrayed the UN as an obstacle to US power. The United States also invaded and then occupied Afghanistan and Iraq and oversaw coups in Venezuela and Haiti (Hallward 2010). Furthermore, the CIA violated the human rights of many of the people it detained as terrorists, employing brutalizing acts of torture, from rectal feeding to waterboarding to sexual humiliation, all to extract intelligence that did not prove useful to stopping terrorism (Ackerman and Rushe 2014). The post-9/11 US Empire fused an extreme form of unilateral US military coercion with neoliberal idealism about the virtues of democracy and free markets and, by doing so, evoked global scorn and galvanized mass protest movements against it.

Despite temporarily inspiring hope for a substantive change to the US Empire during his election campaign, President Barack Obama continued the Bush administration's global War on Terrorism (Ali 2010; Englehardt 2010; Greenwald 2013; Scahill 2013; Street 2010; Turse 2012). In his first term, Obama set out to eliminate the threat of weapons of mass destruction, shift resources from Iraq to Afghanistan and Pakistan to "finish the fight against the Taliban and al-Qaeda," and retain its "first and incontrovertible commitment in the Middle East ... to the security of Israel." Far from being the friend to the Muslim world, feigned in his Cairo public diplomacy speech, and contrary to Tea Party pundits who depict him as a dovish un-American Other, Commander-in-Chief Obama routinely authorized coercive operations to achieve strategic goals in at least seven Muslim countries: Afghanistan, Iraq, Libya, Pakistan, Somalia, Yemen, and Syria. Obama unilaterally ordered the aerial bombing of Syria in the absence of a congressional authorization, a UN resolution, a NATO coalition, and an Arab League resolution. Furthermore, Obama oversaw hundreds of drone killings, the growth of counterterrorism camps across East Africa, in Honduras, Guyana, and elsewhere, and was the first US president to authorize the assassination of an American citizen. The Obama White House has continued to pursue the US national interest in world affairs through joint operations with the DOD, the CIA, and the State Department, unleashing terrifying drone strikes, covert "dirty wars" by special force operatives, training and deploying non-US proxy armies to overthrow non-aligned states, and waging cyber-warfare against the networks of challengers (Englehardt 2010; Scahill 2013; Turse 2012). These coercive acts, combined with intensified attempts to contain Russia and China and its ongoing bombing of Iraq, Syria, and Yemen reflect the US Empire's capacity to impose its will where it wants, when it wants. At the same time, the US maintains its core commitment to building a world liberal capitalist order, as signalled by its pushing of the Trans-Pacific Partnership (TPP) in East Asia to further integrate China, Japan, and other states (Starrs 2015).

The Imperial Hierarchy: Who Makes Foreign Policy Decisions?
Each day, decisions that aim to build and rebuild the US Empire's world order get made. But who actually makes these strategic decisions, and from where are they made? In a democracy, the legitimacy of the state relies on popular consent, meaning there should be an accord between the foreign

policy decisions that state representatives make and the will of the people. The essence of democracy is the right and capacity of citizens to understand and meaningfully participate in making the decisions that affect and shape their lives (Dewey 1985). Yet, when it comes to the empire's policy decisions, most US citizens play a marginal role because the federal government's national security planning structure is hierarchical, centralized, exclusionary, and elitist.

The President
At the top of the US foreign policy decision-making hierarchy is the executive branch of the US state, particularly the president, whose power derives from the constitutionally assigned roles of commander-in-chief, chief negotiator, and chief diplomat. The US was founded on the constitutional separation of powers, with the goal of restraining executive power, but the "predominant pattern to have emerged over American history has been the rise of the presidential office in the formulation of foreign policy" and the "transformation of American government into ... an extensive and centralized system of administration relating to the resources and actions of a world power" (Foley 2012, 112). From the Second World War to the present day, this administrative centralization has been further entrenched, as the president's decision-making power and executive support for it has grown. The post–Second World War rise of the national security state transformed a normative constitutional presidency into an "imperial one" (Schlesinger 1973), enabling the president to exercise near-supreme power over foreign policy decisions (Fisher 2004). Furthermore, the prerogative gives US presidents exceptional and extrajudicial power following their declaration of a national security crisis (Neocleous 2007): following 9/11, the president gained unprecedented powers, first with the 2001 Authorization to Use Military Force doctrine, which allowed then president Bush to authorize attacks on all organizations and individuals, groups, or states associated with or supportive of "terrorism." Then, in 2011, President Obama turned the Authorization into law as the National Defense Authorization Act, acquiring for himself and giving to future presidents the right to exercise military power at their own discretion (Greenwald 2012a). The US public has absolutely no power whatsoever over these executive decisions.

Presidential foreign policy decisions, however, can be influenced by the National Security Council (NSC). Established in 1947 as an interdepartmental body to advise the US president about national security, the NSC includes the president, vice-president, the secretary of state, the secretary of defense, the chairman of the Joint Chiefs of Staff, and the director of National Intelligence. The NSC is the most influential agent in the development of US foreign policy (Best 2009); it proposes foreign policy legislation and sets the foreign policy agenda through its national security strategy. The national security strategy is used by the president's NSC to define and communicate a coherent foreign policy vision to Congress, state, and non-state actors and US and non-US citizens. While the NSC's national security strategy determines US strategic interests, an immense executive bureaucracy – the DOD (the army, navy, and air force), the US Department of State, the US Trade Representative, the Department of Homeland Security, and various "intelligence" agencies (the CIA, the National Security Agency, and the Defense Intelligence Agency) – pursues them. They also conduct global surveillance and generate elite geopolitical knowledge that factors into the NSC's decisions. The NSC, not citizens, authoritatively defines what the "national interest" is, and is not, in world affairs. It is responsible for how the US state acts, to what end, and how it does so. Through the national security strategy, it defines national security "problems" and then organizes and deploys state agencies to "solve" them.

Congress

The executive branch makes the major foreign policy decisions, but US Congress has some power in this area. The US Constitution grants Congress the right "to regulate commerce with foreign nations," "to raise and support armies," and to declare war. The Constitution's division of powers between the executive branch, Congress (the legislature), and the courts (and the judiciary) seeks to establish a system of checks and balances in US foreign policy and functioned as an "invitation to struggle over the making of US foreign policy" (Barrett 1990, 91). Congress has the power to tax, approve budgets, and allocate funds; to raise militaries and declare war; and to deliberate about US foreign policy. The US Senate Committee on Foreign Relations can debate the foreign policy decisions of the executive branch, and the House Committee on Foreign Affairs has the power to pass legislation that impacts US diplomacy. While the "making of sound US foreign policy depends on a vigorous, deliberative, and often combative process that involves both the executive and the legislative branches" in the post-9/11 context, "congressional oversight of the executive across a range of policies, but especially on foreign and national security policy, has virtually collapsed" (Ornstein and Mann 2006). Congress *ought* to hold the executive branch accountable for its deeds and make its deeds subject to public deliberation.

Yet, Congress regularly fails to perform this crucial role; instead, it tends to support executive decisions (Foley 2012, 117). The executive branch is the central locus of foreign policy decision-making and Congress is at best "a junior partner" and at worst a compliant observer (Wilson Center 2011).

Civil Society and Special Interest Groups
Though the US executive branch enjoys considerable independence from the public when making the empire's decisions, there are some opportunities for citizens to influence foreign policy from civil society – that is, from the institutions and networks of socialization distinct from political society or the state's juridical and coercive apparatuses (Gramsci 1971). From civil society, interest groups not directly employed by the state struggle daily to influence the US Empire's policy. The interest groups best able to do so are the resource-rich and organized "corporate citizens," as they have greater power to curry the favour of politicians and shape foreign policy than do the majority of disorganized and resource-poor citizens (Cox 2012; Gilens and Page 2014; Jacobs and Page 2005). Due to the campaign finance reforms that followed the recent *Citizens United v. Federal Election Commission* and the ongoing expansion of the lobby-industrial complex, the US government (Congress and the legislature) is being corrupted by corporate special interest groups, which pay for the policy outcomes they want behind the public's back and often absent public knowledge and informed consent (Lessig 2012; McChesney and Nichols 2012). Corporations bankroll lobbyists to court and convince politicians and policy-makers to do their bidding, advancing private sector interests to the US state as the general "national interest," while insiders influence the political process by going in and out of a "revolving door" between the private and public sectors, switching roles between state administrators for country and chief executive officers for capital (Open Secrets 2014). The political class of Congress people, senators, and governmental insiders often leverage their public service roles to move into more lucrative positions as servants of private corporations (Lessig 2012). Elites and business interest groups have substantial and independent influence over US government policy formation, while the general public has very little. Bluntly, the propertied and powerful few steer and move policy in ways they like and choose; most citizens get the policies they want only if business elites want them too (Gilens and Page 2014). Outwardly, the United States is a democracy, but at the core it is a dollarocracy in which the state's political class is beholden to and a beneficiary of capitalism and big business (McChesney and Nichols 2012). Lobbying by corporations such

as the Motion Picture Association of America, Information Technology Industry Council, National Mining Association, National Defense Industrial Organization, American Petroleum Institute, the Financial Services Roundtable, and the Pharmaceutical Research and Manufacturers of America press and pay for US politicians to support their narrow corporate interests as national interests. Between 1974 and 2002, for example, average citizens had little power to shape world affairs, because US foreign policy was "most heavily and consistently influenced by internationally oriented business leaders" (Jacobs and Page 2005, 107).

Elections
Elections give US citizens a means of publicly representing their foreign policy preferences to the state through the selection of a political leader. Voters may choose their candidate on the basis of retrospective evaluations of foreign policy performance; they may punish incumbent candidates for foreign policy failures or reward them for successes (Seaver 1998, 76). The notion that America (as a collective of citizen-voters) guides presidential foreign policy platforms through the electoral process, however, is unfounded. A little more than half of the citizens of the United States usually participate in elections to select the US president (a pitiful voter turnout for a country that represents itself to the world as a paragon of democratic virtue), and these elections do not really give these citizens the ability to substantively influence US foreign policy. Wittkopf, Jones, and Kegley (2003, 318) agree: "Americans do hold opinions about foreign policy matters, but they are not transmitted into the policy-formation system through the electoral process." Elections do not offer citizens a genuine foreign policy choice, because presidential candidates, while sometimes proposing very different domestic policies, tend to similarly gear their foreign policy to the maintenance of US military and economic dominance vis-à-vis actual and speculative rivals and threats. Presidential candidates may discuss foreign policy tactics with prospective voters, but only as a way to make themselves appear more capable than their opponents in maintaining US supremacy. Elections let citizens select between marginally different domestic policies, but they do not provide them with a meaningful way to determine each party's foreign policy platform or even allow them to choose between substantively different ones. This is because both major parties are *most* responsive to the policy preferences of the corporations that bankroll their campaigns (Gilens and Page 2014; Nichols and McChesney 2013). The PR of presidential candidates does sometimes pander to the foreign policy preferences of citizens

during the electoral campaign, but it has been shown that, soon after being elected, the new leader discounts them or changes the course of action in response to new circumstances. In sum, elections do not give the public an effective means of influencing US foreign policy.

Elite Democracy
Elitists justify the systematic exclusion of the public from foreign policy decision-making by maintaining that ordinary citizens don't possess the time, skills, or knowledge to be capable of deciding what's best for the United States in the world system. They believe an elite few should make foreign policy on behalf of the many (O.R. Holsti 2004). The notion that elites should independently determine US foreign policy rests on a negative post–Second World War discourse about the majority of American citizens as overly emotional, apathetic, and uninformed (Lippmann 1955; Almond 1960). Elitists accept the contribution of citizens to domestic policy, but when it comes to foreign policy, they reject the democratic notion that public opinion should play a role. Walter Lippmann (1955), for example, saw the public as a threat to intelligent foreign policy. "The unhappy truth," he wrote, "is that the prevailing public opinion has been destructively wrong at critical junctures" (16), and the public "has compelled governments ... to be too late with too little, too long with too much, too pacifist in peace or bellicose in war" (27). Hans Morgenthau (1978, 147) said, "The rational requirements of good foreign policy cannot from the outset count on the support of a public opinion whose preferences are emotional." Appearing on CBS talk show *Face the Nation* in March 2006, Bush's vice-president, Dick Cheney, told his interviewer that presidents should not heed public opinion: "I don't think we can pay attention to that kind of thing. The president has got a job to do ... He ignores the background noise that's out there in the polls that are taken on a daily basis" (cited in Wittkopf, Jones, and Kegley 2003, 276). In 2005, David Rothkopf (2005, 4) said the majority of US citizens were basically ignorant of world affairs and as such needed to be led by elites. The notion that a small group of elites should make foreign policy with little to no regard for the citizens they are elected by and accountable to is an autocratic proposition. Yet this position persists, supporting the steering of foreign policy by an elite few from the commanding heights of US society's most powerful institutions.

On the whole, US citizens do not influence the foreign policy decisions that power elites make to plan and steer the US Empire, but the ideology of American exceptionalism teaches them that they should support it.

The US Empire's Exceptional Culture Ideology

The US Empire's growth has been justified by an ideology or a dominant set of ideas and beliefs about America. Said (1993) argues that imperialism is not just what corporations and governments do but also the ideas and beliefs that give legitimacy to what they do in pursuit of power. Steinmetz (2005, 344) contends that the formation of empires is "propelled not just by economic motives but also by diplomatic and military considerations, dreams of national glory, religious or civilizing missions." And critical geographers and post-colonial scholars remind us of how the US Empire is co-constituted culturally (Dalby 2008; A. Kaplan 2002; Park and Schwarz 2005; Shohat and Stam 1994, 2007). The US Empire's dominant culture ideology, which normalizes, legitimizes, and makes empire seem like common sense, is called "American exceptionalism."

At its core, the ideology of American exceptionalism represents the United States as a unique liberal capitalist country in a world system of liberal and illiberal capitalist states, an extra-special nation that is qualitatively different from and better than other nations (K.J. Holsti 2011). One month after 9/11, George W. Bush (2001) asserted his pride in "the exceptional character of the Nation we serve" and said he never felt "more certain about America's goodness or more confident about America's future." Pressed by conservative critics, Obama has talked more about America's exceptional quality than Bush (Schlesinger 2011). From the United States' founding to the post-9/11 War on Terror, the constitutionally inscribed liberal political philosophy, dynamic and immensely productive capitalist economy, and openness to foreigners make it seem, especially when compared with history's aristocracies and autocratic regimes, a unique kind of country. Exceptionalism represents the United States not only as fundamentally different from all other countries but also as inherently *superior* to these countries (K.J. Holsti 2011, 397). This ideology is itself not exceptional (because it has existed in other empires, including the British and Soviet), is not always false (because the United States does possess *some* exceptional qualities), and is not necessarily a tool of elite propaganda (because presidents and their foreign policy advisors may themselves believe it) or bereft of material consequences (because it may shape United States foreign policy decisions). Nevertheless, American exceptionalism legitimizes the US Empire while giving crucial rhetorical support to questionable and often controversial strategic decisions.

American exceptionalists claim the United States has a unique responsibility, obligation, or mission to liberate or save other peoples, cultures, and entire societies that are suffering from some kind of evil, oppression, or exploitation (K.J. Holsti 2011). The US state's expansion of its internal frontier in the nineteenth century, its 1898 colonial war against Spain, its Good Neighbour policy in Latin America, its roles in the First and Second World Wars, its Cold War against the Soviet Union, its human rights wars of the 1990s, and its post-9/11 global War on Terrorism, for example, have all been represented as acts that aimed to liberate or save foreign populations, societies, and even the whole world from various kinds of evil (K.J. Holsti 2011). American exceptionalism makes it seem as though US foreign policy is guided by exceptionally benevolent as opposed to typically self-interested goals. Ironically, though the US claims an altruistic duty to act on behalf of the world, it infrequently asks the world's people's whether or not they so desperately want or need such help.

American exceptionalists also claim that the United States should be free from the external constraints that limit the sovereign powers of most other states in the world system. While institutions of global governance aim to prevent world conflict by curbing each state's sovereign power to act in whatever way it likes, the United States, in addition to trying to make the global governmental rules, often takes exception to them. The US Empire often "claims the authority to make sovereign judgements on what is right and what is wrong" for everyone else, while exempting "itself with an absolutely clear conscience from all the rules that it proclaims and applies to others" (Hassner 2002, 46). After all, massacres, extraordinary renditions, and torture perpetrated by US military personnel are not brought to global justice, because the US state rejects the International Criminal Court's jurisdiction over its military and seems to exempt itself from the Geneva Conventions (Jinks and Sloss 2004).

In addition, American exceptionalists see the world system in a Hobbesian way – that is, hostile state and non-state enemies always exist and threaten the national security of not only the United States but also the entire world. For example, the post–Second World War growth of the Soviet Union did not just challenge the United States' liberal democratic state form and expansionary consumer-capitalist way of life but also sought to enslave and oppress all of humankind; twenty-first-century "rogue states," such as North Korea, and international terrorist organizations, such as ISIS, threaten not just US security but also the well-being of all states and peoples. To the extent that a global threat requires an exceptional global state to eliminate it, the United States' universalization of threats legitimizes its global growth as an empire, as well as its exceptional military presence around the world.

Unfortunately, an empire that perceives itself as permanently threatened by outsiders (and to some extent by insiders) is one that sows mass fear, paranoia, and anxiety among its own population and those living elsewhere; it encourages and expects its population to be ready and waiting for some war, somewhere, with some kind of threatening enemy. Yet, in exceptionalist culture ideology, the United States never uses its power to threaten the security of others; rather, it wages "reactive" wars in response to the threat others pose to it. It does not victimize innocents but is victimized by the hatred and sinister plots of guilty and crazed enemies. The United States is never the bad guy in the Manichean morality plays scripted by exceptionalist speechwriters but instead is a force of absolute good in a bad and mad world. In all the aforementioned ways, the culture ideology of American exceptionalism works to legitimize the US Empire.

The US Empire in Decline? Not So Fast

The United States is an economically and geopolitically expansionist, hierarchically organized, and culturally exceptionalist empire, but might it one day fall? This question is not new or original but one that American politicians and scholars alike have contemplated for decades. In 1960, John F. Kennedy worried that "American strength relative to that of the Soviet Union has been slipping and communism has been advancing steadily in every area of the world" (cited in Rachman 2011). In the mid-1970s, Marxists, observing deindustrialization, the United States' defeat in Vietnam, the OPEC crisis, and stagflation, thought that US Empire had entered a terminal period (Mandel 1999). In the 1980s, Paul Kennedy's (1987) *Rise and Fall of the Great Powers* triggered a lively discussion about whether or not US economic and military hegemony, faced with the rise of West German and Japanese capitalism and burdened by "imperial overstretch," was headed for decline. In the mid-1990s, scholars argued that the United States' unipolar moment that followed the Soviet Union's collapse was over and that America now faced a multipolar world system of states that strove to counterbalance US power (Layne 1993). Since the Great Recession of 2007–8 began, declarations of US decline have permeated society (Chomsky 2012; Zakaria 2008, 2011). What do recent declinist thinkers say?

Externally, the rise of Brazil, Russia, India, China, and South Africa (BRICS), which together account for about 30 percent of world GDP and about 45 percent of the planet's population, supposedly heralds a massive shift in concentrations of global economic, military, and cultural power away from the US toward the BRICS. The BRICS' formation of an energy trading bloc apart from the G7; attempts to free themselves from American-dollar dependency with a new multinational currency regime; establishment of a new development bank; and growth of culture industries and soft power seem to point to a multipolar world system in which the US Empire is counterbalanced (Ismi 2014; Layne 2012). Internally, the United States faces numerous economic problems. America runs a permanent account deficit, annually borrowing more money from the world than it makes by selling to it. In 2011, the US federal debt was $14.3 trillion, 8 percent ($1.2 trillion) of which was held as treasury notes, bonds, and bills by China (Murse 2012). The United States' debt is largely the result of its wars, particularly the Iraq war, which cost taxpayers about $3 trillion (Stiglitz and Bilmes 2008); its subsidization of banks like JPMorgan, Bank of America Corp., Citigroup Inc., Wells Fargo and Co., and Goldman Sachs Group with about $83 billion per year (Bloomberg Business 2013); and, importantly, the fact that tax rates for the United States' 1 percent corporate class have fallen substantially since peaking in the 1940s, leaving middle-and low-income citizens to pay more than their fair share for social programs such as Medicaid, the Supplemental Nutrition Assistance Program (formerly the Food Stamp program), housing assistance, and corporate welfare programs such as infrastructure development and war (Gilson 2011; Stewart 2013). The US government cannot spend as easily as it did in the past, as creditors are losing confidence in the nation's ability to pay back the trillions it owes, and the US dollar's role as the world system's reserve currency is supposedly losing its lustre. In response to its economic woes, the US state could raise taxes on the super-rich with even higher rates of taxation on the biggest incomes (Piketty 2014), but it is instead succumbing to private pressures to implement austerity measures (raising taxes on workers while cutting social programs). This may further weaken the US Empire and open a power vacuum that China and other new old powers will fill (Layne 2012). Overall, declinists say the curtain is falling on the US Empire and that American power elites and the working class will have to grudgingly adjust to the new reality of a multipolar world system in which the United States is no longer *numero uno*.

The world system is undoubtedly undergoing significant changes, and the US Empire is beset by serious external and internal problems that unsettle its long-standing unipolar privilege. But for now, the United States remains the world's only true empire, not least in terms of its economic and military preponderance.

The United States is still the world's biggest national economy. With only 4.6 percent of the world's population, the United States accounts for about 27.5 percent of the world's total GDP. In 2013, the United States' GDP was estimated by the IMF to be $16.2 trillion, almost two times as much as China's ($9 trillion), more than three times the size of Japan's ($5.1 trillion), more than four times the size of Germany's ($3.6 trillion), six times the size of France's ($2.7 trillion), and $4 trillion greater than the combined GDP of its next top five competitors: Brazil, United Kingdom, Russia, Italy, and India (Adelman 2013; Bergmann 2014). In 2014, the GDP was estimated to be $17.5 trillion, a sum greater than the combined GDP of the BRICS countries (Bergmann 2014). In addition to having the largest national economy and the most popular world reserve currency (Conerly 2013), America is home to 543 of the world's top 2,000 largest global corporations; it headquarters more than double the number of global corporations based in Japan (251) and nearly quadruples the total of those based in China (136) (DeCarlo 2013). The United States is the central base of the majority of the world's top 2,000 publicly traded corporations, and these hold dominant positions in aerospace and defence, business and personal services, casinos, hotels and restaurants, computer hardware and software, conglomerates, financial services, healthcare equipment and services, media, pharmaceuticals and personal care, and retail (Starrs 2014, 87). The US is a magnet for foreign direct investment (recently surpassing China), the hub of the world's most extensively developed free-trade spokes, a choice destination for highly skilled knowledge workers, and home to top-tier universities that annually file the most patents (*Forbes* 2014; *Foreign Policy* 2013). Also, many of the transnational corporate class's globe-trotting elites still live in the United States (Starrs 2014), and fourteen of the world's twenty-five richest CEO-shareholders are US citizens: Bill Gates, Warren Buffet, Charles Koch, David Koch, Larry Ellison, Christy Walton, S. Robson Walton, Jim Walton, Alice Walton, Sheldon Adelson, Jeff Bezos, Larry Page, Sergey Brin, and George Soros (Transnational Institute 2013).

The declinist argument that crisis is endemic to capitalism may be correct, but an all-out economic collapse of the US Empire does not seem to be imminent. The billionaires at the top of the US class hierarchy continue to prosper, and the US state has been able to throw water on the flames of catastrophe by managing capitalist crisis after crisis, most often by making the working class pay for each of them. Furthermore, the declinist argument comes across as reductionist, as it posits GDP and other economic measures to be the most important indicators of US power while neglecting other power resources.

The US Empire's apparatus of coercion, for one, is still the world's largest. The US Empire has long used military hard power or the threat of it to pry open regions closed to capital accumulation and to contain the rise of emergent rivals. Today, it continues to back the global expansion of its corporations with the most extensive military the world has ever seen while leading a vast global security alliance through NATO. The US spends more than any other country in the world on preparing for, waging, and recovering from war and accounts for nearly 40 percent of the world's total military expenditure. In 2013, the US defence budget of $682 billion was a sum larger than the combined defence budgets of the next top ten spenders (Rosen 2014). The United States' defence budget is almost four times larger than that of China ($166 billion), the world's second largest spender, and almost eight times the size of Russia's ($90.7 billion), the third biggest spender (Rosen 2014). The US and its allies are responsible for nearly 70 percent of global military expenditure, while US adversaries account for less than 15 percent (Walt 2011). The DOD – the army, navy, marine corps, air force, and coast guard – controls almost 2 million troops (more than 250,000 deployed around the world), a stockpile of about 5,000 nuclear warheads (compared to China's 250 and Russia's 1,500), and a complex for researching and developing some of the most technologically advanced weapons systems in the world (Turse 2008). To protect and promote US interests abroad, the DOD maintains almost 1,000 military bases (compared to Russia's 10; China has none) (Vine 2012). These are protected by a Status of Forces (SOF) agreement, which allows DOD personnel to act as they like without constraint by their host state's own sovereign laws (Johnson 2004). The US Empire of bases stretches far and wide, across many continents connecting 150 of the world's 192 territorial states to the Pentagon's command and control centre.

The US Empire is not as powerful as it once was, nor is it able to achieve every objective it sets for itself, but the BRICS – a collection of quite different countries often mythologized as a counter-hegemonic unity – do not currently or coherently rival the US's economic, military, or media-technological might (Starrs 2014). Sparks (2014, 414) writes that, if "there is a near term challenge to the West, or more specifically to the USA, then it comes from China, not the BRICS as a collective." But China does not pose as a substantive rival to the United States' combined power either (Starrs 2014, 2015; Thompson 2014), nor does it express the United States' exceptionalist will to build, lead, and superintend a world order that looks like itself. As Starrs (2015) says, "China does not have the capacity (nor the will) to create an alternative order to American hegemony—it simply wants to increase its share of the pie."

The Significance of the Culture Industry to the US Empire

Importantly, no country possesses the cultural-industrial reach and power of the United States, and the culture industry is significant to the US in many ways.

Capitalism

The culture industry is economically significant to the US Empire as one of its most profitable capitalist sectors. The Founding Fathers never intended for the US communications system to be completely capitalist, and American media reform movements have at critical junctures proposed and fought for a non-commercial media guided by democratic values (McChesney 1999, 2004, 2008, 2013, 2014b; Pickard 2014). Yet, from the Communications Act of 1934 to the Telecommunications Act of 1996 to the present day, the US government, on behalf of powerful corporate lobbyists, has largely established and enforced, through law, policy, and regulation, a capitalistic mode of media and cultural control that extols markets, private ownership, the profit motive, advertising, and hyper-commercial values (McChesney 2004, 2008, 2013; Pickard 2014). In this model, democratic values such as civics, citizenship, public inclusion, and participation are sidelined by corporate values such as individual self-interest, rampant consumerism, and exclusionary forms of pay-to-belong brand loyalty. Media conglomerates use privately owned capital technology (production studios, distribution chains, and exhibition outlets) and the waged labour of workers they hire to produce cultural goods and then sell (or license) these goods on the market to consumers (e.g., other media corporations such as TV networks, cinema chains, and retailers). The many US-based media conglomerates that sell cultural commodities are engines of US economic growth, job creators, tax revenue generators, buzz-makers, and contributors to the national GDP. In 2013, PricewaterhouseCoopers predicted that global spending for media and entertainment will reach $2.2 trillion in 2017, compared to $1.6 trillion in 2012. The United States, home to powerful horizontally and vertically integrated media conglomerates like Comcast-NBCUniversal, The Walt Disney Company, Time Warner, News Corporation, and Google, is the largest player in this expanding world media market (James 2013). The United States' cultural reach is unparalleled; its media conglomerates account for nearly half of the world's total audiovisual trade, and when it comes to TV shows and films, it "consistently generates a positive balance of trade in every country in which it does business" (MPAA 2014b). In addition to selling cultural goods to consumers and exchanging consumer attention with advertising companies, US culture industry firms are in the business of promoting the ethos of buying on behalf of corporate clients such as Walmart, General Electric, McDonald's, Coca-Cola, Nike, Citigroup, and Fannie Mae. In a world system that depends for its survival on the expansion and legitimization of consumerism as a way of life, the US culture industry profits by supporting the advertising needs of larger corporations and using media products to attract people's attention to branded goods and services (Smythe 2001).

Public Relations: Public Affairs
The culture industry is geopolitically significant to the US Empire as a relay for and accomplice of strategic communication and PR campaigns. The US Department of State's (2014) Office of Public Diplomacy and Public Affairs, for example, seeks to "support the achievement of US foreign policy goals and objectives, advance national interests, and enhance national security by informing and influencing foreign publics and by expanding and strengthening the relationship between the people and Government of the United States and citizens of the rest of the world." This office coordinates the Bureau of Public Affairs (which runs foreign press centres, hosts press conferences, monitors the media, operates websites, manages regional media hubs, pitches interviews with officials to news outlets, places editorials about US strategy in newspapers, makes TV content, and plans social media events), the Bureau of International Information Programs (which orchestrates face-to-face and virtual people-to-people dialogue about America and US foreign policy through various platforms), and the Center for Strategic Counterterrorism Communications (which organizes communications activities that counter terrorist-generated information about America across a wide variety of media platforms). The Department of Homeland Security (2014) houses an Office of Public Affairs that acts as "the primary point of contact for news media, organizations and the general public seeking information about Department of Homeland Security's programs, policies, procedures, statistics and services." The Central Intelligence Agency (2014) has an Office of Public Affairs as well, which sources the news media, the entertainment industry, and networked publics with scripts, videos, and information that puts the CIA in a positive light. The crown jewel of the US Empire's PR apparatus is the DOD's (2014) Public Affairs Office, whose Assistant Secretary of Defense for Public Affairs coordinates "public information, internal information, community relations, information training, and audiovisual matters." The DOD's PR budget is not officially disclosed, but reports suggest expenditures between $4.7 billion and $15 billion annually on everything from

news ops to domestic recruitment ads to foreign psychological operations (AP 2009; Trento, Waltemeyer, and Gaskill 2013). Through the Public Affairs Office, the DOD runs the Defense.gov News and Defense.gov News Photos to source news companies with DOD-promoting press releases, images, audio files, publications, and video news releases. It also has a DOD Special Assistant for Entertainment Media to support culture industry productions of spectacular war-themed TV shows, films, and video games. In addition, the DOD's Defense Media Activity connects and links the millions of active guard and reserve military service members, civilian employees, contractors, military retirees, and their families in the US and around the world via the American Forces Radio and Television Service broadcasts, American Forces Press Service, DOD News Channel, the Stars and Stripes news service, and hundreds of websites. The US Empire's PR apparatus sources the culture industry with content and outsources content-generation jobs to firms with no apparent connections to them, strategies that help it to conceal its influence (Trento, Waltemeyer, and Gaskill 2013). It is an economic boon to the culture industry, doling out big content subsidies to media corporations (in the form of state-generated "free content") and directly paying firms to create strategic cultural products (through state-provisioned PR contracts).

Space of War: Information Operations
The culture industry and networks of communication technologies are geopolitically significant to the US Empire as new mediatized spaces of twenty-first-century warfare that visually integrate the home front and the battlefront, both local and global (Grondin 2011; Stahl 2006). Long ago, McLuhan (1997) described the fusion of "cold wars" (wars fought with industrial weapons technology) and "hot wars" (wars fought through the media and information and communications technology). In 2004, Leigh Armistead, a military instructor and editor of *Information Operations: The Hard Reality of Soft Power*, said, "The global information environment has become a battle-space in which the technology of the information age ... is used to deliver critical and influential content in order to shape perceptions, influence opinions, and control behavior" (xvii). In a period in which US troops are suspected to be intentionally targeting and killing non-aligned war journalists (Lindorff 2012; Paterson 2014) and Fox TV news pundits like retired army Col. Ralph Peters say the US military should do so (Linkins 2009), the notion that the culture industry is a battlefield is not just metaphoric but quite literal. The DOD doctrine for waging war on the mediated spaces of this battlefield is called "information operations" (IO) (US Department of Defense 2003b,

2003c, 2010, 2012). The doctrine of IO has its origins in DOD directives *Joint Vision 2010*, published in 1996, and *Joint Vision 2020*, which was published in 2000 but updated and extended in October 2003, when Donald Rumsfeld signed a seventy-four-page document entitled *Information Operations Roadmap (IOR)* (US Department of Defense 2003b). The *IOR* outlined the DOD's "plan to advance the goal of information operations as a core military competency" (1) and put forward the following policy recommendations: "fight the net" (by targeting cyberspace – a global sphere of anti-war and terrorist organizing – as "an enemy weapons system") (6); "improve psychological operations (PSY-OPS)" (by producing pre-emptive, commercial-quality, and audience-targeted psy-ops cultural products "for aggressive behaviour modification during times of conflict") (6); "improving network and electro-magnet attack capability" (by developing the capacities to disrupt, degrade, and destroy target sectors of the emerging global telecommunications and weapons systems that are dependent on the electromagnetic spectrum) (6–7); centralizing IO planning and leadership (by creating new hierarchically organized IO leadership positions, commanders, and control structures) (7); standardizing IO discourse and cultivating "a well-trained and educated [information operations] workforce" (by preparing new planners, setting up military college IO graduate programs and research institutes, and recruiting students) (12). The *IOR* also presents an all-encompassing definition of IO: "The integrated employment of the core capabilities of Electronic Warfare, Computer Network Operations, Psychological Operations, Military Deception and Operations Security, in concert with specified and supporting and related capabilities, to influence, disrupt, corrupt or usurp adversarial human and automated decision-making while protecting our own" (11). IO is *permanent* (it is used during peace, crisis, and war) and *boundless* (it is not confined to one territory). The *IOR* boldly asserts that "information intended for foreign audiences ... is increasingly consumed by our domestic audience" and that "PSY-OPs messages will often be replayed by the [US] news media for much larger audiences, including the American public" (11).

National Identity
The culture industry is important to the US Empire as a significant means of representing, defining, and distinguishing territorial notions of the American Way from other ways of life. The United States is a territorial state, but "America" is a discursive terrain of struggle between political blocs that position and manoeuvre to rule the state and define the reigning definition of America. The meaning of "America" is not static or rooted in soil but culturally

constructed and transformed through processes of differentiation from others; it is defined through and against what it is not and thus relies on the fixing of a discursive division between an "us" and a "them," a "we" and a "they," an "I" and a "you." In this regard, the culture industry and the many nationally inflected cultural products it makes and sells have the power to get Americans to see, think, and feel themselves to be part of a unified national self, as different from others. The culture industry plays an important role in the making and remaking of territorial notions of American identity (Dittmer 2010), as many news programs, TV shows, films, digital games, and web content address their targets as members of one nation and solicit their identification with a national self (Billig 1995). The singing of the national anthem at televised sporting events like NHL and NFL games, for example, tries to unite all Americans, young and old, men and women, black and white, rich and poor, rival fans, as one "America": "the land of the free and home of the brave." Though many of the US culture industry's nationally inflected products enlist millions of different people across the US in one "imagined community" (Anderson 1991), and many more segment and divide this community into micro-national markets and multicultural lifestyle communities, they do not stay put in the United States. For more than 100 years, the culture industry has deterritorialized its operations, pushing its cultural products beyond the American frontier across countries, continents, hemispheres, and, now, the entire planet. Today, US cultural products carry images of and stories about America, informing, entertaining, and possibly influencing people from China to Chile to the Czech Republic. While other states guard their own national culture industries (often against the presumed or actual threat of Americanization), the global reach of the US culture industry has made mediatized America a kind of "second culture" all over the world (Gitlin 2001). Peoples remain by and large divided by borders, histories, classes, sexualities, ethnicities, lifestyles, and languages yet are increasingly and commonly exposed to American cultural products, which turn them into an audience for media scripts of the empire.

Public Opinion
The culture industry is further significant to the US Empire as a shaper of American and transnational public opinions about what world issues are important to it, why, and how. The culture industry plays an agenda-setting role, as many of its goods tell publics what world issues are significant to think about, and may "shape the outlines of foreign policy issues in the minds" of publics "more or less remote or removed from these particular issues" (Cohen 1963, 199–200). For example, when the *Washington Post* ran op-ed pieces by

Hollywood heartthrob George Clooney about the Darfur conflict, and Clooney himself created a media spectacle by protesting outside the Sudanese Embassy to raise consciousness about genocide, this far-off country, once of little importance to many US citizens, entered the public spotlight as something to think about. A bestselling video game like *Call of Duty: Modern Warfare 2* gets civilians to play as US soldiers in a virtual war between the US and Russia, putting Russians in their digital crosshairs as a present or future threat to US national security. Invisible Children Inc.'s distribution of *Kony 2012* through video-sharing websites such as YouTube and Vimeo turned the once unknown Joseph Kony and his rebel militia group, Lord's Resistance Army, into one of the most tweeted topics in the blogosphere. As an agenda-setter, the culture industry constructs certain people, places, and countries as objects worthy of public attention, telling publics what to think about and impressing on them what others may be thinking too. In addition to telling citizens what world issues they should be thinking about, the culture industry's products tell them *how* they should think about them. News stories, TV shows, films, and video games about war, diplomacy, and national security are neither mirrors that reflect reality nor impartial mediators of the power relations between the United States and other states. Far from acting as transparent windows to the world, the culture industry's products frame the world in partial and selective ways, thereby encouraging people to develop certain kinds of understandings of the world, often at the expense of others (Entman 1993). For example, the *Washington Post*'s favourable coverage of Clooney's activities to raise consciousness of Darfur condones the US state's use of economic sanctions and diplomacy in Darfur in order to bring an end to the genocidal conflict, which has the effect of normalizing "humanitarian intervention." *Call of Duty: Modern Warfare 2* frames war as a permanent, legitimate, and efficient solution to interstate conflicts: diplomacy is not an option. *Kony 2012* takes a clear stand against child soldiering and intends to galvanize young people to pressure the US government, African governments, and the International Criminal Court to capture, arrest, and imprison Joseph Kony. In sum, far from being passive reflections of the world, the culture industry's products actively intervene in, give meaning to, and co-construct events by telling people *what* and *how* to think about them, privileging certain issues for focus and prioritizing specific understandings of them.

Mediascapes and Speculative Empires
The culture industry may have the effect of blurring the lines between the US national security state's actual conduct and fictional constructions of

it with geopolitical TV events, blockbuster films, and games that are designed to be sold, watched, or played for fun. These cultural products feed into "mediascapes" (Appadurai 1997) of the US Empire with scripted stories about what the US Empire once did or is now doing. Though these products may attempt to feign a fit between their fictionalizations of the US Empire and the reality of its past or current events, they never quite do so. *Pearl Harbor* (2001) claims to give its viewers historical accuracy and realism yet distorts and leaves a lot out of the picture (Suid 2001). The online game *Kuma/War* (http://www.kumawar.com/) "attempts to approximate war in real time" (Stahl 2010, 103) by enabling people to replay simulated versions of US military events—from killing Osama bin Laden to helping Libyan rebels kill Muammar Gaddafi—soon after the US news packages them as having happened, but these interactive stories are told from the point of view of the US national security state, not those countries or cultures in which it kills. In addition to representing the US Empire's past and present conduct, the culture industry speculates about the US Empire's future condition with fictions that project, prefigure, and even anticipate what's to come. These cultural products carry worst-case scenarios of possible attacks on US soil, scripts of forthcoming security threats, stories about counter-hegemonic rivalries and enemies-in-emergence, and conjectures about temporally distant wars. A Hollywood film like *The Siege* (1998), for example, fictionally prefigured a terrorist attack on American soil prior to the actual 9/11 attack, and soon after the film's author, Laurence Wright, said 9/11 "looks like a movie, my movie" (BBC News 2002). Many video games imagine and immerse people in future-oriented stories of global war and conflict as well. In *Battlefield 4* (2013), the US state goes to war against China; *Call of Duty: Modern Warfare 3* (2011) simulates the Third World War, between the US and Russia; *Call of Duty: Ghosts* (2013) pits a small US Special Operations unit against a coalition of Latin American states called "the Federation of Americas" that plot to colonize the United States.

Given the culture industry's long-standing production of mediascapes that simulate and speculate about the US Empire, it was not entirely surprising when many survivors and eye-witnesses of the 9/11 attack compared what they experienced to entertainment (BBC News 2002). Nor was it unusual, following the 9/11 attack, that the US national security state was urged to integrate the imaginations of the culture industry's cultural workers into its threat matrix and strategic decision-making apparatus. *The National Commission on Terrorist Attacks upon the United States* (2004), for example, chastised the US national security state's "failure of imagination" (to pre-emptively anticipate the attack) and implied it should have been able to do what author Tom Clancy's novel *Debt of Honour* (1994) had done (imagine a pilot who turns an airplane into a terror weapon). The US national security state strives to influence how it is imagined in the cultural products that media companies produce and sell and relies on the culture industry to imagine fictionalizations of future-oriented threat, crisis, and war scenarios. There is a "complementarity in the media-state nexus and the part played by the culture industry in furnishing the security establishment with the cultural imagination needed to meet its goals" (Kumar and Kundnani 2014). For example, less than a year following 9/11, DOD analysts and culture industry workers like David Ayer (writer of *Training Day*), John Milius (co-author of *Apocalypse Now*), and Ron Cobb (the monster designer for *Star Wars*) got together at the Institute for Creative Technologies to imagine new types of threats so as to help the state pre-emptively prepare for them (Calvo 2002). Orson Scott Card's *Ender's Game* is proposed as recommended reading for US Infantry Leaders (S. Shaw 2013); Michael Macedonia, former director of the army's simulation technology centre, says *"Ender's Game* has had a lot of influence on our thinking" (Harmon 2003). Max Brooks, author of *World War Z*, lectures military brass about the importance of preparing for future threats and credits the zombie apocalypse genre with helping them to do so (Dehart 2013). P.W. Singer, Senior Fellow and Director of the Center for 21st Century Security and Intelligence at the Brookings Institute and member of the US Military's Transformation Advisory Group, helped the video game firm Treyarch develop the bestselling *Call of Duty: Black Ops II* (Peck 2012). Two years later, *Call of Duty*'s director and writer Dave Anthony became a Senior Fellow to the Atlantic Council (AC), a NATO think tank. "I thought someone from a creative industry would be the last person that these people would think of working with," said Anthony. The AC's vice-president Barry disagreed. In fact, he praised Anthony's ability to "excel in imagining future security scenarios that are different from today's challenges" and spoke of how eager the AC was to harness Anthony's "world-class talents for imagining new types of threats to strengthen our work on emerging challenges, disruptive technologies, and security and defense strategy" (Drennan 2014). Clearly, the culture industry's imaginings of the past, present, and future of the US Empire are shaped by the national security state and shaping of its own strategic imagination as well.

In sum, the culture industry is tremendously significant to the US Empire as an engine of capitalist growth, a tool and source for PR, a space of war, a means of building a national identity inside the US territory and projecting it to the world, a shaper of public opinion, and a source of the strategic imagination. In the chapters that follow, I examine in greater depth the history and current workings of the US Empire's culture industry, beginning with the early-twentieth-century rise of public relations.

2

Public Diplomacy and Selling the American Way to the World

On the cusp of the twentieth century, large-scale factories were booming in US cities, drawing millions of workers from all over the world to America with the promise of a better life than the one they left behind. The growth of industries organized around the mass production of commodities required the members of a massive and growing waged working class to see themselves primarily as consumers. After US corporations had Taylorized mass production techniques, they turned their efforts to figuring out the one best way to manufacture a consumerist way of life (Ewen 2001). The sphere of production (waged labour time in factories) was routinized, difficult, and meaningless for many workers, so the captains of industry came to rely on the captains of consciousness (advertising and marketing firms) to get workers to see the sphere of consumption (unpaid leisure time in department stores, supermarkets and plazas) as exciting, convenient, and uplifting.

In the early twentieth century, advertisers rose to the challenge of cultivating consumer demand for an ever-expanding supply of endlessly produced commodities, effectively channelling people's demands for control and freedom in the workplace toward a number of packaged choices in an ostensibly "free" marketplace (Ewen 2001). While the ad industry's "captains of consciousness" met the demand for a society of people with a new "consumption ethic" (Marchand 1986), the United States' burgeoning cultural industry tried to absorb people's leisure wages by selling entertainment to them. Vaudeville theatre acts, the Barnum and Bailey and Ringling Brothers circus spectacles, Buffalo Bill's Wild West extravaganza, comic strips, photographic exhibits, motion pictures, and sporting events like baseball and horse racing fostered in customers the sense that to be a true American was to be a consumer (Rydell and Kroes 2005). The commercial gratifications of the United States' burgeoning culture industry were many but not quite enough to quell worker dissent. As the lack of freedom in waged work became more apparent, the gap between the rich and the poor grew wider, and the democracy of the market belied class conflict, workers formed unions to challenge industry's power and state support for it.

To combat the rising political power of worker and social movements that advocated for democratic reform between 1880 and 1920, corporations looked for new ways of controlling public opinion and behaviour so as to remove from democracy the risk of mass public participation (Carey 1995). Entrepreneurs, theorists, and experts in the new discipline of human psychology dutifully met this emergent corporate demand for techniques of mind management and exploited this area of business by building a large-scale public relations (PR) industry (Ewen 1996). Founded by George V.S. Michaelis in 1900, the Publicity Bureau was the first of many US PR agencies to profit by selling opinion-making services to large-scale corporate clients. Ivy Ledbetter Lee and George Parker formed a second PR company in 1904, called Parker and Lee, which fed press releases, leaflets, and bulletins to journalists about the good deeds of corporate America in hopes of transforming widespread public criticism of their operations into mass approval (Gale 2014). Lee described PR as efforts to place corporations before the public and generate mass support by "placing them before the public in the most favorable light"(Gale 2014).

In 1913, Lee was hired by the billionaire John D. Rockefeller to create a positive image of him as an industrial magnate and to temper rising criticism of his power. In 1914, Ivy was paid by Rockefeller to mitigate public outrage in the wake of the Ludlow Massacre. To protest draconian company rules, unpaid overtime, low wages, dangerous work conditions, and cronyism, the United Mine Workers of America had organized a miners strike at a Ludlow, Colorado, tent colony owned by the Rockefeller family's Colorado Fuel and Iron Company. Rockefeller hired the Baldwin-Felts Detective Agency to break the strike, but the miners persevered. As the conflict escalated, Colorado's National Guard was brought in to put the strike down, which resulted in the fatal shooting of a number of striking miners and their family members. To manage public backlash, Rockefeller hired Lee to launch a PR campaign that secured positive publicity for the Rockefeller dynasty's position by bending "facts" in its favour (Ewen 1996, 80). In 1919, Lee used the small fortune he amassed from Rockefeller to launch a PR "counselling office" called Ivy Lee and Associates, and years later he built Ivy Lee and T.J. Ross, which profited by selling opinion-making services to corporations such as Phelps Dodge, Standard Oil, and United States Rubber (Hiebert 1966).

As corporations welded the techniques of commercially oriented entertainment, advertising, and PR into new machinery for influencing and managing public opinion and behaviour, the very American ideal of a participatory democracy was thrown into jeopardy, rejected by some in favour of elite rule. Lippmann (1922) argued that participatory democracy had become impossible and that this was due in part to the growth and impact of the culture industry. Lippmann (1920, 37) observed how the rise of the culture industry gave the state and commercial entertainers, news organizations, advertisers, and PR firms a powerful tool for shaping public opinion and bemoaned how "the manufacture of consent" had become "an unregulated private enterprise." Lippmann (1922) argued that the citizenry's perception of the world (the "pictures in their heads") was formed through exposure to distorted media representations ("pseudo-environments" and "stereotypes") of it. Moreover, Lippmann said citizens filtered everything they read, saw, and heard through their own subjective prejudices, leading to a doubly distorted view of the world. Even if citizens were capable of discerning objective truth from media distortion, they would still be able to grasp only a partial sense of an immense, over determined, and ever-shifting reality. From this, Lippmann concluded that a self-governing democracy of informed, participating, and rational citizens ("omni-competent citizens") was a myth and impractical. In the place of democracy, Lippmann (1922) proposed a technocratic society ruled by a "specialized class" of elites, a group "composed of experts, specialists and bureaucrats" who would work to achieve benevolent ends in government intelligence organizations. For Lippmann, this post-democratic state would not base its policy decisions on the public opinions of the "bewildered herd" but rather engineer a public opinion that reflected the wisdom of the intelligent few. It would then impress this knowledge on the public mind through communications media. "A revolution is taking place," wrote Lippmann (1922, 248–49), wherein "the knowledge of how to create [public] consent will alter every political calculation and modify every political premise." For Lippmann, the manufacture of consent to elite knowledge was benevolent, so long as it aimed to make the pictures in people's heads better correspond with the world outside. In proposing this technocracy, Lippmann was optimistic that a state equipped with the tools of public opinion-making would serve the public interest. He argued that the state's "manufacture of consent" to elite knowledge about the national interest was both benign and necessary because "the common interests [of the country]" were not obvious to most.

Edward Bernays (1923, 1928) – perhaps the twentieth century's most significant public relations theorist and profit-minded practitioner – twisted Lippmann's claim about the impossibility of democracy into a rationale for his own profit interests as the owner of a public relations firm that profited by servicing the opinion-making goals of numerous industrial clients such as Procter and Gamble, the American Tobacco Company, and General Electric (Ewen 1996). Bernays' firm even helped the United Fruit Company (now Chiquita Brands International) and the CIA to topple democratically elected president of Guatemala Jacobo Árbenz and his social democratic government in 1954, after it had undertaken a few modest land reforms aimed to better meet the needs of the country's many bonded debt slaves. Bernays launched a PR campaign to demonize Árbenz's left-leaning government as a communist menace to America and to whip up public support for the coup that, though condemned by the world, was followed by decades of a civil war that killed hundreds of thousands and rule by US-backed military juntas that helped the United Fruit Company prosper (Schlesinger, Kinzer, Coatsworth, and Nuccio 2006).

In a number of pamphlets and books that promoted his company's services, Bernays depicted democratic self-governance as not only impossible but also a threat to the perpetuation of elite rule in America, which he wished to preserve and promote (Ewen 1996). To defend the elite rule from the destabilizing opinions and actions of mass publics of workers, unions, and democratic socialists, Bernays said that an intelligent few needed to guide the mass of citizens toward proper views and actions (those decided by the elites in conjunction with his privatized public relations counsels). For Bernays, public opinion should not derive from citizens themselves but be determined by "a highly educated class of opinion-molding tacticians" who analyze the "social terrain" and adjust "the mental scenery from which the public mind, with its limited intellect, derives its opinions" (Ewen 1996, 10). Defining PR as "the attempt, by information, persuasion, and adjustment, to engineer public support for an activity, cause, movement, or institution," Bernays (1928, 17) argued that PR professionals were among the intelligent few and advised his elite clients to buy his PR services to "pull the wires which control the public mind." While Lippmann called for undemocratic yet benevolent public intelligence agencies to manufacture consent to expert knowledge, Bernays supported the privatization of the engineering of consent and oversaw PR's growth into a big industry that shaped public opinion on behalf of whatever state or corporate client was willing to pay for this service. Both of these thinkers advocated for a kind of government that is nominally democratic in form but substantively ruled by elites. Both assumed that elites will always already know what's best and, presumably, do what's best for all, naively discounting how power corrupts and how elites often serve themselves. Both argued that political and corporate elites should use the culture industry to engineer public consent to ideas and actions they proscribe. And both Lippmann and Bernays cut their teeth as workers for the Committee on Public information, the US state's first wartime PR agency.

*****

In the early twentieth century, the United States was home to a large culture industry, and its public relations wing took part in the development of a consumer-oriented society flooded with all kinds of sales pitches, spectacles, and spin cycles. Throughout the rest of that century, the marketing, advertising, and branding sectors grew larger and larger while "promotional imperatives" came to "influence the behaviors of whole organizations, professions and institutions" (Davis 2013, 1), including those of the US government. Alongside the growth of these promotional industries, the US government built information, propaganda, and public diplomacy apparatuses that mobilized the cultural workers of these industries to develop and launch campaigns aimed at directly or indirectly influencing public opinions and behaviours. From the First World War throughout the wars of the twentieth century and to this day, PR strategies initially designed to support capitalism's sales effort have converged with and become indistinguishable from large-scale national security state campaigns aimed at selling America and war policy to the world. Facing routinized national security threats and eventually becoming a country at permanent war, the US state recruited the culture industry's writers, radio personalities, journalists, ad-people, musicians, designers, filmmakers, TV personas, hucksters, and spin doctors to sell the empire to the world and, in the process, opened world markets to the culture industry's expansion.

The Committee on Public Information: 1918–19

On April 14, 1917, a week after the US joined the Allied forces by declaring war on Germany, President Woodrow Wilson used his executive power to establish the Committee on Public Information (CPI) for the purpose of rallying US and world opinion to the cause of defeating Germany and promoting the supremacy of the United States' liberal democratic capitalist ideals. This goal faced many obstacles. Many US citizens had elected Wilson due to his promise to keep the United States out of war, and US immigrant and radical working-class organizations viewed the war as an inter-imperialist rivalry between states that served the interests of national industrial elites (Ewen 1996, 105). In a letter to Wilson in the lead-up to war, public opinion guru Walter Lippmann encouraged the government to establish a wartime publicity agency. After the US entered the war, Lippmann submitted to Wilson a plan for this state public relations agency (108). Soon after, Wilson issued Executive Order 2594, "Creating Committee on Public Information," to establish the CPI and appointed George Creel to lead it. Creel, a liberal journalist, seemed to possess the prestige and rhetorical skills to convince skeptical publics that war really was a way to make the world safe for democracy.

In *How We Advertised America*, Creel (1920, 3) says the "recognition of Public Opinion as a major force" made the First World War different "from previous conflicts" in that it necessitated a "fight for the minds of men, for the 'conquest of their convictions.'" Creel says the CPI "was called into existence to make this fight for the 'verdict of mankind,' the voice created to plead the justice of America's cause before the jury of Public Opinion." As a "plain publicity proposition, a vast enterprise in salesmanship," and "the world's greatest adventure in advertising," the CPI recruited young Americans to war, got Americans to buy war bonds, and showcased the United States' military and industry using the total means of communication media: "There was no part of the great war machinery that we did not touch, no medium of appeal that we did not employ," says Creel. "The printed word, the spoken word, the motion picture, the post, the signboard – all these were used in our campaign to make our own people and all other peoples understand the causes that compelled America to take arms" (4). Creel describes the CPI's work as comparable to an "advertising campaign, though shot through and through with an evangelical quality" (155). The CPI boosted war morale in Allied countries, built consent to war in neutral ones, and cultivated dissent in the enemy states with its divisions of Speaking, News, Advertising, Pictoral Publicity, and Films.

The Division of Speaking sought to shape public opinion through face-to-face oral communication, mobilizing influential opinion leaders from a number of civil society groups to rally people to the war. Led by the CPI's Four Minute Men, it mobilized 7,500 speakers in 5,200 communities to give 755,190 speeches in support of the war (Creel 1920, 5). In coordination with state fairs, the CPI organized war exhibits that displayed to the public "guns of all kinds, hand-grenades, gas-masks, depth-bombs, mines, and hundreds of other things" (142). To talk up the US abroad, the CPI selected "Americans of foreign birth, men of achievement in their particular trades and professions," and sent "them back to their native lands for speaking tours" (243). The CPI also recruited men of "native lands" (professors, business owners, religious leaders), gave them the latest "facts and figures," and sent "them out to talk to their own people" (243). These foreign advocates turned out to be the United States' "best propagandists, preaching the gospel of democracy with a fervor and understanding that would have shamed many an heir of Plymouth Rock" (244).

The CPI's Division of News was "machinery for the collection and issuance of the official news of government" (Creel 1920, 70). Run by "newspaper men of standing and ability" who "were sworn into the government service," this division prepared and fed to the commercial press "all news bearing upon America's war effort" (71) on behalf of the White House, the navy, the army, the Department of Justice, the War Industries Board, the War Trade Board, and the National War Labor Board. In addition to sourcing the news media to give "the people a daily chronicle of the war effort" in the form of "more than six thousand [press] releases" (82), the Division of News published its own daily called the *Official Bulletin*, which had "a circulation of one hundred thousand copies a day." It also "gathered together the leading novelists, essayists, and publicists of the land, and these men and women" were to produce "articles that went to the press as syndicate features" (7). Using these strategies, the CPI was able to shape the news media's war agenda. The CPI also targeted the "foreign-language press" by opening press "offices in every capital of the world outside the Central Powers" and sourcing war correspondents with its own content. Through cable and wireless transmission, it gave, for "the first time in history, the speeches of a national executive ... universal circulation" (9). The CPI's foreign news service carried "several thousand words a day to the press of the world" (242). It also operated a foreign mail service that distributed news and feature articles and government bulletins around the world (262). In addition to exporting its content, the CPI brought the newsmakers of the world to the US by inviting the foremost newspaper men of other states – Mexico, France, Spain, Holland, England, and the Scandinavian countries – to tour the country so they might "see with their own eyes, hear with their own ears," the power and resolve of the United States. The importation of foreign public opinion-makers was of "incalculable value" to the United States' ability to influence foreign publics. While travelling the country, the foreign newsmakers sent home daily reports by cable and by mail, and on returning home, they wrote news articles and "even went upon the lecture platform" (226) to promote US aims. And because these journalists were not directly affiliated with the US government, their depiction of the United States seemed more credible and trustworthy: "every column carried weight because it came from the pen of a writer in whom the readers had confidence" (230).

The Divisions of Advertising and Pictorial Publicity created photographs, posters, pamphlets, and magazines. In peacetime, the advertising industry served the needs of capitalism by cultivating mass demand for products and getting people to see themselves as sovereign consumers. During wartime, advertising companies ran a "patriotic campaign that gave millions of dollars' worth of free space to the national service" (Creel 1920, 6). Publishers gave ad space to the CPI at no cost, while advertisers themselves purchased ad space in periodicals "and turned it over to the Division of Advertising to use for government purposes" (158). Posters were designed to recruit soldiers, build national unity, glorify the war, and demonize Germans, and publicists "put into pamphlet form America's reasons for entering the war, the meaning of America, the nature of our free institutions, our war aims" (5). The Foreign Pictorial Publicity division circulated "posters, bulletins and photographs" through the show windows of American businesses operating abroad (243). The CPI also opened up reading rooms "in foreign countries" and furnished them with "American books, periodicals and newspapers," which it also supplied to foreign schools and libraries (10, 244). To teach foreigners how to read these texts, the CPI held American English classes for locals, where exposure to "the history, aims and ideals of America" turned the young men that attended each week into "champion[s] of the United States" (244).

The CPI's Division of Films entered "the motion-picture business as a producer and exhibitor" of films in the United States and worldwide "as part of the educational campaign of the United States" (Creel 1920, 120). Through the motion picture, the United States' war aims, as well as the meanings and purposes of liberal democracy and capitalism, "were carried to every community in the United States and to every corner of the world." While films like *Pershing's Crusaders*, *America's Answer*, and *Under Four Flags* promoted the war, other films represented US capitalist-consumer society, the workings of liberal democratic government, and everyday American life to make the country and culture "vivid to foreign peoples" (8). The CPI distributed films through existing private companies such as Hearst-Pathé and Universal and directly exhibited its films in theatre houses in major cities, pouring a "steady stream of wonderful 'fighting stuff'" or "war pictures" into metropolitan city centres so that "the eyes of the world followed America's war progress" (120, 272). It also licensed its films to travelling exhibitors, who moved across the country with their own projectors (120), and it brought its films from the city to the countryside by "put[ting] a projector on an automobile" and travelling from rural "village to village, delighting the rustic populace with 'the wonders of America.'" To the "literate millions" in cities and to "the millions unable to read" in rural areas, screens "carried the story of America, flashing the power of our army and navy, showing our natural resources, our industrial processes, our war spirit, and our national life" (272). While many of the films promoted the war or showed off the wonders of US capitalist-consumer society, the CPI added to this mix a dose of Hollywood entertainment flicks (274). Hollywood comedy and drama films followed the path of the US military as a result of a mutually beneficial relationship between the CPI and the studios. The CPI helped the studios expedite the process of internationally distributing commercial films, but it ensured the shipments would contain a minimum of 20 percent CPI material. The CPI also prohibited the studios from selling content to foreign exhibitors who refused to show the CPI's material or who screened German war propaganda (275). Films were also exhibited abroad by travelling civil society organizations like the American Red Cross, the YMCA, and the Military and Naval Associations (279).

In addition to mobilizing the culture industry to promote US war aims, the CPI censored it as well. The Espionage Act of 1917 made it a federal crime to produce and circulate false information intended to interfere with the operation or success of the US military or to promote the success of its enemies during war time; the Sedition Act of 1918 added to the list of expression offences "language intended to cause contempt, scorn, contumely, or disrepute as regards the form of government of the US, the Constitution, the flag, the uniform of the Army or Navy, or any language intended to incite resistance to the US or promote the cause of its enemies" (cited in Graber 2011, 411).

The CPI also set up a voluntary censorship system that requested that news journalists voluntarily submit their war stories to the CPI before publishing them. Also, the CPI controlled what the US transnational publics saw on the silver screen by trying to "keep out of world circulation" any films that gave "entirely false impressions of American life and morals," such as those about "the lives and exploits of New York's gun-men, Western bandits, and wild days of the old frontier." Although Creel claims that films "covering every detail of American life, endeavor, and purpose, carried the call of the country to every community in the land, and then, captioned in all the various languages, went over the seas to inform and enthuse the peoples of Allied and neutral nations" (1920, 116), the only films the CPI allowed to be screened were those that it decided were realistic. It reviewed at least "eight thousand motion pictures," carefully deciding which ones could and could not be released for distribution "into foreign countries with the true message from America" (281). The CPI's censorship was combined with coercive responses to anti-war opinion. The CPI framed pacifist-minded US citizens and those who said the war served only the profit interests of industrialists as slackers, dupes, and traitors. Outspoken critics of the war such as socialist leader Eugene Debs were sentenced to years in jail, and many other war critics were demonized.

The CPI mobilized every sector of the US culture industry, especially the PR wing, in order to engineer public consent to its version of America and to censor expressions of dissent. At the end of the First World War, the CPI, the United States' first propaganda or public diplomacy agency, was closed down. But it offered a model for selling America that successive US state agencies would build on.

The Office of the Coordinator of Inter-American Affairs (OCIAA): 1938–41

Throughout the 1920s and early 1930s, US public diplomacy had a largely private character but was supported by the US state, which pushed private trade, investment, and cultural goods abroad (Rosenberg 1982). The first published issue of *Foreign Affairs* featured an article by former US Secretary of War Elihu Root (1922), who claimed that "control of foreign relations by democracies" like the United States would require coordinated efforts in "popular education." In 1936, the US state and private sector efforts toward popular education expanded after the US signed a convention in Buenos Aires to establish cultural exchange and information programs in Latin America (Rosenberg 1982). The Division of Cultural Relations (DCR), housed by the US State Department, was established in 1938 to implement the Buenos Aires agreement and was largely an outgrowth of the "Good Neighbour" policy of Franklin D. Roosevelt, which aimed to open up Latin America to US business. At the start of the Second World War in 1939, Roosevelt came to believe that "American trade and investment seemed to increase or decline along with the expansion and contraction of its communications and culture" and that "America's national security depended on its ability to speak to and to win the support of people in other countries" (cited in Rosenberg 1982, 202). On July 30, 1941, Roosevelt issued Executive Order 8840 to establish the Office of the Coordinator of Inter-American Affairs (OCIAA) and appointed Nelson A. Rockefeller to lead it. As a liaison between the needs of US corporations involved in finance, industry, the culture industry, and US diplomacy efforts, the OCIAA was formed to support US corporate interests in Latin America and to combat Nazi Germany's incursions there (Cramer and Prutsch 2006).

The OCIAA pushed the United States' "Good Neighbour" foreign policy, which sought to develop Latin America into a new market for US goods. A new US public diplomacy protagonist, the cultural attaché, worked for the OCIAA to warm up foreign publics to US business presence by managing cultural events and educational exchanges. The cultural attaché, who possessed generalist knowledge of both the United States and the country in which they were posted, aimed to cultivate relations with local opinion leaders, select people to study in the United States, and coordinate the distribution of US media products to libraries, universities, and other institutions (Thomson and Laves 1963). The OCIAA's Division of Press and Propaganda employed hundreds of US journalists, editors, visual artists, and photographers to produce articles, translate and disseminate Roosevelt's speeches, and create artwork for Latin American newspapers, periodicals, and magazines. The OCIAA's Motion Picture Division commissioned Hollywood studios (The Walt Disney Company in particular) to produce animated films that represented positive relations between the US and its new neighbour. With the OCIAA's support, Walt Disney Company cultural workers travelled to Latin America, filming landscapes and people and then adding to this footage animated characters that were intended to resonate with local viewers. The result of this project was *The Three Caballeros* (1944) and *Saludos Amigos* (1942), glocalized animated films that promoted the United States' Good Neighbour policy (Telotte 2007). At the start of the Second World War, the US also established the Foreign Information Service to coordinate anti-Nazi radio broadcasting in Latin America and Europe, the Coordinator of Information to conduct psychological warfare against enemy states, the International Visitor Leadership Program to bring foreign leaders to the US to see America through carefully planned tours, and the Office of Government Reports to do public opinion research. Prior to the United States' entrance into the Second World War, Latin America was a workshop for US public diplomacy.

The Office of War Information (OWI): 1942–45

The US entered the Second World War on December 8, 1941, the day after Japan attacked Pearl Harbor. Roosevelt closed the OCIAA on June 11, 1942, and on July 13, 1942, issued Executive Order 9182 to establish the Office of War Information (OWI), which aimed to "formulate and carry out, through use of the press, radio, motion picture and other facilities, information programs designed to facilitate the development of an informed and intelligent understanding, at home and abroad, of the status and progress of the war effort and of the war policies, activities, and aims of the government" (Summers 1972, 17–18). Led by the former CBS news journalist Elmer Davis, the OWI steered cultural workers from the news, public relations, and entertainment industries into a global public diplomacy campaign that aimed to undermine enemy morale and lift up that of America around the world. Prior to the war, the OWI's staff had known "how to package and market soft drinks, automobiles, and breakfast cereal for large corporations," but during the war these workers' main "client was the United States government, and their job was to sell Washington's policies on war and peace" (Dizard 2004, 18). To do so, they promoted Roosevelt's Four Freedoms (freedom of speech, freedom of worship, freedom from want, and freedom from fear) as universal freedoms, represented the Second World War as a clash between democracy and dictatorship, and sold US liberal international developmentalism in an attempt to achieve a secure post–Second World War order, led by the United States.

During the war, the OWI's Victory Speakers' Bureau tried to imitate the success of the CPI's Four Minute Men by hiring 100,000 local opinion leaders to carry OWI messages to US citizens at public forums held in venues such as town halls, churches, classrooms, and theatres. The Victory Speakers' Bureau groomed its speakers to become powerful orators and controlled their speeches by providing them with speech outlines and talking points to follow. To deter speakers from going off-script, the director monitored them to ensure they did not break the OWI's rules of censorship or spread misinformation. More expansive than the Victory Speakers' Bureau was the OWI's Radio Bureau, which used this fast and light media to reach listeners in the United States and elsewhere. On the home front, millions of US citizens listened to Roosevelt's "fireside chats," while the OWI and US radio broadcasters integrated war stories into daily variety shows, comedies, soap operas, sports coverage, and news programs. Also, the OWI directly produced radio programs such as *This Is Our Enemy* (naming Germany, Japan, and Italy), *Hasten the Day*, *Sam at War*, and *We Have Met the Enemy* to encourage civilian participation in domestic military programs. In addition, it contracted commercial radio producers like Norman Corwin to make radio shows such as *An American in England*. When Pearl Harbor was attacked, the United States had few foreign radio transmitters, and the ones it did possess were controlled by the OIAA's Foreign Information Service (FIS), which was broadcasting to Latin America. During the Second World War, the FIS became the Voice of America (VOA), an OWI-operated international broadcaster. The VOA leased transmitters from private firms all over the world and used them in every country the war affected to tune the ears of people into US presidential speeches, music, and news updates.

The OWI's News Bureau delivered its content to news readers through supportive US-based national and international news companies. Some newspapers maintained formal editorial independence during the war, but many agreed to voluntarily self-censor according to OWI guidelines. To go global, the OWI organized cooperative arrangements with the Associated Press, United Press, and International News Service, and although these firms initially viewed the OWI as a business competitor, they let the organization use their distribution networks as content pipelines in exchange for a fee. Supported by these news corporations, the OWI operated a global press service that transmitted 100,000 words a day to sixty overseas posts, filtered more than 3 million words from nearly 100 overseas news correspondents, circulated 35,000 photographs, produced thousands of feet of newsreel film, and manufactured and distributed millions of copies of a tabloid newspaper called *L'Amérique en Guerre* in France and published *Sternebanner* in Germany (Dizard 2004, 26).

The OWI also operated visual, graphic, and publishing bureaus. These bureaus worked with the War Advertising Council, a group formed by the US corporate sector in 1942 to service the OWI and to ensure that the representations around the globe of the American Way were firmly aligned with the needs of big business (or "free enterprise") and a consumerist way of life. Between 1942 and 1943, the OWI contracted photographers from the ad industry to make heroic images of American civilians mobilizing for war. It paid illustrators and graphic artists to make the Four Freedoms concept palatable to working people, to portray equality between men and women as achievable through military service, to foment fears that Americans were constantly threatened by an omnipotent enemy, and to normalize the idea that allegiance to the state's war aims trumped civil liberties. The OWI formed alliances with US magazine and book publishers to produce war content and helped these publishers gain a foothold in foreign markets hitherto dominated by European companies (Dizard 2004). Supported by the OWI, US publishers launched international editions of magazines like the *Reader's Digest*. The OWI also directly sponsored the development of Overseas Editions, a book distribution chain that released US books to each country involved in the war. To give US publishing and distribution firms an exhibition outlet, the OWI built twenty-six US information centres around the world (Bogart 1995, xiii). Through these military-made print distribution and exhibition networks, the United States pumped all kinds of American magazines, books, and pamphlets into Europe, Africa, and the Middle East. In fact, the OWI information centres exhibited US history books, literary classics, works in the fields of economics, politics, and sociology, source books in science and technology, text books in medicine, and government documents, reports, and periodicals (Thomson and Laves 1963, 54).

Hollywood also helped the United States fight the Second World War. Two years before the OWI was formed, the Production Code Administration (which enforced the Motion Picture Production Code, also known as the Hays Code, after Hollywood's chief censor Will Hays) had set up the Motion Picture Committee for Cooperating for National Defense in order "to evaluate requests from government public relations offices and to make the appropriate facilities and technical advice available" (Steele 1984, 74). Hollywood studios, including Warner Bros., Paramount Pictures, and Metro-Goldwyn-Mayer, agreed to support US aims should it enter the war (Steele 1984). Before the United States' entry into the Second World War, Harry Warner, the head of Warner Bros., pledged to directly support the US state's public diplomacy effort. Warner said, "Our company is about to start the largest program of pictures for the government that has ever been made by any company in the industry" (cited in Nash 1985, 178). In 1942, the OWI formed the Bureau of Motion Pictures (BMP) to network with Hollywood, which was regarded as an "Essential War Industry" (Short 1985). "The motion picture," said OWI head Elmer Davis, is "the most powerful instrument of propaganda in the world, whether it tries to be or not" (cited in Koppes and Black 1977, 88). He continued, "The easiest way to inject a propaganda idea into most people's minds is to let it go through the medium of an entertainment picture when they do not realize that they are being propagandized" (88). With the support of Hollywood studios, the BMP produced, indirectly censored, and distributed war films to US and international theatres. By working with the OWI, Hollywood secured government support for its trade interests abroad. The OWI annually selected forty Hollywood feature films and then distributed them in neutral foreign states, thereby helping Hollywood gain a foothold in the European film market. The OWI allowed Hollywood films to "be shown in the theatres behind the lines of the victorious US troops: first in North Africa, then in Italy and France, and later in all liberated areas" (Wagenleitner 1994, 39).

The OWI's campaign was the "Strategy of Truth," but the truth the OWI conveyed was assembled from information filtered through the Office of Censorship. Run by Byron Price, former head of the Associated Press, the Office of Censorship "withheld information that would aid the enemy, including defense matters, shipping, weather reports and the president's travels" (Brewer 2011, 100). It prohibited the publication of images of dead US soldiers for almost two years, restricted the flow of evidence that Nazis were exterminating Jews until the war's end, banned scenes of black American soldiers fighting alongside white ones, and depicted pacifists as un-American Nazi pawns and Marxist radicals. Mixing ideological persuasion with censorship, the OWI moved a public that was initially uninterested in seeing the United States enter another European war to become one that accepted the executive's opinion that war was a noble means to protect liberal capitalism from dictatorship and assert the United States' exceptional superpower role in world affairs. By the time the Second World War ended in 1945, 50–70 million people had died, the United States had dropped two atomic bombs on Japan, and a rivalry between the United States and the Soviet Union had emerged. On September 15, 1945, the OWI was closed down and its foreign division was transferred to the State Department's Interim International Information Service. On December 31, 1945, the VOA and OCIAA (renamed in March 1945 the Office of Inter-American Affairs [OIAA]) broadcast services to Latin America and Europe were transferred to the State Department. Despite these changes, US public diplomacy capacity continued to grow. On January 1, 1946, the State Department absorbed the OWI and the OIAA's functions into the new Office of International Information and Cultural Affairs.

Public Diplomacy and the Cold War, 1946–91

From 1945 to 1991, the Cold War raged between the United States and the Soviet Union. US presidents came and went, but all were committed to the use of public diplomacy to smash the Iron Curtain and sell liberal democracy – and more importantly consumer capitalism – to publics around the world. And the culture industry was routinely recruited by the state to help it produce and circulate positive stories about America as a place of freedom, democracy, equality, and social mobility (Cull 2008).

On July 26, 1947, Truman signed the National Security Act to "provide for the establishment of integrated policies and procedures for the departments, agencies, and functions of the Government relating to national security." The act established the National Security Council (NSC) to advise the US president on all policies related to national security and created the CIA to gather security-relevant intelligence and conduct clandestine operations. The NSC issued its first public diplomacy directive (NSC Memorandum 4/4A, "Coordination of Foreign Information Measures") in December 1947 (National Security Council 1947). NSC-4 called for the State Department to do overt public diplomacy, and NSC-4A directed the CIA to "initiate and conduct, within the limit of available funds, covert psychological operations designed to counteract Soviet and Soviet-inspired activities." On January 16, 1948, Congress, pressed by Assistant Secretary of State William Benton, supported the establishment of a permanent public diplomacy agency by passing the Smith-Mundt Act (named after New Jersey Republican Senator Alexander Smith and South Dakota Republican Representative Karl Mundt). Also known as the United States Information and Educational Exchange Act of 1948, the act authorized Congress to allocate public funds to a full-time public diplomacy agency. Section 501 says the act's objective is "to enable the Government of the United States to promote a better understanding of the United States in other countries, and to increase mutual understanding between the people of the United States and the people of other countries." It authorized the secretary of state to prepare and disseminate abroad "information about the US, its people and its policies, through press, publications, radio, motion pictures and other information media, and through information centers and instructors abroad" (Dizard 2004; Thomson and Laves 1963). While section 501 of the act gives the US state the legal power to propagandize foreign publics, it prohibits the circulation of the same propaganda materials in the US: "any information ... shall not be disseminated within the United States, its territories, or possessions." Although the act intended to squelch anxieties about the US state manipulating the minds of US citizens while permitting such ideological manipulation on a global scale, it "blocks out important information to the US public about its government's foreign-policy objectives" (Snow 1998, 619). Basically, the act gave the US executive the power to unilaterally speak for the nation on world affairs without letting US citizens know what it was doing or saying. Interestingly, the act says that the state's public diplomacy agency must not compete with the profit interests of US media corporations but instead should protect and promote them in other countries. Section 1005 declares that the agency must utilize, to the maximum extent, "the services and facilities of private agencies, including existing American press, publishing, radio, motion picture, and other agencies through contractual arrangements or otherwise." Furthermore, the act declares that the agency must contract these media corporations in each "field consistent with the present and potential market for their services in each country" it targeted, a stipulation that basically transformed public diplomacy into the culture industry's global Trojan Horse and the selling of America, a business opportunity. A 1948 US Advertising Council booklet entitled *Advertising, a New Weapon in the World Fight for Freedom: A Guide for Business Firms* enthused that "Selling America through advertising copy lends itself to commercially sponsored broadcasts abroad, to posters and window cards, to pamphlets and leaflets. The field is so broad that there is really no end to the media through which business and industry can help sell the truth abroad" (cited in Summers 1972, 62).

On April 14, 1950, Paul Nitze's NSC-68 called for aggressive overt and covert economic, geopolitical, and psychological warfare to influence hearts and minds in Soviet spheres of influence and to cause social unrest there. Between 1950 and 1953, the Office of International Information supported the United States' role in the Korean War and waged a "Marshall Plan of Ideas" in Western Europe. It also strove to challenge what Senator William Benton called the "Big Lie" of Soviet propaganda, which claimed that the US capitalist system was crisis prone and headed for a crash; that the United States was ruled by warmongers and monopolists; that the United States' rich were getting richer and the poor were getting poorer as a result of capitalism; that the US ideals of freedom and democracy were myths that covered up racial, sexual, and class inequality; and that US culture was shallow, materialistic, and intellectually stunted (Thomson and Laves 1963). In response to these ostensible lies, Truman called for a global "Campaign for Truth." In a speech delivered at the American Society of Newspaper Editors' annual convention in 1950, Truman (1950) said, "I am convinced that we should greatly extend and strengthen our efforts to make the truth known to people in all the world," and he pledged his commitment to "spread the truth about freedom and democracy." He declared that the US "must use every means at our command, private as well as governmental, to get the truth to other peoples" and that the US government would win "the minds of men" by coordinating its public diplomacy activities with private media allies "in a sustained, intensified program to promote the cause of freedom against the propaganda of slavery." This Campaign for Truth attempted to debunk

Soviet claims against the United States and generate worldwide confidence in US leadership of the world by harnessing the promotional services of the culture industry. In a 1951 State Department Bulletin called "The America Idea: Package It for Export," John Beggs explained:

> Your Government recognizes that, in order to achieve the objectives of its foreign policy throughout the world, it must have the cooperation of private enterprise and private organizations whose daily relationships with people in foreign lands contribute to the building of international good will. In this greater struggle, the interests of American Government and American business abroad are synonymous ... Companies selling products overseas can also sell America and our concept of freedom.

Supporting the State Department's effort to sell the truth to the world was the Psychological Strategy Board, which Truman established in 1951 to advise the NSC on how to change minds and behaviours.

When Eisenhower became president in 1953, he established the President's Committee on International Information Activities, chaired by William H. Jackson, to evaluate public diplomacy activities. The resulting *Jackson Report* called for the establishment of a consolidated public diplomacy agency separate from the CIA's black propaganda agencies and the DOD's psychological warfare units. The report advised this new agency, once established, to strategically adapt or localize its activities to the particularities of each country or region it targeted. The report also recommended a strategy of "non-attribution," meaning that propaganda would be attributed only to the United States when this was an asset. Furthermore, the report called for this service's coordination with private organizations like churches, labour groups, and corporations. Finally, it said that the agency should distribute products that contained fair criticism of US society and culture, as this would demonstrate the United States' self-reflexivity, openness to debate, and support for the free exchange of ideas. Eisenhower operationalized the *Jackson Report* by establishing the United States Information Agency (USIA) on June 1, 1953. Beholden to the NSC's direction and accountable to it each year, the USIA's job was "explaining and interpreting to foreign people the objectives and policies of the United States Government"; "depicting imaginatively the correlation between US policies and the legitimate aspirations of other peoples in the world"; "unmasking and countering hostile attempts to distort or to frustrate the objectives and policies of the United States"; and "delineating those important aspects of the life and culture of the people of the United States which facilitate understanding of the policies and objectives of the Government of the United States" (Hansen 1984, 17). When the USIA was established, US educational and cultural exchange programs were handed over to the State Department's Bureau of Educational and Cultural Affairs (Frankel 1965, 26–27). But this was really a formality, as the USIA's overseas posts were still responsible for managing educational and cultural exchanges.

Between 1953 and 1991, the USIA expanded alongside the US Empire in order to bolster the US image, promote its military incursions, and shuttle liberal democratic and capitalist ideal-carrying commodities. The USIA operated a number of bureaus: the Bureau of Information produced media content that expressed and supported the US executive's official foreign policy positions and coordinated the dispatch of US strategic intellectuals to foreign countries to talk up US interests. The Bureau of Educational and Cultural Affairs administered educational and cultural exchanges such as the Fulbright Program (the exchange of students and professors between the United States and other countries to foster mutual understanding) and the Foreign Leaders Program, which became the International Visitors Program (the education of the emerging elites of other countries in the United States with the hope that they would dutifully support US strategic interests when they returned home to rule). The USIA also operated the Office of Research and Media Reaction to conduct public opinion surveillance polling and analysis in other countries so that it could customize its propaganda campaigns to suit local cultural and ideological conditions. USIA Public Affairs Officers ran country-specific teams of persuaders that designed and followed country-specific plans, or blueprints, to influence the opinions of local community leaders, professors, military personnel, politicians, and policy-makers in the target countries (Sorenson 1968, 64). US-based PR companies fully supported the USIA's emergence, since its global Americanization effort was recognized as offering them a lucrative business opportunity. In 1952, PR guru Edward Bernays had led a national committee for an adequate US overseas information program comprised of twenty-eight media industry leaders to lobby for the USIA's establishment (perhaps hoping to reap maximal contracts).

Throughout the Cold War, US presidents supported the USIA's selling effort. In his 1953 State of the Union address, Eisenhower promised to "make more effective all activities related to international information" because they were "essential to the security of the United States" (cited in Sorenson 1968, 31). Kennedy declared the USIA's mission was to "help achieve US foreign policy objectives by (a) influencing public attitudes in other nations and (b) advising the president, his representatives abroad, and the various departments and agencies on the implications of foreign opinion for present and contemplated US policies, programs, and official statements" (cited in Malone 1988, 20). Johnson supported the USIA's use of "modern instruments and techniques of communication" to "reach large or influential segments of national populations – to inform them, to influence their attitudes, and at times perhaps to motivate them to a particular course of action" as a way to get these segments to exert "noticeable, even decisive, pressures on their governments" (US Congress 1994). Under Nixon (and Ford), the USIA supported the Vietnamization of the American War and détente with the Soviet Union and China. Carter renamed the USIA the US International Communications Agency (ICA) and, unlike his predecessors, said this public diplomacy agency should "undertake no activities which are covert, manipulative, or propagandistic." Carter wanted the ICA to help US citizens to "understand the histories, cultures, and problems of others, so that we can come to understand their hopes, perceptions, and aspirations" (cited in Cull 2008). Carter's plan to use the ICA to enable two-way dialogue about US foreign policy between non-US and US citizens was quickly reversed by Reagan, who re-established the USIA and unabashedly conceived of it as an apparatus of ideological warfare to defend the United States from Soviet propaganda and aggressively sell the supremacy of liberal democracy and capitalism to the world. To do so, Reagan issued NSC-77, "Management of Public Diplomacy Relative to National Security," which sought "to strengthen the organization, planning and coordination of various aspects of public diplomacy of the United States government relative to security" by explicitly linking "public diplomacy" to "actions of the US Government designed to generate support for our national security objectives." In 1990, the first Bush administration issued National Security Presidential Directive 51 to affirm the USIA's mission of explaining and promoting America around the world.

All Cold War presidents, Republican and Democrat, used the USIA as an instrument of power. And while the USIA aimed to influence and change the attitudes and behaviours of people to make US interests feel like theirs, it also aided the global growth of US media corporations in the countries it targeted.

The USIA ran its own international news service to bridge the territorial gap between the US Empire's administrative centre and its satellites.

Named after the shortwave wireless transmitters that carried information from Washington, DC, to US embassies during the Second World War, this "wireless file" acted as a feedback loop between Washington's imperial planners and the hundreds of US diplomats stationed abroad. The US executive used the wireless file to guide the conduct of diplomats, keep them informed about changes in US foreign policy, and ensure that their talking points aligned with the president's. Diplomats used this information to keep the executive informed about what was happening "on the ground" in the country in which they were positioned. In addition to connecting Washington elites with their foreign ambassadors, the wireless file was an influential source of official information for commercial news journalists, who craved a ready supply of news stories about US foreign policy and the politics, economics, and cultures of countries affected by it. News organizations all over the world published the contents of the wireless file (which USIA authors conveniently editorialized and translated into the target country's local language) (Dizard 2004, 160). In addition to sourcing news organizations with linguistically adapted wireless files, the USIA started building foreign press centres in major cities in 1961 as a way to corral foreign correspondents into centralized locations so that it could feed them its news. On October 18, 1961, the USIA established the New York Foreign Press Center and started sourcing news journalists with press releases and holding press conferences. Furthermore, the USIA produced newsreels and circulated them to foreign news organizations.

The USIA also supported the globalization of the US publishing industry, acting as a subsidizer, producer, distributor, and exhibitor of books. In 1948, Congress approved Public Law 402, which authorized the USIA's Information Media Guarantee (IMG) program. The IMG was designed to give US commercial publishers an incentive to export and sell American books, magazines, and journals abroad by guaranteeing they would be paid in US dollars in exchange for the foreign currencies – rupees, francs, pesos, and pounds – they received from transnational consumers of these products, who, at the time, were short on US dollars. Between 1948 and 1960, the IMG helped US publishers export $40 million worth of US books to eighteen countries (Thomson and Laves 1963). The IMG subsidy stimulated the global establishment of US publishing houses and supported their foreign sales efforts (Dizard 1961). The USIA also subsidized the publishing industry by underwriting US-based international book reproduction and distribution firms such as Ladder Books and Franklin Publishing, translating

American books aligned with USIA goals from English into foreign languages at no cost to the publisher, contracting US publishers to carry certain titles abroad, and outsourcing the production of its own books to US authors (Sorenson 1968). In addition to greatly supporting the book industry's global growth, the USIA itself acted as an international distributor and exhibitor of books. USIA libraries, reading rooms, and travelling exhibits served as distribution/exhibition points for hundreds of thousands of American printed works: books such as *Forced Labour in Soviet Russia*, *The Communist War on Religion*, *The Threat of Soviet Imperialism*, and *Death of Science in Russia*; magazines such as *Reader's Digest, America Illustrated, American Reporter, World Today, National Review, Life, Time, Newsweek, Ebony,* and *Phylon*; academic journals such as *Problems of Communism*; and comic books, including *Superman* and *Donald Duck*. With help from the USIA, the US publishing industry went global while exposing its readers to US high-, low-, and middle-brow culture.

The USIA operated international radio broadcasting agencies, too, the Voice of America (VOA) being its most important. Founded in 1942 as part of the OWI, the VOA was integrated into the USIA in 1953 and given a charter in 1960. The VOA Charter declared that the "long-range interests of the United States are served by communicating directly with the peoples of the world by radio" and that, "to be effective, the Voice of America must win the attention and respect of listeners." To achieve this goal, the VOA would 1) "serve as a consistently reliable and authoritative source of news" that is "accurate, objective, and comprehensive"; 2) "represent America, not any single segment of American society, and will therefore present a balanced and comprehensive projection of significant American thought and institutions"; 3) "present the policies of the United States clearly and effectively, and will also present responsible discussions and opinion on these policies" (Hansen 1984, 19). Although the VOA charter expressed noble public service broadcasting values (public interests, not private profits) similar to those espoused by Britain's BBC and Canada's CBC, the VOA largely served as the official voice of successive US presidents, who represented the United States' liberal democratic consumer-capitalist society as the apex of world historical development. As such, the VOA targeted many countries with hundreds of thousands of hours of media in various program formats. VOA news shows like *Panorama USA, Press Conference USA, Issues in the News,* and *The Breakfast Show* featured reports, analysis, and discussions about happenings in the United States. Among the VOA's most popular offering to world youth was jazz and rock music, which it licensed from the US recording industry and broadcast around the world. While the State Department financed world tours of Dizzy Gillespie, the Dave Brubeck Quartet, and Louis Armstrong, the VOA hired Washington disc jockey Willis Conover to host *Music USA*, a two-hour nightly jazz show that reached a global audience of listeners. The VOA also broadcast rock and roll to the world in order to attract the youth oppressed by the Soviet Union to American ideals. Nearing the end of the Cold War, the VOA was broadcasting each week in forty-seven different languages, contracting out services to the radio industry, and boosting the profits of the recording industry by licensing songs from some of the United States' most popular recording artists. The CIA's broadcasters, Radio Free Europe and Radio Liberty, also directed numerous psychological warfare campaigns against Soviet-leaning states throughout the Cold War.

The USIA also operated a motion picture and television service. In the year of the USIA's founding, Eric Johnston, president of Hollywood's chief lobby group, the Motion Picture Association of America, said to a US Senate Foreign Policy Committee that "Pictures give an idea of America which is difficult to portray in any other way, and the reason, the main reason, we think, is because our pictures are not obvious propaganda" (cited in Wagenleitner 1994, 229). The USIA commissioned Hollywood studios to produce documentary films in support of US foreign policy goals. Its first feature, *John F. Kennedy: Years of Lightning, Days of Drums* (1964), glorified Kennedy's presidency; *Cuba Waits* depicted the negative effects of communism in Cuba; *Escape to Freedom* encouraged East Germans to immigrate to West Germany in pursuit of freedom; *Integration* celebrated the progress of African Americans toward equality; *American Economy* lauded the United States' burgeoning consumer culture. *Tomorrow in Their Hands* and *Night of the Dragon* supported US war policy in Vietnam (Elder 1968). USIA posts distributed these and hundreds of other films it made through film lending libraries, commercial theatres, and a film mailing service. The USIA even exhibited its films to viewers in rural areas using mobile riverboat and jeep-equipped projectors (Dizard 1961). In 1965, the USIA added TV to its arsenal and distributed TV shows in post-colonial countries. TV documentaries like *Venezuela Looks towards Her Future* and *Guatemala Forges Its Future* conveyed capitalist modernization as the future of Latin America. The USIA produced Spanish-language soap operas (or telenovelas) like *Nuestro barrio*, which framed US capitalist modernization as the development solution to the economic and social problems of the urban poor. In 1980, the USIA established Radio y TV Martí to directly broadcast into Cuba. In 1982, the USIA's *Let Poland Be Poland* was globally broadcast to support Solidarity, the Polish trade union. In 1983, the USIA built WORLDNET Film and Television Service, a global satellite TV operation.

Throughout the Cold War, the USIA used these and all available culture industry resources to attack the Soviet Union and glorify America's model as the best. By 1991, the US had won the global contest of ideologies.

Public Diplomacy after the Cold War, 1991–2000

The end of the Cold War was accompanied by heady claims that humankind had arrived at the end of history, a new period when age-old conflicts between competing ideologies were transcended by a new global order defined by free trade, political interdependence between liberal states, and technological integration. Ben Wattenberg (1991, 20), a neoconservative intellectual, argued that the demise of the Soviet Union meant that the United States had a golden opportunity to aggressively universalize the American way of life: "Only Americans have the sense of mission and gall to engage in benign, but energetic, global cultural advocacy. We are the most potent cultural imperialists in history." The United States emerged from the Cold War as the world's undisputed superpower. In this unipolar moment, public diplomacy was tasked with supporting the United States' New World Order foreign policy. George Bush's (1990) National Security Review 24 re-evaluated US public diplomacy activities, and National Security Directive 51 reaffirmed its main goals: to explain US foreign policy to global audiences, describe US culture, provide information about US and world events, and support surrogate media diffusion in areas of the world where a commercial press did not exist.

Clinton's foreign policy promoted neoliberal democracy and free trade to the world, and the USIA primarily served "the interest of US trade and economic sectors by touting the superiority of US commercial values and economic policies to elite foreign audiences" and by selling a corporate version of America "to the influential markets of the world" (Snow 1998, 623–24). The Clinton administration transformed the structure of the USIA by passing the International Broadcasting Act of 1994 (Public Law 103–236) to establish the nine-member Broadcasting Board of

Governors (BBG), which brought all US international broadcasters (the VOA, WORLDNET, Radio y TV Martí, Radio Free Europe/Radio Liberty, and Radio Free Asia) under one roof. The act gave the president the power to select the BBG's members from among American culture industry workers and established the International Broadcasting Bureau to provide the BBG with support. Following the passage of this act, the USIA was reorganized into four bureaus: 1) Broadcasting (including radio, television, and film), 2) Educational and Cultural Affairs (which handled cultural exchange, arts, library, and book activities), 3) Policy and Programs (including policy guidance, the wireless news file, exhibits, publications, and foreign press relations), and 4) Management (Nakamura and Weed 2009). The steering and action of the USIA was overseen by a number of groups: the Advisory Commission on Public Diplomacy, the Advisory Board for Cuba Broadcasting, the J. William Fulbright Scholarship Board, the Cultural Property Advisory Committee, and a number of private sector committees dedicated to different programs.

In the mid-1990s, the USIA's budget was $1.189 billion (4 percent of the CIA's annual budget). Throughout most of the 1990s, the USIA had 190 offices in 142 countries. Region-specific offices – the Office on African Affairs, the Office of Inter-American Affairs, the Bureau of East Asian and Pacific Affairs, the Office of West European and Canadian Affairs, the Office of East European Affairs, and the Office of North African, Near Eastern, and South Asian Affairs – enabled the USIA to design and implement glocalized PR campaigns on a regional and country-specific basis (Nakamura and Weed 2009). The USIA also built the Office of Affiliate Relations to establish a global network of affiliated radio and TV stations around the world to broadcast its material; launched a weekly TV program in Ukraine called *Window on America*; produced and distributed a documentary about human rights violations in Yugoslavia called *Crimes against Humanity*; and launched a 24/7 English-language news infotainment service called VOA News Now. The VOA transmitted 660 hours of weekly programs in fifty-three languages to numerous countries, Radio y TV Martí sent twenty-four hours of radio and four and a half hours of TV shows in Spanish to Cuba every day, and Radio Free Europe/Radio Liberty beamed more than 500 hours of programs in twenty-three languages to Central Europe, Russia, Iran, Iraq, and the Soviet Union's former republics each week (USIA 1999, 1). Steered by the neoliberal Clinton administration's conflation of the US national interest in world affairs with free markets, free enterprise, and free trade, the USIA of the 1990s functioned to promote and sell an "essentially corporate version of the country to the influential markets of the world" (Snow 1998).

In the late 1990s, Congress reduced the USIA's budget. This decision rested on the assumption that the US government no longer needed an official means of telling and selling "America's story" to the world, because its liberal democratic capitalist story had already become the planet's metanarrative. Congressional cutbacks to the USIA also rested on the assumption that US media corporations, NGOs, and other private actors would autonomously bring positive imagery and messages of America and US foreign policy to the world, even though the US state paid less for them to do so.

Congress' budget crunching efforts came to a head in October 1998, when it passed the Foreign Affairs Agencies Consolidation Act (or Foreign Affairs Reform and Restructuring Act of 1998). The act would abolish the USIA on October 1, 1999, and integrate all USIA bureaus (with the exception of the International Broadcasting Bureau) into the Department of State, putting them under the command of a new under secretary for public diplomacy. Congress' rush to close down the USIA was perhaps short-sighted, as growing global antipathy to the Washington Consensus, heightened fears of Americanization, and cultural nationalist backlashes against the global dominance of US corporate brands such as Coca-Cola, McDonald's, and Nike indicated that the private sector could not sustain transnational support for America. Six months after the passage of the act, recognizing that US imperial hegemony could not last without official public diplomacy, Clinton signed Presidential Decision Directive/NSC-68 International Public Information on April 30, 1999. Its purpose was to build "understanding and support for US foreign policy initiatives around the world" by "countering the growing hostile misinformation about the United States, and more effectively promoting US policy, values and interests to foreign audiences." To ensure that the United States' renewed public diplomacy effort supported national security objectives, Clinton's directive called for the State Department, DOD, and National Security Council to oversee its operations, setting the stage for twenty-first-century US public diplomacy.

Public Diplomacy and the Global War on Terrorism, 2001–9

On September 11, 2001, al-Qaeda hijacked and crashed airplanes into the World Trade Center, a symbol of global finance capital, and the Pentagon, a symbol of US military preponderance. This terrorist attack typified the "propaganda of the deed," a psychological warfare strategy driven by the idea that actions not only speak but also speak louder and more forcefully than words. Though al-Qaeda committed mass murder on 9/11, the group's primary goal was to shatter the United States' image of security and sow mass fear and anxiety among the US public (Kaldor 2007). As both American and worldwide TV networks turned the attack into a global media event, al-Qaeda destabilized the US Empire's image of military invincibility. The Bush administration responded to the attack by declaring a new global War on Terrorism. The US then started fighting this war in Afghanistan and later in Iraq and other countries. Global criticisms of US foreign policy peaked following 9/11, and throughout George W. Bush's first term politicians emphasized the need to rebuild public diplomacy. At a 2001 US House of Representatives Hearing entitled "The Message Is America: Rethinking US Public Diplomacy," Henry Hyde (R-IL) said, "It is by now obvious to most observers that the role of public diplomacy in our foreign policy has been too long neglected." Hyde went on to say that public diplomacy should "enlist the populations of the world into a common cause and ... convince them that the goals that they seek for themselves – freedom, security and prosperity – are the same as those the United States seeks" (US Congress 2001a). To sell these goals, the US State Department again enlisted media corporations. A 2002 Independent Task Force on Public Diplomacy sponsored by the Council of Foreign Relations and entitled "Public Diplomacy and the War on Terrorism" called for "the establishment of coordinating structure, chaired by a principal adviser to the president, to harmonize the public diplomacy efforts of government agencies, allies and private-sector partners." It declared that US "image problems and foreign policy are not things apart. They are both part of an integrated whole" (Peterson 2002, 74). In 2002, *The National Security Strategy of the United States* announced the US state's "need for a different and more comprehensive approach to public information efforts that can help people around the world learn about and understand America" (White House 2002, 31). It stated, "We will wage a war of ideas to win the battle against international terrorism" (6).

While the US state worried that the rising tide of anti-Americanism would inspire future acts of violence toward US life, liberty, or property at home and abroad and greatly diminish its soft power in world affairs, the US corporate class feared that the transnationalization of anti-American hatred would cost them revenue in the numerous markets in which their companies did business. In 2003, *Business Week* asked, "Will the enormous rise in anti-Americanism seen globally as a result of the war spill over to the business realm and cause problems for the continued development of globalization and free markets?" Many corporations surmised that the answer was yes. In response, they formed the Business for Diplomatic Action (BDA) in 2004 "to encourage, develop, collect and disseminate new insights and research related to America's role in the world, public diplomacy, and global public opinion." The BDA was run by blue-chip corporations, including American Airlines, Time Warner, Clear Channel, Google Inc., McDonald's, Microsoft, PepsiCo, The Coca-Cola Company, and Studio One Networks. The BDA also collaborated with think tanks like the Brookings Institution and the Center for a New American Security. Anti-Americanism, the BDA observed, inspired the destruction of US property (ritualistic McDonald's window smashing), increased security costs (more surveillance cameras and guards to police shopping malls), and ignited trade boycotts (e.g., "Drink Mecca Cola, not Coca-Cola"). The BDA believed "the US stands to lose its competitive edge if steps are not made toward reversing the negativity associated with America." In response to this negativity, the task force declared that "American business leaders have the responsibility to use their influence and creative resources to improve the overall reputation of the United States."

Hoping to improve the United States' reputation, US Secretary of State Colin Powell recruited Charlotte Beers as the State Department's under secretary of state for public diplomacy and public affairs on October 2, 2001. Prior to working as the Office of Public Diplomacy's (OPD) leader, Beers had been a powerful advertising executive. Powell's recruitment of Beers reflected his belief that public diplomacy is like branding. At a news conference in September 2001, Powell described why he hired Beers: "I wanted one of the world's greatest advertising experts, because what are we doing? We're selling. We're selling a product. That product we are selling is democracy. It's the free enterprise system, the American value system. It's a product very much in demand. It's a product that is very much needed" (US Department of State 2001).

Powell's notion that nations are brands that can be produced and sold on the world market like Nike shoes, McDonald's hamburgers, and Starbucks coffee was popularized in the late 1990s by the British brand expert Simon Anholt (2008). "Just as companies have learned to 'live the brand,'" says Anholt, "countries should consider their reputations carefully – because ... in the interconnected world, that's what statecraft is all about" (cited in C. Risen 2005). After 9/11, nation branding was embraced by Beers, and in her confirmation hearings, Beers said before the Senate Foreign Relations

Committee that she would sell "not only the facts but also emotions and feelings of what it means to be American," as "these intangibles" were incredibly important to the realization of US interests. "The whole idea of building a brand is to create a relationship between the product and its user," said Beers. "We're going to have to communicate the intangible assets of the United States – things like our belief systems and our values" (cited in Starr 2001, 56). Beers recruited the US Advertising Council to help the OPD rebrand America (Teinowitz 2002).

Though the OPD's post-9/11 branding campaign was global, it focused especially on Muslims. A number of policy reports published between 2001 and 2008, including *Finding America's Voice: A Strategy for Reinvigorating US Public Diplomacy* (composed by an independent task force sponsored by the Council for Foreign Relations), *An Initiative: Strengthening US-Muslim Communications* (drafted by the Center for the Study of the Presidency and Congress), and *Changing Mind, Winning Peace: A New Strategic Direction for US Public Diplomacy in the Arab and Muslim World* (an extensively researched US government document), called for an improved US public diplomacy effort aimed at Muslims all over the world and described ways of sparking pro-US transformation among Muslims. In an October 10, 2001, address to the House Committee on International Relations, Beers outlined three key points she sought to communicate to the Muslims of the world: 1) the attacks on the World Trade Center and the Pentagon were not attacks on America but attacks on the world; 2) this is not a war against Islam; it is a war against terrorists and those who support and harbour them; and 3) all nations must band together to eliminate the scourge of international terrorism (US Congress 2001b). Beers' premier campaign was called the Shared Values Initiative, launched in October 2002.

In an attempt to make a case for the shared values between America and the Muslim world, the OPD contracted the US-based advertising firm McCann-Erickson to produce five TV commercials in which American Muslims (perhaps actors) talk about their happy lives and positive experiences in the United States (Perlez 2002). The videos claim to showcase the everyday lives of four very patriotic Muslim Americans: Abdul Hammuda, a Libyan-born baker; Algerian-born Elias Zerhouni, director of the National Institute of Health; Farooq Muhammed, a New York firefighter; and the Lebanese-born Rawia Ismail, a teacher who socializes with children in her kitchen, at a school softball game, and in front of her elementary school class (Perlez 2002). In each video, American Muslims praise the United States' religious openness, multicultural pluralism, and racial equality. "We are happy to live here as Muslims and preserve our faith. Religious freedom here is something that is very important, and no one ever bothered us," says Adbul Hammuda (Tapper 2003). "I was totally embraced by the people here ... Everybody told me, 'Well, we're all immigrants here, we're all from different places, and we meld together,' and I loved that," claims Elias Zerhouni. "I've never gotten disrespected because I'm a Muslim." "We're all brothers and sisters," says Farooq Muhammed. Each video shows Muslims working, praying, socializing, making music, and working in the United States and conveys an uplifting image of Muslim life in America. The ads do not show the downside of Muslim life in America, such as hate crimes against Muslims, warrantless surveillance of Muslims, incarceration and persecution of Muslims suspected of being terrorists, and right-wing media Islamaphobia. Each of the OPD's ads ends with a tagline saying it is sponsored by the Council of American Muslims for Understanding (a front group funded by the State Department to give its message an air of authenticity) (Rampton 2007). To circulate these videos through sources not obviously affiliated with the US government, the OPD purchased ad space from Middle Eastern TV networks such as Abu Dhabi TV and Al Jazeera. The videos targeted "non-elite" Muslims between the ages of fifteen and fifty-nine and were subsequently viewed on TV by an estimated 288 million people across Africa and Asia (Tapper 2003). The OPD also worked with *Sesame Street*'s executive producers to make a glocalized version of the popular American children's TV show to teach Muslim children about America.

The OPD's Shared Values campaign also launched an Arabic magazine called *Hi*. With an annual production budget of $4.5 million (and contracted out to a private US publishing firm), *Hi* was designed to appeal to middle- and upper-class Muslim teenagers, with flashy images of American consumer culture. The OPD also produced a booklet called *Muslim Life in America*, which reached approximately 288 million people in the Middle East, South Asia, and East Asia with positive stories about Muslim American citizens such as Atlanta Hawks basketball player Shareef Abdur-Rahim and Nobel Prize winner Ahmed Zewail. The OPD bought ad space of pan-Arabist newspapers and filled it with pro-American messages, and a website called Open Dialogue was created to enable discussion between Muslim Americans and Muslims living elsewhere. Its messages were also conveyed through portable "American Rooms" (small centres full of information about American society) abroad, 150 of which had been developed by the OPD and the Smithsonian Institute and placed in libraries and shopping malls in Bangladesh, Oman, United Arab Emirates, Afghanistan, Bulgaria, Uzbekistan, Kyrgyzstan, and elsewhere.

The Broadcasting Board of Governors (BBG) supported the Shared Values Initiative with new TV and radio broadcasters. The BBG used 150 million congressionally appropriated dollars to launch Radio Sawa (Radio Together), an Arabic-language broadcaster whose goal is to "cover US policies and actions" with a "fresh, upbeat American style" that meshes with the "daily lives" of its young listeners (US Congress 2004, 20). Radio Sawa's programs encouraged "audience voting for favourite songs, questions from listeners about American and US foreign policy, call-in discussions, and news stories about young people, women's issues, and health" (Peterson 2002). Radio Sawa was carried on FM transmitters in Jordan, Kuwait, Dubai, Abu Dhabi, Qatar, Bahrain, and Djibouti, as well as Iraq, and was transmitted from Cyprus to reach Egypt, Lebanon, Syria, and Gaza (Djerejian 2003, 30). Radio Farda, another BBG venture launched soon after, was built to broadcast glocalized American programming to Iran.

While the OPD's Bureau of International Information Programs and Bureau of Public Affairs handled the electronic and print components of Shared Values, the Bureau of Educational and Cultural Affairs (BECA) facilitated educational and cultural exchanges between US and Muslim intellectuals through its Partnership for Learning Program. This program targeted young and diverse Muslims through academic and professional exchanges such as the Fulbright, International Visitor Leadership, and Citizen Exchange programs. Fourteen Afghan women (civil servants) travelled the United States to learn about America, and forty-nine Muslim women from fifteen different countries visited the United States to learn about the US election process. The OPD also brought the head of the largest Islamic organization in Indonesia – and the world – to the United States, funded a Rule of Law conference for more than 200 Egyptian judges, brought young Palestinians to the United States, and hosted teachers from Turkey, Uzbekistan, and the Kyrgyz Republic. Middle Eastern journalists and TV producers also travelled to the United States for media training sessions and to explore the country with their cameras (Beers 2002). Muslim academics from Asia and the Middle East were brought to the United States for study tours, and more than twenty principals of Islamic schools in Indonesia visited in the summer of 2002. When Muslims would or could not go to the United States to study the American way of life, the OPD took American education to them. A group called Writers in America (comprised of fifteen established American authors) toured the Middle East to promote American literary humanism. Richard Ford, a member of this group, was quoted in the *New York Times* expressing his eagerness to "go to Islamic nations to help humanize America" (cited in Beers 2002).

The United States' globe-spanning network of American universities also attempted to foster a pro-American intellectual transformation among Muslims of the world. As Beers (2002) said, "The American University of Beirut, the American University in Cairo, and the Lebanese American University – each set up by the private sector and each currently enrolling about 6,000 students – are well positioned to help impart America's values to the Arab and Muslim World." The BECA targeted and sought to change the minds of educated Muslim opinion leaders and tastemakers with the hope that they would change the minds of their followers in their respective countries to support US interests.

The OPD's Shared Values campaign was vast but not effective, as the American brand's attractiveness continued to diminish at the end of 2002. A Pew Research Center (2003) report called *What the World Thinks in 2002* said that world public opinion was against the United States and that anti-Americanism was surging in the "Muslim world." After seventeen months of trying but failing to convince the Muslim world to embrace America and the Bush Doctrine, Beers resigned from the OPD and returned to Madison Avenue (Beers 2003). Beers perhaps recognized that branding an empire is far more difficult than creating brand images for commodities.

Margaret Tutwiler, a diplomat for the Reagan and Bush I administrations in the 1980s and a lobbyist for the Cellular Telecommunications Industry Association (now CTIA – The Wireless Association) in the 1990s replaced Beers in October 2003. In her confirmation hearing, Tutwiler (2003) said public diplomacy needed to focus less on nation branding and more on relationship building through educational and cultural exchanges. With a budget of $685 million, Tutwiler's OPD drastically increased US cultural and educational exchange programs. The Fulbright scholarship exchange program was restarted in Afghanistan after a twenty-five-year hiatus. Through a school Internet connectivity program, 26,000 high school students from the Middle East, South Asia, South East Europe, Central Asia, and the Caucasus collaborated with US students on online projects dealing with business, health, and civics. The Partnership for Learning program began its first high school initiative, recruiting 170 students from predominantly Muslim countries to live with US-located families and study at US high schools. English-teaching programs received an additional $1.573 million to create new regional English-language officers. The BECA worked with the Near Eastern Affairs and South Asian bureaus to establish forty-three more American Corners (city-based information and cultural hubs where locals can learn about America) in the Muslim world (including ten in Afghanistan and fifteen in Iraq). One hundred and ninety-four more American Corners were subsequently opened. American Corners, libraries, and primary and secondary schools, in turn, received thousands of American books from US embassies. By September 2004, embassies worldwide had distributed $400,000 worth of US books. US English teaching programs expanded, and the Culture Connect Program linked US celebrities to hundreds of foreign youngsters (Tutwiler 2004a).

During Tutwiler's brief stint at the OPD, the BBG expanded its broadcasting operations in the Muslim world, developing a US state-owned Arabic-language TV network to rival Al Jazeera called Alhurra (or "The Free One"). Alhurra was launched on February 14, 2004, and began broadcasting to millions of viewers in twenty-two countries across the Middle East. Start-up funds for the $3.5 million venture came from Bush's $81 billion supplemental budget request for military operations in Iraq. BBG chairman Norman Pattiz described Alhurra as being designed to have a hybrid "look of a CNN, a Fox, or an MSNBC" and "the look of Arabic satellite TV stations." In its first year, Alhurra targeted Muslim viewers with a number of news programs modelled on US commercial news shows like ABC's *Nightline*, NBC's *Meet the Press*, and CBS's *Face the Nation* (Bowers 2004). Though Alhurra packaged its content as news, Congress funded it to promote US interests. Pattiz said of Alhurra: "A key part of our mission is to be an example of a free press in the American tradition ... We've assembled a highly professional group of journalists primarily from the region to provide the kind of news and information that will resonate with our viewing audience and enable them to make informed decisions." BBG chairman Kenneth Y. Tomlinson described Alhurra as "a beacon of light in a media market dominated by sensationalism and distortion." Muslim and Arabic-speaking viewers, however, did not feel particularly enlightened by Alhurra or attracted to its content. "People watch it once or twice and then turn to Al Jazeera and Al Arabiya – if they're inclined to look at news," said Edward S. Walker Jr., president of the Middle East Institute (Wright 2004). These Arab-news broadcasters seemed to provide listeners and viewers with more veracious and resonant news.

Despite the efforts of the OPD and the BBG, anti-American sentiment continued to grow globally in 2003 and 2004, following the US invasion of Iraq (Wallerstein 2003, 26). Grisly images of civilian deaths, prisoners being sexually humiliated and tortured at the Abu Ghraib prison complex, people starving themselves to death to protest the illegal prison camps of Guantanamo Bay, and the revelation that the only WMDs in Iraq were those dropped by US fighter jets challenged the OPD's and BBG's feel-good campaign. Perhaps sensing the futility of her job, Tutwiler resigned from the OPD in April 2004. The position of under secretary for public diplomacy and public affairs remained vacant for nearly a year, but on March 15, 2005, US Secretary of State Condoleezza Rice announced the appointment of Karen Hughes to this important post. Hughes was a long-standing close friend and confidante of Bush and had been Bush's director of communications when he was governor of Texas and an agent of strategic communications for Bush's 2004 re-election campaign. During Bush's first eighteen months in office, Hughes had managed the White House Offices of Communications, Media Affairs, Speechwriting, and the Press Secretary. In her confirmation hearing, Hughes repeated a number of public diplomacy clichés: that the US was primarily engaged in a "struggle for ideas" and that, by using "new technologies, the Internet and satellite television" and "people-to-people exchanges," public diplomacy would "partner in common cause with other countries to defeat propaganda with truth." Also, Hughes framed the United States' unilateral invasion and occupation of Iraq as serving the cause of "freedom," a universal value that is God's gift to all of humankind. She said, "Freedom is the universal hope of the human heart, instilled not by any country or government but by the Creator," and the world is "witnessing freedom's power across the world in the courage of the Iraqi people." Obscuring the self-interested geopolitics of the US Empire, Hughes explained, "I have watched President Bush make some very difficult decisions in the cause of freedom" (cited in Rice 2005).

Led by Hughes, the OPD promoted America and US foreign policy with the assistance of some of the United States' leading public relations companies. The Private Sector Summit on Public Diplomacy held at the State Department on January 9, 2007, for example, brought together OPD officials with 160 top PR experts. Secretary of State Condoleezza Rice lauded this "public-private partnership," saying "the solutions to the challenges of the 21st century are not going to be met by government alone" and will require "a close and vital partnership between government and the private sector." Rice spoke of "the global presence, creativity and efficiency of these

[PR] organizations" as "invaluable resources and natural partners" in the state's efforts "to share America's story and ideals with others" (US Department of State 2007, 2). "We have a lot of interests in common and you have the ability to be so vital to what we do," said Hughes to PR executives. "You have employees all across the world who have an incredible reach into their societies," and "your operations touch millions of lives every day" (16). The summit resulted in an action plan for privatized public diplomacy. James Murphy, chair of the PR Coalition, described how corporations would "develop business practices that make public diplomacy a core element of international corporate public action," "promote understanding of American society, culture and values in other countries," and "build relationships of trust and respect across cultures." By helping the state to sell America to the world and counter anti-Americanism, the PR Coalition would help itself to state contracts while helping "American global companies to do business abroad" (4).

On December 11, 2007, business journalist James Glassman became the under secretary of state for public diplomacy. He remained in the position for a mere six months before leaving. At the end of the Bush presidency, the OPD seemed to integrate seamlessly with a network of private PR firms, which helped themselves to contracts to help the state sell "America." The ideological returns, however, were marginal. A 2008 Pew Institute global attitudes poll reported that between 2002 and 2008, positive attitudes toward the US continued to plummet (Schneider 2009). As *The Economist* (2007, 30) lamented, "Across the world, anti-Americanism has increased to the point where the United States is often regarded as a threat to world peace rather than its guarantor."

Public Diplomacy 2.0, 2009–12

The "selling of the president" (McGinnis 1988) is an integral part of domestic political communication, but the selling of brand Obama was a global effort. During the election campaign, Obama's brand managers David Axelrod and David Plouffe paid the PR corporations GMMB, Elevation Ltd., and The Park Group more than $52 million to make Obama's image (Ali 2010). They designed Obama to symbolize a change to America and to the previous eight years of US foreign policy, a president who would lead Americans and the world toward a better future. With oratory flare, charisma, and televisual presence, Obama inspired people to hope for change, and his election as president on November 4, 2008, was hailed by marketing executives and public diplomacy officers alike as a new and better day for America's image in the world market. *Advertising Age* said Obama's election was "An Instant Overhaul for Tainted Brand America" (Wentz 2008).

Yet, Obama continued the Bush administration's War on Terror, coupled with a policy of "engagement." In May 2009, Obama established a global engagement directorate within the National Security Council "to drive comprehensive engagement policies that leverage diplomacy, communications, international development and assistance, and domestic engagement and outreach in pursuit of a host of national security objectives" (White House 2009a). To support this initiative, Obama appointed former CEO of Discovery Communications Judith McHale as under secretary of state for public diplomacy (Kellerhals 2009), and after McHale returned to the private sector in 2011, Obama appointed Kathleen Stephens, a US Ambassador to South Korea, to this post.

In the first four years of Obama's presidency, the OPD tried to engage, inform, and persuade publics all over the world about the virtue of America. The Bureau of International Information Programs ran speakers series through American Corners at American centres in major cities. It produced approximately fifty publications that describe US society and policy in Arabic, Chinese, English, Persian, Russian, French, Spanish, and other languages. It also translated fiction and non-fiction titles by leading US authors into various languages and established joint publishing arrangements with publishing companies in target countries. The BECA continued to support educational and cultural exchanges of at least 300,000 people through the Fulbright Program, the Office of Academic Exchange Programs, the Office of Private Sector Exchange, and the Office of Citizen Exchanges, which brought foreign physicians, athletes, musicians, camp counsellors, choirs, interns, professors, researchers, trainees, and more to work in the United States for anywhere between a few months and a few years. The Bureau of Public Affairs continued to try to set US and international news media agendas through press briefings with American and international journalists, town hall meetings, and speakers events. The BBG continued to transmit radio and TV messages about America to the world through the Voice of America, Worldnet TV, Radio y TV Martí, Radio Free Europe/Radio Free Liberty, Radio Farda, Radio Free Iraq, Radio Free Asia, Radio Sawa, and Alhurra Television. It spent millions of dollars each year to pay for the pilot of a privately owned propaganda plane called AeroMartí to fly around the island of Cuba, directly beaming anti-Castro American TV shows into the country, which were jammed and had no impact (Hudson 2013).

During his brief stint as under secretary of state for public diplomacy in the final months of the Bush administration, Glassman (2008) coined the phrase "Public Diplomacy 2.0." According to Graffy (2009, 47), "Public diplomacy is the art of communicating a country's policies, values and culture to the people of another nation," while "Public Diplomacy 2.0" is the "art of using this new Internet phenomenon [Facebook, blogging, Twitter, MySpace, YouTube, Wikipedia, and more] in order to achieve those objectives – citizen to citizen, person to person." Obama's OPD expanded Public Diplomacy 2.0 by getting diplomats to use Twitter to make a case for America in 140 characters or less and link their tweets to videos "uploaded to YouTube and images posted on Flickr" (Graffy 2009, 52). It also established a digital outreach team that tried to change anti-American opinions through Arabic, Persian, and Urdu blogs, websites, and chat forums (Dale 2009).

"Public Diplomacy 2.0" reflects an attempt by the OPD to sell America by spreading digital imagery and messages about it across many platforms (TV shows, radio, websites, podcasts, blogs, and games), all at once. It tries to get people to interact with, immerse themselves in, and express themselves through OPD-sponsored platforms that cross over into popular social media sites, which embrace them as collaborators, functionalize their interactivity, and put their participatory ethos to work (Comor and Bean 2012). In Obama's first term, the OPD learned to authorize, observe, and exploit the content-generating practices of social media users, harnessing their interactivity as a source of unpaid promotion. However, Public Diplomacy 2.0 talks of supporting genuine engagement, dialogue, and mutual understanding obscured the continuation of public diplomacy's realpolitik and thus its persistence as a means of selling America to the world (Comor and Bean 2012).

Conclusion: The Consequences of Public Diplomacy

The establishment of the Committee on Public Information during the First World War, the Office of the Coordinator of Inter-American Affairs and the Office of War Information in the Second World War, the United States Information Agency during the Cold War, and the Office of Public Diplomacy during the War on Terror established an immense transnational state-corporate PR network for selling images and messages of the US Empire to the world and opening up markets to the US culture industry's expansion. This chapter concludes by highlighting some of public diplomacy's flawed premises and possible consequences.

First, public diplomacy agencies originate in the executive branch and as a result of national security directives. They are established by the executive in response to a perceived threat to national security, funded by Congress, and deployed in support of US Empire. Though public diplomacy personnel may criticize what the US state communicates (or fails to communicate), they are largely emissaries of the US Empire who normalize it as good, right, or necessary in an anarchic world system that presumably longs for US leadership and order.

Second, public diplomacy is coordinated by the executive branch and top-level security agencies, but successive public diplomacy agencies have collaborated with US media corporations to sell America. These state agencies source the culture industry with content and outsource Americanization jobs to its firms by paying them to try to change hearts and minds around the world. In the process, they work to boost the culture industry's global presence and shuttle its products abroad.

Third, public diplomacy seems to rest on an elitist or paternalistic view of non-US publics. Public diplomacy assumes that people need to be informed about America and US foreign policy by the US state and its corporate contractors because they cannot formulate a reasonable understanding of them on their own. It takes it as axiomatic that people do not understand what America or US foreign policy is all about and that the US state must tell them for their own good, not just its own. Public diplomacy basically depicts people who criticize the US Empire as suffering from a "false consciousness" about some truth that US state persuaders know. This is an unfair, untrue portrayal, of course: many people who dislike the US Empire are not irrational anti-American fanatics but rather rational critics of bad policy, not the totality of "America."

Fourth, public diplomacy is dubious; it is often represented as fostering dialogue through two-way and interactive communication in order to build mutually beneficial relationships and greater cross-cultural understanding, but many of its campaigns are designed with the overarching goal of changing how people think about the US Empire. Public diplomacy largely initiates dialogue with others as a means of neutralizing or deflecting criticisms of the US Empire, not to bring about a change in the policies that instigate such criticisms. Public diplomacy officers may employ two-way media platforms, but it is they who decide the goal, the message, the target, and the intended effect.

Fifth, public diplomacy can be ethnocentric. It participates in the US Empire's attempt to universalize its particular societal model as the world model and therefore assumes that other countries should be more like it. It takes for granted the United States' liberal democratic capitalist societal model as the necessary, best, or inevitable future of other countries and seems not to tolerate difference or the prospect of alternative developmental paths. The United States' model of societal development is only one among many, and no singular or universal model of development exists for all to follow everywhere. Yet, public diplomacy pushes the US model as the one which must prevail over all alternatives and finds different societal models as inferior or lacking relative to its own idealized one. While public diplomacy claims to recognize national, regional, and local social and cultural differences (with its country-specific cultural attaches, country plans, country teams, and glocalized PR strategies), it does so in order to more effectively manage, make over, and move these differences into a mould of sameness based on the United States' societal model.

Sixth, although the US state asserts its sovereign right to use public diplomacy to protect and promote its societal model around the world, it can be criticized for not respecting the sovereign rights of other states to resist this process. Public diplomacy often enters other countries without prior consultation, treaties, or agreements and attempts to manipulate the outlook and behaviour of non-US populations so that they will rise up or turn against the national policies of their own states in support of US strategic interests. In this way, public diplomacy disregards and violates the sovereignty of states and can be criticized as a coercive act of cultural imperialism, "a process of social influence by which a nation[-state] *imposes* on other countries its set beliefs, values, knowledge, and behavioral norms as well as its overall style of life" (Beltran 1978, 184).

3

The US Culture Industry
Still Number One

In his famous *Life* magazine article, "The American Century," the mid-twentieth-century media mogul Henry Luce (1941) urged Americans to recognize and "accept wholeheartedly" their "duty" and "opportunity as the most powerful and vital nation in the world and in consequence to exert upon the world the full impact of our influence" (63). Luce described how "American jazz, Hollywood movies, American slang, American machines and patented products are in fact the only things that every community in the world, from Zanzibar to Hamburg, recognizes in common" (65). During the Second World War, Max Horkheimer and Theodore Adorno (1995) called the source of these "things" the "culture industry." These critical theorists coined the culture industry concept to highlight the capitalist system's incorporation of culture into its circuits of accumulation and interrogate the for-profit production, distribution, and marketing of all the world's cultural forms – high and low – as commodities. For them, cultural commodities seemed to help people cope with the alienating work routines they endured each day, concealed the class relations that tore society asunder by portraying America as a harmonious land of happy consumers, closed minds to the badness of present conditions instead of opened them to alternative and possibly better futures, and taught conformity, not critical thinking.

Following the Second World War, the United States was home to the most powerful culture industry on the planet, and it had become the world's centre of culture's financing, production, distribution, and exhibition (H.I. Schiller 1969, 1976). Throughout the Cold War, the US culture industry underwent incredible growth – internally, by developing new sub-sectors, and externally, by expanding operations in Western Europe and moving into Asia, Africa, and Latin America in search of new infrastructural investments, production, and distribution systems to build; sources of ad revenue to extract; and audiences to commodify and sell commodities to (Schiller 1969, 1976). This culture industry's pulp fictions, magazines, films, radio programs, TV shows, and ads, however, were intertwined with the geopolitics of the US state, which sought to sell the American way of life to the world (Bah 2008; Wagenleitner 1994). At the end of the Cold War, this industry further expanded into the former Soviet sphere of influence and continued building its operations in Asia, Africa, and the Middle East (H.I. Schiller 1991, 1992). By the turn of the millennium, the US culture industry and its pop products were criss-crossing nearly all borders to encompass the entire planet (H.I. Schiller 2000).

Decades have passed since Luce spoke of America being a superpower in "all the trivial ways"; since Horkheimer and Adorno (1995) lambasted the culture industry; and since Schiller shed light on this industry's role in expanding the US Empire. Nowadays, the US culture industry's spectacular things are common referents for communities all over the world. The NFL's Super Bowl XLVIII, for example, was broadcast globally by Fox TV networks, reaching 198 countries and connecting about 100 million people as viewers of this bone-crunching American sports media event – a truly global one (Price 2014). American TV shows like *Late Show with David Letterman*, *Friends*, and *Desperate Housewives* travel across borders, too, gathering, entertaining, and possibly influencing audiences, even in Saudi Arabia, where youth watch them uncensored with Arabic subtitles (*Daily Mail Reporter* 2010). In 2014, Hollywood pumped out major motion pictures that brought millions of people into theatres across the world's major cities, from São Paulo, to Moscow, to New Delhi, to Cape Town, to Shanghai. Michael Bay's blockbuster flick *Transformers: Age of Extinction*, for example, was the highest-grossing film worldwide and ranked among the top ten films at the box offices of Brazil, Russia, India, China, South Africa, and even Nigeria. In the same year, Activision's *Call of Duty: Advanced Warfare* was the best-selling video game in the world.

The US culture industry clearly has immense global market power, and American pop culture stretches around the globe. Yet, there are some countervailing trends that complicate the notion that the United States is the single home base of cultural production and the centre from which all cultural goods flow. Over the past four decades, culture industries have grown outside of the United States, and their goods flow in many directions, sometimes even into the United States (Thussu 2007; Tunstall 2008).

We read news stories of made-in-Russia blockbusters like *Stalingrad* (2013) triumphing over Hollywood fare at the Russian box office for the first time since the end of the Cold War (Kozlov 2013), Hong Kong–Chinese fantasy films like *The Monkey King* (2013) and rom-coms like *Breakup Buddies* (2013) encroaching on Hollywood's near-total control of the worldwide box office (Cieply 2014), Mumbai-based Bollywood being "the world's most prolific cinema factory" because it annually makes about 1,000 films, almost doubling Hollywood's yearly output (Ghosh 2013), and Nigeria's Nollywood producing and circulating even more videos via alternative production/distribution networks (J. Miller 2012). These stories point to a world system of many national and regionally situated culture industries, each with its own differential capacity to produce, distribute, and exhibit cultural products for "culturally proximate" audiences who may prefer to consume films and TV shows made by and featuring people "who look the same, talk the same, joke the same and behave the same" as they do (Tunstall 2008, xiv).

Around the world, non-US culture industries do exist in asymmetrically interdependent power relations (Straubhaar 1991). But has the growth of these industries, their products, and the audiences for them really undermined the economic power of the US culture industry and the ubiquity of US pop? *Foreign Policy* stories such as "How Hollywood Conquered the World (All Over Again)" (Galloway 2012) suggest the answer is no, and *New York Times* headlines such as "Hollywood Works to Maintain Its World Dominance" (Cieply 2014) point to the US culture industry's struggle to preside over emerging challengers.

This chapter contends that the US culture industry continues to be number one and explains this top position with regard to the capitalist strategies US media companies use to maintain their grip on markets and the geopolitical strategies the US state employs to help them do so. The first section of this chapter describes the US culture industry's ongoing dominance by profiling some of its most significant media companies. The second section focuses on the capitalist strategies US media companies use to integrate non-US culture industries into their cross-border networks of production, distribution, and exhibition, and the commodity design strategies they employ to gather audiences across borders. The third section highlights the ways that the US state supports the dominance of the US culture industry, focusing on its national and global policies. This chapter's focus on the combined economic and geopolitical strategies that protect and promote the interests of the US Empire's culture industry in other countries helps explain how and why US cultural products overflow into other countries and with little reciprocation of influence by them.

An Oligopoly for Owners

The US culture industry is owned and controlled by a small number of big media conglomerates that have grown more and more concentrated, year after year (Bagdikian 2004; Downing 2011; McChesney 2008; Noam 2009; Winseck 2008). A genuinely competitive media market (one with many sellers of goods and low barriers to entry) is a thing of the past, while an oligopolistic market (one with a few sellers of goods and high barriers to entry) is the norm in the United States (Noam 2009). The pattern of oligopolistic market control is not exclusive to the US culture industry but is replicated across other sectors of the US economy, in manufacturing, banking, retail, health care insurance, transportation, arms, airlines, groceries, beer, and more (Bellamy Foster, McChesney, and Jonna 2011; Weissmann 2013). The condition of an oligopolistic market is the result of years of big media companies becoming even bigger through horizontal and vertical integration strategies (McChesney 2004, 2008). Since the 1980s, media companies that previously operated in only one sector began acquiring a range of media firms in many other sectors, converging the sectors (Winseck and Jin 2011; Jin 2011). Comcast's 2011 takeover of NBCUniversal is the latest of many media mergers and acquisitions that have swept across the United States for the past thirty years (Adegoke and Levine 2011). As a result of these, a few mega-conglomerates control the means of producing, distributing, and exhibiting all kinds of content.

In 2013, the United States was home to the world system's top ten media conglomerates (in terms of sales, profits, assets, and market value): Comcast-NBCUniversal, The Walt Disney Company News Corporation, Time Warner, Time Warner Cable, DirecTV, CBS Corporation, Viacom, Dish Network, and Liberty Global (DeCarlo 2013). US media conglomerates continue to be disproportionately run by white men and staffed by white male cultural content producers (Women's Media Center 2014). The CEOs of these media conglomerates belong to the US power elite and are among the highest-paid people in the United States (*New York Times* 2015). In 2012, the median annual pay of the United States' top twenty media CEOs was about $30 million each, which was approximately $6 million more than the CEOs of technology firms, $12 million more than the CEOs of consumer goods firms, and about $20 million more than the CEOs of US banks like JPMorgan Chase and Morgan Stanley (Carr 2013). In 2013, CBS Corporation CEO Leslie Moonves collected $65.6 million (up 9 percent from the year before); Viacom's CEO, Philippe Dauman, was paid $37.2 million (a raise of 11 percent from the year before); Walt Disney Company CEO Robert Iger took home $34.3 million (up 46 percent); Time Warner CEO Jeff Bewkes banked $32.5 million (a 27 percent pay hike); Comcast CEO Brian Roberts earned $31.4 million (up 8 percent); and Rupert Murdoch, CEO of News Corporation, got nearly $30 million (Patel 2014).

Together, these and other American media CEOs and their shareholders control some of the world's leading TV and film production studios: Universal Studios (Comcast-NBCUniversal), ABC Studios (The Walt Disney Company), Fox Entertainment Group (News Corporation), Warner Bros. Television and CBS Television Studios (Time Warner), Paramount Pictures, and MTV Films (Viacom). They also own the planet's major media distributors: Disney Media Distribution (The Walt Disney Company), Fox Filmed Entertainment (News Corporation), Warner Bros. Entertainment (Time Warner), and CBS Television Distribution and Paramount Pictures Corporation (Viacom). Furthermore, US media conglomerates own some of biggest TV news networks, such as CBS News, ABC News (The Walt Disney Company), CNN International (Time Warner), and Fox News (News Corporation), and many of the world's biggest cable and satellite TV firms and websites.

The United States is also home to Thomson Reuters, The Associated Press, Bloomberg, and Dow Jones and Company, which are among the world's top news companies. Also US-based are two of the world's top five ad corporations (Omnicom Group and Interpublic Group) and eight of the world's top ten public relations firms (Edelman, Weber Shandwick, FleishmanHillard, Burson-Marsteller, Hill + Knowlton Strategies, Ketchum, Ogilvy Public Relations Worldwide, and FTI Consulting), which contribute substantially to the profits of US media firms by purchasing ad space and time from them.

Most of the world system's top information and communication technology, Internet-web, and big data corporations are US-based as well. The

US is home to the world's top three computer hardware firms (Apple, Dell, and Hewlett-Packard), eight of the world's top ten software firms (Microsoft, Oracle, Symantec, VMware, Adobe Systems, Intuit, and Fiserv), three of the world's top ten communications equipment firms (Cisco Systems, Corning Optical Communications, and Motorola Solutions), three of the world's top five semi-conductor companies (Intel, Qualcomm, Micron), the top two computer services firms (IBM and Google), two of the top telecoms (AT&T and Verizon Communications), the top three Internet retail companies (eBay, Liberty Interactive, and Amazon.com) (DeCarlo 2013), and the world's most visited websites (Facebook, Google, YouTube, Yahoo Inc., Wikipedia, eBay) (*Foreign Policy* 2013). Netflix dominates the on-demand Internet video streaming service and boasts more global subscribers than American ones (Hamel 2014). The US Internet service providers market is ruled by Verizon, AT&T, and Comcast, which exhibit the same globalizing tendencies as conglomerates in other sectors. The US basically dominates the global digital platform market (Jin 2013). In fact, Google, which accounts for more than 65 percent of all Internet searches worldwide, recently surpassed US-based DirectTV to become the world's largest media company (in terms of the advertising revenue it generated) (Ben 2013). "Big data," a relatively new buzzword that refers to a rapidly growing US-centred industry that designs and sells software and services for producing, commercializing, managing, processing, analyzing, and selling consumer data commodities, is led by the United States too. According to Network World, fourteen of the world's top fifteen big data firms are based in the United States: IBM, Hewlett-Packard, Teradata, Oracle, EMC, Amazon, Microsoft, Google, VMWare, Cloudera, Hortonworks, Splunk, MongoDB Inc., and MapR. (Korolov 2013). Other massive data aggregation and consumer profile selling companies – Acxiom, Ayasdi, Datalogix, Equifax, Experian, Evolv, Gnip (now owned by Twitter), Inome (previously Intelius), LexisNexis, TowerData, and TransUnion – are also headquartered in the United States. And most of the world's largest data centres that house and power immense data storage systems are US-based and owned: Amazon, Digital Reality, Google, Data I/O Corp, Facebook, Quality Technology Services (QTS), Microsoft, Terremark, and Switch Communications.

Though video games are developed, produced, marketed, published, and consumed all over the world, the United States is a major centre of a games industry that is huge and profitable. In 2014, more than 150 million Americans were playing video games, and over 135 million units were sold (ESA

2015). In a study of the top 100 country-specific video game markets by total revenues in 2014, the US ranked number one ($20.5 billion in revenue); China came in second ($17.9 billion); and Japan was third ($12.2 billion) (NewZoo 2014). Furthermore, the United States is home to Microsoft Studios, Activision-Blizzard, Electronic Arts, and Take-Two Interactive, which were four of the world's top ten revenue generating game companies in 2013 (Statista 2014).

The US culture industry is the largest, richest, and most expansive in the world, but media corporations exist in other countries that, with the help of their own host states, grow in power and profits too. Brazil's Rede Globo; Canada's BCE-CTV, Rogers Communication, Shaw Communication, and Quebecor; China's CCTV, Shanghai Media Group, Phoenix TV, and Xinhua News Agency; France's Vivendi and Agence France-Presse; Germany's Bertelsmann; India's Bennett, Coleman and Co., and Zee; Italy's Mediaset and Inter Press Service; Japan's Sony; Mexico's Grupo Televisa and Azteca; Qatar's Al Jazeera; Russia's Russia Television; and the United Kingdom's BBC, Pearson, and ITV are all examples of powerful national media firms with a global business outlook (Arsenault and Castells 2008). There are rising Internet powers, too, like Baidu (China) and Yandex and VKontakte (Russia). And Japan-based video game companies like Sony Computer Entertainment and Nintendo, and Chinese online game firms such as Tencent, stifle total US digital dominance.

Now, in the early twenty-first century, the US culture industry no longer operates in a near-unipolar global media market. And in a possibly emerging multipolar global media market in which non-US culture industries make more cultural products than ever before, the US culture industry faces the rise of numerous challengers and competitors, perhaps even rivals. The growth of non-US culture industries, however, does not negate the United States' current top position. In 2012, the US culture industry generated $479.23 billion (29.2 percent of the world total)— and by 2017 the US is expected to account for $632.09 billion (29.4 percent of the world total) (Bond 2013). So while significant non-US culture industries exist and continue to grow and interlock all over the world, the US culture industry is still number one and will likely remain so for years to come (James 2013).

The Culture Industry's Power: Capitalist Strategies

The US culture industry continues to be at the top of the world hierarchy of culture industries. What business strategies do its media conglomerates use to expand their power in other countries? In the world system, US media conglomerates have entered other countries and integrated the media firms based in those countries by linking and forming strategic alliances with them (Oba and Chan-Olmsted 2007). Between 2001 and 2005, Time Warner, News Corporation, The Walt Disney Company, Viacom, and NBCUniversal, for example, partnered with a number of non-US culture industry firms, and this enabled them to intensify "their expansion into many emerging economies amid saturating media demand in developed countries" (22). In effect, non-US media firms all over the world "have joined those based in the United States and a few other wealthy nations in widening and deepening the culture market – and extending the entire industry's transnational orientation" (D. Schiller 2007, 120). The US culture industry integrates industries elsewhere into its chains and networks of power through ownership, cross-border production, and distribution/exhibition deals.

Ownership
US media conglomerates enter other countries and integrate their culture industries by organizing and implementing cross-border ownership deals such as mergers and acquisitions, joint ventures, and equity partnerships in order to expand their own operations (Jin 2008, 2012). Through mergers and acquisitions, the US culture industry gains a strong foothold in the media markets of other countries, leveraging new acquisitions to produce and push American content. Joint ventures that enable US and non-US media firms to establish entirely new media corporations that synergistically serve the profit interests of both (Jin 2012). Additionally, US media firms pursue equity alliances with non-US media firms. In these business deals, US media conglomerates acquire a percentage of an existing non-US media firm by investing in it. In sum, mergers and acquisitions, joint ventures, and equity alliances enable the US culture industry to institutionalize its dominance in another country's culture industry and transnationalize its holdings.

Cross-Border Production
US media conglomerates integrate other culture industries into their operations with cross-border media production as well (Miller et al. 2005; Mirrlees 2013a; Scott 2005). In the new international division of cultural labour, US media conglomerates pit smaller culture industries,

states, and cultural workers against one another in competitions to attract footloose Hollywood film and TV productions. In addition, quite a lot of film and TV production begins and ends with the financing and creative power of US-based media conglomerates, but the actual work of creating cultural commodities happens in production networks spanning many countries. US media conglomerates are centralized in terms of capital ownership, creative decision-making, and copyright control, yet they are flexible in terms of the companies with which they work. A cross-border production can take the form of either a "runaway production" or an "equity co-production." In a runaway production, a US-based studio outsources tasks to cultural workers living elsewhere, often in the major cities of other countries. By shooting films and TV shows on-location in other countries, Hollywood studios usually pay less for labour than they would in the US, benefit from state-provisioned subsidies, and also get "more bang for their buck" where currencies are worth less than the US dollar (Miller et al. 2005). In addition to turning to foreign locales in search of lower subsidies and currency deals, and lower-waged workers, US media conglomerates enter and integrate other countries through equity co-productions – financing the production of a cultural property by a non-US company in return for the international distribution rights to it. Runaway productions and equity co-productions help to maximize the profit interests of the US culture industry by transforming other countries into service providers (Hollywood studios maintain control over the finished product's copyright and key creative, financial, distribution, and marketing decisions) (Scott and Pope 2007), reducing place-specific cultural identities (Hollywood regularly makes over other places into body doubles or simulacra of US landscapes) (Elmer 2002), disorganizing cultural workers (Hollywood pits unionized US workers against non-US workers and demands that all of them lower their standards and expectations if they want a job), and accumulating public wealth provisioned by neoliberal states (Hollywood capitalizes on a competitive race to the bottom between states trying to attract production to their territories by offering the largest subsidies) (Miller et al. 2005). Although cross-border productions between the US culture industry and others may at times provide the capital, jobs, and professional skills transfer that fledgling culture industries need to grow, they can also undermine indigenous development and nationally specific cultural products capable of competing with those of the United States.

Licensing Agreement
US media conglomerates also integrate the culture industries of other countries (specifically their distributors and exhibitors) by licensing copyrighted content to them. Through licensing agreements with non-US TV networks and theatre chains, US media conglomerates distribute and get their cultural commodities exhibited in other countries and give the non-US firms a financial incentive to buy from them as opposed to investing in homegrown content. The conglomerates use a cost amortization strategy that works like this: they produce TV shows and films and sell them in the United States; if they are able to recoup production costs and turn a profit by selling to US-based TV broadcasters and theatre chains, they then license their works to non-US TV networks and theatre chains, but at a reduced cost. Given that acquiring a US TV show or film usually costs a non-US media firm less than it would for them to produce an original TV show or film of comparable or greater quality, non-US media corporations eagerly buy from US media conglomerates, loading their schedules with American fare (Doyle 2012). Using licensing agreements, US media conglomerates turn non-US culture industries into exhibition pipelines for streaming their content while these media firms use American content as a magnet for local viewers, whose attention they then sell to advertisers. Licensing content from the US culture industry enables non-US media firms to maximize profit by saving on costs associated with homegrown production and optimizing the capacity for commodifying and selling a large audience. But when non-US exhibitors do not invest a portion of their profit into the production of their own national content, licensing from the US works to diminish non-US production capacity and product availability while further enhancing the market power and cultural presence of US pop (Grant and Wood 2004).

Pervasive cross-border ownership, production, and distribution/exhibition partnerships between the US culture industry and non-US culture industries suggest that the US culture industry's market dominance is not achieved by geopolitical coercion but by capitalist invitation and incorporation. In their struggle to achieve profit goals in many countries, US media conglomerates do not force themselves on non-US states, media corporations, or audiences. They have grown globally by integrating and incorporating non-US culture industries into their vast cross-border networks and chains of financing, ownership, production, and distribution/exhibition.

Designing Cultural Commodities to Go Global: Global Audience Commodification

The US culture industry's control of transnational production, distribution, and exhibition chains supports the global reach of its products. And the complex transnational ownership, production, and distribution/exhibition partnerships between US and non-US firms ensure that US cultural commodities flow through many national media markets. The cross-national presence of US cultural products may be further explained with reference to the design strategies of US media conglomerates. To attract transnational consumers to their cultural products, the US culture industry's conglomerates design blockbuster event films, global-national TV formats, and glocalized lifestyle brands.

The US culture industry seeks to produce globally popular films as opposed to distinctly American popular films. Heeding the "cultural discount" – the notion that a cultural product that exclusively represents one national culture and is originally intended for one national audience will have diminished appeal elsewhere – Hollywood strives to design cultural products with transnational audience resonance. These blockbusters tend to boast huge budgets, transnational audience reach, a global marketing campaign, near-worldwide release, and a massive return on investment. Many global blockbuster films downplay their Americanness by casting international stars (not just US talent), drawing from already familiar stories or pre-sold properties (myths, legends, and books that are not distinctly American), mixing genres (often fantasy and science fiction), abiding by classical narrative structures (story formulas that are conventional and easy to follow and identify with), conveying universal themes (as opposed to themes particular to US society and culture), and generating plenty of visual spectacle (image is privileged over dialogue) (Mirrlees 2013a). Using these textual design strategies, Hollywood studios annually produce blockbuster films that downplay American "nationness" and play up universality. For example, in the first decade of the twenty-first century, the highest-grossing US films worldwide are not explicitly about American people, places, and cultures: *Avatar* (2009), *The Dark Knight* (2008), *Shrek 2* (2004), *Pirates of the Caribbean: Dead Man's Chest* (2006), *Spider-Man* (2002), *Transformers: Revenge of the Fallen* (2009), *Star Wars: Episode III; Revenge of the Sith* (2005), *The Lord of the Rings: The Return of the King* (2003) and *Spider-Man 2* (2004). The top ten highest-grossing films in 2014 were *Transformers: Age of Extinction; The Hobbit: The Battle of the Five Armies; Guardians of the Galaxy; Maleficent; The Hunger*

Games: Mockingjay - Part 1; X-Men: Days of Future Past; Captain America: The Winter Soldier; The Amazing Spider-Man 2; Dawn of the Planet of the Apes; and *Interstellar.* While a few of these globally popular and profitable sci-fi/fantasy flicks briefly represent US people, geography, and culture, many of them downplay recognizable American-ness in order to have cross-border resonance.

A second strategy the US culture industry uses to attract transnational viewers is TV show concepts that national TV networks license from US production houses to be adapted for their own audiences. Following the logic of cultural proximity – the notion that many viewers tend to prefer TV shows that are intended for people with similar cultural tastes and preferences to their own – US TV companies design global TV formats that "can be re-packaged to suit particular [local and national] markets and tastes" (Freedman 2003, 33). The TV format trade is not exclusively US-based, but the United States is home to many TV entrepreneurs who claim proprietary rights to at least twenty-two TV formats, such as US supermodel Tyra Banks' *Top Model* and Mark Burnett's *Survivor, Are You Smarter than a 5th Grader?,* and *The Apprentice.* The TV format trade involves a collaborative global-local business relationship between US TV companies and the national TV networks in other countries, who purchase licences to make national versions of an American TV formats (Moran 2009, 118–19). *Top Model,* for example, is licensed to more than 120 national TV networks. Thus, worldwide, viewers are watching nationally adapted versions of global TV formats, many of which are made in the United States and owned by US media firms. US-owned but nationally adapted TV formats foster the illusion that viewers are watching national TV shows when, in fact, they are watching US culture industry-owned shows.

Glocalization, or the customization of media brands so that they appeal to and abide by different national states and cultures (Aysha 2004), is a third strategy the US culture industry uses to make products with global legs. While the overarching goal of the US culture industry is global market dominance, the media firms that comprise it realize that exporting manifestly American cultural products is not always a solid business strategy. Thus, they glocalize. As *The Economist* (2002) puts it, "Think local: cultural imperialism doesn't sell." Global advertisers also seem to support a strategy of textual glocalization. In 2002, US-based global marketing corporation DDB released a white paper called "America and Cultural Imperialism" to describe how US corporate entry into foreign markets is "made more difficult by the appearance – or reality – of cultural imperialism." The report offers "some practical measures businesses can apply to their product and the market they are pursuing" to mitigate negative perceptions of American brands (DDB Worldwide 2002). One of these "practical measures" was glocalization. Nowadays, the US media giants have adopted a strategy known as "think globally, act locally" to maintain and/or expand their dominance (more) effectively (Jin 2007, 763). For example, aside from its own MTV channels in the United States, Viacom Media Networks (formerly MTV Networks) owns a large number of regional and country-specific MTV channels elsewhere in North America and in Africa, Asia Pacific, Europe, the Middle East, and Latin America (Chalaby 2006; Sowards 2003). For MTV, "thinking globally and acting locally" are central to its rule of transnational pay-TV markets and hold on global youth culture, suggesting that MTV's corporate glocalization is not undertaken to protect or promote the diversity of cultures but, rather, to capitalize on them.

The US culture industry still makes cultural products that represent facets of the American Way, but as detailed above, it is also de-Americanizing its cultural products with global blockbusters, global-national TV formats, and glocalized brands. The US culture industry creates, co-opts, and commoditizes universal and particular stories, transnational and national symbolisms, and global and local motifs to strengthen its grip in markets everywhere. It floods markets with goods that do not always appear to be agents of Americanization. Yet, in an era of endless market segmentation into smaller and smaller niches, and the resulting marketization of cultural difference, diversity-inflected commodities – global, national, or translocal – look more and more the same. The mix of postmodern cultural commodities may excite, annoy, dazzle, or give enjoyment to those who consume them. But the many uses and gratifications that consumers take from the products, and their various effects, belie the products' uniformity of purpose: that is, to cultivate transnational demand for other consumer products made by other industries. As US cultural commodities travel the globe, they attract mass and niche consumer groups to the same advertising message, which in an ever-expanding market system becomes ever more difficult to escape: keep buying!

In addition to being in the business of producing and selling cultural commodities to consumers, media corporations generate revenue by producing and selling audience attention to advertisers (Smythe 2001). The economic function of cultural commodities – whether globalized, nationalized, or glocalized – is largely to attract and expose as many viewers as possible to ads for goods. The films and TV shows scheduled and screened by US and non-US media exhibitors relay people's attention to the dream world of consumerism that drives the capitalist system forward and directs their eyes to idealized, often ecologically destructive, difficult-to-achieve styles of life. Advertising's centrality to the culture industry boom shows no sign of abating. In 2013, global ad spending was at an all-time high, topping $500 billion for the first time, with the BRICS growing rapidly and fuelling media developments there (*Advertising Age* 2013). The United States, however, continues to be the largest ad-spend market in the world, with a per capita expenditure that is "20 times larger than that of China and more than 100 times greater than India's" (Sparks 2014, 400). The world market for ad spending continues to grow while the US culture industry holds court over American audience commodities: global advertising firms spent nearly 180 billion for them in 2014 (eMarketer 2014).

The US Culture Industry's Power: Geopolitical Strategies

The US culture industry uses many capitalist strategies to enter non-US media markets, integrate national culture industries into its networks and chains, and commodify consumers, but these are often supported by the political strategies of the US state, which struggles to maintain and solidify the US culture industry's number one position. Capitalist and political strategies often come together to support the market power of the US culture industry, at home and abroad.

Political economists take it as axiomatic that there is scarcely any aspect of the culture industry which is not supported directly or indirectly, by the US state and policy (McChesney 2004, 2008). The US Treasury, Congress, the Department of Commerce's US Patent and Trademark Office and International Trade Administration, the National Telecommunications and Information Administration, the Federal Communications Commission (FCC), the White House Office of the US Trade Representative, the Homeland Security Immigration and Customs Enforcement agency, and the Department of State all take part in culture industry policy decision-making and implementation. The US state formulates culture industry policies that claim to serve a general "national interest," but this interest tends to congeal the particular interests of the culture industry firms that have the power to advance them to Washington through their well-resourced network of lobby groups. The Motion Picture Association of America (MPAA), the National Association of Broadcasters, the Association of American Publishers, the Recording Industry Association of America, the Software Alliance, the Entertainment Software Association, the Internet Association, and the International Intellectual Property Alliance are culture industry lobbyists whose interests and goals in shaping government policies are spelled out on their websites.

The MPAA says it is "the voice of one of the country's strongest and most vibrant industries – the American motion picture, home video and television industry. We aspire to advance the business and the art of filmmaking and celebrate its enjoyment around the world" (MPAA 2014a). Though located in California, close to Hollywood, the MPAA operates front organizations that push the US culture industry's business interests to the states and publics of least thirty countries, including Brazil (Association for the Protection of Movies and Music), Russia (Russian Anti-Piracy Organization), India (Motion Picture Distributors Association), and China (Motion Picture Association China).

With an annual budget of more than $40 million, the National Association of Broadcasters calls itself "the voice for the nation's radio and television broadcasters." To reap private returns through the control of lucrative government monopoly licences to the public airwaves, it "advance[s] the interests" of its "members in federal government, industry and public affairs" and before "Congress, the Federal Communications Commission and the courts" (NAB 2012).

Paid for by more than 200,000 US book publishers, the Association of American Publishers is the "trade association of US book publishers" and aims to provide "advocacy and communications on behalf of the industry" while representing "the industry's priorities on policy, legislative and regulatory issues regionally, nationally and worldwide" (APP 2013).

The Recording Industry Association of America "supports and promotes the creative and financial vitality of the major music companies" that "create, manufacture and/or distribute approximately 85% of all legitimate recorded music produced and sold in the United States" by working "to protect the intellectual property and First Amendment rights of artists and music labels" (RIAA 2013).

The BSA/Software Alliance, headquartered in Washington, DC, but with operations in more than sixty countries, says it is "the leading advocate for the global software industry before governments and in the international marketplace," and through "government relations, intellectual property enforcement and educational activities around the world" it "protects intellectual property and fosters innovation," "open[s] markets," and "builds trust and confidence in information technology for consumers, businesses and governments alike" (BSA/Software Alliance 2013).

Started by US digital giants like Google, Facebook, Amazon, AOL, Yahoo Inc., Expedia, eBay, Zynga, and others, the Internet Association claims on its homepage to "represent the interests of America's leading Internet companies and their global community of users" (Internet Association 2013).

The Entertainment Software Association (ESA 2014) is "exclusively dedicated to serving the business and public affairs needs of companies that publish computer and video games for video game consoles, personal computers, and the Internet." The association's federal government affairs program seeks to "advance the computer and video game industry's policy priorities with the US Congress and the Executive Branch" and "influence Congress' legislative agenda and the Administration's policy agenda."

The International Intellectual Property Alliance (2013) supports the property rights of "US copyright-based industries in bilateral and multilateral efforts" aimed at improving global "protection and enforcement of copyrighted materials" and aims to open up "foreign markets closed by piracy and other market access barriers."

The above culture industry lobby groups struggle to influence the US state's culture industry policies and regulatory framework by directly approaching legislators, meeting with key political figures, and using their own media networks to cultivate public consent to an image of their interests as being the same as those of America. And US politicians and policy-makers frequently oblige them (Freedman 2008; K. Lee 2008; McChesney 2004, 2008, 2013). Though media democracy groups like Free Press have fought and won important policy battles against culture industry lobbyists, most of the time US culture industry policy is shaped by "corporate insider hegemony" and marked by a "lack of public participation" (McChesney 2004, 7). Together, media companies wield enormous power and influence in Washington; in effect, state agencies and institutions largely facilitate and legitimize the capitalist goals of the culture industry while mediating and managing the sectoral tensions and conflicts between companies within it.

The accommodative relationship between the US state and the culture industry stems partially from the US state's recognition of the culture industry's importance to the overall growth of the US economy. Like other states that push culture industry development, it builds up the culture industry to create jobs, brand places, generate tax revenue, and increase national GDP. The amicable relationship also arises in part from a "revolving door" between Washington and the culture industry: many culture industry lobbyists have worked for the US state, and many policy-makers have worked for the culture industry. For example, Jack Valenti, the MPAA president from 1966 to 2004, was President Lyndon Johnson's adviser. Dan Glickman, MPAA president from 2004 to 2010, was a former congressman. Current MPAA head Chris Dodd is a former senator and congressman. In 2014, Trade Representative Stan McCoy moved from his government job to the MPAA as its new global head (T. Lee 2014). Moreover, lobbyists for the United States' top media conglomerates have held government jobs, rotating from public to private service jobs. For example, in 2013–14, 118 out of 142 Comcast lobbyists were formally employed by the US government; thirty-one of thirty-four Time Warner lobbyists that period had previously worked for the state too; so did twenty-three of twenty-eight News Corporation lobbyists and fifteen out of nineteen Walt Disney Company lobbyists (Open Secrets 2014). These links and ties ensure that policy debates and outcomes are heavily weighted in the culture industry's favour.

What policy tools does the US state use to concretely support the profit interests of the culture industry?

IP Protection and Promotion
First, the US state supports the culture industry by protecting and promoting its property rights. Intellectual property rights (IPR) – copyright specifically – are the legal basis for the culture industry, its existence and growth, and markets for the exchange of its cultural commodities. The culture industry's owners depend on the US state to recognize and legally enforce their copyright. A significant form of intellectual property, copyright gives media corporations the exclusive right to enable or prohibit others from using or copying their cultural goods and gives them the right to sell, license, or trade these rights to others. The US state aggressively protects and promotes the IPR of US media corporations with the force of law while attempting to deter, discipline, and punish those individuals (and governments) that violate these rights (Bettig 1996; Sandoval 2010). Even the White House works on behalf of the culture industry's copyright holders. Its Washington-based office of the United States Trade Representative, for example, monitors copyright infringing activities in the US and around the world and works with and pressures other violating states to recognize and enforce within their own territories American-derived copyright legislation.

With numerous federal-level agencies, the representative serves the culture industry "domestically and abroad, bilaterally, and in regional groupings" by "building stronger, more streamlined, and more effective systems for the protection and enforcement of IPR" (USTR 2015, 80).

Subsidies
Second, the US state supports its culture industry with subsidies that transfer public wealth to private media corporations. From the earliest days of the US Republic, postal subsidies helped underwrite the commercial newspaper and magazine industry; state and party printing contracts subsidized a partisan press; public libraries and schools bought commoditized books and established a national readership for them; federal grants supported the development of the nation's private telegraph system and telephone network; state research and development funds helped build the radio and TV broadcasting industries; and the FCC's allocation of monopoly rights to bits of the electromagnetic spectrum to private broadcasters and cable TV networks helped them grow and prosper (McChesney 2004, 2008, 2013). In addition to funding and pioneering the Internet (Diamond and Bates 1996), US military research and development also supported the foundational technology that underpins the US computer and video game industry (Herz 1997). The US state continues to subsidize the various sectors of the culture industry with income tax credits, property tax abatements, tax exemptions and rebates, cash grants, free services, and more.

Between 2007 and 2011, American cities, counties, and states awarded hundreds of millions of dollars in subsidies to the United States' most powerful media companies. Adobe Systems took in $42.5 million; Amazon was awarded $348 million; AMC Entertainment absorbed $36 million; AT&T collected $24.7 million; Apple chewed up $119 million; CBS received $24.7 million; Cisco Systems enjoyed $3.59 million; Comcast devoured $88.6 million; eBay won a bid for $68.2 million; Dell consumed $61.1 million; Electronic Arts got $30 million; globalizing Hollywood film and TV studios received about $1.5 billion; IBM computed $117 million; Facebook made $54.8 million from three friendly states; Fiserv downloaded $1.86 million; Google processed $107 million; Hewlett-Packard took $21.1 million; Microsoft received $312 million; Midway Games grabbed $2.29 million; Motorola tallied $7.52 million; Oracle received $19.1 million; Time Warner took $48.9 million; Twitter got $22 million; Yahoo Inc.

made $14 million; and Verizon was awarded $65.6 million (Story, Fehr, and Watkins 2012). Starting in 2005, the US state has provisioned tax breaks to video game corporations, which has helped them to deduct more than $6 billion in software development costs and the enormous revenues they earn from online subscriptions and digital downloads; it also gives them tax credits every time they increase research and development expenditure (Kocieniewski 2011). Overall, the US government is a multi-billion-dollar subsidizer of the US culture industry.

Ownership Concentration
Third, the US state supports the culture industry by enabling media corporations to centralize their growth at home and abroad with a concentrating supportive policy and regulatory framework. While anti-trust laws and cross-ownership restraints once prevented corporations from merging their operations, the US state has largely dismantled the policies and regulations that were intended to protect market competition and media source diversity. Prior to 1996, the FCC prevented one media company from owning multiple TV stations in the same community, TV stations in every community in the nation, or TV stations, radio stations, newspapers, and cable TV systems in the same community. But in 1996, Congress passed the Telecommunications Act, overturning this long-standing FCC regulation. The act helped a handful of US media firms gain control over every sector they chose and greatly diminished the diversity of US media sources (Freedman 2008; Noam 2009; H.I. Schiller 2000; McChesney 2004, 2008). Furthermore, since the Communications Act of 1934, which linked a capitalist media model to the American Way, the FCC has capped foreign ownership of US broadcasting firms at 25 percent on the grounds that US ownership supports US national security, and foreign ownership threatens it. Despite a recent debate at the FCC about loosening this nationalist securitization of the US airwaves, the state's protection of American TV broadcasters to keep out non-US owners persists. When considering foreign ownership of the airwaves, the FCC says it "will continue to coordinate as necessary with Executive Branch agencies on issues relating to national security, law enforcement, foreign policy, and trade policy" (Griffin, Capassa, and Cukier 2013).

In sum, by establishing and enforcing intellectual property and copyright, giving massive public subsidies to fledgling and gigantic media companies, and supporting ownership concentration, the US state plays a crucial role in cementing the power of the US culture industry. In addition to solidifying the power of the culture industry at home, the US state boosts the profit interests of its firms abroad with a global neoliberal policy of trade liberalization, deregulation, and privatization.

Liberalization
From the Second World War to the present day, the US state has promoted the liberalization or the opening of other countries to the US culture industry with its free flow of information doctrine. During the Second World War, the US state framed the free flow of cultural goods across the borders as instrumental to its building of a world order of capitalist, liberal democratic, and peaceful states (Rosenberg 1982, 215). After the war, the free flow ideal was supported by the US-built United Nations, which transformed it into a universal human right (Preston, Herman, and Schiller 1989, 37). The UN's embrace of the free flow ideal, however, coincided with the US state's geopolitical efforts to open the world market to the US culture industry (H.I. Schiller 1976, 24). A 1946 memo by Assistant Secretary of State William Benton, for example, said, "The State Department plans to do everything within its power along political or diplomatic lines to help break down the artificial barriers to the expansion of private American news agencies, magazines, motion pictures, and other media of communications throughout the world. Freedom of the press – and freedom of exchange of information generally – is an integral part of our foreign policy" (cited in H.I. Schiller 1984, 6). In 1948, the Department of State started administering the Agreement for Facilitating the International Circulation of Visual and Auditory Material of an Educational, Scientific and Cultural Character to facilitate the "world-wide free flow of audio-visual materials" between countries by providing "favorable import treatment through the elimination or reduction of import duties, licenses, taxes, or restrictions" (Office of the Federal Register National Archives and Records Administration 2013, 244). As the Cold War proceeded, the government used the free flow doctrine to try to break down national barriers to the US culture industry's expansion and boost the flow of its commodities across borders (Herman and McChesney 1997, 17). The US state's free flow of information doctrine has given crucial geopolitical support to the global trade interests of the US culture industry by pushing free trade and obliterating "trade-distorting" cultural policies such as national subsidies, ownership regulations, or content quotas that may help non-US culture industries to grow.

Deregulation and Privatization
The US state's promotion of global cultural and audiovisual free trade is coupled with its pushing of *deregulation*, or the elimination of political constraints on the power of media corporations to maximize profits, and *privatization*, or the transfer of state ownership rights to public telecommunication firms and public broadcasters to privately owned media and culture industry firms.

In the late 19th century and for much of the 20th, telecommunication system of nearly every nation-state was considered a monopoly, territorially bound and regulated by a PTT (Post, Telegraphy, and Telecommunication) (Hills 2002). National telecommunication systems were symbols and agents of national security, cultural-national identity formation, and sovereignty. The capitalist form taken by the US telecommunications system was the exception to the global PTT rule. Yet, the PTT tradition posed an economic barrier to the expansion of US firms. On behalf of US corporations, the state sought to overcome the territorial limit on accumulation posed by the PTT tradition, initiating a neoliberal reform in the telecom industry beginning in 1982, when the Reagan administration opened up AT&T's domestic monopoly to foreign direct investment, and Margaret Thatcher privatized British Telecom (Comor 1997). While foreign cash flowed into the United States and British telecom markets, American and British corporations demanded the telecommunications systems of other countries be opened up too. By deregulating their own national telecom giants, the United States and the United Kingdom established a neoliberal precedent for other states to follow (Comor 1997). Throughout the 1980s, the United States continued to push telecommunications deregulation, targeting the Western European-, Japanese-, and Canadian-based executives of national telecom firms in an attempt to persuade them of the benefits of deregulating and privatizing their home country's systems (Comor 1997, 198). The US has been very successful in achieving this goal, as states have been privatizing telecommunication systems around the planet. Capitalist telecommunications networks are now the norm, and US-originated neoliberal policies played a significant role in spearheading this transformation (Jin 2005). Telecommunication industries were restructured "because governments around the world adopted neoliberal telecom policies, as they confronted intensifying pressure not only from corporations but also directly from international organizations and the US government" (Jin 2005).

The US state also pressures and promotes the global deregulation and privatization of national public radio and TV broadcasters. Following the

Second World War, public broadcasters existed in all Western European nation-states and in several other countries, including Canada, Australia, New Zealand, Japan, and India. Funded by citizens (through taxation or licensing) and mandated to serve the national public interest by informing, educating, and enlightening them, national public broadcasters were the global rule. At that time, the US commercial media model was the exception. But now the US model is fast becoming the global rule, while public models are a quirky exception as public broadcasters rapidly become defunded, deregulated, and privatized. Between the Second World War and the present day, US media firms have spread the capitalist media model to the world and have been supported by the US state. Today, neoliberal state after state has embraced the commercial media model while public broadcasters are attacked by the right for being paternalistic, elitist, and in some instances authoritarian producers of patronizing, boring, and sometimes propagandistic national content. As public broadcasters have declined in number, non-US media companies have grown and integrated with US media conglomerates atop the system. In many different countries, non-US post–public media corporations replicate the US culture industry model and reproduce its capitalist logics by pursuing profit maximization, exploiting waged workers, selling audience attention to advertisers, retransmitting American entertainment, and modelling their own cultural products on those made by US firms.

On behalf of the US culture industry, the US state has battled unilaterally, bilaterally, and multilaterally through a number of global governmental agencies to embed and institutionalize neoliberal policy (K. Lee 2008). For more than 100 years, the International Telecommunications Union viewed national telecommunication systems as state monopolies and public utilities, but in the 1980s and 1990s, it was brought into line with the United States' neoliberal policy (Comor 1997; Hills 2002, 2007; Thussu 2007). The US state has organized the neoliberal World Trade Organization (WTO) to try to dismantle all barriers to the culture industry's expansion and free flow of its cultural products (Hills 2002, 2007). The most significant WTO trade agreements that serve this goal are the Agreement on Basic Telecommunications Services, the General Agreement on Tariffs and Trade, the Agreement on Trade-Related Aspects of Intellectual Property Rights, and the General Agreement on Trade in Services (K. Lee 2008; Puppis 2008). In addition to working through the WTO to achieve its trade goals, the United States has won consent to bilateral audiovisual free trade agreements with numerous countries, including the once resistant South Korea (Jin 2011). Furthermore, the US state pressures the IMF and World Bank to compel developing countries to deregulate and privatize their industries as a condition of their receiving financial loans, aid, and technology transfers (Dizard 2001). The World Intellectual Property Organization has enshrined US intellectual property law as world law, and the US state demands all countries to enforce its homegrown copyright law (Bettig 1996; Ryan 1998).

The US culture industry and its lobbyists have been served well by the state and appear grateful to it for its immense support. As a recent filing to the United States Trade Representative by the MPAA's head says, "On behalf of MPAA and its members, I want to express our appreciation for the critical assistance the US government provides the industry's efforts to grow its foreign sales" (MPAA 2014c, 1).

Non-US state campaigns to protect and promote the development of non-US national culture industries to spite the US culture industry's global sales efforts have ebbed and flowed over the years, but the US state has fought against them. In the mid-1970s, for example, UNESCO became a flashpoint for struggles against the US culture industry's global dominance. To protest the ownership inequalities, cultural trade imbalances, and dependencies that divided the rich US culture industry from those in the poorer post-colonial countries, the Non-Aligned Movement (NAM) proposed a New World Information and Communication Order (NWICO) (Taylor 1997, 47). In response to NAM's grievances, UNESCO formed the International Commission for the Study of Communication Problems (or the MacBride Commission). At the UNESCO General Conference of 1978, the Mass Media Declaration was put forth in order to recognize the role of communication and culture in national development. Fearing that NWICO and the MacBride Commission's recommendations would limit the US culture industry's expansion and foreign sales, US think tanks, media firms, and even the state itself ridiculed and rejected them (Roach 1997). The Heritage Foundation, for example, argued that NWICO's proposals supported state ownership and control of culture and sought to extend and replicate the Soviet Union's propaganda system in developing countries (Roach 1997). The Inter-American Press Association, the International Press Institute, the World Press Freedom Committee, and the US news media echoed these charges. In 1985, the Reagan administration, followed by the like-minded Thatcher government, then withdrew from UNESCO, muzzling its criticisms of US cultural imperialism (Fraser 2003, 143; Taylor 1997, 49).

The Non-Aligned Movement's struggle for NWICO at UNESCO was defeated, but since the early 1990s, many post-colonial and neo-colonial states have joined forces at UNESCO to again contest US culture industry dominance. So while the US state, on behalf of its culture industry, struggles to globalize neoliberal policy, many non-US states have tried to locally resist this campaign by exempting "culture" from trade dealings and declaring their sovereign right to protect and promote their cultures (and culture industries). In 2001, UNESCO's General Assembly adopted the Universal Declaration on Cultural Diversity, which called cultural diversity "the common heritage of humanity." Anticipating that UNESCO would again become a flashpoint for challenging its culture industry's dominance, the US state rejoined the organization in 2003. In the fall of 2005, delegates from over 180 states (led by Canada and France) approved the final document of the UNESCO Convention on the Protection and Promotion of Diversity of the Cultural Expressions. The US (and Israel) voted against it. Nonetheless, states all over the world still protect and promote their national culture industries (and, to some extent, official national cultures). So, though the US state has tried to universalize a neoliberal policy regime on behalf of its globalizing culture industry, it has not been able to achieve this goal due to the ever-persistent sovereignty of territorial states to reject and resist US pressure and persuasion.

Conclusion: The Consequences of US Global Culture Industry Dominance

Even now the US culture industry remains number one in terms of its market power and reach. The world system has many competing culture industries, but the United States' culture industry is still the most central. In many countries, the US culture industry has increased its presence and the flow of its commodities. The market power of the US culture industry in the world system is maintained through capitalist strategies that aim to integrate non-US culture industries into its operations (cross-border ownership, production, and distribution/exhibition deals) and textual design strategies (global blockbusters, global-national TV formats, and glocalized brands) that seek to appeal to and resonate with consumers across borders, not just those in the United States. The power of the US culture industry is further facilitated and legitimized by the policies of the US state, which by and large support the interests of its powerful owning class. By protecting intellectual property rights, allocating huge public subsidies to media firms, and enabling ownership concentration, the US state has helped build up the culture industry's power at home. Abroad, the US state pushes neoliberal policy (liberalization, deregulation, and privatization) to demolish barriers to the globalizing profit interests of its culture industry. The global power of the US culture industry, then, is the outcome a combination of capitalist and geopolitical strategies forged over the long history of the US Empire and cultural imperialism.

What are the consequences of this dominance?

The first effect of US culture industry dominance is the persistence of a largely one-way flow of cultural products between the US and other countries. The United States still exports a far greater number of cultural products to the world than it imports from it, accounts for nearly half of the world's total audiovisual trade, and boasts an audiovisual trade surplus (WTO 2010). In 2012, the US trade surplus in audiovisual services was $13.6 billion (USITC 2014, 15). Of the top thirty all-time highest-grossing films worldwide, only one (*Spider-Man 3*) is made by a film studio (Sony Entertainment Pictures) not owned by US-based media conglomerates. In 2013, all but one (the Russian-made *Viy 3D*) of the top twenty highest-grossing films of the year were Hollywood owned. No Russian films topped the North American box office. The Chinese Communist Party (CCP) blocks the flow of a lot of American entertainment by capping the number of Hollywood films allowed to be screened in China's theatres to thirty-four; yet in 2012, Hollywood films generated more than half of all ticket revenue in China (Tsui 2013). In 2013, Hollywood films took up about 40 percent of China's box office, but no Chinese films were screened by major US theatre chains. Like Hollywood films, TV shows owned by US firms are the most genuinely "global." The EU has an audiovisual trade deficit with the United States of $8–9 billion every year, and half of this sum is accounted for by TV shows (Doyle 2012). Currently, 85 percent of the TV shows exported from one country to another come from the US, while a mere 7 percent are shipped from the UK, the world's second largest TV exporter (Willens 2015). According to Claire Enders, founder of Enders Analysis, "The $400 billion [global] market for television is sustained by American programming" as there seems to be "an inexhaustible demand" (cited in Willens 2015). Though multi-directional cultural commodity flows are growing, they should not be misconstrued as reciprocal flows between the United States and other countries.

A second effect of the US culture industry's dominance is the perpetuation of the extraordinary ability of US media corporations to enter, integrate, and influence the world's many culture industries to increase their own returns. "Increasing returns are the tendency for that which is ahead to get further ahead, for that which loses advantage to lose further advantage" (Arthur 1996). In the world system, all countries have national culture industries that produce national media, but not all countries have the same (i.e., equal) ability to produce, distribute, and exhibit cultural products worldwide. The concept of increasing returns suggests that the ones that do have this ability will continue to use it with relative ease, while those that don't will either face an uphill battle or simply fall further behind. The advantage enjoyed by the US culture industry in world markets is therefore part of a self-reinforcing cycle; the maintenance of US global media strength will largely rely on the relative weakness of non-US culture industries. The top position of US culture industry in the world system's hierarchy gives its firms the ability to asymmetrically exert influence over the internal structure, ownership patterns, distribution, and exhibition process and standards of media quality of other national culture industries without proportionate reciprocation of influence by them. Many non-US culture industries are promoted and protected by the cultural policy of their home states from total control by the United States. At some future point, one or a combination of these state-culture industry complexes may be capable of challenging the US culture industry, but if they do, the US state will likely use whatever means necessary to contain or combat them. So for the time being, non-US media firms, though economically and culturally significant in their own national and regional markets, remain in globally subordinate positions vis-à-vis the US giants. They are formally independent from the United States and pursue their own market goals at home and abroad, yet their growth is semi-dependent on the US culture industry as a major source of foreign direct investments, cross-border production contracts, and a low-cost supply of high-quality cultural content. Driven by the market pressure to compete with national and regional market rivals, non-US media companies will compete and collaborate with each other while increasing returns to the US culture industry as a whole.

A third effect of US culture industry dominance is asymmetrical cultural diffusion and mixing. The exceptional power of the US Empire's culture industry means that it is better able to produce and circulate commercialized representations of its own national identity and foreign policy than other countries. As suggested above, some people on the receiving end of the United States' global over-flow of cultural commodities may perceive them as threats to their own national cultures and call for their home states to defend or protect their way of life from Americanization. Others may embrace US cultural products and see the imagery and messages as a welcome alternative to what their national culture industry gives them (or deprives them of). A local viewer's material circumstances shape receptivity to US cultural products, and the cultural effects of US products in other countries are not predictable. Yet, there may be effects, some invisible and some more palatable than others. Dizard (2004, 176), a former employee of the United States Information Agency (USIA), remarks, "No society ships ... thousands of Hollywood style films without leaving a cultural mark, whether it intends or not." The cultural marks of US culture industry dominance are multiple, hybrid, and often contradictory but certainly not based on a reciprocal exchange or mutually beneficial meeting of equals. As Van Elteren (2006, 351) says, cultural mixings do not take "place on a level playing field" and instead have "frequently been conducted within the language and culture of the greater power, and within a global economic structure in which the other party command[s] only a little power." Because the US culture industry possesses the greatest power to produce and distribute cultural elements to the world, cultural mixing between the US and the rest is often unequal and asymmetrical. The US culture industry has more structural power than others to package and promote the cultural ingredients that people mix with their own. If the situation was reversed, and the United States was saturated with films, TV shows, ads, and digital content made elsewhere and about another nation, it is unlikely that this would be perceived as benign cultural mixing.

Though the US culture industry is globally dominant, the cultural commodities it manufactures and exports to the world don't always carry imagery of and messages about America that align with the state's geopolitical goals. In a 2011 speech to the US Foreign Policy Priorities Committee, then secretary of state Hillary Clinton said, "Our private media, particularly cultural programming[,] often works at counter purposes to what we truly are as Americans. I remember having an Afghan general tell me that the only thing he thought about Americans is that all the men wrestled and the women walked around in bikinis because the only TV he ever saw was *Baywatch* and World Wide Wrestling" (cited in Lubin 2011). While the US culture industry is enormously successful in selling cultural goods to the world, the US state is not always pleased with the imagery of and messages about America these goods carry. The relative autonomy of US media conglomerates from the US state means that there is no guarantee cultural commodities will support US Empire promotion. The following chapters show how the DOD attempts to resolve the contradictory relationship between the deterritorializing profit goals of US media conglomerates and the foreign policy promotion goals of the US state by supporting the growth of a military-industrial-communications complex that boosts militarism and war as a way of life.

4 The DOD–News Media Complex

The US Empire's wars are fought by soldiers, drones, jetfighters, and tanks in distant lands, but these wars are brought home to US civilians by news media corporations. At a safe distance from actual combat, US citizens read about war in print and digital editions of newspapers, listen to war reports on the radio, watch wars being waged in near real time on TV and computer screens, and search for and download information about war using computers, mobile devices, and so on. When the US state goes to war, two kinds of war thus occur: an actual war and a media war (Taylor 1997). The actual war encompasses war's real material referents: the people who fight, bleed, kill, and die in the actual cities, deserts, and jungles in which violent conflict takes place. Most US citizens never see the actual war but instead consume a highly sanitized "media war" (Taylor 1997). This encompasses the conflict agendas the news media set, the frames of fights they make, and the texts, imagery, and videos of battles they produce to be consumed. Though Total Wars – wars in which a state's total population and resources are mobilized for war – have diminished since the Second World War, small wars, hot wars, cool wars, invasions, occupations, insurgencies, black ops, revolutions, drone attacks, counterterrorism, and "humanitarian" interventions are pronounced in the world system, as well as the content of the news media.

Given war's moral gravity, economic weight, and immense human toll, the US state's decision to go to war or not should be the object of public deliberation. In a democratic society, the news media should inform and educate citizens about substantive debates surrounding war policy and shed light on the range of conflicting positions regarding war. Also, the news media in a democracy ought to be a "watchdog" of society's most powerful war decision-making organizations – the state agencies and corporate lobby groups that steer the empire's war policy. A media watchdog is a vital check against the abuse of power by governmental and corporate elites; it effectively holds large, well-organized, resource-intensive public and private organizations accountable for what they do and draws public attention to the instances in which they do not. Indeed, democratic media fend off corruption by monitoring the day-to-day operations of government and corporations and by investigating forms of state-corporate malfeasance. The news media should expose war PR and propaganda, hold the executive to account, and enable the flow of diverse, dissenting, and veracious opinions about war so as to enable citizens themselves to have substantive discussion and debate about war policy. In this context, the essence of democracy and a democratic news media are threatened by state and corporate propaganda and censorship.

This chapter examines a combined threat to democracy posed by the synergistic propaganda and censorship practices of the DOD toward US news media companies, as well as the willingness of these companies to support and extend the DOD's democracy-corroding information war practices. It focuses on how the geopolitical-economic institutions, policies, and practices of the DOD and news media corporations come together to diminish the production and flow of democracy-nourishing and pacifist information about war (through censorship) and increase the production and flow of militarizing and conflict-inducing information (with PR and psy-ops). This chapter scrutinizes the links between the DOD's information operations and news media corporations and the ways that the DOD and news media companies militarize the news in support of the US Empire. It also shows how DOD public affairs agencies and strategies for managing public opinion about war, combined with the media's capitalist orientation, threaten the news media's democracy-nourishing role and extol a culture in which war seems to be normal.

The first section examines the historical development of the DOD's psy-ops and information operations policies, institutions, and practices for managing the news media's coverage of war, from the Second World War to the post-9/11 War on Terror. The second section examines the persuasive and coercive information operation strategies the DOD uses to try to manage the news media at war. The third section examines the economic reasons why news media companies often support DOD information operations. Examples of news and opinion management strategies are derived from DOD practices in the lead up to and during the 2003 Iraq War. Overall, this chapter documents the US Empire's DOD–news media complex and its production of militarizing war products that serve the DOD and US media firms.

DOD Psy-Ops Policy and Practice: From the Second World War to the War on Terror

From the First World War to the post-9/11 War on Terror, the DOD has tried to manage the way the news media frames war policy, personnel, and practices by combining a mix of psychological and censorship operations to manage public opinion about war and liquidate pacifist dissent (Andersen 2006; Carruthers 2000; Taylor 1997). Even though the DOD does not control the news media, it "attempts to get the public to think about war in a way that aligns with its war policy through the privately owned news media," and the media "have generally served the military rather well" (Carruthers 2000, 272–73). This is due to routinized "cooperation, co-optation and blurring of the lines" between the DOD and the news media (Hallin 1997, 209).

Though psy-ops practices go back as far as to the Committee on Public Information during the First World War, the DOD's Psychological Warfare Branch, which included the Joint Psychological Warfare Committee and Joint Psychological Warfare Advisory Subcommittee, was technically the first official psy-ops division, established in the Second World War with the Office of War Information (OWI). At the end of the Second World War, Gen. Dwight Eisenhower noted how this Total War had led to "many great changes in military science," not the least of these being "the development of psychological warfare as a specific and effective weapon" that "proved its right to a place of dignity in our military arsenal" (cited in Paddock 2002, 20).

In the lead-up to the Korean War in 1950, the DOD established the Psychological Warfare Division to support overt and covert propaganda campaigns. The Joint Chiefs of Staff defined this function as "the planned use of propaganda and related informational measures designed to influence the opinions, emotions, attitudes and behaviors of enemy, neutral or friendly foreign groups in such a way as to support the accomplishment of national policies and aims, or a military mission" (Parry-Giles 2002, 83).

On April 4, 1951, the DOD established a Psychological Strategy Board to: 1) provide more effective planning of psy-ops within the framework of approved national security policies, 2) coordinate the psy-ops of all departments and agencies of the government, and 3) evaluate the effectiveness of the national psy-ops effort (DOD 1952). In 1952, the DOD expanded its psy-ops capacities with Directive S-3140.1, which gave the DOD the authority to use its resources to conduct psy-ops when not officially at war and established a DOD Committee on Psychological Operations to coordinate psy-ops with other government agencies involved in persuasion and public diplomacy. In a 1953 National Security Council (NSC) Directive, Eisenhower declared that "psychological operations are established instruments of national power" (National Security Council 1954, 2). Soon after, he established the Operations Coordinating Board (OCB) to integrate psychological operations with national security strategy (Falk 1964). In 1954, Eisenhower distinguished the DOD's psy-ops from the United States Information Agency's (USIA) public diplomacy efforts: the DOD would undertake psychological operations in countries in which its troops were engaged in combat, while the USIA would be responsible for conducting public diplomacy in non-combat zones. In 1958, Eisenhower signed NSC 5812/1, which further specified the psy-ops responsibilities of the DOD and the USIA (National Security Council 1958). Following these NSC directives, the DOD's psy-ops capacities were gradually enlarged over the next sixteen years or so. After being elected president, John F. Kennedy abolished the OCB but supported the DOD's psychological operations activities as part of a broader policy of "counter-insurgency" against communist movements in Bolivia, Columbia, Cuba, Guatemala, Peru, and Vietnam.

During the Vietnam War, the DOD extended its psy-ops program in Southeast Asia (F.F. Barnett 1989; Paddock 2002). Johnson's National Security Memorandums 325, "Informational and Psychological Warfare Programs in South Vietnam," and 330, "Intensified and Expanded Psyops Activities in Vietnam," brought the DOD, the USIA, and the State Department together in a massive counter-insurgency psychological and public diplomacy operation to promote South Vietnam's Ngo Dinh Diem and demonize the communist North (L.B. Johnson 1965). Soon after being elected president, Nixon issued National Security Decision Memorandum 63, "Psychological Operations against Vietnamese Communists," which aimed to manipulate the opinions of the Vietnamese, not Americans. Yet, the DOD's intelligence gathering (spying) and psy-ops efforts (propaganda) criss-crossed the foreign battlefront and the home front, a situation that the Pentagon Papers and the Church and Otis committees of the 1970s scrutinized. At the same time, the DOD imposed an "informal" censorship regime on journalists by withholding "news so that it could not be published," "classifying documents" that made policies seem controversial, and keeping war correspondents "in the dark" and "away from military operations" (Graber 2011, 412). The DOD's psy-ops campaign, however, was challenged by the American and international anti-war movements' peace media, as well as the North Vietnamese and Soviet Union's anti-imperialist propaganda. "During the Vietnam years ... the US military and the government as a whole proved unable to devise and execute an overall strategy that took due account of the vital importance of the psychological-political dimension of the struggle" (Lord 1989, 15).

During the second half of the Vietnam War, the DOD's psy-ops unit, the Joint United States Public Affairs Office, fed information about the war to the public through compliant journalists – but it didn't directly censor them. Few restrictions were placed on the American journalists who toured South Vietnam, and for this reason, they had some autonomy from the state to capture the horrifying human side of war (Taylor 1997). Satellite TV networks beamed grisly videos – self-immolating monks, napalmed children, bleeding soldiers, public executions – across oceans to US suburbs and city centres, visually bringing the war's many brutalities into American homes. The American War in Vietnam was the first televised and, in many respects, "uncensored war" (Hallin 1989). Between 1961 and 1963, much of the American print and TV news mirrored the state's official war policy, but as public resistance to the war exploded and elite divisions emerged in response, the news media started giving expression to more critical and oppositional points of view (Hallin 1989; Hammond 2000). For "most of the war the media shared the same framework for understanding events in South East Asia as the [US] government," but "after public opinion had moved decisively against the war the media [began] to regularly challenge the official explanation" (K. Williams 1993, 306). Following the Tet Offensive in 1968, in which the Viet Cong launched an all-out attack on the South, "television brought into the home not the carnage of war, but the yawning fissure in the American consensus that underpinned this war in the previous period" (Cumings 1992, 84). The media's coverage of the 1968 My Lai Massacre and the 1969 revelation that Nixon had ordered the bombing of Cambodia that year (in violation of international law) to weaken North Vietnamese supply routes strengthened anti-imperialist arguments and galvanized the peace movement. By the early 1970s, it had become clear to US policy-makers that the US Empire had lost the war and that withdrawal was necessary.

Perhaps desperate to explain their defeat in Vietnam to the public as an effect of something other than wrongheaded policy, US military brass started arguing that the news media had turned domestic public opinion against the war, demoralized troops serving abroad, and caused the United States to lose the war. DOD officials, right-wing think tanks, and Republican politicians soon after promulgated the myth that a footloose liberal news media had not supported the Vietnam War (Kennedy 1993) and that pacifist public opinion – a by-product of TV news media coverage – had indeed lost the war. Major Cass D. Howell (1987, 77–78), for example, blamed TV for making US civilians feel that the war was wrong. Howell complained that "nothing happened in the Vietnam War that had not occurred, either in degree or frequency, in any other war in which Americans had fought," but what was new was TV. According to Howell, "television is too powerful – it has too much impact. It is clear that, if we accept this erosion of public will power, our cause, however just and necessary, is doomed. The enemy knows he does not have to win many battles to win the war as long as he keeps the war on television and drags it out interminably."

This explanation of the US defeat in Vietnam is dubious (because the TV news had actually supported US war aims until an elite consensus broke down) and technologically deterministic (because it reduces the US defeat to a singular cause – negative TV news coverage) (Hallin 1989). In any case, the DOD derived two strategic lessons from this myth of the television-driven "Vietnam War Syndrome," which it was largely responsible for creating. First, if anti-war sentiment developed among the public, the DOD's war effort would be jeopardized because domestic political pressure to end the war would grow. Second, if not properly managed, news coverage of war could facilitate anti-war sentiment and lead to public backlash (E. Louw 2003, 216). After Vietnam, these lessons rationalized the rapid growth of DOD psy-ops policies for managing the total news media's coverage of war. In all future US wars, the DOD would ramp up efforts to reduce the news media's autonomy, while enlarging its own power to control the media war.

During the Reagan years, DOD psy-ops capacities grew as a result of a number of National Security Decision Directives (NSDDs). In 1984, Reagan's NSDD 130 ordered the DOD to rebuild its psy-ops capacities and integrate psy-ops into every level of military planning and operations, making it permanent in times of war and peace. Also, NSDD 130 ordered all government propaganda agencies to ensure that when the United States was at war or responding to a global conflict or crisis, all supporting messages were consistent with official policy (R. Reagan 1984). Soon after, the DOD undertook a systematic review of psy-ops and in 1984 published DOD Directive S-3321.1, "Overt Psyop Conducted by Military Services in Peacetime." In 1985, the DOD released the *Psychological Operations Master Plan*, which expanded DOD psy-ops capacities around the world, de-linked psy-ops from special operations to make it permanent, and led to the building of a joint psy-ops centre. Supported by psy-ops during its 1983 invasion of Grenada, the DOD sourced information to news journalists, while forbidding them to be present during its battles (England 1984). In its 1989 invasion of Panama, the DOD established a national media pool to escort journalists (carefully selected by the DOD) to sites of battle. Despite the DOD's promise to help journalists reach the island, it actually left hundreds of reporters stranded in Miami, Florida. As a result, "there were no pictures or eyewitness accounts of three battles the first day, in which 23 US soldiers were killed and 265 wounded" (Kurtz 2003). The DOD combined this restrictive pooling practice with sourcing strategies and in effect got the news media to support another US invasion (Thrall 2000). Using similar psy-ops strategies, the DOD made sure the news media glorified the Nicaraguan contras, demonized the left-wing Sandinistas, and supported El Salvador's military dictatorship against the left-wing Farabundo Martí National Liberation Front (Solomon 1992; Walker 1991).

Nearing the end of the Cold War, the DOD had become skilled at managing the news media war by pooling journalists, restricting their access to its battles, and sourcing them with content in support of official US war aims (Kumar 2006, 50).

In the lead-up to the 1991 Gulf War, Bush's NSC established the Psyop, Public Propaganda, and Public Diplomacy Committee to coordinate efforts to engineer US and global news coverage of the war. The DOD built psy-ops and PR into every stage of the war, from planning, to preparation, to execution, to aftermath, scripting the Persian Gulf War as a spectacle (Kellner 1992). It attempted to produce this media war as a Hollywood film, with a clear beginning, middle, and end, an easily identifiable cast of evil villains (Saddam Hussein and Iraqis) and good guys (George H.W. Bush and Americans), and a dramatic conflict (war) resolved with a "happy ending" (the liberation of Kuwait) (Engelhardt 1994, 92). The DOD's case for the Gulf War was supported by Hill & Knowlton, a US-based PR company whose multi–million-dollar persuasion services were paid for by the Kuwaiti government (Stauber and Rampton 1995). Hill & Knowlton drummed up public support for the war by building a front group called "Citizens for a Free Kuwait," dispatching Kuwaitis to the news, producing and sourcing video news releases (VNRs) and information kits to news organizations, and spearheading "Free Kuwait" rallies across the nation (Stauber and Rampton 1995). The most egregious yet effective PR event happened on Capitol Hill, when the Hill & Knowlton–supported "Congressional Human Rights Caucus" held a hearing starring a fifteen-year-old Kuwaiti girl named Nayirah, who claimed while bawling that Iraqi soldiers were removing Kuwaiti babies from incubators in a Kuwaiti City hospital and leaving them on the floor to die. In fact, Nayirah had fabricated the story. Moreover, she was the daughter of Kuwait's Ambassador to the US and had been coached by Hill & Knowlton prior to her heart-wrenching congressional performance (Stauber and Rampton 1995).

To get the news media to play a supporting role in its theatre of war after it began, the DOD pooled journalists, controlled their movements, decided what they could and could not report, and screened their stories prior to publication. From Iraq, the DOD sourced the media with talking points by camera-ready press officers, computerized war simulations, and visuals from tank-mounted video cameras (Taylor 1992). With help from the news media, the DOD "sought completely to reshape public understandings of war itself, so that civilian audiences would see it as an essentially bloodless, hi-tech enterprise, effected with such precision that only infrastructure, not humans, suffered its lethal effects" (Carruthers 2000, 133). In the Gulf War, "the media were stage managed, manipulated and lied to, and they believed the lies" (Taylor 1992, 220–21). Cumings (1992, 103) says, "The Gulf War sequence reversed Vietnam; whereas television served state policy in the first phase of the war and questioned it in the second (after Tet), Gulf coverage interrogated the war on the months before Desert Storm, and served the state once the storm broke." While the DOD used these and other strategies to manage the news media's representation of the war, "the mainstream media also presented incredible PR for the military, inundating the country with images of war and the new high-tech military for months, while the brutality of war was normalized and even glamourized in the uncritical media coverage" (Kellner 1992, 421).

In the 1990s, US military conduct in Somalia (1992–93), Haiti (1994), Bosnia (1992–95), Kosovo (1999), and East Timor (1999) was spun through the news media by the DOD and its army of PR companies (E. Louw 2003). There was little critical debate over these wars in Washington and in the news media (Mermin 1999). Despite the DOD's success in making and managing the media image of the Gulf War and the many "humanitarian interventions" of the 1990s to manage public opinion, liberal journalists and academics argued that the news media, journalists, and the public had gained new powers to steer the US Empire. For these proponents of the "CNN-effect," the news media shape public opinion about US foreign policy, and this opinion has the power to influence the decisions of the US national security state (Schorr 1991). The CNN effect theory forwards a bottom-up, populist explanation of why the US Empire acts. So, on CNN, American citizens watch Albanian Muslims being "ethnically cleansed" from Kosovo by Slobodan Milosevic and then, as a show of solidarity with their humanity, demand intervention; CNN passes this will on to Secretary of Defense William Cohen, Secretary of State Madeleine Albright, and others who make strategic decisions based on the news' register of the public mood, and, voilà, NATO-approved American and British jets are bombing Belgrade and Pristina to stop the genocide.

The CNN effect is attractive because it seems to confirm the liberal democratic myth that the voice of the people, carried to policy-makers by a pluralistic and responsive news media, is what makes the state act. However, though seductive, the CNN effect theory is not tenable, for news-generated public opinion about world events is not the sole cause of national security decision-making (Gilboa 2005; Mermin 1997; Robinson 2005). As Gilboa (2005, 38) says, "Global television cannot force policymakers to do what they intend to do anyway." Nor can TV force them to do what they don't intend to do. Nonetheless, the CNN effect shares with the media-induced Vietnam Syndrome the myth of US media corporations supporting the workings of a free and independent "watchdog" press that speaks truth to power. The CNN effect, like the Vietnam Syndrome, perhaps raised DOD suspicions that journalists could and would move public opinion in a direction that threatened their psy-ops campaigns and prompted the military to devise more effective strategies for controlling the media war. In "Winning CNN Wars," for example, US Lt.-Col. Frank J. Stech (1994) describes "what policymakers and military leaders [can and should] do to adapt their policies, strategies, campaign plans, and tactics to support their goals in a CNN war."

Soon after the 9/11 attacks, the White House established an information war room to coordinate the Bush administration's "message of the day" to the world about the global War on Terrorism and its October 2001 invasion of Afghanistan (P.E. Louw 2003; Neuman 2001). Jim Wilkinson, head of this information war room, explained: "This is the first war that has a never-ending news cycle. It may be 3 o'clock in the morning in the United

States, but somewhere in the world, a journalist is on a deadline. A 24-hour news cycle required the coalition to set up a 24-hour operation to communicate the facts" (cited in Neuman 2001). Wilkinson said the room aimed to speak to global publics "directly" and to "bury the Taliban lies" about the consequences of the invasion (Neuman 2001). In the months that followed, the DOD established the Office of Strategic Influence to support this campaign. The office was headed by Air Force Gen. Simon P. Worden, who called for everything from black propaganda (official lies planted in the foreign press to embellish US foreign policy aims) to white propaganda (the manipulation of foreign journalists and news organizations to bias their reporting to US goals) (Dao and Schmitt 2002). "It goes from the blackest of black programs to the whitest of white," said a senior DOD official (cited in Dao and Schmitt 2002). Privatizing this psy-ops job, the DOD outsourced it to the culture industry's promotional sector by paying companies to "develop information programs and evaluate their effectiveness using the same techniques as American political campaigns, including scientific polling and focus groups"(Dao and Schmitt 2002).

In addition to sourcing the news media to build support for the war in Afghanistan, the DOD employed subtle censorship techniques to manage how journalists reported it by restricting access to key battle sites in Afghanistan, and "claiming that complete secrecy was required to assure the success of the operation and the safety of the troops" (Graber 2011, 414). After US air strikes killed about forty-eight Afghani civilians celebrating at a pre-wedding party, the DOD restricted the media from representing the deaths by taking just two reporters to the bloody scene and then prohibiting others from sharing these reporters' stories. On December 2, 2002, US soldiers were injured and killed by "friendly fire" (a bomb dropped on them in an area outside of Kandahar). To prevent journalists from capturing the carnage, the US Marines locked photojournalists in a warehouse until the scene was cleared (Synovitz 2002). Also, the DOD bought exclusive rights to all satellite images of Afghanistan – especially the sites the DOD had bombed – from Ikonos. "They are buying all the imagery that is available," said John Copple, CEO of Space Imaging, Inc., the corporate parent of Ikonos. "And they're using it for maps, they're using it for planning, they're using it for damage assessment after they run missions – they're using it in a variety of ways" (cited in Trivedi 2001). Indeed, the DOD bought up the satellite images of the battlefield to prevent journalists from doing the same, thereby subverting the news' ability to acquire and publicize images of the Afghan civilians it had killed.

The DOD's admittance that it and the OSI used black and white propaganda to influence the global news about the Afghanistan invasion, and its censorship, resulted in a public backlash. To the chagrin of Secretary of Defense Donald Rumsfeld, the OSI was closed down in November 2002. An aggravated Rumsfeld commented, "If you want to savage this thing, fine, I'll give you the corpse. There's the name. You can have the name, but I'm gonna keep doing every single thing that needs to be done and I have" (cited in FAIR 2002). Yet, in the interim between the 2001 invasion of Afghanistan and the 2003 invasion of Iraq, the Office of Global Communications (OGC) was established "to inject pro-Americanism into the punishing 24-hour, seven-day news cycle ... [and] include information campaigns about Mr. Bush's domestic policy – like education bills – as well as traditional information about the military, diplomatic, and economic sides of national security policy" (Becker and Dao 2002). The OGC was closed in late 2002, and its functions were integrated into the DOD.

This brief history highlights how the DOD routinely attempts to manage public opinion about war through the private news media and in a way that aligns with official foreign policy goals. Throughout this history, many US news owners, editors, and journalists fell in line behind the DOD's psy-ops, serving as private emissaries and relays for official imagery and messages of war.

From Psy-Ops to Information Operations (IO)

In the late 1990s, DOD strategists replaced the psy-ops concept with a more contemporary term – "information operations" (IO) (US Department of Defense 2003b, 2003c, 2010, 2012). *Joint Vision 2010* (JCS 1996) and *Joint Vision 2020* (JCS 2000) describe IO as the total actions of the DOD to affect an adversary's information systems while defending and enhancing its own information systems. One month following the September 11, 2001, attacks, the DOD issued the *Report of the Defense Science Task Force on Managed Information Dissemination* (DOD 2001a). The report states that "US civilian and military information dissemination capabilities are powerful assets vital to national security. They can create diplomatic opportunities, lessen tensions that might lead to war, help contain conflicts, and address non-traditional threats to America's interests. In the information age, no diplomatic or military strategy can succeed without them" (i). The report continues: "Coordinated information dissemination is an essential tool in a world where US interests and long-term policies are often misunderstood, where issues are complex, and where efforts to undermine US positions increasingly appeal to those who lack the means to challenge American power." The task force report says that US-based news media corporations such as CNN, Time Warner, and others "provide an abundance of credible information" but "cannot and should not be relied on to act as advocates for national security policies." The report concludes that the DOD needs to use IO to "create a context that enhances the achievement of political, economic, and military objectives" (2).

In October 2003, Donald Rumsfeld signed a seventy-four-page document entitled *Information Operations Roadmap* (IOR) (US Department of Defense 2003b), which offers some insight into DOD information operations. The IOR defines information operations as "The integrated employment of the core capabilities of Electronic Warfare, Computer Network Operations, Psychological Operations, Military Deception and Operations Security, in concert with specified and supporting and related capabilities, to influence, disrupt, corrupt or usurp adversarial human and automated decision-making while protecting our own." IO is *permanent* (it is used by the DOD during peace, crisis, and war) and *boundless* (it is not confined to one territory). "Information intended for foreign audiences, including public diplomacy and PSY-OPs, is increasingly consumed by our domestic audience," the *IOR* notes. "PSY-OPs messages will often be replayed by the news media for much larger audiences, including the American public." DOD IO policy traverses boundaries between national and international, civilian and combatant, us and them, and state and private media. In the post-9/11 period, IO was expanded by the DOD.

The DOD (2003c) IO policy doctrine *FM 3–13, Information Operations: Doctrine, Tactics, Techniques, and Procedures* (hereafter FM 3–13), drawn up in November 2003, describes persuasive and coercive IO strategies. FM 3–13 recommends that offensive and defensive IO be used simultaneously. Offensive IO includes strategies that "destroy, degrade, disrupt, deny, deceive, exploit, and influence adversary decision-makers and others who can affect the success of friendly operations." Defensive IO strategies "protect and defend friendly information" (35). IO also covers public affairs, those "public information, command information, and community relations' activities directed toward both the external and internal publics," and "civil-military operations," which intend to "establish, maintain, influence, or exploit relations between military forces, governmental and nongovernmental civilian organizations and authorities, and the civilian populace in a friendly, neutral, or hostile operational area in order to facilitate military operations, to consolidate and achieve operational US objectives" (43). "PSY-OPS" are "planned operations that convey selected information and indicators to foreign audiences to influence their emotions, motives, objective reasoning, and ultimately to influence the behavior of foreign governments, organizations, groups, and individuals" (41). "Physical destruction" is "the application of combat power to destroy or degrade adversary forces, sources of information, command and control systems, and installations" (42). The FM 3–13 says the "information environment" in which the DOD conducts information operations "is the aggregate of individuals, organizations, or systems that collect, process, or disseminate information; also included is the information itself." This means that every person, group, media organization, and state that has the capability to produce and circulate information and that is part of the global "information environment" is a possible DOD target.

In sum, IO encompasses the DOD's *sourcing* of the news media and manipulation of media sources to persuade US and foreign publics to support US war policy; it also involves the DOD's manipulation, censorship, or destruction of news media sources that are perceived as threats to the United States' ability to win the media war.

The power of the DOD IO to occupy the news media battlefield came into full effect before, during, and after the US-led invasion of Iraq on March 20, 2003.

Making "Operation Iraqi Freedom"

More than a decade after the US invaded Iraq, Paul Krugman (2015), a *New York Times* op-ed columnist and Professor of Economics and International Affairs at the Woodrow Wilson School of Public and International Affairs at Princeton University, declared that the "Iraq war wasn't an innocent mistake, a venture undertaken on the basis of intelligence that turned out to be wrong." Rather, "America invaded Iraq because the Bush administration wanted a war. The public justifications for the invasion were nothing but pretexts, and falsified pretexts at that. We were, in a fundamental sense, lied into war."

To create a pretext for a pre-emptive invasion of Iraq, the Bush administration framed Saddam Hussein's Ba'athist state as partially responsible for al-Qaeda's 9/11 terrorist attacks, claimed Iraq possessed biological and chemical weapons of mass destruction and intended to use them against the United States and its allies, and portrayed Iraqis as wanting the United States to liberate them from Saddam's evil dictatorship. The Bush administration's three "official" rationalizations for pre-emptive war were not based on reality, however, but basically invented (Stein and Dickinson 2006). The "Downing Street Memo," a recording of a secret July 23, 2002, meeting between British Labour government, defence, and intelligence elites talking about the US case for war, reveals the M16 head saying, soon after a visit to Washington, that "Bush wanted to remove Saddam Hussein, through military action, justified by the conjunction of terrorism and WMD," and that the "intelligence and facts were being fixed around the policy." The memo also quoted British foreign secretary Jack Straw claiming that Bush had "made up his mind" to invade Iraq but that "the case [for doing so] was thin" (Stein and Dickinson 2006; Rycroft 2005).

To fix Bush's claims as facts and fatten his case for war, the DOD set up the Office of Special Plans (OSP). Between September 2002 and June 2003, the OSP produced and supplied "intelligence" about Iraq to senior Bush administration officials that had not been vetted by the CIA. Former CIA officer Larry C. Johnson claimed that the OSP "lied and manipulated intelligence to further its agenda of removing Saddam" and that it was run by "a group of [neoconservative] ideologues" who took "bits of intelligence to support their agenda and ignore[d] anything contrary" (cited in MacKay 2003). The DOD established the OSP "to find evidence of what Defense Secretary Donald Rumsfeld wanted to be true" (Hersh 2003). The Bush administration also built its case for pre-emptive invasion by relying on bogus WMD information fed to it by a US front group in Iraq called the Iraqi National Congress (INC), which the CIA and the Rendon Group had established following the 1991 Gulf War in order to rally Iraqis against the Ba'athist state. The Bush administration preferred INC-supplied information to intelligence produced by CIA analysts (Dreyfuss 2002). The INC also supplied *New York Times* journalist Judith Miller with the claim that Iraq possessed WMDs, and Bush administration officials cited Miller to corroborate their claim that Iraq was a threat (Foer 2005; Jamail 2007). The INC was the source of at least 108 news stories about Iraq's alleged WMDs (Chatterjee 2004); and Condoleezza Rice, Colin Powell, and Donald Rumsfeld referred to Miller's news articles when they appeared on US and global TV news networks to sell the war (Boyd-Barrett 2004).

The United States' pretext for war was disputed by Iraqi State TV, Iraqi citizens, international peace activists, weapons inspectors like Hans Blix, and intelligence analysts – and rightly so. A link between al-Qaeda and Saddam Hussein did not exist, Iraq did not possess WMDs, and the most vocal Iraqi proponents of the United States' war to liberate Iraq worked for the INC. The Bush administration's war pretext was bogus, but it nonetheless got many Americans to support the march to war. How did the DOD try to manage the news industry's coverage of its invasion of Iraq, and what IO persuasive sourcing and repressive coercing strategies did the DOD use to do so?

DOD Media Persuasion/Sourcing Strategies

In an attempt to set and control the news agenda and frame of war and thereby engineer public consent to Operation Iraqi Freedom (a label that itself is a salient piece of propaganda), the DOD employed a number of *sourcing* strategies that amount to a gigantic information subsidy to news corporations.

Experts
The DOD dispatched numerous "experts" who worked for or were indirectly funded by the DOD to echo and amplify the Bush administration's pretext for war. Retired US military generals and lobbyists for defence corporations were welcomed to the studios of TV news networks and appeared to the US public as non-partisan military analysts (Barstow 2008a). The DOD's assistant secretary of defense for public affairs, Victoria Clarke, launched the made-for-TV "military analyst" program in early 2002 and sought to "spread the [Bush] Administration's talking points on Iraq by briefing retired commanders for network and cable television appearances" (Sessions 2008). The DOD gave its analysts access to hundreds of private briefings with US military leaders and took them on tours to Iraq. Kenneth Allard, an IO instructor at the National Defense University, said the DOD's dispatching of military analysts to newsrooms "was a coherent, active policy." DOD policy documents refer to military analysts as "message force multipliers" and "surrogates" who functioned to deliver strategic "themes and messages" to millions of TV viewers "in the form of their own opinions" (Barstow 2008a). The DOD even hired a private contractor called Omnitec Solutions to monitor its military analysts' TV appearances and measure their effectiveness. These analysts were quoted more than 4,500 times by journalists employed by US radio, network, and cable TV news stations (Newscorpwatch 2008). Never did the TV news disclose these military analysts' ties to the DOD or US arms firms (Barstow 2008a).

The Office of Public Diplomacy furthered the DOD's construction of Iraq as a threat by getting Ken Pollack (2002), a former CIA intelligence analyst and Brookings Institute scholar, to push the argument he makes in *The Threatening Storm: The Case for Invading Iraq* to the US and international media (Stauber 2002).

Embeds
While DOD-employed experts talked up Operation Iraqi Freedom through corporate TV news networks on the home front, the DOD also sought to manage news sources from the battlefront. In Iraq, the DOD controlled what journalists reported about the war and how they represented it by embedding them with combat units. Months prior to Operation Iraqi Freedom, Secretary of Defense Donald Rumsfeld and Chairman of the Joint Chiefs of Staff Gen. Richard B. Myers issued an embedding directive: "We must organize for and facilitate access of national and international media to our forces, including those engaged in ground operations," and "we will commit communications systems and trained joint public affairs teams to facilitate the international press getting a firsthand look at coalition operations" (cited in Miracle 2003, 42). Lacking confidence in the ability of journalists to cover the war in a fair and balanced way, the DOD said, "We need to tell the factual story – good or bad – before others seed the media with disinformation and distortions, as they most certainly will continue to do. Our people in the field need to tell our story – only commanders can ensure the media get to the story alongside the troops" (DOD 2003a, 1). Victoria Clarke, assistant secretary of defense for public affairs, said that embedding journalists with the troops would expose audiences to the United States' involvement in combat and humanitarian operations, demonstrate the military's commitment to avoid or minimize civilian casualties, support the president's case for war, rapidly respond to and refute charges against the United States, enable news media access to the US military, and highlight the professionalism and power of US military forces in action (Rodriguez 2004).

The DOD's embedded journalism policy was an instrument of media sourcing, influence, and control. It enabled the DOD to allocate reporting assignments to specific journalists and determine which journalists would get access to its official view of the war and which ones would not. The DOD gave aligned or cooperative journalists that supported its war effort privileged access to the war as embeds while excluding non-aligned or non-cooperative journalists. The DOD hired the Rendon Group to screen journalists and rank them as "positive" (trusted to represent the DOD in a favourable light), "negative" (not trusted), or "neutral" prior to embedding them, and it embedded only "positive" journalists (Reed 2009; Reed, Baron, and Shane 2009). Although the DOD chose not to embed "negative journalists," it did not prevent news corporations from dispatching their own non-embedded journalists to the battle. However, it warned that the unilateral deployment of journalists would be dangerous, as the safety of non-embedded reporters could not be guaranteed. Furthermore, unilaterally deployed journalists risked being misidentified by the DOD as enemy combatants and treated as such.

The DOD's embedding policy gave news corporations an economic incentive to work with the DOD, as embeds got access to DOD-provisioned information, photo ops, and protection, and non-embedded journalists were denied access to DOD support for their production of the news and put themselves at risk of being shot at by US and Iraqi combatants. Thus, news corporations could either embed their journalists with the US military and enjoy the benefit of free access, content, and security or deploy their journalists unilaterally in the field and resultantly lose out on a big news production subsidy. Embedding was obviously the most profitable option. As a result, hundreds of journalists relinquished their professional autonomy and consented to being embeds.

To gather, audition, and prepare a cast of "positive" journalists for action in Operation Iraqi Freedom, the DOD hosted a number of news media "boot camps" at bases such as Fort Benning in Georgia, Fort Dix in New Jersey, and Marine Corp Base Quantico and Naval Station Norfolk in Virginia. In early February 2003, the DOD gathered fifty-seven US reporters, photographers, and TV pundits at Quantico and gave them "a crash course in all things military" (Jacobs 2003). The DOD immersed journalists in war simulation games, too, teaching them how to apply gas masks in preparation for a chemical weapons attack, paint their faces with camouflage, escape a minefield, perform first aid, use a compass, and build a desert latrine. The DOD also showed journalists its high-tech weapons and trained them to use military acronyms (Jacobs 2003). At these media boot camps, journalists trained with US soldiers in preparation for the media war. "This allowed the reporters and military to build trust in each other and to get familiar with each other's terminology and routines. It also allowed the news organizations and reporters the opportunity to test their new equipment, techniques, and procedures for reporting in what would be a fluid, hectic environment" (Rodriguez 2004). DOD boot camps elicited journalistic identification with US military forces. *Los Angeles Times* reporter John Henderson, who was embedded with the 3rd Infantry Division in Kuwait prior to Operation Iraqi Freedom, said, "When you're living in tents with these guys and eating what they eat and cleaning the dirt off the glasses, it's a whole different experience. You definitely have a concern about knowing people so well that you sympathize with them" (cited in Glassner 2003). The DOD encouraged journalists to feel as though they were part of the DOD's war effort, not detached observers; it trained them to identify with the department and produce pro-war reports, neutralizing their critical faculties and their professionalism.

Following the rehearsal for Operation Iraqi Freedom, the DOD deployed more than 750 journalists alongside US military combat units to Iraq for set periods of time. Eighty percent of embeds were US reporters, 20 percent were non-US reporters, and 10 percent of the total US reporters were selected from local newspapers from military towns (Whitman 2003). The DOD shuttled embedded journalists around Iraq in armoured Humvees and encouraged them to shoot, record, and transmit sanitized, heroic, and spectacular images of US military action in real time, all the time. Embeds captured and broadcast live footage from actual battles, showing TV viewers war from the point of view of the soldiers with whom they were fighting. The DOD sourced journalists with information it deemed relevant to its story-making process and gave them access only to the scenes and sights of war its PA officers saw fit for public consumption. "The Pentagon's embed strategy was ingenious because it increased rather than limited access to information. By giving broadcasters access to highly newsworthy action footage from the front line, the military was encouraging a focus on the actions of US and British troops, who would be seen fighting a short and successful war" (Lewis and Brookes 2004, 298). DOD editorial rules, however, forbade embeds from reporting everything they saw. Embeds were permitted to publish only news content related to approximate troop strength, approximate casualties, location of previous military targets and missions, and the hometowns of military units. Embeds were not permitted to report DOD information that detailed specific numbers of troops, discuss the location of US aircraft, ships, and weaponry, refer to future operations, or comment on the rules of engagement. If journalists refused to abide by these rules, they were disembedded from the action (Sweeney 2006, 190). Military commanders imposed news media "black outs" when journalist transmissions from the battlefield were perceived to jeopardize the actual and media war effort.

Overall, embedding enabled the DOD to ensure that journalists would show news readers and viewers the war in the way the DOD wanted them to see it. David Axe, a US journalist embedded with the military in Iraq, reflected on his experience: "Embedding means working within the rubric of a military public affairs operation," and this "encourages self-censorship" (Axe 2006).

Information Centres
In addition to embedding journalists with combat units, the DOD attempted to carefully manage the international news media's coverage of war by gathering reporters on US battleships, at CENTCOM headquarters in Doha, Qatar, in Kuwait news media staging areas, and at the Pentagon itself. Prior to the invasion, the US military built a Coalition Information Centre (CIP) at the Hilton Kuwait Resort. The CIP was staffed by IO officials trained by the army, navy, air force, and marines. The CIP attempted to manage the international news media's coverage of the war by sourcing it with press releases, casualty reports, conference talks, and interviews between DOD public affairs officers and journalists. The DOD moved the CIP's headquarters to Doha in Qatar just prior to the invasion. There, the CIP sourced 6,500 military-credited international journalists with its own newsworthy war information.

DOD VNRs and Cable TV
The DOD also sourced the United States and international media with video news releases or pre-packaged made-for-TV segments about the war that were created by its own production studios and distribution systems. The DOD's Defense Video and Imagery Distribution System (DVIDS) produced and distributed war video news releases to TV news corporations, free of charge. "We provide the pipe, a trough of products for national, local and military media," said Lt.-Col. Will Beckman, DVIDS director of operations (cited in Zewe 2004). Between 2004 and 2006, the US news media used more than 72,000 video news releases provided by the DVIDs (Julian 2007). Users of DVIDS material were not required to identify DVIDS as the source, meaning that TV networks ran DOD spin and US citizens consumed it as news. By running DVIDS content, US media corporations saved on costs associated with content development, and the DOD got to promote its message to the public through a seemingly "objective" outlet (Metz, Garrett, Hutton, and Bush 2006).

The DOD also established the Pentagon Channel (now called the DoD News Channel), a 24/7 cable TV channel to carry DOD news briefings, interviews with US military personnel, short documentaries, and lifestyle militainment to subscribers. The Pentagon Channel directly disseminated official information to millions of US soldiers and civilians, bypassing professional journalists. Some US TV news networks, however, carried Pentagon Channel content too (Karl 2008). "We're the house organ, we're the megaphone for the Pentagon," said Allison Barber, who was the deputy assistant secretary of defense for internal communications and in charge of the Pentagon Channel (cited in Zewe 2004). Free and accessible to US and international cable and satellite TV providers, the DoD News Channel provisions militarized public media to the world.

Media Pseudo-Events
To make US citizens feel good about the war, the DOD created some militarized events. In a polemic against the news media's ever-growing obsession with "happenings," and "synthetic novelties," Boorstin (1962) famously derided these as "pseudo-events." For Boorstin, a pseudo-event "is not spontaneous, but comes about because someone has planned, planted or incited it"; is made "for the immediate purpose of being reported or reproduced"; has an ambiguous "relation to the underlying reality of the situation"; and is usually "intended to be a self-fulfilling prophecy" (11). In the months following the invasion of Iraq, the DOD produced a number of militarized pseudo-events, which TV networks devoured.

The first was called "Saving Private Lynch." The DOD derived its content for this pseudo-event from an actual incident in Iraq on March 23, 2003, when a US Army maintenance convoy of Humvees drove into Nasiriyah, Iraq, crashed, and then came under fire. A passenger, Private Jessica Lynch, was injured in the crash but soon after rescued by Iraqis who took her to a civilian hospital where she was tended to by Iraqi hospital workers (Kampfner 2008; Kristof 2003). Jim Wilkinson, head of the Coalition Information Centre, revised Lynch's war experience without her consent and without the public's knowledge of what had truly happened, spinning it into a tale of heroism (Neil 2009). Wilkinson's pseudo-event depicts Lynch as a fearless warrior who, after fleeing the Humvee crash, engages in an intense firefight against Iraqi soldiers until her ammo runs out. Lynch is then shot, stabbed, captured, tortured, and raped by Iraqi soldiers. The story set the stage for a made-for-TV rescue video. On April 1, 2003, TV networks ran a DOD-produced video of Lynch being rescued by a Special Forces unit of the US Navy SEALs. The *Washington Post* and other newspapers reported this event as though it were true, generating quite an outpouring of patriotic zeal. Months after the debut of

"Saving Private Lynch," Lynch publicly criticized the DOD for making her into a pseudo-event (Hosenball 2007). She claimed that "They [the DOD] used me to symbolize all this stuff. It's wrong. I don't know why they filmed [my rescue] or why they say these things" (McIntyre 2003). On April 24, 2007, Lynch testified before the US House Committee on Oversight and Government Reform that the DOD had erroneously portrayed her as a "Rambo from the hills of West Virginia" and chided the military for spinning her experience (CNN 2007). The pseudo-event proved more seductive to NBC TV than reality, so NBC produced its own made-for-TV film called *Saving Jessica Lynch* (CNN 2003a).

A second DOD engineered pseudo-event attempted to convey an end to the Iraq war and the beginning of the reconstruction period. On April 9, 2003, the US military marched on Baghdad, and "liberation" was declared. The US and global news ran videos of a US soldier draping an American flag over the face of a Saddam Hussein statue in Firdos Square and a group of Iraqis then pulling down the statue with help from a US tank. This was a pseudo-event *par excellence*, planned and executed by an army psy-ops unit. US Marine Cpl. Edward Chin admitted that he was ordered to wrap the face of Saddam in the US flag and then encourage Iraqis to congregate around and attack the statue (De Rooij 2003). A US M-88 recovery tank then pulled the statue down. The stage for this event was conveniently located near the Palestine Hotel, where most US and global news journalists were staying (J. Cox 2006). On May 2, 2003, nearly a month following this DOD pseudo-event, another one was conducted. President Bush, accompanied by hundreds of sailors aboard the USS *Abraham Lincoln* battleship and standing under a banner proclaiming "Mission Accomplished," declared, "Major combat operations in Iraq have ended."

DOD persuasive info operations transformed the US invasion of Iraq into a "branded war, a co-production of the Pentagon and Newsrooms, processed and cleansed so that it could appeal to the well-established tastes of people who were veteran consumers of popular culture" (Rutherford 2004, 4). The reality of occupied Iraq following the DOD's staged Saddam statue toppling and Bush victory speech was different. The Ba'athist regime had ended, but the Iraqi insurgency was just beginning.

DOD Media Repression/Coercion Strategies

To maintain US consumer confidence in Operation Iraqi Freedom, the DOD employed a number of coercive information operations to manage the news media's war.

Censoring the Dead and Dying

US civilians tend not to want to see the people the DOD kills in their name, and the DOD knows that allowing civilians to see the injured, dying, and dead risks diminishing the public's support for war. So in the early stages of the Iraq war, the DOD censored its deadly reality (Kamiya 2005) and sought to create a sanitized image of war. Days following the start of Operation Iraqi Freedom, the DOD issued the following directive: "There will be no arrival ceremonies for, or media coverage of, deceased military personnel returning to or departing from Ramstein (Germany) airbase or Dover (Delaware) base, to include interim stops" (Milbank 2003). This censorship policy prohibited the journalists from reporting deceased-soldier "homecomings" (Zoroya 2003). The DOD claimed it censored homecomings to protect the privacy of the departed and their families. "The DOD's censorship policy has been in effect since 1991," said John Molino, a deputy under secretary of the DOD. "Quite frankly, we don't want the remains of our service members who have made the ultimate sacrifice to be the subject of any kind of attention that is unwarranted or undignified" (Roberts 2004). But the DOD's censorship policy also masked the human consequences of war so as to maintain public confidence in the power of the US military.

In addition to prohibiting photographs of the returning war dead, the DOD forbade embedded journalists in Iraq from publishing images of injured and dead US soldiers (Rainey 2005). In 2006, the *New York Times* published an image of a mortally wounded soldier that Gen. Raymond T. Odierno said violated DOD policy. "Names, video, identifiable written/oral descriptions or identifiable photographs of wounded service members will not be released without service member's prior written consent," stated the policy. "In respect for family members, names or images clearly identifying individuals 'killed in action' will not be released. Names of KIAs may be released 24 hours after Next of Kin have been notified" (cited in Arnow 2007). In February 2009, Secretary of Defense Robert Gates lifted the DOD censorship policy on photos of dead soldiers to let the families of soldiers decide if their child's death is newsworthy (Mount 2009).

During the early years of Operation Iraqi Freedom, the DOD's censorship eliminated images of injured, dying, and dead soldiers from the news media. In May 2005, the *Los Angeles Times* examined photos of the Iraq War in major newspapers *(New York Times, Washington Post, Los Angeles Times, St. Louis Post-Dispatch, and Atlanta Journal-Constitution)* and magazines (*Time* and *Newsweek*) over a six-month period in which 559 US and US-allied soldiers were killed, but no images of dead troops appeared. The *Seattle Times* was the only newspaper that published an image – of the covered body of a fallen US soldier – and very few images of wounded US soldiers were fit for print (Rainey 2005). In 490 visuals circulated by the Associated Press dealing with "casualties in Iraq" between March 2003 and June 2005, none portrayed dead or injured soldiers. Arnow (2007) observed, "While flag-draped coffins and respectful photos of funerals abound (one even shows a soldier in an open coffin), just three wounded Americans appear in pictures. Two are in hospitals, and one is in the field."

Spotlight on the US Living and the Iraqi Dead
In addition to prohibiting the flow of images of injured, dying, and dead US soldiers, in late 2005 the DOD strategically placed many living soldiers in the news media spotlight. This IO homecoming program was called "Operation Homefront." The DOD ordered soldiers returning to the US from Iraq to give interviews to their hometown newspapers and TV stations and directed them to praise the US war effort in Iraq. "I've been promised an early release if I do a good job promoting the war," said one reservist. A detailed set of pre-organized DOD talking points encouraged soldiers to 1) admit initial doubts about the war but claim conversion to a belief in the virtue of the mission, 2) praise military leadership in Iraq and throw in a few words of support for the Bush administration; 3) claim the effort to turn the security of Iraq over to the Iraqis is working; 4) reiterate that America must not abandon its mission in Iraq and must stay until "the job is finished"; and 5) talk about how "things are better" now in Iraq (cited in D. Thompson 2005). Operation Homefront resulted in front-page stories in daily and weekly newspapers and upbeat reports on local TV stations. Not all returning soldiers, however, consented to being wrapped up by the DOD as militainment infomercials for the US Empire that Christmas season.

The DOD allowed images of dead Iraqis to be published but encouraged the news media to frame Iraqi death and suffering as a result of Sunni-Shia factional violence. The DOD tried to represent US soldiers as neutral agents occupying Iraq to keep the peace while presumably barbaric, disorderly, and war-loving Arab Muslims slaughtered each other. By portraying US soldiers as passive peacemakers rather than active war-makers, these images attributed responsibility for thousands of Iraqis killed following the US invasion not to the US but to Iraqis themselves. The DOD also encouraged the news media to publicize images of high-profile dead Iraqis. In 2003, the DOD released a CD-ROM of digital images of Saddam Hussein's sons' mutilated corpses to the US and international news media, soon after US forces killed them in a gunfight (CNN 2003b).

Flacking Non-Aligned Journalists
The DOD waged a flack campaign against news organizations that did not play a subservient role in their media war. The DOD's treatment of the Qatar-based Arab television news network, Al Jazeera, is exemplary. While US TV news networks produced Operation Iraqi Freedom as a sanitized spectacle, Al Jazeera represented the human consequences of the US invasion: suffering, injured, and dead Iraqi civilians. For this apparent travesty, the DOD framed Al Jazeera as "an enemy propaganda station, putting out devastating accounts of Iraqi civilian casualties to a vast Arab audience, thus fueling anti-American sentiments" (Knightley 2003, 10). Al Jazeera's coverage of the human consequences of the US invasion threatened the DOD's image of a "clean war." After the US state asked Al Jazeera to cease promoting its brand of war journalism and Al Jazeera refused, the DOD tried to discredit the news station (J. Wolf 2003). In an interview with Fox News on July 20, 2003, Paul Wolfowitz, US Deputy of Defense, claimed that Al Jazeera incited anti-American hatred by "slanting news incredibly" about the war in Iraq (BBC News 2003a). Without providing any evidence, Rumsfeld labelled Al Jazeera as "violently anti-coalition" and claimed it was an accomplice to terrorists (BBC News 2003b). Colin Powell, who presented bogus evidence of Iraq's "WMD" program to the UN, also chimed in: "They tend to portray our efforts in a negative light" (cited in J. Wolf 2003).

Killing Non-Aligned Journalists
The DOD is suspected to have coerced the non-aligned journalists and news organizations that did not perform the way it wished in its media war. As Paterson (2005, 23) observes, "A repertory of coercion – much of it already applied within the United States – has been employed to silence or 'correct' such journalism, seemingly with coordination and sophistication." Journalists who worked outside of DOD media-management mechanisms faced danger and exposed themselves to attacks by Iraqis and by the DOD (Knightley 2003; Paterson 2014). For example, on April 8, 2003, a US tank fired on the Palestine Hotel in Baghdad, killing Reuters cameraman Taras Protsyuk; that same day, an A-10 warthog blasted Al Jazeera's office in

Baghdad and killed its correspondent Tariq Ayyoub (Goodman 2003). On November 13, 2002 – the day before the United States occupied Kabul – the US military bombed the BBC's broadcasting facilities and the Al Jazeera bureau (US officials claimed that the Al Jazeera compound was being used by al-Qaeda) (Weissman 2005). Other reporters in Iraq were harassed and jailed too. Sami al-Hajj, for example, was imprisoned at Guantanamo Bay (Khanfar 2005). Nawfal al-Shahwani was arrested in the northern Iraqi city of Mosul (BBC News 2003a). In August 2003, the award-winning Palestinian cameraman Mazen Dana was shot dead by US forces while filming a scene outside the Abu Ghraib torture prison (J. Wilson 2003). Between 2003 and 2005, the following news workers were reportedly slain by the US military: Taras Protsyuk (Reuters), José Couso (Telecinco), Mazen Dana (Reuters), Ali al-Khatib (Al Arabiya), Ali Abdel Aziz (Al Arabiya), Terry Lloyd (ITN), and Bourhan Mohammad Al-Luhaybi (ABC News) (Reporters without Borders 2005). In 2007, the Committee to Protect Journalists, an independent, non-profit organization that promotes press freedom worldwide by defending the rights of journalists to report the news without fear of reprisal, claimed that "the US military poses" a "threat to journalist safety" because "at least 16 journalists have been killed by US forces' fire since March 2003" (CPJ 2005, 2008). Italian journalist Giuliana Sgrena and her Iraqi cameraman were shot by US troops that were said to have "accidentally" mistaken the camera for an insurgent's gun (Cozens 2005). Wikileaks' "Collateral Murder" video drew public attention to the DOD's use of deadly force against news organizations by showing a US AH-64 Apache helicopter gunner firing on Reuters journalists Saeed Chmagh and Namir Noor-Eldeen in an Iraqi suburb.

In addition to shooting them, the US military detained and harassed numerous journalists. In 2005, the DOD detained eight journalists after accusing them of colluding with the Iraqi insurgency. Among the detainees were Ammar Daham Naef Khalaf and Fares Nawaf al-Issaywi of Agence France-Presse and Hassan al-Shammari of the privately owned satellite TV station Diyar TV (CPJ 2005, 2008). The DOD has even coerced independent US journalists by destroying their communication and recording technology. When anti-occupation forces shot down a US Army helicopter in early November 2003, for example, US troops took cameras away from David Gilkey, a photographer for the *Detroit Free Press* and ordered the Knight Ridder news service to delete all of his photos. In the same month, representatives of thirty news organizations complained that they had "documented numerous examples of US troops physically harassing journalists and confiscating or ruining equipment, digital camera discs and videotapes"(Solomon 2005). The DOD either denied its role in journalist deaths or rationalized them away as unique cases of US troops misidentifying journalists as enemy combatants. Paterson (2011, 182), however, argues that these coercive incidents represent "a plausible indication of a shift in [US] policy toward the treatment of journalists as enemy combatants." Possibly, by using coercion, the DOD tried to scare journalists into staying put in DOD-sanctioned sourcing zones and to deter them from travelling to areas to interview Iraqi sources who might challenge the DOD line. By doing this, the DOD's coercive IO strategies influenced the news coverage of the war. In the media battlefield, it seems the line between civilian journalist and enemy combatant has blurred, as any source of information that challenges the DOD may be being treated as a threat and dealt with as such (Paterson 2014).

Why Do Media Corporations Support DOD IO?

Operation Iraqi Freedom was a brutal display of DOD IO. By combining persuasive sourcing strategies with coercive repression strategies, the DOD was able to set the news media agenda and get it to frame the war on its own terms. Kamiya (2007) says the US print and TV news media's coverage of the US invasion of Iraq represents "one of the greatest collapses in the history of the American media. Every branch of the news media failed, from daily newspapers, magazines and websites to television networks, cable channels and radio." The news media's failure to serve democracy is not only an effect of the DOD's IO but also a result of economic factors. The concentrated corporate ownership of the news and its dependency on advertising revenue/rating, professionalism, competition, and ideology encourage journalists to report the world as the DOD sees it.

Ownership
Many US news media companies are owned by larger media conglomerates that depend on the US state to facilitate and legitimate their profit interests at home and abroad (see Chapter 3, this volume). As a result, many of the media owners share a common interest in the maintenance of US economic and military supremacy and are eager to rally around the state at war. That said, media owners do not all directly control what's fit to print but delegate this control to the workers they hire (editors, journalists, ad people, technicians, and so on). Owners could support the full independence of editors

and journalists to report the news, but given that they have political views on issues like US foreign policy and war and possess the power to influence what and how their firms frame these issues, they often use this power. As Snow and Taylor (2006, 396) point out, "News organizations are often willing colluders with governments and militaries in efforts to censor because major media owners are members of the political elite themselves and therefore share similar goals and outcomes." Ownership gives a small group of people the power to support the US Empire's war policies through the editorials and ideological frames of the newspapers and TV networks they control. For example, Fox News advocated for the invasion of Iraq partly because its owner, Rupert Murdoch, agreed with the Bush administration (Greenslade 2003). To bolster the US invasion, Murdoch directed Fox News CEO Roger Ailes to circulate an executive memo among Fox News staff that demanded that they promote the war. In effect, "Fox News set the standard for patriotic television with an editorial policy that echoed the Bush Administration's official stance, making any challenge to the White House's plans for war seem tantamount to treason" (Calabrese 2005, 167). The major US news networks chased Fox News' skyrocketing ratings, which resulted in more and more pro-war spin.

Concentrated ownership has also compromised the ability of journalists to make quality news about the world. Due to media conglomeration and cost-cutting strategies, news media corporations have downsized their ability to produce high-quality news, and journalists have fewer resources available than they did in the past for informing the public about world affairs. In fact, the US news media has significantly reduced its coverage of world events over the past thirty years (Enda 2011). From 1985 to 2010, foreign news stories in numerous US daily newspapers, including the *Philadelphia Inquirer*, the *St. Louis Post-Dispatch*, the *Dallas Morning News*, and others declined in number by 53 percent (Kumar 2011). A 2004 Pew Project on Excellence in Journalism study found that front-page news stories about foreign affairs had dropped to an all-time low (Starr 2009, 31). Between 2005 and 2008, newspapers like the *Philadelphia Inquirer*, the *Baltimore Sun*, and the *Boston Globe* and TV news networks like CBS, NBC, and ABC closed their foreign bureaus and got rid of many foreign correspondents (Starr 2009, 31). As news companies close foreign bureaus and fire foreign correspondents, they come to rely on DOD source material or parachute journalists that land in and fly out of countries, covering events but often without a proper historical, political, and cultural understanding of them. Trento, Waltemeyer, and Gaskill (2013) state, "Media budget constraints has [sic] created an opening for government contracted propagandists to supplant genuine reportage with internally produced news packages and feel good stories." As the corporate ownership model compels news workers to deliver more content with fewer resources in shorter and shorter periods of time, they write stories derived from the scripts of foreign policy sourced to them by DOD PR agencies.

Advertising

The news media's competition for ad revenue is the second economic factor that predisposes journalists to support the DOD's war policy. As profit-seeking businesses, news companies exist to serve the interests of advertising corporations, which are their main revenue source; they sell space and time to advertising firms, which pay to place ads between the news on behalf of their corporate clients. The bottom line dictates that news companies treat content as bait to attract viewer attention to ads for commodities. During wartime, news companies lure viewers into an ad flow by exploiting their interest in and anxiety about state violence. The news media tends to promote DOD war goals because fiscally responsible marketing managers assume that US viewers will be automatically patriotic or in support of the war. In this respect, pro-war news stories are safe business decisions, while news stories that are critical of US foreign policy are not, due to their potential to disturb the militarized mindset of the target audience commodity.

In the lead-up to the Iraq invasion, US TV news networks customized their content to resonate with an assumedly pro-war audience. Fox News maximized its profit by adopting a pro-war editorial policy; it was the premier platform for Bush administration officials and pro-war guests to spread propaganda and demonize pacifists as un-American and "the great unwashed" (Rutenberg 2003). Fox was simply abiding by the market logic of branded infotainment, which reduces the news to a niche product customized to attract select lifestyle groups of consumers to advertisements. By supporting the DOD's IO campaign, Fox News commoditized and exploited a right-wing, Republican, conservative American niche audience (Arsenault and Castells 2006, 301). Rival TV news networks then tried to replicate Fox News' commercial "success" in a competitive race to the bottom to become the most watched channel by war-primed viewers. The corporate competition to control audience commodities and ad revenue drove all major US TV news networks to adopt a pro-war position. CBS titled its reports "America at War"; CNN used the heading "Strike on Iraq"; Fox, NBC, and

MSNBC even used the DOD's official name for the invasion: Operation Iraqi Freedom. "The networks," claims Calabrese (2005, 168) "went to great lengths to seamlessly blend their patriotism, technological prowess, and professionalism, which in the long run has the potential to yield market advantages."

Professionalism/Competition
A third reason why journalists may support DOD policy is because professionalism teaches them to work with official sources (i.e., from organized and resource-rich state and corporate institutions) and ignore non-official sources (i.e., from disorganized and resource-poor citizens). At the same time, the capitalist organization of the news puts increasing, competitive pressure on journalists to produce more news stories in less time, which, combined with the downsizing of newsrooms, encourages them to depend on Washington and DOD press handlers for source material. By sourcing information to professional-minded journalists, the DOD helps news media companies reduce news production costs and thereby increase the likelihood of its official frames being reproduced. As a result, Bennett (1990, 106) says, "mass media news professionals, from the boardroom to the beat, tend to 'index' the range of voices and viewpoints in both news and editorials according to the range of views expressed in mainstream government debate about a given topic."

In every ABC, CBS, and NBC TV evening news story about Iraq in the eight-month lead-up to the invasion, for example, Bush administration and DOD officials were the most frequently quoted sources, and anti-war voices and oppositional Democrats were barely recognized (Hayes and Guardino 2010). The Center for Public Integrity documented 935 false statements (and hundreds of questionable claims) by these sources (Lewis and Reading-Smith 2008). In 576 news stories about Iraq published by elite daily newspapers (*New York Times, Washington Post*, and *Wall Street Journal*) and two weekly magazines (*Time* and *Newsweek*), almost all "conveyed Administration pronouncements and rationale without much critical commentary" (Gelb and Zelmati 2009, 11). A Fairness and Accuracy in Reporting study of TV news shows about the invasion of Iraq that were aired on ABC *World News Tonight*, CBS *Evening News*, NBC *Nightly News*, CNN's *Wolf Blitzer Reports*, Fox's *Special Report with Brit Hume*, and PBS's *NewsHour with Jim Leher* during the three-week period following the first day of bombing (March 20, 2003) found that 1,617 on-camera sources (interviewees) appeared in the stories, and 63 percent of all sources were current or former US state employees, either civilian or military, more than half of whom were current or former US officials (Calabrese 2005, 166).

Although sourcing puts Washington and the DOD in a powerful position to manage the news media's frames of war, not all journalists are dupes of or ciphers for state sourcing activities. The endless market segmentation of viewers into niche markets and the need for media firms to address, albeit often in skewed ways, the interests and preferences of various news readers create some space for dissenting voices (Freedman 2009). Though all journalists depend on official sources, not all journalists will necessarily repackage the official source as news or neglect alternative sources: "source dependence does not guarantee journalistic compliance with this or that source's perspective" (Sparks 2007a, 78). Kofi Annan's 2004 claim that the Iraq war was illegal did get covered by the US news media (Phillips and Gardiner 2004), and the anti-war statements of Hollywood celebrities – Janeane Garofalo, Tim Robbins, Mike Farrell, Rob Reiner, Martin Sheen, Susan Sarandon, and Michael Moore – did appear on mainstream TV news networks and in elite newspapers before and after the 2003 invasion (Fox News 2003; M. Wilson 2002). However, the news media do not give dissenting sources equal weight to those controlled by the DOD, and dissenting perspectives are often flacked and marginalized (Dardis 2006). Yet, some journalists do give voice to widespread dissent, and this may not be simply a by-product of elite disagreement but rather an effect of the contradictions of news markets (Freedman 2009).

Ideology/Self-Censorship

A fourth reason the news media support US war policy is ideology, which shapes how journalists perceive the world and write about it. Journalists sometimes act as mouthpieces for DOD spin because they already share with it the same deeply entrenched exceptionalist view of the US role in the world. To be fair, not all journalists share the same outlook as the US power elite, and some may even conflict with the DOD, citing values like professionalism and autonomy in struggles to resist the attempts by the powerful to influence or censor what they say. Yet, many US journalists have perpetuated the DOD's official line, and when the US state has declared war, journalists have been all too willing to support DOD war policy. During Operation Iraqi Freedom, for example, some US journalists deferred to the DOD's war aims because of their prejudice as American citizens. In an interview on CNN's *Larry King Live*, CBS *Evening News* anchor Dan Rather said, "Look, I'm an American. I never tried to kid anybody that I'm some internationalist or something. And when my country is at war, I want my country to win, whatever the definition of 'win' may be. Now, I can't and don't argue that this is coverage without prejudice. About that I am prejudiced" (quoted in Rendall and Broughel 2003). Pandering to the lowest common denominator of national chauvinism pays, as American exceptionalism is what many viewers believe to be true. Conversely, faced with the above IO and corporate control strategies, journalists may come to fear the repercussions of (i.e., career-ruining flack and employment deprivation) and exercise self-censorship. As Graber (2011, 417) says, "It is not unusual for the news media to censor their coverage when they deem it essential for security interests, specifically when they agree with the government's objectives and face condemnation and economic penalties for voicing [anti-war] dissent."

Conclusion: The Consequences of the DOD-News Media Complex

Journalists stand between the US Empire's real wars and the media wars consumed by readers and viewers in the US and elsewhere, influencing what and possibly how the public thinks about wars and why they happen. But while they may influence public opinion about war, they themselves can be influenced by larger geopolitical and economic institutions, policies, and practices, namely the DOD and its persuasive and coercive IO strategies for managing the news media's war and the corporations that hire their labour to report it. War-promoting news is as much the result of actors, policies, and practices external to media companies – DOD IO – as it is shaped by internal factors such as ownership, advertising dependency, news routines, and nationalist ideology.

Democracy requires an investigative watchdog press that is free from and critical of state and corporate power, especially in times of war. But the relationship between the DOD and news media corporations at war is largely defined by cooperation, not conflict. The DOD–news media complex undermines media for democracy, tries to manipulate public opinion, censors war's human consequences and embodied trauma, and encourages citizens to consume war as an entertaining spectacle, not something requiring deep deliberation about structural causes or human-level effects. Now, the Internet enables citizens to generate and disseminate their own propaganda for and against official war policy, interactively support and contest mainstream news agendas, and reactively tweet back at the power elite. The DOD–news media complex may no longer have as much reach, control, or influence as it once did, and principled journalists may try to resist DOD IO.

Current technological changes and conscientious journalists, however, have not instigated the end of the US Empire or changed the fact that an elite few decide to go to war and rely on an army of DOD mind managers to convince the world why America must. So long as the US Empire is at war, the DOD–news media complex will exist, with DOD-employed PR experts and corporate-minded journalists continuing to serve on the frontlines of its war policy sales effort.

5
The DOD-Hollywood Complex

Year after year, Hollywood studios produce TV shows and films that represent the DOD and the CIA travelling the globe and targeting and obliterating threats to US security. ABC's action series *Alias* shows CIA agent Sydney Bristow (Jennifer Garner) concealing her career from friends and family members and undertaking clandestine operations against threats to America. Fox Network's *24* depicts Counter Terrorist Unit (CTU) agent Jack Bauer (Kiefer Sutherland) using all means necessary – torture, assassination, and psy-ops – to foil attempts by terrorists to assassinate the US president, detonate "WMDS," and destroy the US cybergrid. *Homeland*, Showtime's remake of the popular Israeli drama by the same name, validates the CIA's violation of civil liberties and abuse of human rights by framing controversial acts such as surveillance and torture as necessary and effective means for preventing terrorist attacks. The 2007 blockbuster film *The Kingdom* depicts US FBI agents in intense shootouts with al-Qaeda in Saudi Arabia. *Argo*, the 2012 recipient of an Academy Award for Best Picture, dramatizes the CIA's extraction of six US diplomats from Iran during the country's revolution against the US-backed shah. *Zero Dark Thirty*, a nominee in 2012 for five Academy Awards, dramatizes the US state's hunt for, surveillance of, and eventual killing of Osama bin Laden at a compound in Pakistan.

Far from being trifling entertainment that offers viewers a blissful escape from the politics and practices of the US Empire, many Hollywood

TV shows and films tell stories about the coercive agents of the US state that legitimize war and covert ops by making them seem normal, necessary, and good. Hollywood TV shows and films are pernicious forms of PR for the US Empire. How do the DOD and the CIA try to get Hollywood studios to make such products, and why do Hollywood studios often support them?

This chapter examines the DOD-CIA-Hollywood complex – the institutional links between the DOD, the CIA, and Hollywood studios that encourage the production of entertainment in support of US war policy and that discourage the flow of pop culture that is critical of it. The chapter's first section presents a brief history of the DOD-Hollywood complex. The second and third sections examine the DOD's and CIA's public affairs institutions, policies, and practices that influence Hollywood's scripts and analyze a few DOD and CIA Hollywood products: *Transformers* (2007), *Act of Valor* (2012), *Argo* (2012), and *Zero Dark Thirty* (2012). The fourth section considers the structural reasons why Hollywood supports the DOD's and CIA's public relations efforts, and the conclusion critiques this complex. Overall, this chapter examines a symbiotic relationship between the security state and Hollywood, which encourages the production of entertainment that glorifies the US Empire's coercion and discourages the flow of goods that criticize it.

The DOD-Hollywood Complex: A Brief History

The emergence of the motion picture coincided with the growth of late-nineteenth-century colonial empires and the rise of the movie theatre as a major attraction to the United States' urban working class (Shohat and Stam 1994). During the 1898 Spanish-American War, US media mogul William Randolph Hearst financed a number of filmic newsreels that glorified the United States' first colonial conquest. "Film was born at a moment when a poem such as Rudyard Kipling's 'White Man's Burden' could be published, as it was in 1899, to celebrate the US acquisition of Cuba and the Philippines" (Shohat and Stam 1994, 100). Burgeoning US motion picture companies deployed cameramen to Cuba to film the war (Musser 1990, 240), and soon after the United States declared war on Spain, they released films like *Tearing Down the Spanish Flag* (1898) to drum up public support for the war. Motion pictures helped the US state win public support for the war in the Philippines, Guam, and Cuba while idealizing Europe's colonial wars against "primitive" civilizations. "For the working classes of Europe and Euro-America," say Shohat and Stam (1994, 100), "photo-genic wars in remote parts of the empire became diverting entertainments, serving to neutralize the class struggle and transform class solidarity into national and racial solidarity." In 1911, the US Army recruited filmmakers to make *The Military Air-Scout*, a story set in 1914 about a future inter-imperial war between the US and European states.

The first time the US military supported a feature-length film was in the lead-up to the First World War, when David Wark Griffith, a good friend of US President Woodrow Wilson, started working on *The Birth of a Nation* (1915). Griffith's Civil War and reconstruction period epic was assisted by the West Point engineers, who gave Griffith technical advice on battle tactics and provided some artillery for combat scenes (Rydell and Kroes 2005). *The Birth of a Nation* conveyed a white-supremacist interpretation of the US Civil War that was championed by the Ku Klux Klan; it filled cinemas in the United States and attracted viewers across Europe and in South Africa. *The Birth of a Nation* "helped the fledgling film industry gain legitimacy in precisely the same way that many other mass culture industries had won approval – by lending legitimacy to dominant racist presumptions" (Rydell and Kroes 2005, 81). The film was screened at the White House for President Wilson and members of the US Congress and Supreme Court. William Brady, head of the National Association of the Motion Picture Industry, Hollywood's lobby group at the time, sent a memo to the White House that read "The motion picture can be the most wonderful system for spreading national propaganda at little or no cost" (cited in Fraser 2003, 40).

At the outset of the First World War, Wilson seemed to agree with this assessment of the propaganda value of film. In a wartime speech, he declared, "The film has come to rank as the very highest medium for the dissemination of public intelligence ... And since it speaks a universal language, it lends itself importantly to the presentation of America's plans and purposes" (cited in Fraser 2003, 40). As discussed in Chapter 2 in this volume, the Committee for Public Information (CPI) mobilized Hollywood to sell the war, and Hollywood was eager to screen it for a price. In a 1917 editorial, the *Motion Picture News* proclaimed that "Every individual at work in this industry" has promised to provide "slides, film leaders and trailers, posters ... to spread that propaganda so necessary to the immediate mobilisation of the country's great resources" (cited in Klindo and Phillips 2005). Hollywood studios abided by the CPI's motion picture censorship department's content guidelines and turned over films to this agency for a look prior to distributing them abroad. The CPI approved films for export that supported the US war effort, while restricting the free flow of films that might, regardless of the director's intent, undermine it. The CPI banned films that represented US "forts, coast defense or other fortifications," that might "bring the United States Army into ridicule," and that depicted class inequality or portrayed pacifist activists that might "injure the feelings of neutrals or our allies" (Rydell and Kroes 2005, 138).

In the interwar period, some films criticized war, such as *All Quiet on the Western Front* (1930), but the US military and Hollywood continued to collaborate. *Wings* (1927), the first film to win Best Picture at the Academy Awards, featured dogfight scenes with planes supplied by the US military. And the US Navy and Marines worked with director Frank Capra on a trilogy of films that show off military technology: *Submarine* (1928), *Flight* (1929), and *Dirigible* (1931). Lloyd Bacon's *Here Comes the Navy* (1934) and *Devil Dogs of the Air* (1935) were also the outcome of military partnerships (T. Shaw 2007, 201). Despite the fond relationship between the military and Hollywood, conservative anxieties about the potential for Hollywood films to cause US citizens to think and act in immoral ways led to the Motion Picture Production Code, also called the Hays Code, after Will Hays, president of the Motion Picture Producers and Distributors. The Hays Code was a set of industry self-censorship guidelines that influenced the content of most films made by major US studios between 1930 and 1968; it prevented Hollywood studios from producing movies that depicted the US government in ways that, though potentially true to reality, might be perceived as negative.

From 1930 to 1938, most Hollywood studios did not oppose the rise of Nazi Germany (nor did many other US industrial giants like IBM, General Motors, and Ford Motors) (Black 2012). The US national security state had not yet declared Germany an enemy of America, and US corporations treated Germany as a large market for American products, including films. In order to protect their profit interests in the large Nazi Germany film market, Hollywood studios acquiesced to Nazi censors and even cooperated with them (Urwand 2013). Following the outbreak of war in 1939, however, Hollywood turned against Nazi Germany. Warner Bros. released *Confessions of a Nazi Spy* (1939), and the Producers Releasing Corporation launched *Hitler, Beast of Berlin* (1939) (C.J. Miller 2006). By the early 1940s, Hollywood was releasing films like *I Married a Nazi* and *A Yank in the R.A.F.* that further demonized the Nazis.

In 1940, Hollywood helped promote the US military's first peace-time effort at conscription. To make the September 16 Selective Training and Service Act (or forced conscription for men 18–35 years old) seem fun – even funny – Hollywood studios made comedies in 1940–41 about military service: Universal Pictures released *Buck Privates, In the Navy,* and *Keep 'Em Flying* (starring Abbott and Costello); Paramount Pictures put out *Caught in the Draft* (starring Bob Hope); Warner Bros. launched *You're in the Army Now* (starring Phil Silvers and Jimmy Durante); Columbia Pictures sold *You'll Never Get Rich* (starring Fred Astaire) and *Boobs in Arms* (with The Three Stooges); and 20th Century Fox circulated *Great Guns* (starring Laurel and Hardy). Hollywood also introduced US citizens and new enlistees to the trials and tribulations of military training with films like *The Bugle Sounds* (featuring actual US cavalry), *Parachute Battalion* (featuring paratroopers of the 501st Parachute Infantry such as Gen. William C. Lee, who doubled as the lead character in some scenes), and *I Wanted Wings* (showing Randolph Field and featuring 1,160 US Air Corps airplanes, 1,050 cadets, 450 officers and instructors, and 2,543 enlisted men) (Thompson 2002, 36). *Dive Bomber*, a film about training for air combat, was based on a story by a US Navy commander named Frank Wead and fully supported by the US Navy. Shot at NAS North Island in San Diego and on the famous Second World War battleship USS *Enterprise*, *Dive Bomber* allowed the Navy to showcase Vought SB2U Vindicator dive bombers, Douglas TBD Devastator torpedo bombers, and hundreds of US pilots. The Navy set up recruiting booths at the theatres where the film was screened (Orriss 1984, 25–27).

Following the United States' 1941 entrance into the Second World War, the Office of War Information's (OWI) Bureau of Motion Pictures (BMP) mobilized Hollywood to make films that supported the American war effort. According to Doherty (1993, 5), Hollywood became "the preeminent transmitter of wartime policy" to ensure "when the worker leaves the factory that he does not leave the war." To encourage Hollywood to depict the war in a way that aligned with war policy objectives, the BMP supplied Hollywood studios with the *Government Information Manual for the Motion Picture Industry*, which "offered guidance to film makers on major themes like democracy, the homeland and the role of the United Nations in promoting a view of America's involvement in World War II as a people's war for democracy and against fascism" (Koppes and Black 1977, 66–67). The BMP asked studios to consider seven significant questions when conceptualizing film scripts:

1) Will this picture help win the war?
2) What war information problem does it seek to clarify, dramatize or interpret?

3) If it is an "escape" picture, will it harm the war effort by creating a false picture of America, her allies, or the world we live in?
4) Does it merely use the war as the basis for a profitable picture, contributing nothing of real significance to the war effort and possibly lessening the effect of other pictures of more importance?
5) Does it contribute something new to our understanding of the world conflict and various forces involved, or has the subject been adequately covered?
6) When the picture reaches its maximum circulation on the screen, will it reflect conditions as they are and fill a need current at that time, or will it be out-dated?
7) Does the picture tell the truth or will the young people of today have reason to say they were misled by propaganda?

Between May 1942 and August 1945, the BMP reviewed 1,652 scripts (Koppes and Black 1977, 103) and asked studios to revise scripts if they depicted the United States as lawless, classist, corrupt, or racist, if they portrayed US citizens as oblivious to the war, or if they depicted US allies negatively. Hollywood abided by the BMP's specifications and made approximately 500 war-themed pictures, including comedies such as *Blondie for Victory*, musicals such as *Star-Spangled Rhythm*, and combat documentaries such as Frank Capra's *Why We Fight*. In 1943, Warner Bros. produced Irving Berlin's *This Is the Army* (starring Ronald Reagan), one of the most profitable war films ever made. Warner Bros. then donated $10 million from its box office profits to the Army Emergency Relief fund.

During the war, the Department of War and the Navy Department also worked with Hollywood studios to produce newsreels, documentaries, and training films such as *Flight Command* (1940) and *I Wanted Wings* (1941). The Walt Disney Company produced films that helped the military train and indoctrinate soldiers, while films like *Casablanca* (1942) (a military romance whose premiere coincided with the US and Allied invasion of North Africa and the capture of Casablanca), *Sahara* (1943) (a film about the US and British defeat of German forces in North Africa, which featured US tanks and soldiers from the US IV Armored Corps), and *Since You Went Away* (1944) (a melodrama about the war-time duties of US citizens) helped promote the war (Larson 1948).

Ronald Reagan, then a young Hollywood actor, worked for the DOD's First Motion Picture Unit in Culver City, California, where he helped produce hundreds of war training films for the US Air Force like *Beyond the Line of Duty* and *This Is the Army*. During the Second World War, a "number of prominent film directors offered their services to various branches of the Armed forces" and were "assigned to make training films as well as documentaries explaining war-related issues" (Kispal-Kovacs 2010, 123). For example, the DOD commissioned Frank Capra to make *Why We Fight*, a seven-part series of war propaganda films that described to US soldiers and citizens the qualities of the democratic capitalist system the United States was fighting for and those of the autocratic fascist system they were fighting against; Britain's, Russia's, and China's battles against Germany, Italy, and Japan; and the need for the United States to reject isolationism and embrace its role as a world leader (German 1990; Rollins 1996). The DOD hired John Ford to direct *The Battle of the Midway* (1942), a documentary montage of air battle footage and shots from under bombs falling from planes, and *December 7th* (1943) and *They Were Expendable* (1945). It paid William Wyler to film B-17 bombers unloading their cargo on occupied France in *The Memphis Belle: A Story of a Flying Fortress* (1944) (Harris 2014). In the middle of the Second World War, Col. K.B. Lawton, chief of the Army Pictorial Division, said this about the political leanings of Hollywood's cultural workers: "I have never found such a group of wholehearted, willing, patriotic people trying to do something for their government" (cited in Sklar 1975, 249).

However, not all of these patriotic people's reel wars made the DOD's cut. In 1942, the US Army commissioned director and writer John Huston to make three documentary films about the Second World War: *Report from the Aleutians* (1943) (about soldiers training for combat), *The Battle of San Pietro* (1945) (about US intelligence failures that led to the deaths of many soldiers), and *Let There Be Light* (1946) (about seventy-five US soldiers being treated for and recovering from post-traumatic stress disorder in a psychiatric hospital following the war). Because the realism of these films betrayed the army's attempt to package such portrayals, the army deemed them to be controversial. They were not released to the public, on the grounds that they would demoralize America and harm future recruitment efforts.

When the Cold War began, the already cooperative arrangement between the US DOD and Hollywood grew stronger. In 1946, the US War Department and the Navy Department set up Hollywood film review offices that granted Hollywood production companies assistance – access to hardware like shops, tanks, or planes, troops, and technical knowledge – so long as they agreed to represent the military and US foreign policy in a positive way (Suid 2002). In 1948, the DOD's Public Affairs branch opened the Motion Picture Production Office (MPPO) and hired Donald Baruch, a former New York theatre producer to head it in 1949 (Suid 2002). Baruch became the DOD's liaison with Hollywood, reading, vetting, and co-producing war scripts with Hollywood for the next forty years (Suid 2002). Any Hollywood studio requesting assistance from the DOD was required to submit a script to Baruch, who would then read it, recommend it for production with the army, navy, or air force, ask for script changes to be made before offering support, or refuse support to scripts that did not represent the military in the best possible light (Suid 2002). By 1950, Baruch controlled the means of provisioning military assistance to Hollywood studios, which eagerly capitalized on this relationship.

The MPPO's establishment of an enabling market environment for pro-war films following the Second World War was abetted by the Motion Picture Alliance for the Preservation of American Ideals (formed in 1944) and the House Committee on Un-American Activities (formed in 1947). These organizations publicly persecuted socialist cultural workers who might make films critical of US Empire and thereby established a major deterrent to anti-war films. The Hollywood moguls' defeat of the Conference of Studio Unions strike in 1945 and the lockout of 1946 combined to form "the death knell of the Hollywood Left" (Buhle and Wagner 2002, 376). In 1947, Congress found a group of ten US cultural workers (who belonged to the American Communist Party) in contempt for refusing to answer questions about their political leanings and then jailed them for one year. Fearing further government investigation, Hollywood moguls met at the Waldorf Astoria Hotel in New York City and agreed to a policy of denying employment to all workers who were known or suspected as communist sympathizers (Horne 2001). Hollywood's Red Scare had taken off, and in 1950 the right-wing journal *Counterattack* released the Red Channels pamphlet, which labelled an additional 151 workers "Red Fascists." Though failing to prove Hollywood's Red takeover, the Motion Picture Alliance for the Preservation of American Ideals and the House Committee on Un-American Activities pushed for the employment deprivation of left-leaning workers, which sent an ideological chill throughout Hollywood's networks of power. While US public diplomacy agencies represented America as a beacon of free speech and free-wheeling creative expression abroad to distinguish the American Way from the Soviet one, at home industry censors ensured that motion pictures would support the ideology of the state. Hollywood's capitalist logics and Red purge deracinated film's capacity to critique the US Empire and ensured that most films would cast a positive light on the military for years to come.

From the beginning of the Cold War until the mid-1960s, all the major war films produced by Hollywood received technical assistance from the MPPO (Suid 2002, xii). *The Flying Leathernecks* (1951) (about US fighter pilots battling the Japanese during the Second World War) was shot at Marine Corps bases Camp Pendleton and El Toro and featured DOD-owned Grumman F6F Hellcats flown by servicemen (Orriss 1984); *From Here to Eternity* (1953) (about the daily lives of US soldiers stationed in Hawaii in the lead-up to the Japanese attack on Pearl Harbor) was shot with US Army support at the Schofield Barracks in Hawaii. *The Caine Mutiny* (1954) (about mutiny on a US destroyer and the consequences faced by those responsible for it) was shot with navy assistance at the Naval Station Treasure Island in San Francisco and Pearl Harbor, on the island of Oahu in Hawaii. *Away All Boats* (1956) (about US naval warfare against the Japanese in the Pacific during the Second World War) was filmed aboard the USS *Randall* and with help from Ralph Scalzo, a navy coxswain. *The Bridges at Toko-Ri* (1955) (about a troubled US Navy pilot who bombs Korean bridges during the early stages of the Korean War) was filmed aboard US destroyers and features US aircraft; *Run Silent, Run Deep* (1956) (about a submarine commander who seeks and achieves vengeance against a Japanese destroyer that sank his boat in a Second World War naval battle) was supported by Second World War submarine veterans and shot on the USS *Redfish*.

In the early 1960s, the DOD-Hollywood complex was criticized due to the MPPO's support for Darryl Zanuck's D-Day film, *The Longest Day* (1962). Senate politicians complained that the DOD was allocating scarce and costly public resources to Hollywood; DOD weapons technology and personnel paid for by the people to secure them from threat were serving to secure the profit interests of Hollywood instead. As New Jersey senator Clifford Case said, "The practice of making facilities of the defense establishment available for any private ownership, for commercialization and commercial profit, is one to be examined and should be permitted only in a situation in which their use would not in any way endanger the security of the United States" (cited in Suid 2002, 181). Also, Zanuck agreed to conform to DOD script guidelines in exchange for support but then refused to delete dialogue and scenes the DOD did not approve of before releasing *The Longest Day* to the market. The MPPO wanted Zanuck to remove "casual profanity" from dialogue like "crap, muck it, mother lover, bastards, damn, hell, and lines like 'they couldn't sink the clucking can if they tried to.'" It was also concerned about "the excessive amount of slaughter in this story" and urged Zanuck "to minimize the dramatizations of personal killings," saying the film should "avoid the 'bloodbath' effect" (cited in Suid 2002, 177). Zanuck ignored these requests, which further frustrated politicians and made the MPPO seem to be a Hollywood pawn. In response to Zanuck's refusal to play by the DOD's rules, the DOD implemented a new film policy in January 1964 to guide all future DOD-Hollywood co-productions (Suid 2002). Arthur Sylvester, who became assistant secretary of defence for public affairs in 1961, evaluated the DOD-Hollywood relationship and established a more strict set of guidelines, an official militarized film policy, to guide the conduct of Baruch's MPPO and its relationship with Hollywood. Sylvester said, "The United States military can't be rented by anyone. They are not going to be turned over to motion pictures indiscriminately" (cited in Suid 2002, 193). The new militarized film policy formalized the DOD's power to give or withhold support to Hollywood based on the extent to which it applied DOD-requested script changes. It also said that companies would have to ensure the safety of the US service members when filming, that DOD assistance must not interfere with the "operational readiness of the armed forces," and that studios must pay the DOD for the use of its resources (Suid 2002). Moreover, studios would have to apply to use DOD equipment, locations, and personnel on specific dates and at specific times, so as to give the DOD the time it needed to prepare for the shoot (Suid 2002).

Some Hollywood firms, disconcerted by the illiberal prospect of DOD script control, loosened their political ties with the DOD and took flight to Europe to shoot their war films there. Others complied with the DOD's new militarized film policy, resulting in DOD-supported films like *In Harm's Way* (1965) and even spy-genre Bond films like *Goldfinger* (1964) and *Thunderball* (1965). All in all, the DOD-Hollywood complex produced only a dozen or so war films in the 1960s. *Captain Newman, M.D.* (1963) was filmed at the US Army's Fort Huachuca complex in southern Arizona; *A Gathering of Eagles* (1963) was supported by the US Strategic Air Command and its head, Gen. Curtis LeMay (T. Shaw 2007, 202). *The Dirty Dozen* (1967), a film in which twelve convicted murderers are trained by the US Army to assassinate German officers during the Second World War, starred veterans Lee Marvin, Robert Webber, and Robert Ryan (US Marines); Telly Savalas (US Army); Charles Bronson (Army Air Forces); Ernest Borgnine (US Navy), and Clint Walker (Merchant Marine). Though these Second World War films had box office success, the US Empire's hot and dirty wars in Latin

America, the Middle East, and Africa were withheld from the public record and so ignored by Hollywood. The Cold War clash between capitalism and communism was, however, allegorized in westerns (Corkin 2000). In *High Noon* (1952), *Shane* (1953), and *The Searchers* (1956), for example, the west symbolizes the post-colonial states in which the US and Soviet Union vied for hegemony, a chaotic frontier zone in which US heroes exert their power and impose order. *The Alamo* (1960), financed and directed by the staunchly pro-military celebrity John Wayne, was about Texans fighting for independence against Mexico in the 1830s but was also perceived by Wayne as a way to "sell America to countries threatened by communist domination" (cited in T. Shaw 2007, 207).

In the early stages of the American War in Vietnam, Hollywood released a few films that framed Vietnam as strategically important to the United States' fight against communism like *China Gate* (1957), *The Quiet American* (1958), and *Five Gates to Hell* (1959). With help from Hollywood, the DOD made the documentary *Why Vietnam?* (1965) to convince the public that the US military needed to expand its operations into South Vietnam (Springer 1991). Hollywood also worked with the USIA to make *Night of the Dragon* (1965), a propaganda film narrated by Charlton Heston that framed North Vietnam's attacks against civilians in the South as a pretext for US humanitarian intervention.

Hollywood majors largely dealt with the Vietnam War indirectly by making films about the Second World War, such as *Catch-22* (1970), and about the Korean War, such as *M*A*S*H* (1970). An exception was *The Green Berets* (1968), directed by and starring John Wayne. Based on a book by the same name that the Kennedy administration had used in 1961 to spin the United States' growing presence in Vietnam, *The Green Berets* repackaged the Domino Theory, the notion that if Vietnam fell to communism, the entirety of Southeast Asia would too. Wayne, an ardent supporter of the war, felt that in the wake of a growing and vocal anti-war movement, *The Green Berets* film could inspire "a patriotic spirit" among Americans regarding the Vietnam War and tell the world "why it is necessary to be there" (cited in T. Shaw 2007, 211). Jack Valenti, special assistant to Lyndon Johnson and soon-to-be head of the MPAA, urged Johnson to grant Wayne permission to make the film, and Johnson did. The MPPO supported the film on the condition that it could change the script to its liking. All references to the Vietnamese conflict being a civil war were cut because this challenged the US foreign policy frame of South Vietnam as an independent country under attack by an aggressive neighbour that was a pawn of Chinese and

Russian communists. Scenes in which the Green Berets abuse Viet Cong prisoners of war were cut because they risked confirming the belief among anti-war activists that the US was committing war crimes in Vietnam. After these and other script changes were made, *The Green Berets* was shot at Fort Benning and Fort Bragg and with DOD-provisioned jeeps, weapons, tanks, helicopters, 350 army personnel, and a platoon of Hawaiian American soldiers that performed as the Vietnamese (T. Shaw 2007, 215). *The Green Berets* was a box office hit in 1968, as it seemed to tap into the pro-war ideology of some Americans. Though not about Vietnam, the Second World War film *Patton*, released in 1970 and supported by the DOD, responded to public angst about the Vietnam War by promoting war as glorious and killing for one's country as noble. Nonetheless, the decline of Hollywood's moguls, changing public attitudes toward US foreign policy, and New Left anti-war activism enabled some creative resistance to the DOD's film policy and opened more space in media markets for non-DOD supported films.

Soon after the United States' withdrawal from Vietnam in 1975, a new generation of directors, screenwriters, and actors responded to public distrust of the US military and the peace activism that had shaken the nation years earlier with a number of films that dealt with the turmoil and trauma experienced by Vietnam War veterans. *The Deer Hunter* (1978), *Apocalypse Now* (1979), *First Blood* (1982), *Rambo: First Blood Part II* (1985), *Full Metal Jacket* (1987), *Casualties of War* (1989), and *Born on the Fourth of July* (1989) meditate on the war's dehumanizing and disabling effects on US soldiers and offer a sobering rejoinder to jingoistic films like *The Green Berets*.

While these films address the tortured minds and brutalized bodies of the US soldiers who fought in Vietnam, they fail to shed light on the capitalist drive of US war policy, the flawed technocratic outlook of the US power elites that steered the war, the atrocities and crimes perpetrated by US soldiers against the Vietnamese, and the systematic devastation of Vietnam's habitat by Agent Orange and carpet bombing. Kispal-Kovacs (2010, 226) states, "Most American films about the Vietnam War are largely self-absorbed ruminations on the ill effects it had on Americans and hence are incapable of offering a more objective view of what happened to the people of Vietnam." Furthermore, future soldiers often took these ostensibly anti-war films as pro-war statements. As former US Marine Anthony Swofford (2005, 6) writes in *Jarhead*, a book about his experience as a sniper during the 1991 Gulf War, "Vietnam war films are all pro-war, no matter what the supposed message." Soldiers watch these films and "are excited by them, because the magic brutality of the films celebrates the terrible and despicable beauty of their fighting skills. Fight, rape, pillage, burn. Filmic images of death and carnage are pornography for the military man." During the 1980s, Hollywood made a few pro-Vietnam war films, like *Uncommon Valor* (1983) and *Missing in Action* (1984). These films attempt to re-establish an image of the American soldier as having power over Vietnam by depicting them as vigilantes, single-handedly blasting their way through this socialist republic in search of US POWs.

The most popular and profitable DOD-Hollywood co-production of the 1980s was *Top Gun* (1986), starring Tom Cruise (as Lt. Pete Mitchell). This film is about a hot-headed, egotistical, womanizing US fighter pilot who competes with other men to be "the best of the best." To do so, Mitchell must learn to temper his youthful passions, instruct others at the flight academy, and win dogfights. When approached by Hollywood producers Jerry Bruckheimer and Don Simpson, the US Navy saw this story of a fighter pilot school as an opportunity to promote its image and recruit young men. Phil Strub, the DOD's Hollywood liaison officer, said, "*Top Gun* was significant to me and to others because it a marked a [post–Vietnam War] rehabilitation in the portrayal of the military. For the first time in many, many years, you could make a movie that was positive about the military, actors could portray military personnel who were well-motivated, well-intentioned, and not see their careers suffer as a consequence" (cited in LaRocque 1997). Paramount "paid the military $1.8 million for the use of Miramar Naval Air Station near San Diego, four aircraft carriers and about two dozen F-14 Tomcats, F-5 Tigers and A-4 Skyhawks" (Lamar 1986). *Top Gun* helped revitalize the US military's image, boosted US public confidence in US air-strike and combat capabilities, prepared it for the first Gulf War, and led to a surge in flight training enlistees. Paramount Pictures proposed placing a ninety-second Navy recruitment ad at the beginning of the *Top Gun* videocassette in exchange for $1 million in credit toward their debt to the Navy for its assistance. The DOD rejected the offer, saying that the film is itself "already a wonderful recruiting tool for the Navy" and "to add a recruiting commercial onto the head of what is already a two-hour recruiting commercial is redundant" (cited in Robb 2004, 81). US Navy recruiters set up shop outside of the theatres in which *Top Gun* was screened. Following *Top Gun*'s release, recruitment reportedly increased 500 percent (Kellman 2005). *Top Gun*'s box office success gave Hollywood studios a big incentive to work with the DOD on war scripts. In 1986, the navy's Hollywood liaison officer, Sandra Stairs, was pleased that Hollywood production companies were flocking to the DOD for technical assistance: "I've seen ten times more scripts now than in the previous two years" (cited in Lamar 1986). According to Mace Neufeld, producer of *The Hunt for Red October* (1990), a film that also got DOD support, Hollywood in the post–*Top Gun* period operated according to an implicit business rule: get DOD assistance "or forget about making the picture" (cited in Sirota 2011b).

In the 1990s, the DOD-Hollywood complex grew larger, and amicable relations between the DOD and Hollywood studios became standardized and routinized. Following the collapse of the Soviet Union, the United States faced a world in which it could no longer attack other states on the basis of containing the Soviet communist threat to the so-called Free World. The US state started focusing on "terrorism" as the post–Cold War threat, and Hollywood responded with a cycle of films about US protagonists battling terrorists at home and abroad. Throughout the 1990s, the United States battled Columbian drug terrorists in *Clear and Present Danger* (1994), neo-Nazi terrorists in *Die Hard with a Vengeance* (1995), homegrown terrorists in *Under Siege* (1992), international terrorists in *Under Siege 2* (1995), Russian terrorists in *Air Force One* (1997), and Bosnian terrorists in *The Peacemaker* (1997). Islamic terrorists were depicted as anti-American evil-doers in *True Lies* (1994), *Executive Decision* (1996), and most infamously *The Siege* (1998). During this period, the DOD supported many of these films (Robb 2004).

In addition to screening the United States' new fight against a roster of post–Cold War enemies, Hollywood returned to the past by making blockbuster Second World War films like *Saving Private Ryan* (1998) and *U-571* (2000), which were both supported by the DOD. While the Vietnam War films of the 1980s had made war seem bad, *Saving Private Ryan*, with its focus on a small band of comradely soldiers engaged in ground combat and fighting for their lives against an evil enemy for a just cause, made US state coercion seem "good again" (Canby 1998). Though effective at portraying intense battle scenes, *Saving Private Ryan* and other Second World War combat genre films and TV shows like HBO's *Band of Brothers* individualize the war and revel in a sentimental masculine militarism that venerates male authority (Young 2003, 255). To make the world safe for capitalism in the late 1990s, the US military needed new recruits, and Hollywood icons seemed happy to help convert its consumers into new combatants. In 2000, Spike Lee and James Brolin appeared in DOD-placed TV commercials to pitch military service. US Secretary of Defense William S. Cohen enlisted celebrities, including Julia Roberts, Tom Cruise, Robert De Niro, Harrison Ford, Sidney Poitier, and Will Smith, to go on national TV, radio, and the

Internet to encourage US citizens to enlist in the army, navy, marines, and air force. "You've got to get the people of influence," said Cohen (cited in Becker 2000).

Following 9/11, the DOD commissioned two dozen Hollywood screenwriters, including Steven E. de Souza (*Die Hard, Die Hard 2*), Joseph Zito (*Delta Force One, Missing in Action*), David Fincher (*Fight Club, Alien 3*), Spike Jonze (*Adaptation, Being John Malkovich*), and Mary Lambert (*Pet Cemetery I* and *Pet Cemetery II*), to brainstorm future threat and attack scenarios at the DOD-funded Institute for Creative Technologies (BBC 2001). To get Hollywood to portray its new global War on Terror as heroic and to encourage Hollywood to "rally round the flag in a style reminiscent of the early days of World War II" (Bart 2001), the Bush administration arranged two meetings with media executives. Ken Lisaius, a White House spokesperson, said the meetings briefed "studio executives on the war on terrorism" and advised them on "future projects that may be undertaken by the industry." He stated that the Bush administration "has great respect for the creativity of the industry and recognizes its impact and ability to educate publics at home and abroad" (cited in Lyman 2001).

The first meeting occurred in October 2001. Lead representatives of the Bush administration were Chris Henick, deputy assistant to the president, and Adam Goldman, associate director of the Office of Public Liaison. Hollywood elites in attendance were lawyer Bruce Ramer and writer-director Lionel Chetwynd; Chris Albrecht, president of HBO Original Programming; Colin Callender, president of HBO Films; Leslie Moonves, president and CEO of CBS Television; Jerry Offsay, president of programming for Showtime; Peter Roth, president of Warner Bros. TV; Bryce Zabel, chairman of the Television Academy of Arts and Sciences; and Craig Haffner, CEO of Greystone. The meeting aimed to create a strategic "arts and entertainment task force" that would be an intra-agency bridge between Washington and Hollywood. "We need to tap into the creativity and energy of this community," said one government official. Hollywood seemed eager to commit its creative energy to state PR goals. "I think you have a bunch of people here who were just saying, 'Tell us what to do. We don't fly jet planes, but there are skill sets that can be put to use here," said Moonves. "We have not done a good job communicating to people about who we are when so many people in the world think ill of us, and many wish us harm," said Zabel. "It's possible the entertainment industry could help the government formulate its message to the rest of the world about who Americans are and what they believe" (cited in Rutenberg 2001).

A second Washington-Hollywood meeting happened on November 8, 2001, in Beverly Hills. Karl Rove, a senior White House adviser, facilitated a high-powered discussion about how Hollywood might help sell the United States' War on Terror. Rove encouraged Hollywood to 1) make films that communicated that the country's war on terrorism was not a war against Islam but rather terrorism, 2) rally US citizens around the flag and potentially aid military recruitment efforts, 3) emphasize that US troops and their families need support, 4) frame the 9/11 attacks as an attack against civilization that required a global response, 5) emphasize that children need to be reassured of their safety and security in the wake of the attacks, and 6) suggest that the global War on Terror is a good war against evil and not a war between friendly and civilized nation-states. Rove stressed that the US state would not censor films or force Hollywood to make propaganda. "The industry will decide what it will do and when it will do it," said Rove following the meeting. Furthermore, Rove suggested that Hollywood should avoid making films with simplistic one-dimensional messages. "The world is full of people who are discerning, and we need to recognize that concrete information told with honesty and specificity and integrity is important to the ultimate success in this conflict," advised Rove, cognizant of the "active audience" and how Hollywood imagery has complex political effects in reception contexts (CNN 2001).

Some Hollywood executives heeded Rove's request. Walt Disney Company chairman Robert Iger said that Hollywood films could help unite the US population in the global War on Terror: "This is a recognition that September 11 was a day that changed the world, and if we can step forward and help our country contend with how the world has changed, I think that's the patriotic thing to do" (cited in M. Armstrong 2001). Studio executives offered to produce war documentary films, public service announcements, and ads that promoted national security goals (Lyman 2001). In the months following 9/11, Hollywood produced two propaganda films: *The Spirit of America* (a montage of clips from previous US Hollywood action, drama, and war films intended to energize patriotism) and *Operation Enduring Freedom* (an explanation of the US global War on Terror intended to promote the invasion of Afghanistan). The largest theatre chain in the US – Regal Entertainment Group – showed *Operation Enduring Freedom* before all featured films on its 4,000 screens.

For six years following 9/11, however, Hollywood did not produce any explicit feature films about the global War on Terror, the 2001 invasion of Afghanistan, or the 2003 invasion of Iraq. This temporal gap between actual US war policy and Hollywood's reel wars was not unusual, though, as studios in the past had tended to wait until a war was over before throwing their money behind a script about it. Since the Second World War, films about the United States at war have tended to be released many years after the war ends, when historians, policy-makers, and citizens have had some time to digest its meaning. And given that the United States' post-9/11 wars were met with condemnation by people all over the world, Hollywood studios, globalized and motivated by money, perhaps realized that War on Terror flicks were a risky business venture.

Hollywood studios instead put their money behind a number of films that returned to past wars, purging them of their complexity and horrors and promoting them as good wars, driven by benign US foreign policy intentions. George W. Bush referred to the terrorist attack on the World Trade Center as another Pearl Harbor, and Hollywood capitalized on this sentiment with Second World War nostalgia films like *Pearl Harbor* (2001). The DOD supported *Pearl Harbor* and other films, about the Vietnam War (*We Were Soldiers*, 2002), its interventions in Africa (*Tears of the Sun*, 2003, and *Black Hawk Down*, 2001), and about air skirmishes with North Korea (*Behind Enemy Lines II*, 2006) (Forsyth 2005). Doherty (2004, 15) says that post-9/11 films about the United States' past wars conveyed "expressions of a renascent nation ready to kick ass" and "a respect for public servants in uniform, a sympathy for military codes of conduct, and a celebration of the virtues forged in the crucible of combat." Hollywood studios also packaged fantasy films that offered allegories of war (*The Lord of the Rings* trilogy, 2001–3), fictionalizations of the so-called West versus East clash of civilizations (*The Kingdom of Heaven*, 2005, and *300*, 2006), films about the rise and fall of ancient empires (*Troy*, *Alexander*, both 2004), and sci-fi spectacles in which the US DOD teams up with robots to save the world (*Transformers* movies, 2007–14).

Hollywood's first major films about the 9/11 terrorist attack were released in 2006 (*World Trade Center* and *United 93*), and Hollywood waited until 2007 to fictionalize the United States' global war on Islamic terrorists (*Rendition, A Mighty Heart, The Kingdom*). In 2007, 2008, and 2009, Hollywood studios released a cycle of films about the US wars in Afghanistan and Iraq (*Lions for Lambs, Redacted, In the Valley of Elah, Grace Is Gone, Stop-Loss, The Lucky Ones, The Hurt Locker, Brothers*, and *The Messenger*). These films dealt with war's consequences from the point of view of US soldiers and addressed complex topics, including "grief, desertion, battlefield murder, rape, post-traumatic stress disorder and so-called blowback repercussions from botched, covert interference abroad" (Patterson 2007). But like the presumably anti–Vietnam War films of an earlier era, these products individualize these wars; fail to address the controversial policies, shaky legal frameworks, and corporate interests that supported them; and say nothing about the horrifying impacts they had on Afghani and Iraqi civilians. Though many of these war films were critically acclaimed by reviewers (and travelled well in international film markets), most were flops at the US box office (Steyn 2007). For more than 100 years, Hollywood had produced racist Orientalist films that portrayed Arabs and Muslims as "heartless, brutal, uncivilized, religious fanatics" (Shaheen 2003, 171). But in the post-9/11 era, Hollywood resisted the temptation to cash in on war films that depicted Muslim and Arab peoples, cultures, and states as enemies of America. Conservatives interpret this as a sign of Hollywood's liberal bias, when in fact it meshes with the Bush administration's public diplomacy strategy in the Muslim world and Karl Rove's post-9/11 request that Hollywood studios *not* produce war films that depict the War on Terror as a war against Muslim Arab peoples. Though Hollywood largely refrained from demonizing Arabs and Muslims as terrorists in its films made for the big screen, TV networks made and scheduled TV shows that on smaller screens did, like *24, The Agency, The Grid, Sleeper Cell, The Path to 9/11,* and *D/C 9/11: Time of Crisis.*

This brief history of the DOD-Hollywood complex suggests that, far from being an outpost of anti-war radicalism, Hollywood often supports the US at war. In this complex, the power of US military coercion and the persuasiveness of film pervade one another, allowing the DOD to promote its image of violence to the public and Hollywood to secure profits. The political and economic reasons why Hollywood glamorizes and glorifies US war policy are discussed further in the following section, which unpacks the DOD's film-policy regime and the resulting co-production relationship between the DOD and Hollywood.

The DOD-Hollywood Complex: Institutions, Policy, Practice, and Products

The DOD boasts a centralized Hollywood liaison office that is linked to every US military branch. Headed by Phil Strub and Terry Mitchell, the Department of Defense Special Assistant for Entertainment Media (DODSAEM) is the largest and most resource intensive Hollywood liaison office. The DODSAEM is located in the Pentagon, Washington, DC, a few doors down from the DOD public affairs office and the briefing studio where US defence secretaries issue sound bites about US national security threats and frame US foreign policy for the news media. The DODSAEM is the go-to place for Hollywood production companies that wish to produce a blockbuster war film or TV series. The DODSAEM oversees the Hollywood liaison offices – the Office of Army Chief of Public Affairs, the Navy Office of Information West, the Office of Public Affairs–Entertainment Liaison Office (air force), the Public Affairs Motion Picture and Television Liaison (marines), and the Motion Picture and TV Office (coast guard). All of these offices are located in the same place, at 10880 Wilshire Boulevard in Los Angeles. These liaisons provide Hollywood with the footage and military capital it needs to make blockbuster war films and TV shows. The DODSAEM grants Hollywood access to military locations (bases, barracks, battlefields), personnel (actual US officers and soldiers), software (knowledge about military protocol, chain of command, systems operation, troop lingo, drill routines), and, most important, hardware (real battleships, jet fighters, tanks, helicopters, and guns). Not every Hollywood production company, however, gets DOD assistance.

The DOD works with Hollywood production companies only when their war scripts fulfill the DOD's content requirements, which are outlined by DOD Directive 5410.16, "Department of Defense Assistance to Non-Government, Entertainment-Oriented Motion Picture, Television and Video Productions," issued on January 26, 1988. This directive is presently operative and "outlines the policies and procedures governing DOD assistance to non-Government theatrical and television motion pictures, television mini-series, network, cable, syndicated television, or direct video release productions that are primarily entertainment oriented" (1). The DOD-Hollywood filmmaking procedure works like this: the Hollywood production company first must submit a "letter describing the proposal to produce a specific motion picture, television program, or video product, stating the story/project objectives and identifiable benefits for the Department of Defense," and it must submit "five copies of the script for review and evaluation" (7). In collaboration with the liaison officer serving the DOD unit represented by the script, the DODSAEM then subjects the war script to a rigorous review and assessment process. The DOD not only reviews existing war scripts but also may proactively approach "non-Government producers, scriptwriters, etc., in their efforts to develop a script that might ultimately qualify for DOD assistance" and give "guidance, suggestions, access for technical research, etc." (4). DOD Directive 5410.16 outlines a framework for a collaborative, as opposed to a competitive, relationship with Hollywood: "Official personnel services and DOD material shall not be employed in such a manner as to compete directly with commercial and private sectors" (3).

The DODSAEM approves or disapproves of DOD support for Hollywood production based on the nationalist content criteria that it employs when assessing the quality of a war script. According to DOD Directive 5410.16, DOD assistance is provided to Hollywood film, TV, or video productions "when cooperation of the producers with the Government results in benefitting the Department of Defense or when this would be in the best national interests." The "national interest" is an ideologically loaded term, but according to the DOD, the war scripts that are in the "best national interests" are those that "authentically" represent "actual persons, places, military operations, and historical events" and those that "depict a feasible interpretation of military life, operations and policies." In addition, the DOD says war scripts are in the "best national interests" when they are "of informational value and considered to be in the best interest of public understanding of the US Armed Forces and the Department of Defense." DOD supported war scripts should also "provide services to the general public relating to, or enhancing, the US Armed Forces recruiting and retention programs" (2). Lastly, it is in the "best national interests" that the war script "not appear to condone or endorse activities by private citizens or organizations when such activities are contrary to US Government policy" (20). Basically, the DOD may approve a Hollywood war script if it represents the DOD "accurately" and "feasibly," supports recruitment, and promotes US Government policy. When a Hollywood war script fulfills these DOD content criteria, it may be approved. As a result, the film project will get full DOD assistance, including special access to DOD facilities, technology, personnel, and expert knowledge about DOD operations.

DOD script approval amounts to a big war film production subsidy to Hollywood. According to DOD Directive 5410.16, "the [approved] production company shall not be required to reimburse the Government for military or civilian manpower ... when such personnel are officially assigned to assist in the production" (10). This means that, when the DOD flies jet

The DOD-Hollywood Complex 183

fighters or helicopters, drives tanks, or sails battleships for the camera, the production company is not charged. The costs of these activities are accounted for by the DOD as "normal training and operational missions [and expenditure] that would occur regardless of DOD assistance to a particular production [and] are not ... chargeable to the production company" (10). The DOD provides Hollywood with soldiers-cum-actors that train/act for the camera; it also encourages Hollywood to hire "military personnel in an off-duty, non-official status ... to perform as actors, extras, etc., provided there is no conflict with any existing Service regulation" (2). The DOD does not charge Hollywood for shooting images of its multi-million-dollar weapons technology: "Beyond actual operational expenses, no charges shall be levied for asset usage (i.e., rental and/or depreciation factors)" (10). However, Hollywood must reimburse the DOD for "any additional expenses incurred as a result of assistance rendered" (2). These additional expenses include "petroleum, oil, and lubricants for equipment used," "expendable supplies," "lost or damaged equipment," and travel costs for the DOD liaisons and equipment shipping.

To ensure Hollywood makes a war film that abides by the DOD's content requirements, the DOD assigns to the production a project officer who is "present during filming of all scenes pertinent to the DOD" and whose function is to "advise the production company on technical aspects and arrange for information necessary to ensure accurate and authentic portrayals of the DOD." The project officer enforces Hollywood's "proper selection of locations, appropriate uniforms, awards, decorations, grooming standards, insignia and set dressing applicable to the military aspects of the film." If the production company fails to comply with the approved script, the project officer can withdraw support. DOD Directive 5410.16 says the project officer may suspend DOD "assistance when action by the production company is contrary to stipulations governing the project and to the best interest of the DOD" (6). The DOD can call for war script revisions and screen the film before public release: "The production company must arrange for an official DOD screening in Washington, DC, before delivery of the production for general public release" (8). If the film is approved for release, the project officer promotes the DOD through Hollywood marketing by "attend[ing] pertinent preproduction and production conferences" and attending "the approval screening of the product" (6). DOD Directive 5410.16 clearly highlights the DOD's policy and practices for intervening in and attempting to influence Hollywood's entertainment market.

A for-profit sub-sector of military cultural intermediaries has developed around the DOD's liaison offices and studios to advise cultural workers on how to script war's "accuracy and authenticity." For example, Capt. Dale Dye, a retired US Marine and Vietnam War veteran, is founder and owner of Warriors, Inc. (http://www.warriorsinc.com/), a company that sells "technical advisory services to the entertainment industry worldwide," including "performer training, research, planning, staging and on-set advisory for directors and other key production personnel" (Warriors, Inc. n.d.). As a business, Warriors, Inc. is motivated by profit, but by selling advice to Hollywood it also seeks to use Hollywood to influence public perceptions of US military personnel. The Warriors, Inc. website outlines the motives of this company:

> Captain Dale A. Dye, USMC (Ret) came to Hollywood with a vision. He had a single mission in mind ... to change how American civilians view the common grunt. Having been around infantrymen all his life and having been one himself, he knew that the majority are intelligent, creative, and full of heart ... and the image of the dumb cannon-fodder blindly following orders not only was not true ... but was a grave disservice to those brave servicemen who had risked and often gave their lives so that our nation could survive and prosper. So he looked for the best medium available to reach the hearts and minds of the public, and chose the film and television industry to spread his message. Welcome to Warriors, Inc.

Warriors, Inc. has worked with Hollywood on the development of blockbuster war films like Steven Spielberg's *Saving Private Ryan* (1998) and popular Second World War TV shows such as HBO's *Band of Brothers* (2001) and *The Pacific* (2010). Dale has even acted in numerous war films and TV shows.

Brian Chung, a former US Army captain, and Greg Bishop, a former US Army lieutenant-colonel, are also military cultural intermediaries who, after serving in Iraq, turned their experience of war into a culture industry business venture. They established a firm called MUSA in 2009. This company is "owned and operated by seasoned military veterans with modern tactical combat experience and broad entertainment experience" and sells "strategic, tactical and modern military consulting services to the film, television, gaming, advertising and technology industries." MUSA's website (http://musaconsulting.com/) promotes itself to Hollywood production companies by saying it "bridges the gap between the military and entertainment," helps filmmakers "enhance productions" by "achieving accurate and authentic portrayals of military personnel and equipment," and saves production companies "time, money and stress by navigating" them through the DOD's "military support approval process." MUSA packages and sells a number of services to Hollywood firms that wish to co-produce war films with the DOD. These include 1) technical advice to "ensure authenticity of all military-related material"; 2) DOD packaging/support to "eliminate DOD roadblocks by preparing and packaging your project, providing DOD 'production assistance agreement' consultation and DOD relationship management"; 3) military liaisons who are trained to "ensure clear lines of communication between the production company, the supporting DOD service and local military commands"; 4) actor training, "including 'basic training,' dialogue coaching, weapons familiarization ... so actors shoot, move and communicate like real troops"; 5) IP script development to "achieve faster and smoother DOD support"; 5) combat choreography; 6) wardrobe, props, and weapons; 7) post-production advising; 8) location consulting that helps production companies compare "preferred shooting locations" with "DOD equipment and personnel needs and advise which locations are most conducive to the budget"; 9) marketing that leverages "expertise in communicating to military audiences via traditional media, military targeted media, DOD-run media and social media"; and brand integration that helps production companies integrate their brand into other projects. MUSA has cashed in on DOD-Hollywood film productions such as *The Day the Earth Stood Still* (2008), *Transformers: Revenge of the Fallen* (2009), and *G.I. Joe: The Rise of Cobra* (2009).

Since 9/11, the DOD's official film liaison officers and sub-contractor intermediaries like Dale, Chung, and Bishop have helped Hollywood studios make a number of blockbuster war films. These include *Pearl Harbor* (2001), *Enemy at the Gates* (2001), *Black Hawk Down* (2001), *Bad Company* (2002), *Behind Enemy Lines* (2002), *Windtalkers* (2002), and *Captain Phillips* (2013). The DOD's support for some of these films was based on the ostensible "accuracy" of their scripts, but the DOD plays fast and loose with the term. In fact, it has taken to co-producing fantastical films that promise the biggest box office bang among youth such as *Iron Man* (2008), *Iron Man 2* (2010), *Battle: Los Angeles* (2011), *Battleship* (2012), and *Man of Steel* (2013).

Another major DOD-Hollywood co-production, *Transformers* (2007), was based not on realism but on toys imported to the United States from Japan in the 1980s. *Transformers* is a fantastical sci-fi film with a simplistic narrative structure and unrealistic plot: a wayward but good-hearted teenager teams up with good alien robots (Transformers) and the US Navy, Army, and Air Force to fight a war against evil alien robots (Decepticons) that threaten the world, and together they save the world. Owned by Paramount Pictures, directed by Michael Bay, and produced by Steven Spielberg, *Transformers* is a product placement bonanza for the US auto industry: Optimus Prime is a Peterbilt 379, Bumblebee is a Chevrolet Camaro, Jazz is a Pontiac Solstice, Ironhide is the GMC Topkick. The film also spun off toys, a comic book series, a novel, and a video game. While Hollywood designed *Transformers* as a trans-media synergistic franchise to maximize profits, the DOD cashed in on the film's global publicity power. "I wanted the story to have global impact," said director Michael Bay, "so I was dead set about getting military cooperation"(cited in Miles 2007). The DOD supported Bay's live-action filming at the Edwards Air Force Base in California, at the White Sands Missile Range, at the Holloman Air Force Base, and in New Mexico (which "body doubled" for Qatar). The DOD also assisted with on-location shots at the Hoover Dam and the Pentagon. Three hundred actual US soldiers performed in action sequences in which the film's protagonists fearlessly fight Decepticons. The DOD also provisioned the F-117 Nighthawk, the CV-22 Osprey, the F-22 Raptor, the A-10 Thunderbolt IIs, and the Lockheed AC-130s (Miles 2007). Lt.-Col. Paul Sinor, the army Hollywood liaison officer, helped Bay ensure the military's core values, tactics, dialogue, and uniforms were accurately portrayed (Kruzel 2007). "Without the superb military support we've gotten on this film, it would be an entirely different looking film," said Ian Bryce, one of *Transformers*' producers. "We want to cooperate with the Pentagon to show them off in the most positive light, and the Pentagon likewise wants to give us the resources to be able to do that" (cited in Smith 2006).

By DOD content policy criteria, the *Transformers* war script should not have been supported, as it is not an "accurate" or "feasible" representation of the DOD or the US at war, since the United States has never been attacked by robots from outer space and probably never will be. Yet, the promotional material accompanying *Transformers*' release unflinchingly emphasizes the film's "realistic" portrayal of the DOD. "Even though it's a fantasy, they understood that our depiction of the military is grounded in reality and they wanted an accurate portrayal of their personnel and technology," said Bryce (cited in Cochran 2006). Some military PR clarified that the film was not an attempt to create verisimilitude but rather a future-oriented war simulation. "The Army has never fought giant robots, but if we did, this is probably how we'd do it," claimed Sinor (Smith 2006). Other military spokespeople highlighted the film's promotional benefit to recruiters. "The special effects are definitely going to draw the younger crowd, and then they'll be able to see just how the Air Force operates," said Chief Master Sgt. Mike Gasparetto, a career field manager for Air Force Recruiting Service. "I think it will be a great branding tool for the Air Force" (cited in Kruzel 2007). Following the completion of *Transformers*, the DOD invited above and below the line production members to visit the 9/11 Memorial Chapel. *Transformers* was screened at the Pentagon and then released on July 4th to celebrate America's independence.

A more recent DOD-Hollywood co-production is *Act of Valor* (2012), a film in which US Navy SEALs and Navy Special Warfare Combatant-Craft crewmen do battle with an American-killing Chechen terrorist and a Russian drug smuggler while on a covert mission to rescue a kidnapped CIA agent. Andersen (2014, 22) writes that *Act of Valor*'s (2012) "aestheticization of war sanitizes and celebrates significant yet contentious transformations in US foreign policy, denies the human, moral and political consequences of these transformations and supports the growth and maintenance of a war society."

What's interesting about this film is not just its aestheticization of war, its first-person perspective violence, high-altitude parachute jumps, or jungle scenes (the film feels like an immersive first-person shooter war game but without the controls, as it is shot from the Zeiss Ze cameras mounted on each SEAL's helmet), but rather its initiation by the DOD. In 2008, Navy Special Warfare started soliciting proposals for a film about the SEALs that would support its recruitment effort, honour its dead, and correct media misrepresentations of its conduct. In return, the company would receive full SEALs production support. The Bandito Brothers, a production company run by Mike McCoy and Scott Waugh, militainment entrepreneurs who in 2007 were hired by the navy to create a recruiting video, got the contract. The Bandito Brothers cast actual SEALs – not Hollywood celebrities – in *Act of Valor*. The names of the SEALs/actors do not appear in the film's credit role, but the Naval Special Warfare members killed since September 11 do (Jurgensen 2011).

Act of Valor was distributed by Relativity Media, a medium-size US film production/distribution company. Tucker Tooley, Relativity's president of Worldwide Production, gushed, "*Act of Valor* is truly one-of-a-kind-ripped from today's headline-making heroic missions, an incredibly crafted film featuring active duty Navy SEALs, in a remarkable and fast-paced story that will give audiences an authentic inside glimpse and make them proud of America's finest. We're honored to add this unbelievably entertaining and gripping film to Relativity's 2012 slate" (cited in Fleming 2012).

Act of Valor was released on President's Day weekend. To promote the film, McCoy recycled the myth that Hollywood is against war and presented his company as bucking this anti-military trend. "The Vietnam legacy has been this fog that wouldn't lift for 40 years," and "no one had the balls in Hollywood to go the other way," boasts McCoy (cited in Warren 2012). Waugh placed a recruitment message into his publicity for the film, saying, "We take our freedom too much for granted. I now feel that all young people should serve our nation in some capacity" (McHugh 2011). Following the SEALs' killing of Osama bin Laden, trailers for *Act of Valor* filled Super Bowl TV ad spots. The film was pre-screened at SHOT, the United States' annual trade show for the gun industry, and it eventually premiered in New York City on the USS *Intrepid*.

The CIA-Hollywood Complex: Institutions, Policies, Practices, and Products

The CIA is a relative newcomer to Hollywood's business of filmmaking – publicly, that is (Jenkins 2009, 2012). Throughout the Cold War, the CIA sought to influence public opinion and elicit public consent to US war policy through film. In 1950, it established the Congress for Cultural Freedom to recruit unwitting left-leaning intellectuals and use them to fight its cultural battle against the Soviet Union (Stoner Saunders 1999). That same year "the CIA bought the rights to George Orwell's *Animal Farm* and then funded the 1954 British animated version of the film"; also, the Congress for Cultural Freedom's US branch oversaw the production of *1984* (1956), based on George Orwell's novel about a totalitarian police state (Graham 2008; Stoner Saunders 1999).

Throughout the 1950s, the CIA worked with anti-communist cultural workers in Hollywood like John Ford and John Wayne and studio bigwigs like Cecil B. DeMille, Darryl Zanuck, and Luigi Luraschi. Through Luraschi, head of Paramount Pictures' domestic and foreign distribution arm, the CIA managed many filmic representations of America that moved around the world. Luraschi reviewed every script for scenes that he thought would make America look bad or offend another country. He released films for export that framed US policy in a positive light and held back from international distribution those that did not. Luraschi even had Hollywood filmmakers plant well-dressed and happy African Americans in films like

Sangaree (1953) and *The Caddy* (1953) to counter the Soviet propaganda emphasis on US race segregation.

Though the CIA has been operating behind the scenes of Hollywood studios since the 1950s, in 1996 it made its contribution to Hollywood magic public by appointing a Hollywood liaison officer named Chase Brandon, a veteran CIA agent (Jenkins 2009, 2012). In 2007, Brandon was succeeded by Paul Barry, also a former covert agent. Barry heads the CIA Entertainment Industry Liaison Office (EILO), which is run by the CIA's Public Affairs Office, an agency that "oversees the [CIA's] daily interaction with the media, the general public and the CIA's workforce" and manages the CIA's "cadre of speechwriters." The Public Affairs Office website (https://www.cia.gov/offices-of-cia/public-affairs/entertainment-industry-liaison) describes the EILO's goal as follows:

> As an organization that plays a key role in America's defense, the CIA is a frequent subject of books, motion pictures, documentaries, and other creative ventures. For years, artists from across the entertainment industry – actors, authors, directors, producers, screenwriters, and others – have been in touch with the CIA to gain a better understanding of our intelligence mission. Our goal is an accurate portrayal of the men and women of the CIA, and the skill, innovation, daring, and commitment to public service that defines them. If you are part of the entertainment industry, and are working on a project that deals with the CIA, the Agency may be able to help you. We are in a position to give greater authenticity to scripts, stories, and other products in development. That can mean answering questions, debunking myths, or arranging visits to the CIA to meet the people who know intelligence – its past, present, and future. In some cases, we permit filming on our headquarters compound. We can also provide stock footage of locations within and around our main building. Intelligence is challenging, exciting, and essential. To better convey that reality, the CIA is ready for a constructive dialogue with a broad range of creative talents.

The CIA's EILO is modelled on the DOD's; its officers grant Hollywood companies insight, agency shooting locations, props, and technology to make films and TV shows about this executive branch agency. Before provisioning these public resources, the CIA liaison reads and vets the project's script to make sure that it will depict the agency and its operations and personnel in a positive light. If it does not, the EILO will ask for script changes or refuse to support the production. The EILO even pitches script ideas.

"Looking for inspiration for a new film or book?" the EILO website asks. "Our Entertainment Industry Liaison offers recommendations here."

The EILO's effort to get Hollywood to make a positive portrayal of the CIA aims to change negative public opinions of it (Jenkins 2012). During the Cold War, the CIA supported a reign of terror against countries inimical to US national interests. It funded Cuban exiles to destabilize Castro's regime; detained, tortured, and murdered thousands of South Vietnamese supporters of the Viet Cong with its Phoenix Program; orchestrated coups that overthrew democratically elected socialist leaders in Iran, Guatemala, and Chile; oversaw Iraq's use of chemical weapons against Iran; funnelled money to Islamic jihadists in Afghanistan to fight the Soviet Union; and armed the contras to fight the Sandinistas in Nicaragua. Though motivated by US national security, these and other declassified CIA missions undermined the United States' credibility as a benign leader in the eyes of millions of people. At present, the CIA continues to operate in a clandestine fashion, running extra-juridical torture cells and drone assassinations around the world in the absence of congressional oversight and popular consent. Hollywood has capitalized on the CIA's shady status in the public mind by making films like *Three Days of the Condor* (1975) and *JFK* (1991) that recognize public anxieties about the CIA's dirty deeds. Until the late 1990s, Hollywood had represented the CIA as "an outfit (1) intent on assassination, (2) comprising rogue operatives who act with little oversight, (3) failing to take care of its own officers and assets, (4) operating on morally ambiguous and perhaps morally reprehensible grounds, or (5) bedevilled by its own buffoonery and hopeless disorganization" (Jenkins 2012, 11).

In an effort to counter and politically correct Hollywood's negative media representations, the CIA started working with studios to change its image and, by doing so, public opinion (Jenkins 2009, 2012). "I made that a big priority, and we did a lot more with Hollywood than ever before," said Bill Harlow, the CIA's Public Affairs Office head from 1997 to 2004. "The reason is that the American public gets a lot more of their information about the CIA from Hollywood than it does from the news media, and much of what they see about the agency [films and TV shows] is negative and wrong" (cited in Dilanian and Keegan 2012). EILO's Paul Barry says, "Hollywood is the only way that the public learns about the Agency" (cited in Jenkins 2012, 32). To help the public "learn" about the CIA in the way it wants it to, the CIA's EILO has worked with Hollywood to make films and TV shows, including *JAG* (1995–2005), *Enemy of the State* (1998), *In the Company of Spies* (1999), *The Agency* (2001–3), *Alias* (2001–6), *24* (2001–10), *Bad Company* (2002),

The Sum of All Fears (2002), *The Recruit* (2003), and *Covert Affairs* (2010–14) (Jenkins 2012, 1). In what follows, I offer a brief reading of the production and promotional work of two recent CIA-Hollywood complex films: *Argo* (2012) and *Zero Dark Thirty* (2012).

Argo is a CIA-supported film about the CIA's response to the Iranian hostage crisis in 1979. Adapted from CIA agent Tony Mendez's 2000 book, *The Master of Disguise*, and a 2007 *Wired* article by Joshuah Bearman called "The Great Escape," *Argo* says it is "based on the true story" of the November 4, 1979, Iranian takeover of the US Embassy and Mendez's exfiltration of six US diplomats from the Canadian Embassy in Tehran, where they hide out and await rescue. The film begins with a brief nod to how the CIA deposed of Iran's democratically elected president in 1953 and replaced him with the autocratic shah, whose rule fomented the 1979 revolution. With help from his Hollywood allies John Chambers (a makeup artist) and Lester Siegel (a producer), Mendez (played by Ben Affleck) establishes a fake Canadian film production company and enters Iran to ostensibly scout out exotic locations to shoot for a *Star Wars*-esque science fiction film called *Argo*. Once inside Iran, Mendez dresses up the anxious US diplomats as Canadian filmmakers, gives them travel documents, helps them dupe a group of menacing revolutionary guards at Tehran's airport, and then boards a plane and flies back to the United States with them.

Argo does a lot of ideological work for the CIA. First, though *Argo* presents itself as a piece of true CIA history, it embellishes this history to make the CIA look more important than it actually was. *Argo* portrays Mendez as a maverick agent who, against all odds and a skeptical bureaucracy, single-handedly hatches and executes a plot to rescue his fellow Americans. In reality, the Canadian government and the Canadian Embassy led the exfiltration initiative, first sheltering the US diplomats and then supplying them with travel documents. The CIA got involved in the exfiltration only one week before the US diplomats escaped, and Mendez showed up at the Canadian Embassy for one day and then oversaw the Americans' departure from the Tehran airport, where they passed through the gates with no life-or-death interrogation by the revolutionary guards (Houpt 2013). *Argo* revises history to inflate the role of the CIA and diminish the role of Canadians in helping US diplomats escape Iran. In addition to misrepresenting history to make the CIA look more substantial to the mission's success than it was, *Argo* depicts Mendez as a courageous and affable family man who risks his own life, and it depicts Iranians as a crazed horde of radical Islamist enemies who burn American flags, spit and yell at Americans, and destroy the US Embassy. While *Argo* contains some truth, set in the present context, the film perpetuates the United States' stereotype of Iran and its people as a collective threat to America, Israel, and world security. Though *Argo* is not a documentary film about Iran or its revolution, its claim to be "based on a true story" and its inter-splicing of historical footage within the film further encourage viewers to perceive it as history.

The positive light *Argo* casts on the CIA was duly recognized by the White House. Arriving at the 2012 Oscars through a live video feed from the White House, surrounded by a bunch of medalled US soldiers, First Lady Michelle Obama cheerfully announced that *Argo* had won Best Picture.

Another controversial Hollywood-CIA film is *Zero Dark Thirty* (2012), based on the CIA's post-9/11 decade-long attempt to locate and kill al-Qaeda leader Osama bin Laden. Like most Hollywood films that simplify a complex political reality into a pleasing and palatable format, *Zero Dark Thirty* (written by Mark Boal and directed by Kathryn Bigelow) compresses ten years and the labour of hundreds of CIA agents into a 157-minute film about the individual service of Maya, an attractive twenty-something CIA agent (played by Jessica Chastain). Since graduating from high school, this heroine has been obsessed with gathering intel on Bin Laden. As a CIA agent, Maya interrogates and tortures people, survives a hotel bombing and a gunshot wound, convinces her superiors to pursue her theory about Bin Laden's whereabouts till it is proven true, and then oversees the SEALs' infiltration of Bin Laden's Pakistan compound and assassination of the man himself. The film's prologue reminds viewers of the terrorist attack of 9/11, playing chilling recordings of calls from the World Trade Center's victims to 911 emergency operators. Horrified screams, whimpers, and pleas for help set the stage for a story about CIA surveillance, torture, and extra-juridical acts of killing that claims to be "based on first-hand accounts of actual events." This film frames the United States' global War on Terrorism as an act of vengeance, obscuring the bigger economic and geopolitical stakes involved. It depicts a good CIA agent doing and observing bad things for her country and for the world. Though torture is a human rights violation and often fails to generate usable intelligence, *Zero Dark Thirty* makes the crime of torture seem a legitimate and effective tool in the United States' War on Terror. "Like the bin Laden killing itself," says Greenwald (2012b), "this is a film that tells Americans to feel good about themselves, to feel gratitude for the violence done in their name, to perceive the War-on-Terror CIA not as lawless criminals but as honorable heroes." One CIA official described the CIA's support for the film as a way to "get behind the winning horse" – the "first and biggest" Hollywood film about the hunt for bin Laden (Hastings 2013). While several Republican politicians expressed concern that the CIA exposed classified information when working with Bigelow and Boal on their film (Cieply 2012), this did not happen, and the CIA's support for the film was not unusual. Like *Argo*, *Zero Dark Thirty* works to re-brand the CIA in the public mind as a benign entity.

Why Does Hollywood Support DOD and CIA PR Goals?

The DOD and CIA clearly have an interest in managing public opinion about their agencies and operations through Hollywood entertainment. But why do Hollywood studios, which are not owned by state agencies or subordinate to their PR goals, consent to co-produce pro-war and security films with them? Six factors explain why Hollywood studios so frequently work with the US national security state.

First, Hollywood studios work with the DOD and CIA because these agencies give them a powerful economic incentive to do so – a huge subsidy. When manufacturing war and security-themed films, Hollywood studios seek access to state resources, actual or simulated: military installments and security locations, state personnel, knowledge about protocol and strategy, and, most important, weapons technology. To acquire these resources, Hollywood production companies could build base, barrack, and battlefield set pieces in some studio backlot, hire actors to play military personnel, do in-depth research about military conduct, and engineer scaled-down models of hardware or purchase hardware from Lockheed Martin, Northrop Grumman, Boeing, or Raytheon. But this would be very costly. The F-22 Raptor jet fighter costs $150 million per unit. The standard US Navy battleship costs approximately $100 million per unit. The Blackhawk helicopter costs $4.4 million per unit, and the M-1 Abrams Tank costs about $4.3 million per unit. The average Hollywood war film budget is usually between $75 million and $200 million (BBC News 2004), but the price of one battleship or jet fighter exceeds the total budget of most war films (e.g., *Black Hawk Down*'s budget was $92 million; *Saving Private Ryan*'s budget was $70 million). Instead of buying military technology, the Hollywood production company could employ computer animators to simulate hardware and personnel. However, the DOD provides Hollywood with a more cost-efficient option: co-production. By making war films with DOD and CIA support, the Hollywood production company can save on costs associated with location, below-the-line labour, software, and hardware. Mace Neufeld, a Hollywood executive who co-produced many war films with the DOD, says, "You can do anything in the movie business if the money is big enough. But it's much easier with Pentagon approval" (cited in Stainburn 1997). Hollywood studios also co-produce war films with the DOD and CIA because they believe the product will be perceived by viewers as "realistic." Paramount Pictures' co-president Tom Jacobson says being able to get state assistance adds value to the film product: "With space travel, an FBI Investigation or a counterterrorist operation, the facts make the story better, the reality makes the story better" (cited in Hail 2005).

Second, DOD and CIA subsidies give Hollywood studios less or no incentive to produce films that cast the DOD and CIA in a negative light. Phil Strub says the Department of Defense Special Assistant for Entertainment Media does not "cooperate with a production when we feel that the military portrayals are so unrealistic, so wildly unrealistic that it goes beyond artistic license, and drama, and action into a realm of such pure fancy that we think it's actually misleading" (cited in LaRocque 1997). For Strub, an unrealistic war script is one that criticizes the military and entails a modestly anti-war message, while a "realistic" war script is one that communicates a pro-military and pro-war message. "It's quite true that we look for realism, military realism, within the narrow limits of dramatic movie making. We understand that there's artistic license and these are not documentaries. So in our opinion, if you depict the US military as unrelentingly negative, that's not realistic. So yes, in a sense, we're looking for positive portrayal," says Strub (cited in Millar 2002).

Thus, for the DOD, reality is relative to the political position on war that a production company takes. A war script that entails a critical account of US military conduct, anti-war themes, or pleas for pacifism is classified as unrealistic and does not get DOD support. War scripts that glorify US military conduct, convey pro-war themes, and naturalize militarism are classified as realistic and receive full DOD support. Hence, Robert Aldrich's *Attack!* (1956) did not receive DOD assistance; its story about a US troop that kills an incompetent officer did not seem accurate or in the public good. *War Hunt* (1962), *The Victors* (1963), and *The War Lover* (1964) were denied DOD support because these films scripted soldiers as having "inaccurate" characteristics like cowardice and resistance to authority. *Apocalypse Now* (1979), *Deer Hunter* (1978), and *Platoon* (1986) – critically acclaimed films that represent a grim view of the Vietnam War – did not get DOD support because they did not reflect the DOD's version of realism (Campbell 2001). *Dr. Strangelove* (1964), *Catch-22* (1970), *Full Metal Jacket* (1987), and *The Thin Red Line* (1998) were also "unrealistic" and denied support (Campbell 2001). More recently, the DOD refused to support the modestly critical Iraq War film *In the Valley of Elah* (2007) (Barnes 2008). In all of the aforementioned examples, war's reality is in the eye of the DOD script reviewer, not in the eyes of US citizens, soldiers, or scriptwriters. The DOD and CIA film policy sends a basic message to profit-seeking Hollywood production companies: war scripts that promote the DOD and the US at war will get a big subsidy, cost less to produce, and gain the stamp of official "realism"; war scripts that question the DOD and criticize the United States at war will not be subsidized, will cost more to produce, and will be framed as "unrealistic."

While the DOD and CIA subsidies give Hollywood studios incentive to create entertainment that supports their PR and no incentive to make films and TV shows that do not, additional economic factors explain why Hollywood makes entertainment that helps the state manage opinion.

Third, Hollywood's major studios are owned by vertically and horizontally integrated mega-conglomerates that support and benefit from the broad US foreign policy goal of globalizing liberal democratic capitalism. News Corporation, Time Warner, Sony Corporation of America, and other US-based media conglomerates sit on the Council of Foreign Relations (2012), a major US foreign policy think tank. Furthermore, US media conglomerates depend on the US state for favourable media policy and regulation (see Chapter 3, this volume). Given the important links between the US state and media conglomerates and the state's support for global media business interests, it is no surprise that Hollywood studios align themselves with foreign policy and are often willing to work with and for state PR agencies. In the aftermath of 9/11, Motion Picture Association of America head Jack Valenti thus characterized the Washington Hollywood relationship as "a seamless web of unity that was really quite affectionate to behold" (CNN 2001). In a Fox News interview, Valenti called on Hollywood's creative elites to overcome their ideological divides by supporting the US state's post-9/11 foreign policy goals: "I think I feel a lot like most of the people in Hollywood. This is about our country. This isn't about ideology. This isn't about Republicans and Democrats. This isn't about President Bush. I think most of us know we only have one president at a time. And, therefore, you must rally around the cause … So I find this to be something that Hollywood, secure in the comfort of our little lean-tos along Sunset Strip, can do something for their country." In another interview, Valenti claimed that the Motion Picture Association of America would encourage "movie stars to send messages to our armed forces out there saying, 'We love you, we care about you. Thank you for what you are doing. We haven't forgotten you.'" Valenti also pledged to help the US state "prepare the American public" for the prolonged War on Terror that will "take casualties" to win. He claimed that Hollywood would make sure that "all the people are rallied behind" the United States and would "shore up that will, especially as the passions of September 11 fade over the long time it will take to exterminate Al Qaeda" (Global Viewpoint 2001).

Fourth, Hollywood supports the US Empire because of the political leanings and power of its cultural elites. This claim runs contrary to the conservative belief that Hollywood is ruled by left-wingers who impose their liberal ideology on a helpless public through the media they make (Eberhard 2004). No doubt there are some lefties in Hollywood, and some use their celebrity power to challenge conservative visions of America and air liberal protests of US war policy (Dickenson 2006). In the lead-up to the 2003 invasion of Iraq, Martin Sheen, who played the American president in *The West Wing*, launched a "virtual march" on Washington against the war. Other Hollywood liberals organized Artists United to Win without War and publicly declared that "a pre-emptive military invasion of Iraq will harm American national interests" (Walsh 2002). Michael Moore used his 2003 Oscar acceptance speech for *Bowling for Columbine* to castigate Bush for dragging Americans into Iraq: "We live in a time where we have a man sending us to war for fictitious reasons ... Shame on you, Mr. Bush, shame on you!" A Hollywood Left exists, but it is small. And the existence of liberal-minded cultural workers in Hollywood does not make Hollywood essentially liberal. For there are many conservatives in Hollywood too: Bruce Willis, Gary Sinise, James Woods, Lionel Chetwynd, and Patricia Heaton, to name a few. And the Hollywood Congress of Republicans (http://hollywoodrepublicans.com/) organize conservative film festivals such as the American Film Renaissance and the Liberty Film Festival.

The existence of conservative elites in Hollywood, however, is nothing new. Ross (2011) shows that while "the Hollywood Left has had the political glitz ... the Hollywood Right sought, won and exercised political power." To prove the point, Ross (2011) historicizes the political power of ten major Hollywood celebrities, five of them left (Charlie Chaplin, Edward G. Robinson, Jane Fonda, Harry Belafonte, and Warren Beatty) and the other five right (Louis B. Mayer, Ronald Reagan, George Murphy, Charlton Heston, and Arnold Schwarzenegger). The Hollywood left promoted various liberal reformist causes (like regulated capitalism and social democracy, worker rights, civil rights, women's rights, world peace, and internationalism). The Hollywood right fought to defend and preserve the imperial-capitalist status quo by supporting conservative causes (like unregulated capitalism and anti-communism, union-busting, low taxes for corporations, radical individualism, evangelical Christianity, war, and so on) (Ross 2011). While the Hollywood left used its appeal to win hearts and minds, the Hollywood right won the political power to govern.

Fifth, when it comes to US foreign policy, though political divisions within Hollywood suggest that it is not an ideological monolith and draw attention to how Hollywood studios and their output can be the terrain of political struggle, a space where the past, present, and future of US national values are fought over, left and right Hollywood elites are often unified in their support for the US Empire. Boggs and Pollard (2007, 16–17) write, "Many filmmakers who are ordinarily inclined toward liberal or progressive scripts on domestic issues often suddenly lose that same critical edge once matters reach the water's edge: patriotism nearly always trumps progressivism when it comes to global politics." No US film executive, filmmaker, or cultural worker thinks and acts without being influenced, if only in small ways, by the ideologies of capitalism and American exceptionalism that are part of the country in which they live. In the United States, mainstream political debate about foreign policy is framed by the two-party system, and Hollywood cultural workers rarely escape the cage of a bipartisan ideological consensus about the virtue of capitalism and American exceptionalism. Cultural workers do not need to be ordered or censored by the DOD and CIA to generate stories that convey and legitimize the US Empire's dominant ideologies. As Boggs (2005) says, Hollywood's support for war "flows from the larger political and media culture that is the repository of imperialist ideology. So attached are many Hollywood filmmakers to the combat spectacle with its enduring assumptions of superpower benevolence that they rarely wander far from the bipartisan foreign policy consensus." Intended or not, Hollywood studios capitalize on exceptionalist ideology that is already part of US society.

Sixth, Hollywood studios make media products that support US foreign policy because producers and distributors assume that this is what the majority of consumers in the United States will want. Even though Hollywood is global, the United States continues to be Hollywood's largest and most lucrative TV and film market (China is the second) (B. Strauss 2013). Films and TV shows that affirm US foreign policy and war are considered safe business decisions because they are assumed to express a deeply ingrained "common sense" among American consumers about the exceptional role of the United States in the world, while media products that convey stories that are critical of US foreign policy are considered threats to the bottom line.

Guided by industry assumptions about the exceptionalist mindset of the American consumer and marketing research that attempts to gauge what the world's largest audience wants, Hollywood studios engage in a form of self-censorship, giving US consumers what they think they want. Following 9/11, for example, Hollywood executives decided that American consumers couldn't handle films portraying "terrorism, explosions, hijackings and the kind of jokey violence popular in the films of the 1990s," so instead it backed "patriotic stories, family dramas touching on parents and children and escapist comedies" (Weinraub 2001). Furthermore, Hollywood altered, cancelled, rescheduled, delayed, or accelerated at least forty-five films and TV shows, worrying that they might upset American consumers in the years following the attacks (O'Donnell 2004). A *Law and Order* mini-series scheduled for May 2002 about a biological warfare attack on New York was cancelled. A reference to Osama bin Laden in a new CIA-CBS co-produced drama about the CIA called *The Agency* was deleted. Darren Star, creator of HBO's *Sex and the City*, had editors remove images of the World Trade Center from numerous episodes. The release of *Black Hawk Down* was sped up to sate the assumed desire of the American viewer to see US troops do good abroad, while the exhibition of *Collateral Damage* was delayed so as to avoid upsetting the American viewers' presumed distaste for scenes of terroristic violence at home (O'Donnell 2004). The premiere of *The Quiet American* – a film critical of CIA involvement in Vietnam – was delayed for a year by Miramax because executives feared a negative audience reaction to the film. Harvey Weinstein, Miramax's co-chairman, told the *New York Times* that the studio had concluded that "you can't release this film now; it's unpatriotic. America has to be cohesive and band together. We were worried that nobody had the stomach for a movie about bad Americans anymore" (cited in Weiner 2002). In sum, assumptions about the cultural values and political preferences of US consumers encourage Hollywood to produce and distribute pro-war films.

Conclusion: The Consequences of the DOD-CIA-Hollywood Complex

This chapter has shown how the growth of the DOD-CIA-Hollywood complex encourages the production of militainment, which supports the DOD and CIA's public opinion management campaigns while discouraging the flow of entertainment media that criticizes or frames these agencies in a negative way. I conclude with a brief overview of this complex's legal and political consequences.

First, the DOD-CIA-Hollywood complex arguably violates the First Amendment, which forbids the US state from favouring one kind of speech over another. The DOD and CIA selectively allocate public funds to media projects they favour while refusing those same subsidies to others (Robb 2004; Jenkins 2012). In effect, they support militarized speech (pro-DOD and -CIA films) and withhold support from pacifist speech (films that criticize the DOD and CIA). If the DOD and CIA subsidized hawkish entertainment *and* the dovish work of lefty filmmakers like Michael Moore or anti-imperialist authors like Noam Chomsky, there wouldn't be a violation. But as it stands, the DOD and CIA fund filmmakers that support their ideological goals and withhold funds from those who don't and privilege imperial speech over pacifist speech.

Second, the DOD-CIA-Hollywood complex produces cultural products that are deceptive. DOD and CIA media policy calls for "accurate," "authentic," and "feasible" portrayals of their operations, but to please the script reviewers, Hollywood studios change plot lines, scenes, character descriptions, dialogue, and even history (Robb 2004). For example, Capt. Matt Morgan, the marine corps' project officer on *Windtalkers* – a film about US Marine sergeants assigned to protect Navajo code talkers during the Second World War – called for the removal of a scene in which a marine named "The Dentist" takes a gold filling from the mouth of a dead Japanese soldier. Though this actually happened during the Second World War, Morgan said the scene had to be removed because "the activity is un-Marine" (cited in Robb 2002). Again, while state script reviewers say they are interested in realism, they uphold a militarized and securitized vision of realism that portrays their agencies in the best possible light.

Third, the DOD-CIA-Hollywood complex aestheticizes the violence of the state as a way to glorify it; its products show the world the violence of the US Empire to sanction and legitimize it, not to oppose or encourage democratic deliberation about it. Though the DOD and CIA claim to use film and TV shows to inform and educate citizens, their products are designed to manage public opinions. In effect, the DOD-CIA-Hollywood complex subverts US publicity and propaganda laws, which "forbid the government from engaging in self-aggrandizing and covert communication" (Jenkins 2012, 12) with public resources and without proper public oversight. The DOD and CIA do not always release information about the specific ways they shape film and TV scripts, and Hollywood does not always credit DOD and CIA officers for the films they help make.

These are serious political concerns, but there is no sign of the DOD-CIA-Hollywood complex being dismantled. Backed by the US Empire's power elite, the DOD-CIA-Hollywood complex will continue to simplify the history, the present, and the imagined futures of the US Empire, redact criticism of US foreign policy, revise bad wars into good ones, and turn US soldiers into caricatures of themselves.

Yet, the DOD and CIA do not *force* Hollywood to make propaganda or directly censor content that challenges official policy, but instead they give its firms economic incentives to produce content that supports their goals. This, combined with Hollywood's capitalist logics, ensures a supply of media products that glorifies the military. A few major and independent studios have now and again produced liberal films that scrutinize certain aspects of the US Empire. Since 9/11, Hollywood has produced a few films that criticize the global War on Terror and Iraq War (*Fahrenheit 9/11, Redacted*), express anxiety about the CIA's black ops (the *Bourne* trilogy), lambaste the military-industrial complex (*Lord of War*), and parody militarism (*Team America, Tropic Thunder,* and *War, Inc.*). Yet, the DOD's and CIA's subsidy program, combined with Hollywood's own profit goals, will likely ensure the continued roll out of militainment that promotes the US Empire to the world.

6
The DOD–Digital Games Complex

On July 22, 2011, Anders Behring Breivik car-bombed a government building in Oslo, Norway, killing eight people; he then infiltrated the Norway Labour Party's Worker's Youth League camp on the island of Utøya and shot 69 teenagers. Breivik, a right-wing nationalist and Christian fundamentalist, says he planned and committed this violence as a way to draw the attention of world publics to his 1,500-page manifesto "2083: A European Declaration of Independence," in which he calls on people all over the world to take up arms in a war against groups he frames as the "enemies" of "Western civilization" – that is, Muslims and "cultural Marxists." Breivik says, "The operation was not intended to kill as many people as possible, but to give 'a sharp signal' to the people that can't be misunderstood" (cited in Kremer, Stigset, and Treloar 2011). By destroying public property and assassinating the children of Norway's Labour Party, Breivik perpetrated what military strategists call "propaganda by the deed": the use of violence as a means of communication (Garrison 2004, 265). Breivik anticipated that news corporations would transform his made-for-TV terrorist attack into a spectacular global media event, and they did; through repetitive and sensational coverage, news firms transmitted the fallout of Breivik's terror – corpses, grief, outrage, confusion, analysis, and attempts at explanation – around the world, amplifying his message.

While Breivik used the symbolic power of global TV to publicize his manifesto, he prepared for his violent assault with help from a relatively new and globally profitable interactive media form: the video game. In his first court appearance, Breivik claimed he used the war-themed video game *Call of Duty: Modern Warfare 2* (*COD: MW2*) to train for his terrorist operation (Pidd 2012). In his manifesto, he says *COD: MW2* is "the best military simulator out there" and admits he sees the game "as more as a part of my training simulation than anything else." Breivik seems to derive pleasure from this militarized training tool: "I've still learned to love it though and especially the multiplayer part is amazing. You can more or less completely simulate operations" (cited in Gaudiosi 2011a). He even encourages those who might follow in his footsteps to train themselves on this game by making "arrangements ... with the local gun club, the local gym and an internet café" to host *COD: MW2* "multiplayer simulation" sessions. He says that target practice with "a real assault rifle" is important but that simulated killing with *COD: MW2* is "a good alternative as well." Breivik's terrorist attack and the trial that followed supposedly reopened the public "debate on violent video games" and presented "frightening new evidence for why the video-game industry should be more strictly regulated" (Sutter 2012). Norwegian game retailers pulled *Call of Duty* franchise games from their shelves (Phillips 2011), and a number of UK MPs called for a ban on violent video games (C. Williams 2012).

What global economic and geopolitical structures put *COD: MW2* into Breivik's hands and possibly encouraged Breivik to see *COD: MW2* as a means of training for what he perceived to be a new "global war"? For starters, *COD: MW2* is a US digital commodity that was developed by Infinity Ward and published by Activision Blizzard, two US-based digital game firms with global reach. With $775 million in sales in its first five days of circulation, worldwide sales of over 22 million copies, and gross profits nearing $800 million, *COD: MW2* is the eighth highest-grossing game of all time (Douglas 2012). The global power of US game corporations and their vast production, distribution, exhibition, and marketing networks made *COD: MW2* available to Breivik. His notion that *COD: MW2* could be used as a war training platform was learned from "armies throughout the world," the US army specifically (cited in Pidd 2012). The *Call of Duty* franchise to which *COD: MW2* and many other digital war games belong, for example, are played by US soldiers when preparing for war and following a battle, for relaxation and fun. As retired US Army lieutenant-colonel Hank Keirsey says, "I just got back from Iraq," and *COD: MW2* "was extremely popular amongst troops coming back from patrol. They'd lost friends from improvised explosive devices and it was a very entertaining medium for them" (cited in Farrier 2010). And the Marine Corps Motion Picture and TV Liaison Office lists *COD* franchise games as recipients of support. The intertwining of the profit-maximization goals of US digital game firms with the military imperatives of the US state and Breivik's violent uses of and gratification from *COD* highlight how digital war games are not just kid's stuff but part and product of the US Empire.

War video games are sometimes spoken of as only crass and simple simulations that actual wars exceed in their complexity and moral gravity. In response to Republican criticisms of his foreign policy toward Iran, for example, Obama stated, "These aren't video games that we're playing here" (Lexington 2012). Recently, the *Washington Post*'s national security commentator Walter Pincus (2014) declared that the "air war against the Islamic State is not some video game that the US military is being asked to play and quickly win." The war-is-not-a-video-game motif reminds us that war is not exactly like a video game, yet it works to obscure the existing nexus of real war and war games. Since 9/11, some of the world's most popular and profitable digital games have enabled civilians in the US and all over the world to pick up controllers and play war as imperial grunts. *Fugitive Hunter: War on Terror* (Encore, Black Ops Entertainment, and CDV Software) and *Tom Clancy's Splinter Cell* (Ubisoft) immerse players in the United States' global War on Terrorism. Gotham Games released *Conflict: Desert Storm II: Back to Baghdad* in tandem with the 2003 US invasion of Iraq. In 2003, three of the top twenty console titles in the US market were military-themed (Peterson 2005). "War-based games are doing particularly well, and I'm sure that some of it can be attributed to the current world climate," said Will Stahl, design director of the Xbox game *Full Spectrum Warrior* (cited in Snider 2004). Millions of people in the United States and around the world play video games in their leisure time, and war games are "perhaps the most important part of the global [games] market" (Singer 2010a). In addition to being a source of super profits for US digital firms, war games are the US Empire's ideal-type militainment commodities, which, forged in the nexus of the DOD and culture industry, are transforming the civic and visual experience of war (Huntemann and Payne 2010; Power 2007; Stahl 2010).

To show how, this chapter examines the DOD–digital games complex or the relationships between the DOD and digital game companies that integrate the DOD's war machine with corporate game machines, actual warfighting, and the war games civilians play. This chapter documents how integral digital games have become the way the twenty-first-century DOD conducts war, the linkages between the DOD and game corporations, and the DOD–digital games complex's production of violent video games that glorify permanent war, violence, and militarism as a way of life. The first section reviews key junctures in the development of a symbiotic relationship between the DOD and US digital corporations. The second section examines the DOD's uses of digital war games across four strategic contexts: 1) recruitment, 2) training, 3) public relations, and 4) rehabilitation. The third section examines the modalities of military realism in war simulation games. The conclusion discusses some of the potential political consequences of war games.

The DOD–Digital Games Complex: A Brief History

Following the Second World War, the DOD's research and development agencies, such as the Defense Advanced Research Projects Agency, NASA, and US universities – including Harvard, Stanford, the University of California at Los Angeles, Johns Hopkins, and MIT – began stimulating, with public dollars, the development of the US computer industry. From the late 1950s to this day, the DOD has provisioned physical space, personnel, start-up capital, and grants to technology corporations and has acted as an important driver of digital capitalism (D. Schiller 2008b).

The software and hardware of modern video games are derived in part from DOD-sponsored research and development geared toward innovating new weapons of war, and much of the hardware and software employed by the digital game industry were pioneered by and spun off from DOD subventions (Halter 2006, 4; Herz 1997, 205). From the nexus of the DOD, US technology corporations, and MIT emerged *SpaceWar!* (1962), the first video game. *SpaceWar!* connected computer interface controls with a visual cathode ray tube monitor, bridging the hand and the eye in the space of a screen. By enabling a handheld navigation device to feign the manipulation of symbols on-screen, *SpaceWar!* simulated real-time movement; it laid "the foundation of digital interactive entertainment – the crucial core design subsequent hardware and software designers would work up and sophisticate through generations of games" (Kline et al. 2003, 87).

Throughout the 1960s, the DOD poured funds into Harvard professor Ivan Sutherland's head-mounted display project, the first attempt to produce virtual reality for military training purposes (Halter 2006). By the late 1960s, Sutherland and his student Bob Sproull had coined the term "virtual worlds." These worlds enabled soldiers to be immersed in an interactive environment completely constituted by images of objects that looked real. In 1968, Sutherland and Dave Evans founded the first computer science program at the University of Utah and then established the Evans and Sutherland Computer Corporation, which constructed flight and tank simulators. These simulators were purchased and used by the DOD (Lenoir 2000), which financially underwrote the innovation of technologies inextricably tied to modelling and simulation for war gaming purposes. Many DOD-employed computer scientists became digital capitalism's premier bourgeoisie. David Rosen, a US soldier-turned-businessman, started a pinball machine company named Rosen Enterprises. Soon after, Rosen's firm merged with a Japanese electronics firm called Service Games to form Sega Enterprises Ltd. In 1966, Sega released an electronic shooting gallery game called *Periscope* (Kline et al. 2003, 90–91). In 1967, Ralph H. Baer, chief engineer at a DOD-contracted electronics firm called Sanders Associates, began working on the "brown box" prototype, which linked the screen display of the TV set to a game console. The next year the US Patent and Trademark Office granted Baer the intellectual property rights to this "television gaming apparatus," which he sold in 1971 to the TV firm Magnavox. In 1972, the Magnavox Odyssey was being sold as the first home video game system. Nolan Bushnell, another US military scientist-turned-businessman, adapted *SpaceWar!* into a coin-operated arcade game called *Computer Space* in 1970, then founded Atari and developed the popular tennis video game *Pong* (Kline et al. 2003, 90–91).

During the 1970s, the DOD contracted fledgling video game corporations to produce war simulation machines for combat training purposes. Under contract with the DOD, Baer's Kee Games developed a number of simulation machines such as the combat engineer vehicle trainer, the interactive video systems rifle training system, the light anti-tank weapons simulator, and the tank, which was later converted to a commercial Atari game (Halter 2006, 84–86). Simulation Publications, Inc., a firm started by James Dunnigan in 1969, developed a war simulator called *Firefight* under contract to the US Army Infantry School. Dunnigan was soon after recruited by US Army Lt.-Col. Ray Macedonia to help the army connect with corporate game developers. In 1977, the Office of Naval Research sponsored the Theatre Level Gaming and Analysis Workshop Force Planning conference to bring military personnel and game designers together (Lenoir and Lowood 2002, 5). In the 1970s, the US DOD developed *Maze Wars*, a first-person shooter game. This game was played by soldiers on ARPA-net, the US military prototype of today's Internet. Soon after, computer scientists at the University of Illinois developed *Empire*, the prototype of the first online multiplayer game on the PLATO computer network (built under contract to the army, navy, air force, and National Science Foundation) (Halter 2006, 127–28). In 1977, another PLATO-network war simulator, called *Panzer PLATO*, was engineered so that tank-gunners could hone their killing skills, which then inspired the Atari tank-hunting arcade game, *Battlezone*. Impressed with *Battlezone*, the army's Training and Doctrine Command contracted Atari to turn the game into a Bradley infantry fighting vehicle simulator. *Battlezone*'s virtual artillery graphics were enhanced, and handheld joysticks were replaced by a steering wheel-like device to simulate tank controls. *Army Battlezone*, an addictive and cost-saving war simulator, was the result of this modification (135). In the 1980s, the DOD continued to contract corporations to develop war simulation games while also adapting commercially available war games as modifiable training simulators. The Reagan administration emphasized the magic of the free market but actually allocated a tremendous amount of public wealth to the DOD, which continued to subsidize the United States' fledgling digital game industry (Lenoir 2000). As war-themed coin-op games and military war simulators came to resemble each other, the DOD's recruiters began hanging out at shopping mall arcades; there they used Atari's *Army Battlezone* to connect with and recruit bored working-class kids to meet their quotas. "After all," Halter (2006, 138) writes, "if operating a tank were really so much like playing a video game, then the malls of America were filled with prospective enlistees."

In 1990, the US military launched SIMnet, or "simulation network," a project initiated in 1982 by US Army Maj. Jack Thorpe (Lenoir 2000). SIMnet was developed to facilitate a collaborative training experience between soldiers in a shared virtual space (Halter 2006, 154). US corporations such as Perceptronics, BBN Laboratories Inc., and SAIC (Science Applications International Corporation) were contracted to develop SIMnet (Lenoir 2000). The army applied SIMnet's software, which trained hundreds of soldiers in a shared virtual environment, for the development of combat simulation hardware called a Close Combat Tactical Trainer. Unlike previous combat simulators that resembled clunky rides at amusement parks, the hardware was a grey fibreglass box. The interior resembled actual military combat vehicles – tanks, Humvees, and aircraft. The false windows of these machines were large computer screens, which allowed trainees to gaze into SIMnet's interactive battlefield, which simulated actual places

(Halter 2006, 154). Networked sociality comparable to that enabled by contemporary massive online multiplayer role-playing games such as *World of Warcraft* had also been established. The United States' 1990 Persian Gulf War was fought by soldiers trained on SIMnet and directed by DOD strategists trained on Operation Internal Look, another simulator (Herz and Macedonia 2002). Following the Gulf War, the Institute for Defense Analyses Simulation Center employed SIMnet to simulate the Battle of 73 Easting, in which the US 2nd Armoured Cavalry Regiment defeated the much larger Iraqi force. This gave the DOD the ability to play and replay war history in preparation for war's future (Lenoir and Lowood 2002). Nintendo, Sega, and PC publishers sold commercial games that encouraged US gamers to replay the Persian Gulf War as well. Absolute Entertainment published *Super Battletank: War in the Gulf* and *Super Battletank 2*; Electronic Arts published *M-1 Abrams Battle Tank*; Sega, with help from Lockheed Martin, released *Desert Tank*, a coin-operated war simulator.

Throughout the 1990s, the DOD continued to subsidize the US digital industry, whose firms were outmatched by Japan-based Sega, Sony, and Nintendo. In 1994, the Federal Acquisition Streamlining Act reoriented "defense research spending so that [scientific] research not only served national defense but also that it ultimately [directly] benefited the commercial sector" (Lenoir and Lowood 2002, 17–18). In addition to granting research and development contracts to US digital corporations, the DOD purchased hardware and software from these corporations (Lenoir 2000). The DOD had traditionally preferred to develop and use its own technology, but throughout the 1990s, it became a major consumer of technology sold by digital firms, routinely purchasing and modifying commercialized technology (Lenoir 2000). In the 1970s and 1980s, digital game designers envied the work of the DOD, but throughout the 1990s, DOD procurement officers walked into retail games stores and purchased digital war games that had better graphics and A.I. than their own. As Michael Zyda, the director of the Navy Modeling, Virtual Environments and Simulation Institute, explained, "We'd show our stuff to generals and they'd say, 'Well[,] my son is playing something that looks better than that, and it only costs $50'" (cited in Thomson 2004). The US Army's Simulation Training and Instrumentation Command recruited many contract-hungry corporations, like San Diego-based SAIC and Lockheed Martin, to develop hardware and software for militarized simulation games (Lenoir 2000).

And the DOD purchased commercial games, modified them, and then used them for training purposes at a substantial cost savings. They also started approaching corporate game studios and providing incentives for collaboration.

The DOD assessed the value of commercial war games based on their potential to function as combat trainers. In 1993, the Marine Corps Modeling and Simulation Management Office undertook a study of commercial war games called the *Personal Computer Based Wargames Catalog*, but none of the thirty-plus PC war-themed games were viewed as usable training tools (Halter 2006, 165). In 1996, the DOD authorized soldiers to use government-owned computers for approved PC-based war games (Lenoir 2000). Such games, following the directive of Charles C. Krulak (1997), a marine corps commander general, "provide[d] great potential for Marines to develop decision-making skills, particularly when live training time and opportunities are limited." In 1997, id Software's first-person shooter PC game *Doom* was turned into a training game. Lieutenants Dan Snyder and Scott Barnett bought a shareware version of *Doom* for $49.95 and programmed a modified version called *Marine Doom*. In a *Wired* interview, Barnett explained, "Kids who join the marines today grew up with TV, videogames, and computers. So we thought, how can we educate them, how can we engage them and make them want to learn? This is perfect" (cited in Riddell 1997).

The symbiotic relationship between the DOD and digital corporations was made official in a 1997 policy report entitled "Modeling and Simulation: Linking Entertainment and Defense," published by the National Research Council after a conference attended by representatives of the DOD, US media corporations (film, television, video games, and amusement parks), and US universities. In the report's executive summary, Michael Zyda (1997) states, "The entertainment industry and the US Department of Defense (DOD) – though differing widely in their motivations, objectives and cultures – share a growing interest in modelling and simulation." Zyda continues: "In entertainment, modelling and simulation technology is a key component of a $30 billion annual market for video games, location-based entertainment theme parks, and films. In Defense, modelling and simulation provides a cost-effective means of conducting joint training: developing new doctrine, tactics and operational plans; assessing battlefield conditions; and evaluating new and upgraded systems." The report identifies common areas of research and development such as technologies for immersion (immersive virtual worlds that allow participants to enter and navigate); networked simulation (enhanced networking capabilities enabling the simultaneous linkage of hundreds or perhaps thousands of participants in a virtual universe from different access points); interoperability standards (the production of virtual worlds that flourish and continue to develop as individual participants enter and exit); computer-generated characters (reproductions of artificially intelligent designs of human characters); and technology transfers (the dual-use hardware and software that flow between the DOD and the digital market). The report's conclusion says that, while the DOD and digital industry have different institutional "cultures" that reflect the two spheres' different "business models, capabilities and objectives" (DOD's research and development efforts are well-funded, meticulously planned according to national interests, and forward-looking, while the media industry's efforts are fast-paced, dynamic, and shaped by the flexible logics of profit), these differences could be "a source of strength." The report formalized a symbiotic relationship between the DOD and digital capitalism.

The Bush administration's declaration of a global "War on Terrorism" following 9/11 paved the way for an even tighter symbiosis between the DOD and digital game firms. While the DOD had long contracted game corporations into its operations, after 9/11, game designers started approaching the DOD and offering their services. "It was a reversal of the cultural flow," said Michael Zyda (cited in Thomson 2004). In fact, to demonstrate its patriotism and position itself to reap the benefits of DOD contracts, the Interactive Digital Software Association, a lobby group that represents the interests of Microsoft, Nintendo, and Sony, donated consoles and games to the DOD. "Our armed forces have always shown remarkable skill and dedication to protecting our country and the world from all manner of threats," said the group's president, Douglas Lowenstein. "While overseas on active duty, our troops can't enjoy many of the things they relax with at home, so we decided to bring the games they love to them as our small way of saying 'thanks'" (cited in Paschall 2002). Gifting war games to the DOD was a way that large and fledgling game companies tried to get recognized by the DOD and possibly enter its portfolio of larger allied corporations. In 2008, TopWare Interactive donated over 10,000 units of its sci-fi futuristic shooter title *Chrome Specforce*. "It is our distinct pleasure to support the armed services of our country in any small way we can," said James Seaman, managing director at TopWare Interactive (IGN 2008).

The Structure of the DOD–Digital Games Complex

At present, the DOD has a number of agencies that initiate digital research and development projects, contract digital corporations to make war games, and use or procure the war simulation games produced by US firms. The Modeling and Simulation Coordination Office – previously called the Defense Modeling and Simulation Office – administers DOD modelling and simulation initiatives and supports various agencies that do research and development, purchase, and use digital war games based on modeling and simulation technology. The most significant agencies are the US Army's Program Executive Office for Simulation, Training and Instrumentation (PEO STRI); the Simulation and Training Technology Center (STTC); the Institute for Creative Technologies (ICT); and the Modeling, Virtual Environments and Simulation (MOVES) Institute. In what follows, I describe each of these DOD war simulation research and development agencies.

PEO STRI is the US Army's centre for military simulation training technologies. Established in 1974 and headquartered in Central Florida's Research Park, PEO STRI annually supports projects valued at more than $2.7 billion. PEO STRI is responsible for thousands of procurement contracts, supports 5,500 training systems in eighteen countries, and coordinates foreign military sales in fifty-one countries. The PEO STRI's website (http://www.peostri.army.mil) declares its mission is to "Acquire and Sustain Training and Testing Solutions for the Army," and its motto is "Putting the power of simulation into the hands of our Warfighters." To empower America's warfighters, PEO STRI empowers digital capitalism, annually spending millions on the acquisition of commercialized digital war simulation hardware and software (Robson 2008; Singer 2010a). Lt.-Col. Gary Stephens, a product manager at PEO STRI says, "We own gaming for the army, from requirements through procurement" (cited in Robson 2008).

Located in Orlando, Florida, and part of US Army Research, Development, and Engineering Command (RDECOM), the Simulation and Training Technology Center (STTC) aims "to enhance Warfighter readiness through research and development of applied simulation technologies for learning, training, testing and mission rehearsal." The STTC was the driving force behind the creation of the Institute for Creative Technologies (ICT), an important research and development link between the army, the culture industry, and academia at the University of Southern California, near ICANN (the world's only Internet governing body) and Electronic Arts (one of the United States' largest video game publishers). Established in 1999 with a military grant of $45 million and sustained by military provisioned millions each year, the "ICT brings USC's computer scientists together with artists, writers and cinematographers, creating compelling and immersive training systems" (USC ICT 2011). According to its website (http://ict.usc.edu/), the ICT aims "to explore a powerful question: What would happen if leading technologists in artificial intelligence, graphics, and immersion joined forces with the creative talents of Hollywood and the game industry? The answer is the creation of engaging, memorable and effective interactive media that are revolutionizing learning in the fields of training, education and beyond." At the ICT, US soldiers and cultural workers, military technocrats and digital capitalists, and professors and public relations experts work together on a variety of military simulation games.

Founded at the Naval Postgraduate School at Monterey, California, in 2000, the Modeling, Virtual Environments and Simulation (MOVES) Institute brings together US military personnel, digital game firms, and academics "to enhance the operational effectiveness of our [US] joint forces and our allies by providing superior training and analysis products, education, and exemplary research in the field of modeling and simulation." According to its website (https://www.movesinstitute.org/), MOVES develops "combat modeling systems, training systems, virtual environments, augmented reality, web technologies, networks, and interoperability" and also "excel[s] in agents and artificial intelligence, human-computer interaction and human factors, education and distance learning."

These formal linkages between the DOD and the digital games industry are coupled with ad hoc and informal ones such as meetings, trade shows, and conferences like the I/ITSEC in Orlando, Florida. The DOD also dispatches its soldiers to advise corporate war game designers and brings in civilian game designers.

These linkages between the DOD and the digital game industry annually channel billions of dollars to the development of war simulation technology. In fact, the DOD is estimated to spend between $4 billion and $7.5 billion annually on modelling and simulation technology, research and development, and products (NTSA 2011, 5). The recipients of this public money are most often the subsidiaries of large-scale military-industrial complex corporations such as Lockheed Martin Global Training and Logistics and Northrop Grumman, but DOD research and development contracts, procurement contracts, and intellectual property support fledgling digital game firms too. Clearly, the DOD and the digital industry have a symbiotic relationship, which is framed as integral to US national security. In 2007, the US government officially recognized modelling and simulation as a "national critical technology," and House Resolution 487 acknowledged nearly seven decades of US government and especially DOD support to modelling and simulation technology in a number of areas, including nuclear testing and disarmament, space exploration, homeland security, and entertainment (NTSA 2011).

The DOD uses digital war simulation games in four strategic contexts: 1) recruitment, 2) training, 3) public relations, and 4) rehabilitation. In what follows, the DOD's uses of digital war games are examined in detail.

Recruitment

An empire at permanent war requires the DOD to be engaged in a permanent recruitment drive because most young working people do not want to risk their lives for a nationalistic ideal or be put in a situation where they must kill or be killed. And since the DOD's end of the draft and the establishment of an all-volunteer military in 1973, the department has brought billions of dollars to bear on recruitment. Throughout the 1990s, the DOD was having a hard time recruiting and retaining personnel, and it seemed that fewer US citizens wanted to "be all they could be" in the US Army. A 1996 RAND Corporation report observed that, following the fall of the Soviet Union and the Persian Gulf War, the DOD's recruiting resources had been cut, and it advised the DOD to increase its recruiting resources, specifically its advertising and public affairs budget (Rand Corporation 1996). In 1999, the army's Strategic Studies Institute issued a report entitled *Population Diversity and the US Army* in which some of the reasons for the DOD's recruitment problem are described. The collapse of the Soviet Union in 1991 gave Americans the impression that there was no perceivable threat to US national security; the unemployment rate for youth between the ages of sixteen and nineteen was quite low; and young people seemed to prefer popular brand culture to world policing and flex jobs in the creative economy to a military salary. The DOD seemed to have lost touch with US youth culture, as many young people had become skeptical of the DOD and the United States' superpower role in world affairs (Matthews and Pavri 1999).

In response to its diminishing ranks, the DOD poured more money into its recruitment drive and devised new strategies for filling its ranks with young people, many from poor minority groups (Mariscal 2007; Wyant 2012). To give poor and racialized youth an incentive to join the army, the DOD offered an immediate $3,000 bonus to every person who joined, and increased the army college fund from $40,000 to $50,000. Also, it lowered the bar for enlistment, taking in marginally unqualified recruits so long as they completed some remedial education, and raised efforts at outreach programs to tap youth culture (Matthews and Pavri 1999). Noticing how embedded brand images were in youth culture, the DOD hired private-sector marketing corporations to compete for attention with American brands and convince young people that soldiering was cool. The DOD formed a marketing strategy office (MSO), which launched multimedia "branding campaigns" that targeted young working-class and racialized men (van der Graaf and Nieborg 2003, 5–6).

The MSO's Army Marketing Research Group paid Leo Burnett, a global advertising agency whose clients include McDonald's and Coca-Cola, $100 million to rebrand the army so it would appear more attractive to young people (Dao 2001). A new logo for the army was developed and promoted through an "Army of One" multimedia advertising campaign (Dao 2001). This campaign took notes from the countercultural industry, which had long ago commodified images of dissent, by depicting the army as the site of cool and hip individualism and war as a source of exciting and self-actualizing experiences (van der Graaf and Nieborg 2003, 2). The Army of One brand was peddled to youth by recruiters at shopping malls, high schools, and NASCAR racetracks. Advertisements on TV, in movie theatres, and on billboards encouraged young people to differentiate their identities, not by buying into the lifestyle packaged by Nike or Starbucks, but by joining the Army of One brand community. The pinnacle of the Army of One recruitment campaign was a digital war game called *America's Army* (Hodes and Ruby-Sachs 2002; van der Graaf and Nieborg 2003). Of the concept, Col. Wardynski said, "A well-executed game would put the Army within the immediate decision-making environment of young Americans. It would thereby increase the likelihood that these Americans would include soldiering in their set of career alternatives" (cited in M.B. Reagan 2008). *America's Army* was designed to serve this goal.

America's Army was developed by MOVES at the Naval Postgraduate School and is currently managed by the Office of Economic and Manpower Analysis at the US Military Academy at West Point, New York. A Freedom of Information Act request by GameSpot, a video game promotional website, shed light on how *America's Army* cost the DOD $32.8 million over ten years (Sinclair 2009). US-based video game corporations like Epic Games, THX Division, Dolby Laboratories, Lucasfilm Skywalker Sound,

HomeLAN, and GameSpy benefited from this public expenditure, as the DOD had contracted them to design *America's Army* (Turse 2003a). In 2002, the DOD launched *America's Army* at E3, an annual video game convention in Los Angeles that drew about 60,000 people. There, "young gamers mixed with camouflaged soldiers, Humvees and a small tank ... A giant video screen flashed the words: 'Empower yourself. Defend America ... You will be a soldier'" (M.B. Reagan 2008). In the years that followed, the army rolled out new and improved versions of *America's Army*: in 2003, it launched *America's Army: Special Forces* to increase the number of recruits to special forces (Barbaro 2008); in 2008, it released *America's Army 3*; and in 2013, it released *America's Army: Proving Grounds* to widespread acclaim.

The army distributes *America's Army* to the world as a free download through its own website (http://www.americasarmy.com/) and as a CD-ROM at military recruitment offices, air shows, amusement parks, sporting events, and shopping malls. The DOD also licensed the *America's Army* concept to the US game firm Ubisoft for $2 million (and 5 percent of royalties per game sold), which then modified and sold commercialized versions of the game such as *America's Army: Rise of a Soldier* (2005) for the Xbox and *America's Army: True Soldiers* (2007) for the Xbox 360.

The web platform for playing *America's Army* is designed as a gateway to recruiting a new kind of post-Fordist soldier, a militarized cognitariat (Allen 2014). Before logging on to the game, users must connect through the army's website and submit personal information (Singer 2010). According to Colonel Casey Wardynski, the game's founder, "players who play for a long time and do extremely well may 'just get an email seeing if [they'd] like any additional information on the Army'" (cited in M.B. Reagan 2008). Before, during, or after playing *America's Army*, players can click a hyperlink to the army's GoArmy.com website. Once there, they can learn about the army, the financial, educational, and medical benefits of army service, "Ways to Serve," how to "Become an Officer," and the range of "Technical Careers." And if visitors to the website have questions, they can chat with SGT Star, the army's artificially intelligent "virtual assistant." Army recruiters also travel from town to town, especially to those where job growth is low and the unemployment rate is high, and introduce high school students and adults to army careers by way of *America's Army* tournaments at local community centres where recruiters serve up war games, soda, and pizza. Furthermore, the army holds *America's Army* LAN parties – game-centric virtual gatherings. "Events like LAN parties are useful because we want [the recruits] to see the recruiters as regular folks, just like themselves ... and to help future soldiers stay the course," says Army Public Affairs officer Richard Beckett (cited in M. Thompson 2008).

Soon after its launch, *America's Army* became one of the web's most popular digital war games. Its July 4, 2002, debut resulted in 50,000 downloads. In 2002 the game accumulated 4.7 million players with an average of 30,000 players logging on to the website per day (Schiesel 2005). By January 2009, the game had more than 9.7 million registered users, and gamers had spent more than 230.9 million hours playing it (Mezoff 2009). In 2012, *America's Army* had been downloaded more than 42.6 million times and was the world's most downloaded digital war game. Casey Wardynski has said that *America's Army* is "the most authentic console game about soldiering in the US Army." Yet, the game has been criticized for offering a "sanitized version of war to propagandize youth on the benefits of an Army career and prepare them for the battlefield"(Barbaro 2008). Indeed, *America's Army* immerses players in a positive story of war that is told from the point of view of the US security state.

In addition to using its own game to recruit teenage gamers, the DOD sometimes embeds recruitment ads in commercial war games. *SOCOM: US Navy SEALs* (2002), a tactical third-person shooter game franchise developed by Zipper Interactive and published by Sony Computer Entertainment, is a good example of this practice. In the early twenty-first century, *SOCOM* was one of the most widely played console war games, and according to Sony's president and CEO, Kaz Hirai, *SOCOM* was the PlayStation 2's "platform defining franchise" (cited in Peterson 2005). But it was developed with help from the military. Prior to co-founding Zipper Interactive in 1995, CEO Jim Bosler had had contacts in the US Navy SEALs and was keen on developing a SEAL-themed game. "The SEALs hadn't been done before in a big way," explained Bosler. "And they're really the most elite of the Special Forces. They're doing it all – sea, air and land" (cited in Mirrlees 2009). Zipper Interactive's vice-president, Brian Soderberg, was previously employed in engineering and management positions for US defence contractors, including Loral and Boeing. He also managed the program design of SIMnet (Mirrlees 2009). These two entrepreneurs were well-positioned to secure game development help from the Naval Special Warfare Command (NSWC) in 1999. Cmdr. May and Rear-Admiral Olson, two US Navy SEALs, were dispatched to Zipper Interactive as video game consultants; Zipper Interactive game's designers, in turn, were granted access to a SEAL base in San Diego to conduct research (Benedetti 2002).

The NSWC envisaged *SOCOM* as a promotional and recruitment tool. "There is a recruiting benefit for us, absolutely," said a US Navy spokesperson (cited in Benedetti 2002). Indeed, numerous NSWC recruitment messages were encoded in *SOCOM II*'s instruction manual. Chapter One, entitled "The Ultimate Evolution in Combat," introduces players to the rules of the game and lauds the SEALs' teamwork: "While a single SEAL is dangerous, an entire fire-team is even more so. When the smoke clears, SEALs are victorious because of teamwork." Chapter Twenty-Three, entitled "Are You Interested in a SEAL Career?," advises players to take what they've learned from playing *SOCOM* and join the real SEALs. Following a passage that glorifies the actions of SEALs, *SOCOM*'s instruction manual asks its readers

> Are you motivated to succeed? Are you determined to persevere? Are you ready to accelerate your life? NSW is seeking smart, fit, hardworking young men from all backgrounds to join its elite team of special operations forces. SEAL training is extremely demanding, both mentally and physically. It's meant to be. The end result is the cadre of the best trained-warriors in the world.

The last page in the manual encourages players "to find out more about becoming a SEAL" by visiting the NSW's official website. *SOCOM*'s main menu also features a twenty-minute recruitment video. Over the course of the narrative, SEALs discuss why they enlisted: "Before joining, I didn't feel like I was making a difference. I wanted to do something meaningful." Challenging SEAL training exercises are depicted as pleasurable tasks, like playable and conquerable levels in war games. "The tougher it gets, the funner it is," exclaims a SEAL. Images of skydiving, speedboat driving, and firing machine guns are juxtaposed with discussions of the importance of teamwork. Retired SEALs describe the "no SEALs left behind" attitude that helped them survive the wars in Vietnam and Grenada. SEAL service is represented as a job: "When it comes to action and challenge, few jobs are demanding and tough as being a Navy SEAL," declares a confident young SEAL.

Branded by Sony Computer Entertainment as a realistic war game and encoded with NSWC's branded SEAL recruitment messages, *SOCOM* is a digital mix of interactive entertainment and military recruitment propaganda. Reconciling the imagined antagonism between the US state and "the free market," *SOCOM*'s logo assimilates the US Navy SEALs' official insignia, an anchor intertwined with a golden eagle. *SOCOM* marketing material, however, carried this disclaimer: "The US Navy provided technical assistance, but does not officially endorse this product" (cited in Halter 2006, 261). But as the *SOCOM II* instruction manual and *SOCOM I* documentary show, Sony and Zipper Interactive clearly endorsed *SOCOM* as a US military branding tool.

In August 2008, the army opened the $12 million, publicly subsidized Army Experience Center (AEC), a 14,500-square-foot virtual PR and recruitment facility at the giant Franklin Mills Mall in Pennsylvania (Hurdle 2009). The Army Experience was staffed by more than twenty trained recruiters (McLeroy 2008). By October 12, 2009, the AEC had registered nearly 13,000 new visitors and contracted a total of 149 recruits (134 for active duty and 15 for reserves) (Frontline 2009). Before being granted access to the AEC, people had to first provide the army with personal information, including their name, date of birth, address, and education level. Once inside, civilians were allowed to play with the "Global Base Locator," which locates US bases around the world. At the Career Exploration Area, recruiters talked up the benefits of army careers. In the Gaming Area, civilians played *America's Army* and commercially popular digital war games for the Xbox 360 and PlayStation 3. The centre even let people try out actual training simulators for the Apache helicopter, a Black Hawk helicopter with four door gunner positions, and an armored Humvee with driver and gunner positions (Johnston 2010). "What we are doing here is reaching out to Americans, giving them the opportunity to understand their Army," said Maj.-Gen. Thomas P. Bostick, head of the US Army Recruiting Command. In 2010, the AEC closed its Pennsylvania location and moved on to another state. AEC spokesman Capt. John Kirchgessner said that digital games helped the AEC recruit teenagers and were "a much better way to share our Army story than to simply smile and dial and ask someone if they thought about joining" (cited in Johnston 2010).

By 2011, the DOD's recruitment goals were met (Blottenberger 2011). "We are very proud that our all-volunteer force can still be successful in a wartime environment," said Douglas Smith, a spokesman for the army's Recruiting Command. In the context of the economic downturn, more young people, desperate to meet their subsistence needs and secure a stable wage, entered the DOD. Digital war games like *America's Army* helped the DOD introduce military service to them as a pleasurable and exciting career option rather a life-threatening and psychologically calamitous experience. In 2008, 30 percent of all Americans aged sixteen to twenty-four gained a positive impression of the army because of *America's Army* (Singer 2010), and its players rank as the second most likely group to enlist in the army, surpassed only by kids from military families (P. Miller 2009).

Training

After being enlisted into the military, new civilian recruits are drilled physically and psychologically to establish their competencies as soldiers. Through training, the DOD transforms civilians into soldiers, hardening them to the routinized conduct of killing and making them submissive to a hierarchical chain of command. New recruits then undergo advanced training. The army, navy, air force, and marines annually train more than 3 million soldiers how to fight, complete job-specific tasks, and use military technology. The DOD annually spends billions of dollars on digital war games that train soldiers, sailors, pilots, and tank drivers to master weapons of mass destruction, develop warfighting competencies and skills, and understand new battle doctrines.

In 2002, the army trained soldiers for urban combat in Afghanistan and Iraq using a "modded" version of *Tom Clancy's Rainbow Six: Rogue Spear* (Turse 2003a). In 2003, Synthetic Environments for National Security Estimates (SENSE) trained a US-friendly business and state elite to rule and reconstruct Iraq. In "Iraq: The Computer Game; What 'Virtual World' Games Can Teach the Real World about Reconstructing Iraq," Plotz (2003) says, "These games – in which societies are built from nothing – may offer useful lessons for rebuilding broken nations in the real world." The navy uses Virtual Battle System (VBS), a war simulator derived from Bohemia Interactive Australia's commercial game *Operation Flashpoint: Cold War Crisis* (2001), to train Marines. In 2003, There Inc. signed a $3.5 million, four-year contract with the Army Research, Development and Engineering Command to develop *There*, which trained soldiers in virtual cities – Baghdad, for example – prior to their deployment (Turse 2003b). In 2006, DARWARS, an army research and development program, launched *DARWARS Ambush!*, a multiplayer, first-person shooter game that teaches troops how to respond to convoy ambushes (McLaughlin 2009). In 2007, Sentient World Simulation was used to train DOD Information Operations personnel

(Baard 2007). In 2009, another nation-building (after destruction) simulation game called *UrbanSim* was used to train battalion commanders (preparing for deployment in Iraq) to secure the virtual city of Al-Hamra. *UrbanSim* tasked players with killing insurgents, establishing civil security, and winning the "hearts and minds" of the urban civilians, all in fifteen days! In 2011, US Navy SEAL Team Six trained to kill Osama bin Laden on "computers and some live training on a mock-up environment" designed by Northrop Grumman (Burnett 2011). That same year, the army issued a $57 million dollar contract to Intelligent Decisions to develop the Dismounted Soldier Training System, powered by CryEngine, the technology behind the popular commercial PC, Xbox 360, and PlayStation 3 game *Crysis 2*. *BiLAT* and *Tactical Iraqi* and *Tactical Pashto* trained soldiers to be culturally sensitive when communicating with the Afghani and Iraqi "other." The reason for this was strategic: soldier ethnocentrism, racism, and patriotic jingoism impede the DOD's ability to win peace through hearts and minds in post-war and post-conflict occupation scenarios (McLaughlin 2009).

The DOD uses digital games to train soldiers for three reasons: 1) to save money and lives, 2) to model future war scenarios, and 3) to make training for war "fun."

Training with simulation games costs less than training with actual military machines. Actual jets, tanks, and submarines need to be refuelled; their simulated equivalents do not. Real bullets cost money and are finite; virtual bullets cost nothing and are infinite. Furthermore, by acquiring commercial digital war games and modifying them, the DOD saves on costs associated with software development. While the cost-saving benefits of digital war games to the DOD are regularly lauded by industry PR professionals, the DOD is spending more money on training simulation technology than ever before.

Training with simulators is touted as less dangerous and cheaper than live training exercises, which put people at risk of injury or death and military machines at risk of damage or destruction. During training, new pilots risk crashing planes, snipers may accidentally shoot fellow soldiers, and soldiers may hurt themselves when practising new battle doctrines. "Virtual mission-rehearsal training is the wave of the future ... It is also cost-effective. It saves on the wear and tear of equipment, much of which is already stressed by the wars," says Chris Stellwag, a marketing director for a war simulation game manufacturer (cited in Burnett 2011). Furthermore, digital games allow the DOD to model any terrain, country environment, or location in the world as a possible site of US combat and can be used to prepare US military personnel for future war or conflict anywhere in the world but without adversely affecting present-day international relationships or destroying actual physical environments. Digital games allow the DOD to train personnel in ways that are often difficult, if not impossible, in actual battlefields. Highways in Iraq and cities in Afghanistan can be simulated. Oceans filled with Somali pirates can be too. "You can't simulate the dust, dirt, heat, and stresses that you inevitably feel in combat situations," says 1st Lieut. Roy Fish, a US commander in Afghanistan, "but I think the simulation gets as close as you're ever going to get in North Carolina to Afghanistan" (cited in Martin and Lin 2011).

The DOD also uses digital war games to prepare soldiers for different battle scenarios. By allowing soldiers to play battle scenarios, explore contingencies, and discern the consequences of different actions, the war games attempt to optimize the soldier's performance in an actual war. They enable soldiers to memorize, through routine and repetition, ways of fighting so that, when they fight an actual war, they will feel and act as if they have already experienced both place and action. "Once they get into combat, they have seen almost every possible scenario," says Leslie Dubow, project director for Games for Training, the army's game acquisition program (cited in Martin and Lin 2011). The routinized experience of virtual war encourages soldiers to act and react in specific ways when fighting actual wars. As Heather Kelly, spokeswoman for Lockheed Global Training and Logistics says, "By immersing trainees into situations and environments they may face, mission rehearsal allows the armed forces to train exactly as they fight" (cited in Burnett 2011). In the lead-up to an actual war, digital war games are used to pre-emptively minimize a soldier's apprehension, doubt, or fear while maximizing his or her bravery, confidence in abilities, and calm in the execution of functions.

In addition, the DOD uses digital war games to make training "fun" for the cohort of soldiers who grew up playing commercial war games on PCs and consoles. "There's been a huge change in the way we prepare for war, and the soldiers we're training now are the children of the digital age who grew up with GameBoys," says Fred Lewis, a thirty-three-year US Navy veteran who heads the National Training Systems Association, a trade group that annually sponsors the Interservice/Industry Training, Simulation, and Education Conference (cited in Vargas 2006). Fun digital war games give soldiers an incentive to self-train. "Fun is central," contends Col. Casey Wardynski. "A fun training system means keeping soldiers engaged voluntarily. This situation makes for better training, and can even extend the training day into the barracks where soldiers can continue to train in their off-time" (cited in Halter 2006, 204). Thus, the DOD encourages soldiers to perceive war as fun and virtually preps them to experience actual killing as a pleasurable game-like activity: describing shooting an Iraqi, Sgt. Sinque Swales said, "It felt like I was in a big video game. It didn't even faze me, shooting back. It was just natural instinct: Boom! Boom! Boom! ... It was like *Halo*" (cited in Vargas 2006). Sgt. Sean Crippen, another US Iraq War veteran, described a battle in Iraq as feeling like he "was playing *Ghost Recon* at home" (cited in Vargas 2006). Also, the DOD is making war fun by equipping weapons systems with control pads comparable to those used by civilians when playing games on commercial consoles. Commercial controllers, such as that of the Xbox 360, are converted into the unmanned aerial vehicle interface soldiers use for flying and weapons operation. Mark Bigham, director of business development for DOD contractor Raytheon Tactical Intelligent Systems, says, "There are a lot of important lessons to learn from the gaming community. In the past, the military outspent the gaming industry on human-interface technology, but that's changed. It's never going to go back the other way" (cited in Derene 2008).

Some DOD digital war games designed for dual DOD and corporate use cost the US citizen much and corporations very little. At the Institute for Creative Technologies in 2001, experts from the US Army Infantry School at Fort Benning, Georgia, and designers from Pandemic Studios, a Los Angeles-based game firm, co-produced *Full Spectrum Warrior* (Slagle 2003; Turse 2003a). The Institute paid Pandemic Studios $45 million to develop the game as a realistic combat simulator and brought in combat experts from the Infantry School to provide design oversight. "We had subject matter experts assigned by the Army to the project from the very beginning all the way through," said Josh Resnick, president of Pandemic Studios. "It was the only game that actually was commissioned by the US Army" (cited in Ross and Rackmill 2005).

The game trained US infantry commanders in urban warfare tactics, but after its utility expired, the DOD gave the intellectual property rights to *Full Spectrum Warrior* to THQ and Sony Pictures Imageworks, which then sold the game to civilians in 2004. In the commercial version of the game, the US Army travels to Tazikhstan, a fictional post–Cold War Islamic enemy state wedged between Afghanistan, Pakistan, and China. Tazikhstan is ruled by Mohammad Jabbour Al-Afad, the leader of a group of Mujahideen fighters. Pitted against this Islamic enemy is a multicultural cast of US soldiers – a comedic Jew from Philadelphia, a gun fanatic from the US

South, an ex-cop New Yorker, a liberal American Muslim, and a tattooed Asian American – who resolve their small differences to defeat Al-Afad's US-hating regime. In the first year of its release, the game generated $50 million in revenue for THQ. In 2006, THQ released a sequel to the game called *Full Spectrum Warrior: Ten Hammers*.

In sum, the DOD uses video games to train its soldiers how to fight and kill while the digital corporations that co-produce such training games capitalize on DOD development contracts.

Public Relations and Censorship

Since 9/11, digital war games have intersected with DOD PR by popularizing the military and engineering public consent to otherwise controversial US war policy decisions. At the same time, the conduct of the US Empire has supported the growth of commercial markets for militainment products: consumer anxiety stemming from the state's permanent wars "over there" is responded to by companies with a supply of simulations of war made for consumers "over here."

In 2000, the Joint Chiefs of Staff commissioned Rival Interactive Games to develop *Real War* and *Real War: Rogue States*, which after 9/11 were marketed and distributed by Simon and Schuster Interactive. In the games, players have a "god's eye" surveillance view and omnipresent control of a variety of military forces in a virtual battlefield and are ordered to decimate a terrorist group called the Independent Liberation Army. A spokesperson for Simon and Schuster Interactive said, "It's a very pro-American game that shows how powerful the US military is ... And it's cathartic to blow up terrorists" (cited in Halter 2006, 171).

Another popular war-on-terror-themed game released after 9/11 was *Fugitive Hunter: War on Terror* (2003). In it, players assume the role of Jake Seaver, a former US Navy SEAL and fugitive recovery agent. Throughout the game, the player must travel around the world and kill a number of US enemies – terrorists, drug cartel leaders, militia leaders, bank robbers – who are all foils in a grand global terrorist plot orchestrated by Osama bin Laden from his hideout in Afghanistan. Michael Bell, the CEO of Encore, commented on *Fugitive Hunter*'s popularity:

> In today's world, we have to deal with the daily threat of global and domestic terrorism. For most people, there is no real way to release some of the

frustration and anger they feel toward the direct source of this terror. *Fugitive Hunter: War on Terror* allows them to take out some of this frustration and feel a sense of satisfaction by bringing fugitives to justice. (cited in Calvert 2003)

Approximately one year prior to the 2003 occupation of Iraq, Gotham Games released *Conflict: Desert Storm* (2002). In this game, civilians can play as either US Delta Force soldiers or British Special Air Services soldiers. They defend Israel by disabling Iraq's Scud missiles and assassinate Iraq's previous foreign minister, Tariq Aziz. Anticipating the unilateral military stance of the Bush administration, ads for *Conflict: Desert Storm* read, "No Diplomats. No Negotiation. No Surrender." Gotham Games released *Conflict: Desert Storm II: Back to Baghdad* in 2003, which encouraged players to join the US occupation. Like the Bush administration's propaganda apparatus, Gotham Games' product description for *Conflict: Desert Storm II* inflated the threat posed by Saddam Hussein's Ba'athist regime: "At the height of the 1991 Gulf War, 300 clicks into the heart of Iraq, you must command your squad of Special Forces operatives to strike at Iraq's evil dictator, and his fascist regime. Armed with an authentic arsenal of high-tech weapons and vehicles, your squad will face impossible odds in this battle against tyranny." If US citizens became cognizant of the historical fact that Iraq did not have or intend to use WMDs, was not a threat to US national security, and proved a relatively easy (and nearly defenseless) state to topple, players could overcome cognitive dissonance by squaring off against a hyper-real version of the Republican guard – a powerful military force more difficult to defeat virtually than it actually was.

In addition to capitalizing on the post-9/11 US invasions of Afghanistan and Iraq, digital corporations sold consumers Second World War–themed games that reproduce the myth of the "Good War" (Canby 1998). In Ubisoft's *Brothers in Arms* (2005), players assume the role of Sgt. Matt Baker, a D-Day paratrooper squad leader who moves "through real battlefields" based on "true stories" and "historical events." Acclaim Entertainment released *Combat Elite: WWII Paratroopers* (2005), which immerses players in D-Day and the Battle of the Bulge. By far the most popular Second World War nostalgia game and commercially successful franchise of all time is EA's *Medal of Honor* (*MOH*). Since 1999, EA has mined the history of the Second World

War as well as its protagonists, antagonists, and battles for content and transformed partial and selective facets of this war into games that are played worldwide. Except for *MOH: Operation Anaconda* (now called just *Medal of Honor*) (2010) and *MOH: Warfighter* (2012) (both war in Afghanistan games), *MOH: Underground* (2000), *MOH: Allied Assault* (2002), *MOH: Frontline* (2002), *MOH: Rising Sun* (2003), *MOH: Infiltrator* (2003), *MOH: Pacific Assault* (2004), *MOH: European Assault* (2005), *MOH: Heroes* (2006), *MOH: Vanguard* (2007), *MOH: Airborne* (2007), and *MOH: Heroes 2* (2007) enlist players as American heroes in the Second World War. As digital properties, all of these *MOH* war games have supported EA's business interests. At the same time, these games have inadvertently supported the DOD's promotional goals by making US military personnel look good, representing the Second World War as an inherently "good war," and embedding patriotic messages that commemorate the history of US war policy and venerate the sacrifices made by troops for America's "freedom" throughout the game. Video game corporations also invite players to blast away whatever is left of the "Vietnam War syndrome" in *Shell Shock: Nam '67* (2004), *Shellshock 2: Blood Trails* (2009), and *Conflict: Vietnam* (2004).

Many digital games glorify black operations: a clandestine act of state coercion that is outside of standard military protocol or even against the law. Published by Ubisoft, *Tom Clancy's Splinter Cell* franchise (2002–10) immerses players as Sam Fisher, an agent of the NSA. To win this game, the player must perfect political assassination – neck-breaking, throat-cutting, and sniper fire. *Mercenaries: Playground of Destruction* (2005) casts players as US mercenary fighters hired by the UN, the US, and South Korea to invade and destabilize communist North Korea, circa 2007. *Mercenaries 2: World in Flames* (2008) takes aim at Venezuela; players must invade the country and assassinate its president to gain control of the oil industry. In *Just Cause* (2006), players – cast as Rico Rodriguez – covertly invade a small tropical island comparable to Cuba called San Esperito. The goal is to overthrow the country's socialist dictator. With cash and weapons in hand, Rodriguez incites rebellions, antagonizes the island's political factions, and builds alliances with drug cartels and local rebels. In *Just Cause 2* (2010), Rodriguez topples another dictator. In all of these games, the US achieves strategic goals using coercive force, not diplomacy, and players must execute virtual war crimes. Counter-insurgency tactics, once the secret of Cold War technocrats, reappear in these games as pleasurable state conduct. The most audacious virtual legitimization of state terror is *Call of Duty: Black Ops* (2010). More than 25 million copies of this war game circulate worldwide, enlisting players from all over the world as virtual US Special Forces operatives in black-op Cold War operations (de Matos 2011). *Call of Duty: Black Ops* virtually renders extra-juridical infiltration, spying, sabotage, and killing as not only legitimate but also fun. *Blackwater* (2011), co-created by Erik Prince, former US Navy SEAL and founding owner of the mercenary corporation of Academi, lets Xbox 360 players virtually join his firm as a contractor tasked with protecting Western aid workers and dignitaries against a North African dictator. "The physical, visual and virtual feel of participating in a mission brings a level of excitement and realism to the game that is hard to match," says Prince. "And frankly, it's fun" (Gaudiosi 2011b).

Clearly, in the post-9/11 period, numerous commercially available digital war games gave consumers a virtual means to destroy terrorist threats, secure American and world security, and extend US world military power. They acted as indirect instruments of US military PR that promoted military values, ideology, strategy, and war policy to people in the United States and all over the world.

Some digital war games, however, were censored by the DOD for enabling "enemy" war play scenarios. The case of EA's *MOH: Operation Anaconda* (*MOHOA*) is instructive in this regard. *MOHOA* invites prospective players to "battle through a single-player campaign developed with Tier 1 Operators and inspired by real events" and to "fight today's war in Afghanistan in heart-pounding 24-player online warfare." EA's promotional material for the game emphasizes the EA-Tier 1 partnership that shaped *MOHOA* and says that *MOHOA* allows players to "step into the boots of these warriors and apply their unique skill sets to a new enemy in the most unforgiving and hostile battlefield conditions of present day Afghanistan." The web promo continues: "From story to dialogue to weaponry and technique, these elite Operators guided the action on the screen to help best represent the action on today's battlefield." In an "EA Showcase" interview, *MOHOA*'s executive producer, Greg Goodrich (dressed up as "Dusty," a Tier 1 hero in the game), also highlights the help from the DOD by recounting that EA was "introduced to these Tier 1 operators" who "happened to be operating in Afghanistan," and "these guys ... came into the studio and started interacting with the team," and this helped the developers "find the backbone of our narrative." Goodrich says Tier 1 operatives "helped quite a bit, not only in the story telling, but also, in terms of weapons systems, gear and just helping us keep it authentic" (Mirrlees 2014).

However, *MOHOA*'s multiplayer online mode of the game was developed without military assistance. While the single-player mode of the game enlists players as good US soldiers fighting against the bad Taliban, the multiplayer mode enables players to take up virtual arms as either Tier 1 forces or the Taliban. *MOHOA*'s enemy play option is typical, a genre convention of many violent first-person shooter games. After learning about the Taliban-play option, the DOD decided that this design feature was not in good taste, perhaps even dangerous, and so launched a flak campaign against EA, claiming that video games should not let people play as enemy forces when the United States is at war, as this is insensitive to the US soldiers actually injured or killed by the Taliban and the families and friends of these soldiers (Nowak 2010).

The brass of US-allied NATO states joined the DOD's flak of EA's game, framing *MOHOA*'s multiplayer mode as a tasteless and unpatriotic. The United Kingdom's defence secretary, Liam Fox, said it was "shocking that someone would think it acceptable to recreate the acts of the Taliban against British soldiers ... It's hard to believe any citizen of our country would wish to buy such a thoroughly un-British game. I would urge retailers to show their support for our armed forces and ban this tasteless product" (BBC News 2010). Canadian defence minister Peter MacKay chimed in: "Canadian and allied efforts to bring peace and stability to Afghanistan, a country that has known only war and oppression for far too long, is not a game," he said. "I find it wrong to have anyone, children in particular, playing the role of the Taliban. I'm sure most Canadians are uncomfortable and angry about this" (cited in Wylie 2010).

The DOD (and NATO) flak campaign was followed by censorship of the game on US military bases. The army, navy, air force, and coast guard banned all retailers on all of their bases from selling *MOHOA*. "Out of respect to those we serve, we will not be stocking the game," said Maj. Gen. Bruce Casella, commander of the Army and Air Force Exchange service. "We regret any inconvenience this may cause authorized shoppers," he continued, "but are optimistic that they will understand the sensitivity to the life and death scenarios this product presents as entertainment" (cited in Sulzberger 2010). "We have done this [censorship] out of respect for our men and women who serve," said Kathleen Martin, a spokesperson for the US Navy. The DOD also suggested EA remove the game from the marketplace and redesign it to avoid further offence.

EA responded to the DOD's flak and censorship campaign by saying the game was intended to promote the US war in Afghanistan, not the Taliban. EA spokesman Jeff Brown said, "This year's game, set in Afghanistan, pays homage to today's soldier" (cited in Sulzberger 2010). Brown even emphasized the game's deference to the military by reiterating that several war veterans participated as consultants on the game's design. Perhaps fearful that the DOD would not assist its future war game developments and desperate to deter and contain a symbolic threat to *MOH*'s brand equity, EA eventually caved to DOD pressure. EA removed the Taliban play option from the multiplayer mode and renamed the Taliban avatars "opposition forces." Though the DOD put top-down pressure on EA to make this change, Goodrich publicly claimed that EA itself had decided to modify the game content in response to bottom-up "feedback" from the friends and family members of fallen soldiers. Feigning responsiveness to the tastes and preferences of this consumer group's political sensitivities, Goodrich said this group is "a very important voice to the *Medal of Honor* team," a voice "that has earned the right to be listened to" and that "we deeply care about," especially "because the heartbeat of *Medal of Honor* has always resided in the reverence for American and Allied soldiers." Goodrich continued, "We are making this change for the men and women serving in the military and for the families of those who have paid the ultimate sacrifice – we appreciate you, we thank you, and we do not take you for granted. And to the Soldiers, Sailors, Airmen and Marines currently serving overseas, stay safe and come home soon" (cited in Snider 2010). Overall, EA's publicity aimed to frame itself as supportive of the DOD's war policy and respectful of military personnel.

The case of *MOHOA* shows the DOD's power to shape the content of digital war games and discourage the flow of games it disapproves of. The DOD's flak and censorship campaign against *MOHOA* conveyed a subtle directive to EA and other US video game companies: design games that enable people to play as protagonist US and NATO allies and you will receive DOD support, business, and acclaim; design games that enable people to play as America's enemies and you will lose our support and face public ridicule. From this, it seems that digital war games that enable people to play as current enemies of the United States and commit virtual violence against US and allied forces will be condemned and censored by the DOD, while digital games that allow people to commit virtual violence against non-US enemy states and peoples are sanctioned to freely flow in media markets. A clear double standard exists that highlights a contradiction in the argument to censor violent video games as a way to prevent violence among America's youth (assuming that violent games cause players to act violently). The argument tends not to be for the censorship of all violent video games but, rather, for the censorship of some video games whose simulated violence is said to affront good taste, community norms and standards, and, in some respects, state power. Games that enable players to commit virtual violence on the home front (e.g, *Grand Theft Auto*) or on foreign battlefront against the US state (i.e., *MOHOA*) are the sites of moral panic. But those games that enlist players as agents of state coercion and compel them to invade, occupy, attack, and kill others inside and beyond the US territory easily pass through the conservative screens of moral panic. Perhaps this is because the US Empire requires this type of violence – and the normalized violent attitudes and behaviour it enables – as a functional, even necessary, part of its maintenance and expansion.

Rehabilitation

Virtual war may be played as fun, but real war causes psychological trauma. When soldiers experience trauma during war – seeing a comrade shot in the face, killing a civilian, being deafened by a blast, or ambushed while sleeping – their minds are unable to fully assimilate the shocking experience that occurs. Weeks, months, and even years later, the traumatic experience returns to them as memories, nightmares, flashbacks, and hallucinations. During the US Civil War, traumatized soldiers were said be suffering from "hysteria"; during the First World War, they had "shell shock"; in the Second World War, veterans experienced "combat fatigue." Following the Vietnam War, the American Psychiatric Association classified it as post-traumatic stress disorder (PTSD), a consequence of real war. Hundreds of thousands of US war veterans and active duty personnel suffer from PTSD, which is a cause of suicide. Almost every sixty-five minutes, a US veteran commits suicide, and in 2012 there were 349 suicides among active-duty personnel, almost one per day (Haiken 2013). More US soldiers kill themselves because of the traumatic experience of war than are actually killed in combat (Haiken 2013).

One of the DOD's technological fixes to the problem of soldier suicide is video games. So while the DOD uses war games to recruit and train soldiers to kill, it also uses digital war games to prevent soldiers from killing themselves. Invented by Albert Rizzo, a clinical psychologist at USC and affiliate of the Institute for Creative Technologies, *Virtual Iraq* is an "immersion therapy video game" designed to help Iraq war veterans cope with PTSD by enabling them to virtually replay parts of the war until they are manageable (Halpern 2008; Ziezulewicz 2009). The DOD uses other digital games to curb soldier suicides (suicide scenarios are simulated to help soldiers confront, work through, and overcome suicidal thoughts) and to help soldiers reintegrate into society (everyday life scenarios – for example, family and interaction with friends – are simulated to re-equip soldiers with pro-social competencies). The Afghani and Iraqi victims of the United States' wars, however, receive no such virtual therapy and their suffering remains largely invisible.

Modalities of Digital Realism

The DOD-digital games complex's commercial war games are marketed to consumers as being "realistic." "The big trend has been more realistic (shooting) games where it is actually similar to real-life combat," reports David Cole, an analyst for DFC Intelligence, a game industry research firm (cited in Snider 2004). "Realism" is used by game firms to distinguish the games they sell from those produced by competitors. To give their digital war games an aura of realism, game production companies enlist DOD personnel as design consultants, as we have seen above. By co-producing games with the DOD, video game firms are able to brand their war games as "realistic" in intense market wars for consumer dollars. For example, in the 2011 market war between EA's *Battlefield 3* and Activision's *Modern Warfare 3*, EA CEO John Riccitiello claimed that *Battlefield 3* was "more authentic" and therefore better (Brightman 2011). *SOCOM II*'s box reads, "Association with the Naval Special Warfare Command ensures realistic SEAL gameplay and mission design," and "the title offers a detailed look at what it is like to be a real Navy SEAL."

The DOD and game corporations try to cultivate consumer desire for the digital war games they manufacture by emphasizing their "realism" and encourage players to assess a game's quality according to militarized reality criteria. On the Yahoo Answers! website, players recently debated which digital war game is "most realistic." Dabomb88 says *Call of Duty 4: Modern Warfare* (2007) is "the most realistic" because it "was written and designed with the US Army as well as the British SAS in mind." IndieMalu93 claims that *America's Army: Rise of a Soldier* (2005) "is absolutely the most realistic war game out there ... People are shooting at you every second of the game, and you need to break, you use real guns and real army tactics, in realistic fiction-based Iraq/Afghanistan 2000-era. It's made by the US Army."

The DOD marketing hype that surrounds digital war games with reality claims, however, is misleading. Though virtual wars attempt to "create a fidelity between the representation and reality of war" (Der Derian 2001, xx), they fail to do so. Few digital war games abide by the rules of engagement or deal with interpersonal challenges and even fewer feature civilians. They do not immerse players in a "real war" but enable *virtual wars*. A "real war" refers to the scents, sights, sounds, and feelings of war as it is physically and cognitively experienced by actual soldiers and civilians, who face physical injury, emotional trauma, and death. A virtual war refers to simulation models of war that are pleasurably played by civilians far removed from actual battles. In real war, death is final; in virtual wars, death is infinite. Gamers can pause, save, and replay virtual war experiences; soldiers deployed in real wars cannot. Gamers feel little remorse for their virtual war crimes, while soldiers with a moral conscience develop PTSD. Gamers do not shoot real guns, kill real people, and destroy entire cities, but soldiers do. The virtual wars packaged by digital war games recruit and train civilians and soldiers to support or participate in real wars, but they are abstracted from its embodied, psychological, and geographical consequences. Digital war games immerse their civilian players in a simulated substitute for a brutalizing reality that only soldiers know and feel.

That said, though digital war games are not real wars, they are designed with different "modalities" of realism: geopolitical and temporal, audiovisual, functional, and subjective (Halter 2006; King 2007).

Digital war games, for example, claim to have real-world referents. The real-world *geographical referent* is a world system of antagonistic nation-states in which the United States is the superpower. The *temporal referent* point is the past, present, and future of war. Bestselling franchises such as *Call of Duty*, *Medal of Honor*, and *Battlefield* are based on the First World War. Others claim to simulate the Second World War, the Cold War, the Vietnam War, and those in Afghanistan and Iraq. *Six Days in Fallujah* (2009), for example, was co-designed by dozens of US 3rd Battalion 1st US Marines who in 2004 fought a six-day battle in this Iraqi city. Some games pre-emptively anticipate future war scenarios. In *Call of Duty 4: Modern Warfare* (2007), players fight a new Cold War against Russia. The future-oriented referent, combined with the future-orientation of game play, legitimizes the United States' pre-emptive security logic, which claims that America is permanently threatened by terrorist networks and rogue states. "Mission 58: Assault on Iran" of *Kuma/War* (2004), a game whose missions are modelled on US news stories, allows gamers to invade Iran to destroy its nuclear energy facilities. EA's *Battlefield 3* (2010), which sold 5 million units in its first week globally, is also set in Iran.

Digital war games also claim *audiovisual realism*. The sounds of real US military personnel firing weapons, walking and running, and speaking and shouting are recorded and patched into game play, and the faces and physical movements of soldiers are modelled using face and body scanning technologies.

Descriptive or *functional realism* is also a factor, as much gameplay is modelled on actual US military tactics and strategies. *Close Combat: First to Fight* (2005), a game co-produced by the US Marines and Destineer Studios for use by the US Marines and civilian gamers on the Windows, Macintosh, and Xbox platforms, simulates marine tactics. Many digital war games simulate network-centric warfare (Cebrowski and Garstka 1998). Using weaponized information and communication technology and small and flexible fighting units, US soldier-cognitariats conduct reconnaissance missions, hostage rescue missions, and clandestine attacks. Just-in-time interventions, customized demolitions, and targeted snipes are routine. In multiplayer environments, information age soldiers must work together to collaboratively fight and swarm enemies.

Digital war games furthermore claim *subjective realism*. They construct different types of protagonists – soldiers, space-warriors, tank-gunners – for players to identify with and actively manipulate based on military discourses and practices. Militarism is a patriarchal enterprise (Enloe 1989), and military service is often framed as a way for men to prove their masculinity. The games most often reinforce patriarchal militarism by casting players in hyper-masculine soldier roles (Kline et al. 2003, 254). Digital war games model DOD "cyborg-soldier" prototypes too. *Ghost Recon: Future Soldier* (2012) – developed by Ubisoft and inspired by the US Army's Future Soldier research and development initiative – claims to put players in "the shoes of a Special Forces soldier in a near future scenario" (Brandon 2011). The US Army and *Ghost Recon*'s soldier protagonist is equipped with thermal vision, unmanned aerial vehicles, augmented reality, real-time audiovisual intelligence feeds, and adaptive camouflage.

Digital war games additionally claim *experiential realism:* gameplay is designed as immersive and interactive so as to give players the real-time feeling of being in war. Indeed, games are designed to facilitate a qualitatively different sensorial experience than that offered by war films and TV shows. Distinct from spectators, players actively move through, as opposed to being moved by, the virtual images of combat displayed before their eyes. Digital war games engage and extend the player's corporeal senses – sight, hearing, and touch – in ways that war films and TV shows do not. The games' pixelated gore captures sight; the mechanized firing of guns and screams of injured enemies mobilize the ear; the controller mobilizes touch with shaking, rattling, and vibrating in tandem with the audiovisual military action in which the player is immersed. The interplay of the digital war games' interactive apparatus (controller) and immersive structure engages and extends players' senses into a battlespace of virtual war, which feeds back into the place of play, seamlessly connecting the two spheres. The content (messages about why, who, and how the United States fights) and form (the kinds of war play) work together as well, blurring actual and virtual wars. As Huntemann and Payne (2010, 3) say, "Instead of watching military professionals execute their routines and maneuvers from a distance, civilians are invited to play the military, using the very same technologies, tactics, and discourse employed by the Armed Forces in simulated and, more pointedly, real contexts." Bogost (2007, 142) states, "Videogames that engage political topics codify the logic of a political system through procedural representation." Digital war games integrate players into a rule-bound "procedural rhetoric" of how the US military fights. Mike Thompson (2008, 144) elaborates:

> In many ways, the structure of military computer games mimics the process of actual military planning and execution. The introduction to the game explains the grand strategic vision and the aim of the overall mission, whilst at the beginning of each mission or level within the game, the context of the mission is set, the player is given objectives and aims to be achieved, is equipped with the assets that are needed to achieve these aims, and is informed on the challenges that he will be faced with. In addition, games often begin with a training level which introduces the player to the tactics which are needed in order to successfully complete the game. The procedural logic of military computer games is therefore revealed by these structuring rules; the player is presented with an objective, and then guided and instructed by the game in how best to achieve this objective using the tools at his disposal. In order to complete the game, the player must learn and internalize these rules of warfare and therefore learn how to win wars according to the logic of the game.

This "procedural logic" ensures that the interactive experience of war games does not facilitate free-flowing experiments in identity or pose threats to the DOD's virtual command and control structure. Just as actual US soldiers must obey a military command structure, with its rules, regulations, and technologies, virtual soldiers must conform to the game's design structure. In most digital war games, choices are engineered outcomes, options are rules, and autonomy exists within a pre-given structure. These games require virtual soldiers to obey orders, follow rules, and kill to complete a mission. Obedience and deference to the code's power let them play another round, get high scores, proceed to the next level, and win the game. Virtual soldiers who refuse to submit to this structure die, lose, and cannot move forward. Sgt. Sean Crippen puts the power of militarized procedural rhetoric more bluntly: "You're practically doing the same thing: trying to kill the other person. The goal is the same. That's the similarity" (cited in Vargas 2006).

Conclusion: The Consequences of Digital War Games

Digital war games are an integral part of the US Empire's ways of life and war. The DOD–digital games complex encompasses symbiotic relationships between the DOD and digital corporations that cover research and development funding, procurement contracts, and war game co-productions. The DOD utilizes digital war games to recruit teenagers as soldiers; train soldiers how to fight; promote its personnel, policy, and practice; and rehabilitate traumatized war veterans. At the same time, the DOD supports the economic growth of the video game industry by allocating billions of public dollars to research on and development of simulation and modelling technologies for military purposes and supports this industry as a big consumer of its products. By acting as a market for war games, it gives video game companies financial incentive to design games that glorify war and disincentive to make games for peace. The DOD's provisioning of assistance to video game corporations that make war games further encourages them to make war games that cast the DOD in a positive light. And the wars the DOD fights support this industry, not only as a source of project ideas for new war games, but also as a generator for a digital market of consumers that want to buy and virtually play war, as it is really happening. The DOD is thoroughly intertwined with digital capitalism's profit goals; the business of war feeds an expanding marketplace of violent war games, and this marketplace feeds back into the virtual veneration of state coercion, as well as the DOD's command and control networks.

While digital war games attempt to simulate war, they fail to capture the traumatic experience of war by encouraging players to perceive real and simulated violence as the same thing. Yet, as Scarry (1985, 83) reminds us, "The severe discrepancy in the scale of consequence makes the comparison of war and gaming nearly obscene, the analogy either trivializing the one or, conversely, attributing to the other a weight of motive and consequence it cannot bear." Indeed, violent war games risk desensitizing players to war's embodied horror and deterring public deliberation about war. The efficacy of the citizen in democracy requires both a space in which public deliberation about state violence can occur and a clear demarcation between the political role of the citizen (who deliberates) and the apolitical role of the soldier (who takes orders) (Stahl 2006). But digital war games close the gap between civilian and soldier and are significant tools of propaganda that disinform people about the reality of war all the while promising to immerse them as virtual citizen soldiers in it (Stahl 2006, 2010). Digital war games not only encourage a "militarized worldview" (Payne 2009, 241) but also prepare players, ideologically and practically, for the empire's ongoing wars, transform war into something fun while obscuring its trauma, and glorify the pleasures and thrill of war while hiding its human horrors. The DOD–digital games complex sells to players "a sanitized fantasy of war whose seductive pleasures are felt at the expense of the capacity for critical engagement in matters of military might" (Stahl 2006, 126), and its games bring the "citizen into proximity to a vision of the soldier and battlefield," all the while moving them "further away" from the point of public deliberation about state violence and toward the point of this violence's execution (Stahl 2010, 65).

Why, then, might so many US civilians on the home front be so attracted to video games that simulate war on global battlefronts? The reason is possibly that the games give civilians who will likely never face a draft or directly experience a real war an opportunity to pretend to be a US military hero. Civilians can play through and purge anxieties associated with US Empire maintenance and expansion in a world in which enemies never go away, threats are permanent, and war is the norm. They can temporarily resolve their worry about the waning status of US military power by exaggerating its invincibility. In digital war games, the US is the exceptional state, and the DOD easily occupies countries, defeats multiple enemies, and wins wars on many fronts, all in a matter of hours.

As global blowback against the US Empire mounts, the virtual veneration of the empire's violence may further exacerbate anti-Americanism.

Mercenaries 2: World in Flames (2006) enlists players in a violent coup of a Venezuelan president (loosely modelled on the late Hugo Chavez), raising the hackles of Venezuelan congressman Ismael Garcia, who said the game was part of a US campaign of "psychological terror" (Sanders 2006). *Call of Duty: Black Ops* challenged players to kill Fidel Castro (prior to his actual death), fanning the flames of Cuban anti-Americanism and inspiring the Cuban government to issue this invective: "What the United States government did not achieve in more than fifty years, it now tries to do virtually" (Gabbatt 2010).

The emerging criticisms of the US Empire's war games are sometimes met with smug reminders that they are "just games" and shouldn't be taken so seriously. Yet, one wonders how the US state would respond if Venezuela or Cuba sold millions of copies of video games all over the world that enlisted people in heroic missions to assassinate the American president, eliminate the 1 percent that currently run the country, nationalize the big industries, and gear production to meet social needs? Would such violent video games be casually dismissed as "just games," not anti-American politics by virtual means, and allowed to freely flow in markets?

However, digital war games can offer some criticism of war. As of late, a few video game companies have cashed in on the sorrows of the empire, perhaps in response to the public's growing war fatigue. *Special Ops: The Line* (2012), for example, questions the means and ends of US war policy in the Middle East and grapples with war's horrors for civilians (who are indiscriminately massacred) and soldiers (who suffer PTSD) (Payne 2014). This game might be capable of turning players against war or, at least, encouraging them to develop a critical view of it (Morwood 2014). And *This War of Mine* (2014) casts players not as soldiers but as innocent civilians struggling to survive an urban war as it is happening; scavenging for food and securing shelter, not killing, is key to winning. As novel and innovative as these apparently anti-war games are, they are not the norm; they circulate as aesthetic anomalies and creative exceptions to a digital gaming culture that, ruled by symbiotic market and military relations, marches lockstep with the US Empire.

Conclusion
US Empire, Cultural Imperialism, and Cultural Policy, at Large

Herbert I. Schiller passed away on January 29, 2000, a little less than a year before the 9/11 terrorist attack and the Bush administration's declaration of a global War on Terrorism. Schiller's final book, *Living in the Number One Country: Reflections from a Critic of American Empire*, was published soon after. Schiller did not live to see the drastic expansion of the US national security state in the post-9/11 period and the new alliances between the US state and media corporations. Nor did he see the United States' invasions of Afghanistan and Iraq, which tore off the seemingly neutral mask of liberal internationalist globalization theory to reveal the empire beneath. Throughout this book, I've tried to show how the geopolitical-economic structures of the US Empire's culture industry that Schiller analyzed long ago haunt the world system in old and new ways.

I conclude this book by elaborating on its key claims, which may be useful to further critical twenty-first-century research on the US Empire's culture industry and cultural imperialism.

The world system continues to be a structural hierarchy of states – dominant imperial powers, sub-imperial or middle powers, and subordinate ones – that in pursuit of their interests engage in conflicted and sometimes collaborative relations with each other. In this world system, the United States is the economically, militarily, and culturally dominant imperial power. As a capitalist empire without colonies, the US state's struggle to achieve its national interests in world affairs supports the deterritorializing economic goals of US corporations as they pursue their worldwide profit interests. And as the state facilitates and legitimizes the business interests of US corporations around the world, the vast expansion of state and corporate power is legitimized by American exceptionalism, a culture ideology that represents the United States in comparison to other countries as fundamentally different and superior and having a special mission to liberate or save peoples from themselves and bad or threatening others.

Twenty-first-century declinists say the United States is a waning empire due to the rise of the BRICS and because of over-extending the military, neoliberal dysfunction, and debt. Declinists are correct to say that the United States is not as powerful as it once was in this still hierarchical world system of many competing and sometimes collaborating states, but for the near future, the United States will likely retain its position as the world system's top imperial power. We can recognize the remarkable rise of the BRICS without denying the persistence of the US Empire. Nevertheless, as non-US corporations align with their host governments and strategize to strengthen their economic position outside their home markets, conflict between the United States and other nation-states will likely continue to grow due to competitions to control markets, especially in the world's poorer regions. As China rises and other states try to counterbalance the US Empire, the US state will try to integrate them into its world liberal democratic capitalist order; if it fails to deter a new round of rivalry, another world war may be on the horizon. Driven by corporate competitions to control scarce resources, labour, and emerging markets, interstate conflicts are for now taking the form of overt and covert military, economic, and ideological warfare. In response to the antagonistic character of the world system, the US Empire will likely continue to try to impose order and integrate rivals and incumbents into a political-economic and ideological framework that it is comfortable with and from which it will continue to benefit. There is no guarantee the United States will be able to do this, but the historical record of its conduct suggests that it will certainly try.

The US Empire is internally ruled by power elites from the commanding institutions of the US state, military, and corporate sectors. Decision-making power – the power to decide for everyone else what the "national interest" is and is not – is highly concentrated (Domhoff 2013). US elites are not always unified on domestic issues, but with regard to the maintenance of the United States' top position, there is often a broad consensus. So long as the United States is an empire, US state and corporate cultural imperialism will persist in the form of various coercive and persuasive means and practices that aim to impose and elicit consent to a way of life (i.e., production modes, political and legal norms, policies, language, customs, and ideas) packaged as "America" in other countries, with the goal of influencing and changing their ways and without reciprocation of influence by them.

The US Empire's culture industry, a significant instrument and agent of US cultural imperialism, is constituted by the confluence of US state attempts to engineer consent to America and US foreign policy in the United States and the wider world and transnational corporate media efforts to sell cultural commodities in markets. Though the US government and US media corporations are different and driven by different interests (the US state is motivated by "national security" and media corporations by profit), there are symbiotic relations between them in cultural imperialist campaigns.

The US Empire's culture industry remains integral to US economic, military, and ideological power. From the Creel Committee of Public Information in the First World War, to the Office of the Coordinator for Inter-American Affairs in the interwar period, to the Office of War Information in the Second World War, to the United States Information Agency in the Cold War, and to the Office of Public Diplomacy in the US War on Terror, the executive branch has consistently established, through periods of national security crisis and war without end, public diplomacy agencies to promote America around the world.

US public diplomacy uses the culture industry's public relations techniques to build global support for US moral leadership, outsources "Americanization" PR campaigns to the culture industry, and shuttles its products to the world. Public diplomacy is a process of influence by which the US Empire's culture industry imposes on publics in other states ideas about America with the goal of making them more like or accepting of it. In the process, it subverts the sovereignty of non-US states to protect their own national cultures. Public diplomacy uses magazines, newspapers, books, radio programs, TV shows, films, video games, and websites to communicate the virtues of the US societal model to citizens in other countries, and much public diplomacy discourse frames the people who disagree with US foreign policy as having a flawed understanding of America that needs to be changed.

Dubiously, public diplomacy aims to change public perceptions of the US Empire without changing the foreign policy decisions that may cause anti-American feelings. So long as public diplomacy's words do not reflect the concrete deeds of the US state, its practitioners will face difficulties fulfilling their objectives and successive rounds of anti-American blowback. Though public diplomacy is sometimes talked about by its practitioners as something that fosters dialogue and builds mutually beneficial relationships and greater cross-cultural understanding, most public diplomacy campaigns – save cultural exchanges (Snow 2008) – aim to persuade publics to support the US Empire. For the most part, public diplomacy does not listen to public opinion so as to responsively change US foreign policy, but aims to know public opinion so as to better control it. The US, however, is not the only state involved in public diplomacy. The BRICS nations and many more countries operate public diplomacy agencies that will, in the future, likely conflict with the United States' soft push to universalize its particular interests.

The United States is home to the world's largest and most economically powerful media conglomerates such as Comcast-NBCUniversal, The Walt Disney Company, and News Corporation and is also home to some of the world's most powerful digital media giants like Apple, Microsoft, IBM, Google, eBay, Amazon.com, Facebook, YouTube, and Yahoo Inc. These conglomerates compete and collaborate with non-US culture industries in pursuit of global market control. To increase profits and establish a transnational network that enables the flow of US cultural products, the US culture industry has integrated non-US media firms by acquiring them and by coordinating cross-border production, distribution, and exhibition deals. To tap into transnational viewer tastes and preferences, the US culture industry designs post–American media forms like blockbuster films, global-national TV formats, and glocalized lifestyle brands. Though these products do not carry explicit representations of America to the world, they support an ideological environment in which capitalism and consumerism may appear to viewers as the ideal, though no longer an exclusively American, way of life.

The global prosperity of the US culture industry is not simply the result of free-market logics but is also supported by the geopolitical power of the US state, whose media policies are often shaped by media lobbies. Beholden to lobby pressure and influence, the US state supports the intellectual property rights of the culture industry, allocates millions of dollars in subsidies to its firms each year, enables firms to further centralize and converge their operations, and opens markets to their dominance by pushing audiovisual trade liberalization, deregulation, and privatization of telecommunications and public broadcasters in other countries bilaterally and multilaterally through the International Telecommunications Union, the World Trade Organization, the International Monetary Fund, and the World Intellectual Property Organization. The effects of US media imperialism – the intertwining of the US state's pursuit of its national interests with the business interests of the US culture industry – are the persistence of a largely one-way flow of US cultural products and increasing returns to the US culture industry. In response to these effects, non-US states will continue to devise strategies for protecting and promoting their national culture industries, which will drive further interstate culture industry policy and regulatory conflicts.

Even though the US state facilitates and legitimizes the global profit interests of media corporations, the commercial output of these corporations (i.e., the content of the news and entertainment) does not necessarily or automatically contribute to state-defined war PR and propaganda goals. Moreover, many non-US media corporations represent the world in ways that may challenge or offer counterpoint to the strategic geopolitical interests of the US national security state. The growth of non-US culture industries makes it impossible for the US Empire to totally control the global communication and cultural scene, and it finds itself competing for attention, credibility, and prestige with a number of state and non-state media actors; some are friends, and others are foes.

To try to get US media companies to produce cultural products that frame the US state in ways that do support official war policy, assuming that media markets will fail to generate PR externalities on their own, the national security state, especially the DOD, employs public affairs agencies that link, overtly and covertly, with the US culture industry's conglomerates. The result of such linkages since 9/11 has been a vast expansion of the military-industrial-communications complex and with it the DOD's power to influence public opinion through the news media, popular TV shows and films, and video games. The DOD–news media complex, the DOD-Hollywood complex, and the DOD–digital games complex point to a number of symbiotic relationships between the national security state and culture industry firms that support the production, distribution, and exhibition of militainment products that aim to engineer public consent to war as a normal way of life. Though the DOD and media corporations are motivated by different priorities, the workings of these complexes demonstrate how the DOD recruits media corporations to fulfill its publicity objectives and how media corporations often rally round the DOD to realize their profit interests. The casualty of these complexes is a media that serves democracy and mainstream cultural products that contest and forward alternatives to war as a way of life.

In a democratic society, the news media should act as a "watchdog" of the government and corporate actors that make and shape war policy and inform and educate citizens about war with a range of veracious viewpoints. Yet, the DOD-news media complex gears news media content to serve the DOD's engineering of public consent to war and the corporate goal of maximizing profits. To get the news media to set its policy agenda and frame representations of war in the way it wants, the DOD sources journalists with information about war and national security policy using a number of strategies. The DOD deploys public affairs officers to the news media, embeds journalists with troops, uses information centres to gather international reporters, generates its own video news releases, runs its own cable TV channel, and stages militarized pseudo-events to create militainment hype and buzz. The DOD also exerts subtle forms of censorship over journalists and has harassed and even killed news workers in war zones (Paterson 2014). These components of DOD information operations interact with the capitalist logics of news media corporations – concentrated ownership, advertising dependency, professionalism, competition, and exceptionalist ideology – to shape the definition of what is newsworthy and what is not. In contexts in which there is an elite consensus about war, the DOD's information operations and the news media's profit motive make war propaganda the nation's most newsworthy and commercially viable product.

Democracy requires an investigative, pluralistic, and critical press that is free from political and corporate control, especially in times of war. But the notion that an overly oppositional news media exists to impede the DOD's war aims is invalid, as the relationship between the DOD and news media corporations in times of war and elite consensus is clearly cooperative, not conflicted. The DOD–news media complex supports the engineering of public consent to imperial war policy and encourages citizens to passively watch and enjoy war as a commercial spectacle while basking in profit and power. Yet, this complex faces challenges to its frames by US media reform groups like the Free Press, alternative media organizations like The Real

News and Democracy Now!, the news media firms of other countries like Russia Television and Al Jazeera, and activist Internet users.

Hollywood studios produce a lot of TV shows and films to entertain and amuse consumers in markets all over the world with the goal of making their corporate parents as much money as possible. The DOD-Hollywood complex manufactures entertainment that aims to both make the DOD look good and get Hollywood studios a lot of money. The DOD has developed significant capacity for influencing how their agencies, personnel, and operations look on screens, big and small, by linking their liaison offices to Hollywood companies. Hollywood studios have access to DOD equipment, knowledge, and even personnel in exchange for the power to tinker with films and TV show scripts. The giant subsidization policy of the DOD's public affairs agencies gives Hollywood studios a powerful economic incentive to make films and TV shows that serve these organizations' publicity goals while discouraging the flow of oppositional media products that challenge them.

Furthermore, Hollywood's dependency on the US state for favourable media policy and regulation; the political affinities between Hollywood's owners, producers, actors, and US foreign policy elites; exceptionalist ideology; and industry assumptions about US consumer preferences further entrench a symbiotic relationship between the DOD and Hollywood studios. The DOD does not *force* Hollywood studios to make propaganda or directly censor content that challenges the DOD, and a few major and independent studios have even made "liberal" films that scrutinize US security policy. But the DOD-Hollywood complex is deceptive because it uses popular culture, which consumers may perceive as "just entertainment," to engineer public opinion in support of political goals. Moreover, by supporting militarized speech (pro-DOD films) and withholding support from pacifist speech (films that criticize the DOD), the DOD-Hollywood complex arguably violates the First Amendment's prohibition of the US government from favouring one kind of speech over another. Also, the DOD-Hollywood complex subverts US publicity and propaganda laws, which forbid the US government from engaging in covert self-promotion using public resources. As the DOD occupies Hollywood, and Hollywood colonizes the screens of America and the world, militainment designed to sell US Empire flows around the world. But there is no guarantee that these products have ideological effects, as viewers on the receiving end of militainment can and often do challenge and contest their preferred meanings. And even some Republicans have challenged the DOD's subsidies to Hollywood's war screens, as with the Stop Subsidizing Hollywood Act, introduced by Congresswoman Jenkins in 2011.

The DOD–digital games complex turns interactive play into a means of making "play killing" for and/or as the US military seem fun. The DOD supports the video game industry with its Program Executive Office for Simulation, Training and Instrumentation; the Simulation and Training Technology Center; the Institute for Creative Technologies; and the Modeling, Virtual Environments and Simulation Institute. These DOD agencies fund military modelling and simulation research and development, contract digital corporations to make war simulation games, and procure such games from them. By subsidizing video game corporations, the DOD gives them great incentive to manufacture militarized video games. Furthermore, digital games have become integral to the way the DOD wages war, as the DOD utilizes them to recruit players as soldiers, train soldiers how to fight, sell its image to the public, and virtually rehabilitate war veterans. The DOD–digital games complex transforms war, a serious act of state requiring serious public deliberation by citizens, into something simplified and pleasurable; blurs the important line between real war by making it seem identical to a game; immerses players in virtual wars that distance them physically, experientially, and emotionally from war's real consequences; represents war and even the violation of international law as the only and inevitable solution to interstate conflicts; and connects with other complexes to narrow the democratic and public space for deliberating about who, where, how, and why the United States fights.

Yet, the empire's digital war games are being opposed by a plurality of groups. The American Civil Liberties Union claims that the *America's Army* game, for example, violates the Optional Protocol to the Convention on the Rights of the Child on the Involvement of Children in Armed Conflict, which protects the human rights of children under the age of seventeen from military recruitment and deployment to war (M.B. Reagan 2008). In 2007, ninety members of Iraq Veterans against the War peacefully protested at a Black Expo job fair in St. Louis, where the army's recruiting booth was using video games like *America's Army* and *Call of Duty: Modern Warfare 2* to attract and enlist youth. The Yes Men (2009) – well-known American pranksters – challenged the militarization of digital play in their famous fake *New York Times* issue dated July 4, 2009. The headline: "Popular *America's Army* Video Game, Recruiting Tool Cancelled: New Game Will Recruit Young Diplomats."

Despite mounting resistance, the US Empire's culture industry continues to perform a "double service" for its state and corporate rulers. In the US, it helps the political class to manage public opinion about US foreign policy and "help to overcome" the "lack of popular enthusiasm for the global role of imperial stewardship." In world affairs, the culture industry is used for the empire's "defence and entrenchment wherever it exists already and for its expansion to locales where it hopes to become active" (H.I. Schiller 1976, 47). And the culture industry supports these ideological goals while its owners accrue incredible wealth to entrench their position at the top of the class hierarchy.

The larger the gap between the US Empire culture industry's representation of America and what's happening on the ground in the United States and in the countries in which the US state intervenes, the more likely US cultural products will be scrutinized as shallow propaganda, lacking credibility. The more there is a lack of correspondence between the US Empire's culture industry representations of the American Way and the lived and embodied consequences of US security policy and capitalism, the more the empire will appear hypocritical and be rejected. An honest and credible communications campaign would show the US Empire, "warts and all." It would speak frankly about the US class structure and its internal social problems, move beyond the culture-ideology of American exceptionalism, and elevate for public deliberation above liberal platitudes and neoconservative hubris the real local and global consequences of the US Empire. But this does not seem forthcoming.

Dismantling the US Empire: Democratizing the National Security Policy, the Culture Industry, and Cultural Policy

As the peace movement against the American War in Vietnam was gaining steam, Senator William Fulbright (1967) said that to "criticize one's country is to do it a service and to pay it a compliment. It is a service because it may spur the country to do better than it is doing; it is a compliment because it evidences a belief that the country can do better than it is doing." From its earliest days, the US Empire, as an ideal and actuality, has been contested by anti-imperialists at home and abroad (Tyrell and Sexton 2015). Since 9/11, many American anti-imperialist scholars and peace activists have done the republic a service and paid it a compliment by calling for the US Empire to be "dismantled" (Bacevich 2010; Johnston 2010), and for good reason. The ongoing growth of the US Empire chains the nation's youth to a future of debt, transfers public wealth from citizens to the defence industry, expands a class divide between the elite who benefit from ongoing wars and the many who bear its costs, supports a violent and security-obsessed culture, impoverishes deliberative discourse at home, and fuels anti-American angst abroad. As the empire convulses, mounting metropolitan discontent at the prospect of maintaining the US Empire grows more intense. In an interview with *Democracy Now!*, Jeremy Scahill says, "Unless we, as a society, completely re-imagine what an actual national security policy would look like … unless we're willing to re-imagine how we approach the world, we're doomed to have a repeat of a 9/11-type attack or something that's smaller-scale but constant" (Democracy Now! 2013) If the status quo persists, the United States' future will be one of unending conflict between the political and economic elites who are the beneficiaries of the US Empire and the publics afflicted by it.

The US Empire's culture industry tells US citizens they must continue waging wars "over there" so that they do not have to fight "over here"; the internationalist strategy for dismantling the US Empire advises US citizens to peacefully struggle against the power elite over "here" while supporting democratically minded anti-imperialists "everywhere." Instead of focusing externally on trying to fundamentally change other societies, Americans should focus internally on changing themselves. A democratic and socially just republic at home cannot exist alongside an empire abroad, and if the United States were to live up to its best ideals, it might one day be a model worthy of emulation. American progressives therefore face the challenge of dismantling the empire from within, and they can do so in solidarity or affinity with progressives around the world. As McChesney (2014a, 33) puts it, "If a viable pro-democracy, anti-imperialist movement can emerge here, it will improve the possibilities dramatically for socialists and progressives worldwide."

The peaceful path to dismantling the US Empire moves toward a "post-capitalist democracy" (McChesney 2014a), and along the way, the democratization of national security is a crucial step. The notion that a small elite should decide for everyone else what's to be done in world affairs must be challenged, and the executive branch's centralized, hierarchical, and secretive structures of national security decision-making will need to be democratized and opened up to public deliberation. The democratization of national security policy affirms that the essence of democracy is the right and capacity of citizens to understand and meaningfully participate in making the decisions that affect their lives and therefore necessitates a struggle to transform how national security decisions are made. The fullest participation of citizens in national decision-making, through direct and indirect channels, is not only democratic but the only way, save violent revolution, to dismantle the empire. National security *should* be the object of public deliberation and responsive to the public opinion of the majority of citizens. The US state *should* consult, heed, and respond to the public opinion of citizens before acting in the country's "national interest" in the world system.

The backwards-looking defenders of the status quo say that national security policy *cannot* be democratized because most citizens lack the knowledge, time, and even interest to deliberate about world affairs and that foreign policy *should not* be democratized because it is best left to the few who know what's best for the many. Forward-leaning progressives counter that citizens are capable of forming intelligent opinions about foreign policy matters and could, if given a chance, deliberatively determine what their nation's security interest is and is not (Page and Bouton 2011). The security ideas of the majority of citizens may even be much more enlightened – pacifist, egalitarian, internationalist, and culturally informed – than those held by the empire's power elites. If granted the proper resources required to participate (i.e., a quality internationalist education, a democracy-serving media system, a civic life free from the chains of necessity), citizens could, through deliberative processes, develop positions and proposals that reflect their own security interests. Possibly, publicly determined American security interests would have little to do with the geopolitical economy of empire maintenance and a lot to do with effectively meeting social needs, provisioning quality public education and health care, uncorrupting the political system, building a vibrant news media and culture, and achieving ecological sustainability.

The democratization of national security would be challenging, since, as mentioned earlier, not all citizens possess the same kind of knowledge about the world, time to deliberate, or interest in doing so. Furthermore, the democratization of security would raise a number of practical questions. Which issues, among the hundreds of issues available for deliberation, should be prioritized? Which ones are the most relevant and why? How to coordinate national security deliberation? The democratization of national security would be difficult, indeed, but it poses not only a challenge but also an opportunity, not another elitist rationale for excluding public participation. As O.R. Holsti (2004, 24) says, "There is more to fear from processes and policies that blatantly disregard public sentiments than from those that make a serious effort to engage the public in discussions of such central questions as the scope and nature of American interests."

Furthermore, the dismantling of empire and the democratization of national security are progressive goals that must be coupled with the democratization of the culture industry and its government cultural policy apparatus. The US Empire's geopolitical-economic problems are exacerbated by the culture industry, which tries to get citizens to accept the calamitous status quo as normal and unchangeable. Any struggle to dismantle empire and democratize national security must coincide with a well-organized movement to democratize the culture industry and the cultural policy that supports it. To do so, neoliberal and neoconservative myths about the relations between the culture industry and the government will need to be debunked and more veracious premises established.

For much of the twentieth century, the United States' culture industry was held out to the world as the freest and most democratic, a model that other states and peoples were expected to emulate (Hardt 1988). At present, it is common to assume that, because the US culture industry is part of a capitalist and liberal democratic country, forms of propaganda and censorship characteristic of autocratic states do not exist. The US culture industry is different from those apparent in autocratic states like Nazi Germany (with its Ministry for Public Enlightenment and Propaganda), Fascist Italy (with its Ministry of Popular Culture), or Soviet Russia (with Glavlit and *Pravda*). The US state does not own or control the total media and cultural environment, utilize all cultural products as propaganda instruments, or attempt to censor all cultural content that challenges the imperial "party line." The US culture industry's capitalist character makes it quite different from those in autocratic countries, which are owned and controlled by states. The Walt Disney Company, Time Warner, News Corporation, and other conglomerates, not the US federal government, own the US culture industry. Most of the cultural commodities flowing from the culture industry are designed to serve the profit maximization goals of their owners, not the propaganda goals of the state. When censorship happens in the United States, it is often due to commercial factors, sometimes state coercion, and the First Amendment supports the rights of citizens to create content that is critical of the US government and corporate power. It would be unreasonable to claim that *all* news stories, TV shows, Hollywood films, video games, and digital content that represent "America" and US foreign policy align with the state, especially in this era of post-network TV, globalized Hollywood, and Web 2.0 user-generated content.

Yet, this book has explained why and how empire-affirming cultural commodities flourish and flow. The lion's share of the US culture industry is controlled by corporations, but US state agencies (and their contractors) routinely try to bend the content of some news, entertainment, and digital media products to their liking. And far from being bastions of watchdog journalism and socialist subversion, US media companies all too often comply with the national security state's propaganda and censorship activities. In sum, US state policy and practice, combined with the corporate profit motive, clearly encourages the creation and circulation of US Empire–supporting culture.

These circumstances put to the lie the conservative myth of the US culture industry being ruled by "liberals" or left-wing elites who make media that is overwhelmingly critical of the US Empire. Michael Medved (2006, 2), for example, says that, while the United States was engaged in "World War IV," in Iraq, Afghanistan, and all over the world, "trying to keep us Americans safe" from "Islamic and fascist" enemies that "aim at our annihilation," Hollywood made films "that depict[ed] the American military as unrepresentative and twisted, America as a malignant force in the world and all wars as pointless." Richard Kimball and Joshua Muravchik of the American Enterprise Institute say the US media firms vilify the United States, and this encourages hostility toward US foreign policy (Wellemeyer 2006). These and other conservatives seem to have a problem with the US culture industry's independence from the national security state and take issue with popular culture that doesn't mirror official policy. While conservatives espouse free-market ideals when calling for cuts to public education, health care, welfare, the PBS, NPR, the National Endowment for the Arts, and so on, when it comes to empire, they seem to want the culture industry to make or support government propaganda. Strangely, they depict the culture industry's minor expressions of dissent against the empire as a "market failure" of sorts and put forward an autocratic view of culture's role in society that is, by their own laissez-faire standard of judging the public media of other countries, very un-American.

The notion that the culture industry should support the official war policies of the US state is an affront to democracy and a self-governing citizenry. The idea that it fails to do this circulates across Facebook pages like "Send Hollywood a Message: Stop Making Anti-American, Anti-Military Movies!," is carried by right-wing blogs like AmericanThinker.com, and is reproduced in the day-to-day conversations of ordinary US citizens, who, repeatedly exposed to this idea, may believe it to be true. Some US cultural products *do* put a critical spotlight on aspects of the US Empire and war, and there sometimes are tensions between the profit goals of US-based media companies and the geopolitical PR goals of the US state. Yet, the weight of evidence points to the culture industry and the national security state coming together to make imperial commodity culture so as to make an imperial nation. Far from being a mouthpiece for anti-imperialism, the US Empire's culture industry routinely packages and sells the empire as a way of life.

This book's findings also suggest that the US federal government does cultural policy, despite arguments to the contrary. Cultural policy scholars examine how culture (as a whole way of life), the culture industry (the system of producing and distributing media and cultural goods), and the national representations carried by cultural products (stories and symbols) are shaped and supported by state agencies, policies, and regulations (Lewis and Miller 2003; Throsby 2010). The US has no official, centralized, and federally administered cultural ministry like Canada (the Department of Heritage) or France (the Ministry of Culture), and the US federal government seems not to use cultural policy to compel media conglomerates to make cultural products that promote and protect a distinctive American Way. The US government does not use a screen content quota system to ensure that a portion of the cultural products daily exhibited in theatres and by TV networks help Americans tell their stories to each other. We do not hear pleas by US citizens to defend America's cultural sovereignty against the corruptive or polluting threat posed to it by imported Canadian, Bollywood, Swedish, or Chinese TV shows, films, and news products. When contrasted with *dirigiste* states that use federal cultural policies to govern their culture industries, the US state appears to support laissez-faire.

Yet, this book has shown that the US state intervenes in and shapes the culture industry to influence the way America is screened and perceived. It provides assistance to media conglomerates (huge subsidies) to encourage the production of certain kinds of (imperial) cultural products at the expense of others. And it supports the flow of certain representations of America in society while tacitly restricting others. So while an explicit US cultural nationalist policy is difficult to find, the US federal government does cultural policy but without calling it "cultural policy" and has cultural policy agencies that are not called "cultural policy" agencies – the State Department, the DOD, and the CIA.

What, then, are the characteristics of the US Empire's cultural policy? Napoli (2008) says that normative, democratic cultural policy-making derives from principles and values like diversity, localism, access, and quality. The principles and values of the US Empire's cultural policy, however, do not align with these. Democratic cultural policy says the state should provide citizens with access to a diverse array of cultural products when the market fails to do so, but imperial cultural policy depicts the market as failing when it does not produce propaganda. When media corporations fail to produce representations of America that serve propaganda goals, the US state takes it on itself to intervene in markets and establishes incentives that entice media corporations to do so. Imperial cultural policy does not attempt to fulfill the democratic principles of the marketplace of ideas but rather attempts to control it. Democratic cultural policy seeks to 1) encourage a diversity of cultural expressions, while imperial cultural policy positions itself against diversity when it challenges the status quo; 2) provide all citizens in a democracy, regardless of their class, sex, ethnicity, creed, or location with access to cultural expressions, while imperial cultural policy makes propaganda products available to citizens so as to manipulate them; 3) make judgments about the quality of cultural expressions based on what citizens need to function as informed and engaged participants in democracy, while imperial cultural policy makes value judgments about the quality of cultural expressions based on their "propaganda value" (i.e., how well media products cast America in a positive light and are effective in manipulating people); 4) be committed to fairness, but imperial cultural policy is unfair as it supports trickle-up wealth redistribution from the public to the culture industry's paid propaganda providers.

Furthermore, democratic cultural policy is bottom-up, participatory, and inclusive, but imperial cultural policy is top-down, elitist, and exclusionary. Democratic cultural policy relies on a democratic and deliberative process that includes many diverse social groups in decision-making, but imperial cultural policy is made by and for elites. Imperial cultural policy shapes the imagining of America, represents America in partial and selective ways, and projects this America to the world in commodity forms, but the majority of US citizens have no input whatsoever into how their nation is represented. Imperial cultural policy is administered by a small number of state and culture industry elites who speak for America and decide what America is and is not without even consulting the people who actually constitute America. In imperial cultural policy, the majority of US citizens do not speak but are spoken for; they do not represent themselves but are represented. Overall, the US Empire's cultural policy does not support the principles and values of normative democratic theory but rather expresses the anti-democratic theory of America as a society in which the elite few determine the national security interest and then use the culture industry as a tool of propaganda to integrate this interest into the whole way of life of the many.

Clearly, the US Empire's culture industry is not natural or the outcome of free markets but is shaped significantly by the federal government's imperial cultural policy and propped up with gargantuan subsidies, paid for by the public. The problem is not that federal cultural policy and subsidies exist but that they exist without the public's informed consent and thwart democracy by buttressing complexes that manufacture media to manipulate the public and make money at its expense.

Fortunately, there exists at present a burgeoning US media reform movement that possesses the resources and capacities for challenging and possibly even transforming the US Empire's culture industry. For more than a decade, Free Press (http://www.freepress.net/) has fought tirelessly to build a media system that serves the democratic needs of a self-governing people (McChesney and Nichols 2002, 2010; McChesney 2014a, 2014b). McChesney (2014a, 20) says the goal is to develop an "independent, uncensored, non-profit, and non-commercial news media that would have sufficient public funding but whose content the government could not control." Free Press's push for democratic media encompasses a number of components, including struggles over media policy and legislation; building independent media agencies; popularizing media education; and organizing with, and learning from, all of those cultural workers who create content. Free Press has spearheaded numerous significant media reform initiatives (McChesney 2014b), and now the time is ripe for it to take on the US Empire's culture industry with a campaign to democratize the US Empire's cultural policy apparatus (by opening it up to public participation) and democratize the multi-billion-dollar subsidy it provisions to industry (by giving citizens something that expresses their needs in return for their enormous gift to media conglomerates).

At present, federal cultural policies and subsidies support a culture industry that pumps out empire-promoting and -protecting cultural products that serve the interests of the few, but this policy apparatus and subsidy system could be transformed to support diverse means of producing and distributing cultural goods that express the interests of the many. A small or large portion of the public resources allocated to the US Empire's culture industry could be redirected toward a diversity of public and non-commercial media and cultural organizations that make democracy-enriching content. A reduction of subsidies to the profit-seeking companies that produce militainment could free up public resources for public broadcasting, non-profit media, and community media. Proposals for a "voucher system" (McChesney and Nichols 2010) and "public commissioning" (Hind 2010) for funding public, civic, and democracy-serving media exist. A pittance of the US Empire's multi-billion-dollar public affairs budget could support vouchers that let citizens each annually contribute $200 to public, non-profit media and community media organizations of their choosing. These could generate informational and cultural expressions that more adequately represent the real material concerns, experiences, and aspirations of citizens than the US Empire's culture industry does, while speaking truth to and holding accountable its rulers.

The problems of the US Empire, its culture industry, and imperial cultural policy are many, but they are not inevitable or immutable. The barriers to social change are high, but history teaches us they can be surmounted. The democratization of the culture industry and cultural policy, which shape and are shaped by the geopolitical economy of the US Empire, is a step toward this goal. On the road to dismantling the US Empire, imperial cultural policy resources allocated to the industry that engineers consent to the state's deployment of violence abroad should be shifted toward democratic cultural policy that encourages the production and distribution of public cultural goods that represent the diversity and struggles of US cultural life at home. What is thought and known in America, about America, by the people, for the people, not the power elite, ought to be a cultural policy priority.

Coda: *Welcome to America, I Am Legend*

Welcome: Portraits of America is a global media campaign produced and launched by the US Department of Homeland Security and the US State Department (2007) in partnership with Walt Disney Parks and Resorts. Comprised of a photography exhibit and a companion seven-minute film, *Welcome* presents itself as a scrapbook-style homage to the American people and landscapes, a visual tourist trip across the multiple vistas and cultures of the country. As viewers of *Welcome*, we are shown Latin American marriage festivities, blue-collar truck drivers socializing at rural truck stops, and African American children skipping rope in steamy urban streets. We are taken to Wall Street, where traders frantically work to keep pace with global finance capitalism, then on to Coney Island, the playground of happy nuclear families that stroll among the boardwalk's candy-striped amusements. High above the Grand Canyon we soar with an American eagle, swooping down on shimmering lakes and through luminous forests, where grizzly bears fish salmon from bubbling, peat-smudged streams. As we visually travel across the United States, we see people from all walks of life: firemen and fishermen, cowboys and boxers, carnival workers and Elvis impersonators, Napa Valley vineyard workers and a Sudanese "Lost Boy." The American landscape is as diverse as its people. Yellow corn fields and golden beaches, public baseball diamonds and the Vegas Strip, farmlands and the Hollywood Hills blend seamlessly. *Welcome*'s visual tour ends where many foreigners' "American dreams" begin: the Statue of Liberty, towering over the New York City harbour. *Welcome* enables millions of non-US citizens to view America without actually travelling there and proceeds almost entirely without dialogue, making it accessible to viewers around the world. Indeed, only one word is uttered during the entire film, at the very close: simply, "welcome."

In the same month of *Welcome*'s debut, *I Am Legend*, a science-fiction-horror-action film directed by Francis Lawrence and starring Will Smith, appeared in cinemas around the world. This globally popular blockbuster's image of America is far less welcoming than *Welcome*'s. The year is 2012 and the US has collapsed. We see New York City emptied of human life, littered with skeletons and desiccated machinery. America has been the victim of some kind of attack. The culprit is not global terrorists, communists, or some alien monstrosity but the engine of US technological modernity itself: scientific research and development. A genetically re-engineered measles virus intended to cure cancer has mutated into a malignant super-pandemic and wiped out 90 percent of the world's population. The remaining 10 percent is split between survivors (humans who are immune to the virus and spend the days trying to meet their subsistence needs) and Darkseekers (a hoard of violent beasts that hunt and kill the other survivors). *I Am Legend*'s protagonist is Col. Robert Neville, a US military virologist who led the government's attempt to combat the pandemic but failed. Day after day, Neville struggles to survive. He broadcasts short-wave radio messages to fellow survivors and works in his lab to find a cure. Neville eventually meets Anna and Ethan, two other survivors, and soon after discovers the cure. The Darkseekers become more threatening and frequently attack Neville, Anna, and Ethan. *I Am Legend*'s plot climaxes in a violent conflict between Neville and the Darkseekers. Neville uses a grenade to blow up himself and the Darkseekers, saving Anna and Ethan, who flee with the cure to a survivor colony in Vermont. Neville's self-sacrifice allows New York City, the US, and the wider world to be rebuilt. Neville becomes a global legend.

Welcome and *I Am Legend* have much in common. Each film's financing came from a US-based media corporation. The Walt Disney Company, possibly the world's largest media conglomerate, financed *Welcome*; and Time Warner, another global media giant, backed *I Am Legend*. *Welcome* and *I Am Legend* are cultural products that travelled across national borders. In 2007, *Welcome* was viewed for free by millions of non-Americans at over 200 foreign US consulate offices, from Kigali to Sarajevo. It was also exhibited by the customs facilities at major US airports and through social media platforms such as YouTube. Paying viewers at cineplexes in countries as diverse as Canada, Iceland, India, Malta, and Venezuela watched *I Am Legend*. That same year, as a non-Christmas-themed film exhibited in December, *I Am Legend*'s profitability set a global box-office record: it grossed $256 million domestically and a whopping $329 million internationally. *Welcome* and *I Am Legend*, however, are more than just globalizing cultural products. They were shaped by the US state as instruments of publicity to convey a positive image of America to the world.

Welcome was directed by Federico Tio. Prior to working for the US government, Tio marketed popular Walt Disney Company films such as *Finding Nemo* and *The Lion King*. Karen Hughes (2007), former US secretary of public diplomacy under the Bush administration, commented on the political function of Tio's film: "*Welcome* intends to establish a warm first impression [of America] ... Attracting people to our country is vital to our economy, our national interests, and especially to public diplomacy." Jay Rasulo, chairman of Walt Disney Parks and Resorts, agreed: "We are proud to partner with [the] US Government to extend a world class welcome to America's guests. This project showcases America's greatest asset: the ordinary people who make this nation extraordinary" (cited in Disney 2007). Disney produces and circulates culture as a commodity; Rasulo treats diverse American people as "assets" in the arsenal of US public diplomacy. Here the global promotion of America by the US state is modelled on the marketing of commodities by corporations, and the US state's attempt to cultivate the goodwill of foreign publics mirrors the strategies of corporations to engineer brand loyalty.

I Am Legend was developed with help from numerous US state agencies. To clear some of New York City's busiest blocks and secure some of the most iconic New York City landmarks – Grand Central Terminal and

Washington Square Park – for the shoot, *I Am Legend*'s production team worked with New York City Mayor Michael Bloomberg's Office of Film, Theatre and Broadcasting. On behalf of Warner Bros., the New York Police Department Aviation Unit, the Army Corps of Engineers, and the Department of Environmental Conservation transported a barge into the harbour to construct the pier on which most of the live action of *I Am Legend* was shot.

The DOD participated in the production of *I Am Legend* as well. DOD-owned hardware – Black Hawk and HH-65 Dolphin helicopters, Humvees, and armored Stryker assault vehicles – is featured in nearly all of the film's spectacular action sequences. About 150 real US soldiers appeared in the film too. They operated military helicopters, tanks, and boats for the camera. "Everybody agreed it was important to use real troops in the scenes, for their expertise and for authenticity's sake," says Samuel Glen, a US military and weapons consultant. "New York's famous 69th Infantry Division, under authority from the DOD, was kind enough to allow us to hire their troops on off-duty status as background extras. They are trained for urban peacekeeping so it adds another layer of realism to everything" (cited in Hollywood Tonight 2007). Warner Bros. Pictures used actual military property and shot US military personnel at little cost, while a DOD film officer recommended a few script changes that supported its broader PR campaign.

As cultural products that were influenced by both US media corporations and US government agencies, *Welcome* and *I Am Legend* buttress the United States' culture-ideology of exceptionalism. In *Welcome*, the US is framed as a benevolent "nation of immigrants" that welcomes all. US citizens are a diverse bunch of people, but they nonetheless cohere as one, with little conflict. This unity in diversity makes the US special, uniquely universalistic, fit to lead. *Welcome* invites its foreign viewers to imagine themselves as imminent American citizens, patriots in waiting.

While *Welcome*'s America is exceptional because of its multicultural universalism, *I Am Legend* represents the US as exceptional because of its military. In *I Am Legend*, the US military resolves a world crisis. Humanity faces extinction. The United States must lead. One man, a US military soldier-scientist, is uniquely destined, if not fated, to secure the world. The survival of the human species and future of the planet depend on the brawn and brainpower of one exceptional American military hero. The US state, symbolized by Neville, is martyred; America saves the world, and the story becomes legend.

In addition to promoting the doctrine of American exceptionalism, *Welcome*'s and *I Am Legend*'s narrative contents intersect with and sugar-coat the actual policies of the post-9/11 US national security state. *Welcome*'s image of America reflects the exigencies of the Rice-Chertoff Initiative: established in 2006, this Homeland Security policy proposes to secure US borders from the presumed threat of "illegal immigrants" while also trying to successfully lure "legitimate" foreigners (i.e., low-waged migrant labourers, the city-slicking creative class, and tourists with disposable income) to the homeland for work, play, and shopping. The slogan is "Secure Borders and Open Doors." Since 2001, the state has spent billions of dollars to consolidate US border security, closing down America to all but those people the state deems welcome. America, as portrayed by *Welcome*, is a deceptive image of openness in a period when US borders are more barricaded by multi-million-dollar surveillance systems and policed by often intimidating US border guards, drones, and right-wing militia than ever before. Furthermore, *Welcome*'s image of America as a land of multicultural diversity and abundant employment mystifies the reality of the United States as a radically unequal country where dreams of upward mobility are regularly crushed by the class system.

While *Welcome* conveys an idealistic image of America to the world, *I Am Legend* intersects with the US state's post-9/11 focus on biological weapons of mass destruction as a new security threat. In 2003, to build public consent to a pre-emptive military invasion, the Bush administration claimed that Iraq threatened the United States and its allies with biological weapons. In 2008, a congressional committee claimed that the United States would "likely" be the victim of a biological terrorist attack by 2013. "The consequences of a biological attack are almost beyond comprehension. It would be 9/11 times 10 or a hundred in terms of the number of people who would be killed," said former senator Bob Graham (cited in Meserve 2008). In response to the supposed bio-terrorist threat, the US state has allocated more than $50 billion to the emerging field of "bio-defense" research and development, which is led by US military scientists and biotechnology corporations (Gottron 2007). Critics worry that the Bioshield program masks a dubious bio-weapons program (Borger 2002). Since 1972, the Biological Weapons Convention has prohibited the development of bio-weapons, but this hasn't stopped the United States.

I Am Legend's futuristic narrative of America being annihilated by disease resonates with twenty-first-century cultural anxieties about the threat of biological terrorism, giving popular legitimization to biodefence expenditure. *I Am Legend*'s noble Neville, the principled and handsome US military scientist who independently toils away in his lab, humanizes the US military-industrial complex.

As imperial cultural products, *Welcome* and *I Am Legend* benefit The Walt Disney Company and Time Warner, two profit-seeking media corporations. As geopolitical representations, the two films intersect with the US state's struggle to promote America and US foreign policy to local and global publics by transcoding the general ideology of American exceptionalism and specific doctrines of US national security into captivating and entertaining forms. *Welcome* and *I Am Legend* demonstrate that the US state works with private media corporations to produce cultural products that convey positive representations of America. The US culture industry is not just a factory for producing commodified mass entertainment or part of an inherently laissez-faire market; it is something that is interwoven with the geopolitical strategies of the US national security state. *Welcome* and *I Am Legend* represent a confluence of interests between the US government and media corporations, not an antagonism between these geopolitical and economic actors. *Welcome* and *I Am Legend* show that the US state and media corporations work together to achieve mutually beneficial goals. The two films are much more than run-of-the-mill cultural goods; they are imperial cultural commodities that are designed to serve the strategic interests of the US Empire. And they are only two among hundreds of such products – TV shows, films, news programs, video games, and more – which convey imagery of and messages about America to citizens in the United States and all over the world.

These products spring from the US Empire's culture industry – a topic whose critical study, though instigated by Herbert I. Schiller's contribution to the geopolitical economy of communications nearly fifty years ago, continues to be important today.

References

ACC Public Affairs. 2013. "Hometown News Service Shares Military Accomplishments Globally." US Army, www.army.mil, December 3. http://www.army.mil/article/116403/Hometown_News_service_shares_military_accomplishments_globally/.

Ackerman, S., and D. Rushe. 2014. "Senate Report on CIA Torture Claims Spy Agency Lied about 'Ineffective' Program." *Guardian*, December 9. http://www.theguardian.com/us-news/2014/dec/09/cia-torture-report-released.

Adegoke, Y., and D. Levine. 2011. "Comcast Completes NBC Universal Merger." Reuters, June 29. http://www.reuters.com/article/2011/01/29/us-comcast-nbc-idUSTRE70S2WZ20110129.

Adelman, J. 2013. "Why the US Remains the World's Unchallenged Superpower." *Forbes*, November 24. http://www.forbes.com/sites/realspin/2013/11/24/why-the-u-s-remains-the-worlds-unchallenged-superpower/.

Advertising Age. 2013. "10 Things You Should Know about the Global Ad Market." December 8. http://adage.com/article/global-news/10-things-global-ad-market/245572/.

Airlie, C. 2011. "Global Advertising Spending Rose in 2010, Nielsen Says." Bloomberg Business, April 4. http://www.bloomberg.com/news/articles/2011-04-03/global-ad-spending-in-2010-rose-11-on-soccer-s-world-cup-neilsen-says.

Ali, T. 2010. *The Obama Syndrome: Surrender at Home, War Abroad*. New York: Verso.

Allen, G., and M. Stamm. 2014. "Preconference Call for Papers: Communications and the State: Toward a New International History." 65th Annual Conference, Communication across the Life Span, 21–25, San Juan Caribe Hilton Hotel, Puerto Rico. http://www.icahdq.org/conf/2015/CommStateCFP.asp.

Allen, R. 2014. "America's Army and the Military Recruitment and Management of 'Talent': An Interview with Colonel Casey Wardynski." *Journal of Gaming and Virtual Worlds* 62: 179–91.

Almond, G.A. 1960. *The American People and Foreign Policy*. New York: Praeger.

Andersen, R. 2006. *A Century of Media, a Century of War*. New York: Peter Lang.
–. 2014. "*Act of Valor*: Celebrating and Denying the Brutalities of an Endless and Global US War." *Democratic Communiqué* 26 (2): 22–38.
Anderson, B. 1991. *Imagined Communities*. New York: Verso.
Ang, I. 1985. *Watching Dallas: Soap Opera and the Melodramatic Imagination*. London: Methuen.
Anholt, S. 2008. "From Nation Branding to Competitive Identity: The Role of Brand Management as a Component of National Policy." In *Nation Branding: Concepts, Issues, Practice*, ed. K. Dinnie, 22–23. Oxford: Butterworth-Heinemann.
Appadurai, A. 1997. *Modernity at Large*. Minneapolis: University of Minnesota Press.
Armistead, L. 2004. *Information Operations: Warfare and the Hard Reality of Soft Power*. New York: Brassey's Inc.
Armstrong, M. 2001. "Hollywood, White House, Talk Terrorism." *E!* November 12. http://www.eonline.com/news/42446/hollywood-white-house-talk-terrorism.
Armstrong, S. 2012. "Top Video Game Markets in the World." *Christian Science Monitor*, March 6. http://www.csmonitor.com/USA/Society/2012/0316/Top-video-game-markets-in-the-world/United-States.
Arnow, P. 2007. "From Self-Censorship to Official Censorship: Ban on Images of Wounded GIs Raises No Media Objections." *FAIR*, April 1. http://www.fair.org/index.php?page=3095.
Arsenault, A., and M. Castells. 2006. "Conquering the Minds, Conquering Iraq: The Social Production of Misinformation in the United States; A Case Study." *Information Communication and Society* 9 (3): 284–307. http://dx.doi.org/10.1080/13691180600751256.
–. 2008. "The Structure and Dynamics of Global Multi-Media Business Networks." *International Journal of Communication* 2: 707–48.
Arthur, W.B. 1996. "Increasing Returns and the New World of Business." *Harvard Business Review*, July–August. http://hbr.org/1996/07/increasing-returns-and-the-new-world-of-business/ar/1.
AP (Associated Press). 2009. "Pentagon Spending Billions on PR to Sway World Opinion." Fox News, February 6. http://www.foxnews.com/politics/2009/02/05/pentagon-spending-billions-pr-sway-world-opinion/.
–. 2014. "US Secretly Created 'Cuban Twitter' to Stir Unrest." CBC News, April 3. http://www.cbc.ca/news/world/u-s-secretly-created-cuban-twitter-to-stir-unrest-1.2596612.
APP (Association of American Publishers). 2013. *About*. http://www.publishers.org/about/.
Axe, D. 2006. "Embed Who Ran Afoul of Military in Iraq Reflects on His Experience." *Editor & Publisher*, February 27. http://www.editorandpublisher.com/PrintArticle/Embed-Who-Ran-Afoul-of-Military-in-Iraq-Reflects-on-His-Experience.
Aysha, E. 2004. "The Limits and Contradictions of 'Americanization.'" In *The New Imperial Challenge: Socialist Register 2004*, ed. L. Panitch and C. Leys, 245–61. London: Merlin Press.
Baard, M. 2007. "Sentient World: War Games on the Grandest Scale. *Register*, June 23. http://www.theregister.co.uk/2007/06/23/sentient_worlds/.
Bacevich, A. 2004. *American Empire: The Realities and Consequences of US Diplomacy*. Cambridge, MA: Harvard University Press.
–. 2005. *The New American Militarism: How Americans Are Seduced by War*. New York: Oxford University Press.

—. 2010. *Washington Rules: America's Path to Permanent War*. New York: Metropolitan Books.
Bagdikian, B. 2004. *The New Media Monopoly*. Boston: Beacon Press.
Bah, U. 2008. "Daniel Lerner, Cold War Propaganda and US Development Communication Research: An Historical Critique." *Journal of Third World Studies* 25 (1): 183–98.
Baker, C. E. 2002. *Media, Markets and Democracy*. Cambridge: Cambridge University Press.
Barbaro, M. 2008. "U.S. Military Recruits Children." Truthout.com, July 23. http://truthout.org/archive/component/k2/item/79257:us-military-recruits-children#D.
Barkawi, R., and M. Laffey. 2002. "Retrieving the Imperial: Empire and International Relations." *Millennium* 31 (1): 109–27. http://dx.doi.org/10.1177/03058298020310010601.
Barnes, J.E. 2008. "Calling the Shots on War Movies." *Los Angeles Times*, July 7. http://articles.latimes.com/2008/jul/07/nation/na-armyfilms7.
Barnett, F.R. 1989. "Afterword: Twelve Steps to Improving American PSYOP." In *Political Warfare and Psychological Operations: Rethinking the US Approach*, ed. F.B. Barnett and C. Lord, 209–24. Washington, DC: National Defense University Press.
Barnett, T.P. 2004. *The Pentagon's New Map*. New York: Penguin.
Barrett, D.M. 1990. "Presidential Foreign Policy." In *The Making of US Foreign Policy* by John Dumbrell, 65–95. Manchester: Manchester University Press.
Barstow, D. 2008a. "Behind TV Analysts, Pentagon's Hidden Hand." *New York Times*, April 20. http://www.nytimes.com/2008/04/20/us/20generals.html?pagewanted=all.
Bart, P. 2001. "Nets, Studios Answer Call to Arms in Fight Against Terrorism." *Variety*, October 17. http://variety.com/2001/voices/news/h-wood-enlists-in-war-1117854476/.
Baudrillard, J. 1995. *Simulacra & Simulation*. MI: University of Michigan Press.
BBC News. 2001. "Hollywood: The Pentagon's New Advisor." BBC News World Edition, *Panorama*, March 24. http://news.bbc.co.uk/2/hi/programmes/panorama/1891196.stm.
—. 2002. "September 11: A Warning from Hollywood." BBC News World Edition, *Panorama*, March 24. http://news.bbc.co.uk/2/hi/programmes/panorama/1875186.stm.
—. 2003a. "Rumsfeld Blasts Arab TV Stations." BBC, November 11. http://news.bbc.co.uk/2/hi/middle_east/3238680.stm.
—. 2003b. "U.S. Attacks 'Biased' Arab News." July 27. http://news.bbc.co.uk/2/hi/middle_east/3101387.stm.
—. 2004. "Hollywood Film Budgets Top $100m." March 24. http://news.bbc.co.uk/2/hi/entertainment/3564377.stm.
—. 2010. "Liam Fox Defends Call for Ban of *Medal of Honor* Game. August 23. http://www.bbc.co.uk/news/technology-11056581.
BBG (Broadcasting Board of Governors). 2012. *US International Broadcasting: Engaging and Empowering Our Audience, Broadcasting Board of Governors, 2012 Annual Report*. Washington: BBG.
Becker, E. 2000. "Armed Forces to Try a Hollywood Pitch for Luring Recruits." *New York Times*, January 29. http://www.nytimes.com/2000/01/29/us/armed-forces-to-try-a-hollywood-pitch-for-luring-recruits.html.

Becker, E., and J. Dao. 2002. "Bush Will Keep Wartime Office Promoting US." *New York Times*, February 20. http://www.nytimes.com/2002/02/20/international/20INFO.html?pagewanted=print.

Beers, C. 2002. "Public Diplomacy after September 11." US Department of State, December 18. http://2001-2009.state.gov/r/us/16269.htm.

—. 2003. "Interview on CNN's *NewsNight* with Aaron Brown." US Department of State, January 16. http://2001-2009.state.gov/r/us/16735.htm.

Begg, J.M. 1951. "The American Idea: Package It for Export." *Department of State Bulletin* 24: 409–23.

Bellamy Foster, J., R.W. McChesney, and J. Jonna. 2011. "Monopoly and Competition in Twenty-First Century Capitalism." *Monthly Review* 62 (11). https://monthlyreview.org/2011/04/01/monopoly.

Beltran, L.R. 1978. "Communication and Cultural Domination: USA-Latin America Case." *Media Asia* 5 (1): 183–192.

Ben. 2013. "Google Takes Top Position in Global Media Owner Rankings." Zenith-Optimedia: The ROI Agency, July 9. http://www.zenithoptimedia.com/google-takes-top-position-in-global-media-owner-rankings/.

Benedetti, W. 2002. "Zipper Takes Aim at Global Market with Ultra-Realistic Games." *Seattle Post Intelligencer*, August 26. http://.seattlepi.nwsource.com/lifestyle/84294_zipper27.shtml.

Bennett, W.L. 1990. "Toward a Theory of Press-State Relations in the United States." *Journal of Communication* 40 (2): 103–27. http://dx.doi.org/10.1111/j.1460-2466.1990.tb02265.x.

Bergmann, A. 2014. World's Largest Economies. CNN Money. http://money.cnn.com/news/economy/world_economies_gdp/.

Bernays, E.L. 1923. *Crystallizing Public Opinion*. New York: IG Publishing.

—. 1928. *Propaganda*. Brooklyn: IG Publishing.

Best, R.A. 2009. *The National Security Council: An Organizational Assessment*. Congressional Research Service Report for Congress. Washington, DC: Congressional Research Service.

Bettig, R.V. 1996. *Copyrighting Culture: The Political Economy of Intellectual Property*. Boulder, CO: Westview Press.

Billig, M. 1995. *Banal Nationalism*. London: Sage Publications.

Black, E. 2012. *IBM and the Holocaust: The Strategic Alliance between Nazi Germany and America's Most Powerful Corporation*. Westport, CT: Dialog Press.

Bloomberg Business. 2013. "Why Should Taxpayers Give Banks $83 Billion a Year? February 20. http://www.bloomberg.com/news/2013-02-20/why-should-taxpayers-give-big-banks-83-billion-a-year-.html.

Blottenberger, D. 2011. "All Branches Meet Military Recruiting Goals." Stars and Stripes, January 14. http://www.stripes.com/news/all-branches-meet-military-recruiting-goals-1.131869.

Blum, W. 2004. *Killing Hope: US Military and CIA Interventions since World War II*. Monroe, ME: Common Courage Press.

Bogart, L. 1995. *Cool Words, Cold War: A New Look at USIA's Premises for Propaganda*. Washington, DC: American University Press.

Boggs, C. 2005. "Pentagon, Strategy, Hollywood and Technowar." *New Politics* 11 (1). http://newpol.org/content/pentagon-strategy-hollywood-and-technowar

Boggs, C., and T. Pollard. 2007. *The Hollywood War Machine: Militarism and Popular Culture*. London: Paradigm Publishers.
Bogost, I. 2007. *Persuasive Games: The Expressive Power of Videogames*. Cambridge/London: MIT Press.
Bond, P. 2013. "Study: Global Media Industry Poised to Top $2 Trillion in 2016." Hollywood Reporter, June 4. http://www.hollywoodreporter.com/news/study-global-media-industry-poised-562694.
Boorstin, D.J. 1962. *The Image*. London: Weidenfeld & Nicholson.
Boot, M. 2001. "The Case for American Empire." *Weekly Standard*, October 15. http://www.weeklystandard.com/Content/Public/Articles/000/000/000/318qpvmc.asp.
Borger, J. 2002. "US Weapons Secrets Exposed." *Guardian*, October 29. http://www.guardian.co.uk/world/2002/oct/29/usa.julianborger.
Bourdieu, P., and Wacquant, L. 1999. "On the Cunning of Imperialist Reason." *Theory, Culture and Society* 16 (1): 41–58.
Bowers, F. 2004. "Al-Hurra Joins Battle for News, Hearts and Minds." Global Policy Forum, February 24. http://www.globalpolicy.org/empire/media/2004/0224battle.htm.
Boyd-Barrett, O. 1977. "Media Imperialism: Towards an International Framework for the Analysis of Media Systems." In *Mass Communication and Society*, ed. J. Curran, M. Gurevitch, and J. Woolacott, 116–35. London: Arnold Publishers.
—. 1998. "Media Imperialism Reformulated." In *Electronic Empires: Global Media and Local Resistance*, ed. D.K. Thussu, 156–76. New York: Arnold Publishers.
—. 2004. "Judith Miller, *The New York Times*, and the Propaganda Model." *Journalism Studies* 5 (4): 435–49.
Brandon, J. 2011. "Ghost Recon: Future Soldier: The Real Military Tech Behind the Game." *Popular Mechanics*. http://www.popularmechanics.com/technology/gadgets/video-games/the-real-military-tech-behind-ghost-recon-future-soldier.
Brennan, T. 2003. "The Subtlety of Caesar." *Interventions* 5 (2): 200–6. http://dx.doi.org/10.1080/1369801031000112932.
Brewer, S. 2011. *Why America Fights: Patriotism and War Propaganda from the Philippines to Iraq*. New York: Oxford University Press.
Brightman, J. 2011. "EA CEO: Activision Knows It's 'Threatened' by Battlefield 3." *Business Insider*, June 13. http://www.businessinsider.com/ea-ceo-activision-knows-its-threatened-by-battlefield-3-2011-6.
BSA/Software Alliance. 2013. "About Us." http://www.bsa.org/about-bsa.
Buhle, P., and D. Wagner. 2002. *Radical Hollywood: The Untold Story Behind America's Favorite Movies*. New York: New Press.
Burnett, R. 2011. "Simulation Industry Hopes Special Missions Training Spares It from Military Cuts." *Orlando Sentinel*, September 26. http://articles.orlandosentinel.com/2011-09-26/business/os-military-training-special-missions-20110926_1_military-training-industry-simulation-industry-lockheed-martin-global-training.
Bush, G.W. 2001. Remarks to Members of the Senior Executive Service. October 15. http://www.presidency.ucsb.edu/ws/?pid=62808.
Business for Diplomatic Action. 2004. "Who We Are." http://www.businessfordiplomaticaction.org/who/.

Business Wire. 2007. "Disney Partners with the United States Government to Welcome International Visitors." *Business Wire*, October 27. http://www.business wire.com/news/home/20071022006072/en/U.S.-Government-Partners-Disney -International-Visitors#.VXDno89VhBc.

Butler, J. 2010. *Frames of War: When Life Is Grievable*. New York: Verso.

Calabrese, A. 2005. "Casus Belli: US Media and the Justification of the Iraq War." *Television and New Media* 6 (2): 153–75. http://dx.doi.org/10.1177/1527476404273952.

Calvert, J. 2003. "Fugitive Hunter Signed by Encore." Gamespot.com, October 15. http://www.gamespot.com/articles/fugitive-hunter-signed-by-encore/1100-6076865/.

Calvo, D. 2002. "Coming to an Army Near You." *Los Angeles Times*, July 19. http://articles.latimes.com/2002/jul/19/nation/na-institute19.

Campbell, D. 2001. "Top Gun versus Sergeant Bilko? No Contest, Says the Pentagon." *Guardian*, August 29. http://film.guardian.co.uk/News_Story/Guardian/0,4029,543821,00.html.

Canby, V. 1998. "Saving a Nation's Pride of Being; The Horror and Honor of a Good War." *New York Times*, August 10. http://www.nytimes.com/1998/08/10/movies/critic-s-notebook-saving-nation-s-pride-being-horror-honor-good-war.html.

Carey, A. 1995. *Taking the Risk Out of Democracy: Corporate Propaganda versus Freedom and Liberty*. Chicago, IL: Chicago University Press.

Carpentier, N., ed. 2007. *Culture, Trauma, and Conflict: Cultural Studies Perspectives on War*. Newcastle upon Tyne: Cambridge Scholars Publishing

Carr, D. 2013. "For Media Moguls, Paydays that Stand Out." *New York Times*, May 5. http://www.nytimes.com/2013/05/06/business/media/for-media-moguls -paydays-that-outstrip-other-fields.html?pagewanted=all&pagewanted=print.

Carruthers, S.L. 2000. *The Media at War*. New York: Palgrave MacMillan.

Cassidy, J. 2014. "Forces of Divergence." *New Yorker*, March 31. http://www.newyorker.com/arts/critics/books/2014/03/31/140331crbo_books_cassidy?currentPage=all.

Cebrowski, A. K. and Garstka, J. J. 1998. "Network-Centric Warfare: Its Origin and Future." *Proceedings*, January. http://www.usni.org/Proceedings/Articles98/PROcebrowski.htm.

CIA (Central Intelligence Agency). 2014. Public Affairs Office. https://www.cia.gov/offices-of-cia/public-affairs.

Chalaby, J.K. 2006. "American Cultural Primacy in a New Media Order: A European Perspective." *International Communication Gazette* 68 (1): 33–51. http://dx.doi.org/10.1177/1748048506060114.

Chatterjee, P. 2004. "Rendon Group Wins Hearts and Minds in Business, Politics and War." Corp Watch, August 4. http://www.corpwatch.org/article.php?id=11486

Chomsky, N. 2002. *9–11: Was There an Alternative?* New York: Seven Stories.

–. 2012. "'Losing' the World: American Decline in Perspective, Part 1." *Guardian*, February 14. http://www.guardian.co.uk/commentisfree/cifamerica/2012/feb/14/losing-the-world-american-decline-noam-chomsky.

Cieply, M. 2012. "Film about the Hunt for Bin Laden Leads to a Pentagon Investigation." *New York Times*, January 6. http://www.nytimes.com/2012/01/07/movies/film-on-bin-laden-hunt-leads-to-pentagon-investigation.html?_r=2&ref=petertking&.

–. 2014. "Hollywood Works to Maintain Its World Dominance." *New York Times*, November 3. http://www.nytimes.com/2014/11/04/business/media/hollywood-works-to-maintain-its-world-dominance.html?_r=0.

Clearwater, D.A. 2010. "Living in a Militarized Culture: War, Games and the Experience of US Empire." *TOPIA* 23/24: 260–85.
CNN. 2001. "Hollywood Considers Role in War Effort." CNN.com, November 11. http://articles.cnn.com/2001-11-11/us/rec.hollywood.terror_1_war-effort-hollywood-community-families-need-support?_s=PM:US.
—. 2003a. "NBC to Make Movie about POW Jessica Lynch." CNN.com, April 11. http://www.cnn.com/2003/SHOWBIZ/TV/04/11/lynch.movie.reut/.
—. 2003b. "US Releases Photos Said to Show Saddam's Sons' Bodies." CNN.com, July 24. http://www.cnn.com/2003/WORLD/meast/07/24/sprj.irq.sons/.
—. 2007. "Soldier: Army Ordered Me Not to Tell Truth about Tillman." CNN.com, April 25. http://www.cnn.com/2007/POLITICS/04/24/tillman.hearing/index.html?_s=PM:POLITICS.
—. 2012. "CNN Is Undisputed #1 News Brand in Africa in EMS Africa Survey." CNN.com, July 19. http://cnnpressroom.blogs.cnn.com/2012/07/19/cnn-is-undisputed-1-news-brand-in-africa-in-ems-africa-survey/.
Cochran, J. 2007. "The Making of the Transformers Movie." *ENI*, June 15. http://enewsi.com/news.php?catid=190&itemid=11213.
Cohen, B. 1963. *The Press and Foreign Policy*. Princeton, NJ: Princeton University Press.
Colás, A. 2008. *Empire*. Malden, MA: Polity.
CPJ (Committee to Protect Journalists). 2005. "CPJ Calls on US, Iraqi Authorities, to Explain Journalist Detentions." Global Policy Forum, May 12. http://www.globalpolicy.org/security/issues/iraq/media/2005/0512disappear.htm.
—. 2008. "Attacks on the Press 2007: Iraq." CPJ, February 5. http://www.cpj.org/2008/02/attacks-on-the-press-2007-iraq.php.
Common Dreams. 2012. "Dystopia: Corporate Rule Breeding 'Global Class War.'" January 25. https://www.commondreams.org/headline/2012/01/25-1.
Comor, E. 1994. *The Global Political Economy of Communication*. New York: St. Martin's Press.
—. 1997. "The Re-Tooling of American Hegemony: US Foreign Communication Policy from Free Flow to Free Trade." In *Media in a Global Context: A Reader*, ed. A. Sreberny-Mohammadi, D. Winseck, J. McKenna, and O. Boyd-Barret, 194–206. New York: Arnold.
Comor, E., and H. Bean. 2012. "America's 'Engagement' Delusion: Critiquing a Public Diplomacy Consensus." *International Communication Gazette* 74 (3): 203–20. http://dx.doi.org/10.1177/1748048511432603.
Conerly, B. 2013. "Future of the Dollar as World Reserve Currency." *Forbes*, October 25. http://www.forbes.com/sites/billconerly/2013/10/25/future-of-the-dollar-as-world-reserve-currency/.
Corkin, S. 2000. "Cowboys and Free Markets: Post–World War II Westerns and US Hegemony." *Cinema Journal* 39 (3): 66–91. http://dx.doi.org/10.1353/cj.2000.0007.
Costa, D. 2007. "This Is No Video Game." PCMag.com, September 26. http://www.pcmag.com/article2/0%2c2817%2c2190739%2c00.asp%20%3E.
Council of Foreign Relations. 2012. "Corporate Members." Council of Foreign Relations http://www.cfr.org/about/corporate/roster.html.
Cox, J. 2006. *Information Operations in Operations Enduring Freedom and Iraqi Freedom: What Went Wrong?* Monograph. Leavenworth: US Army Command and General Staff College.

Cox, M. 1995. *US Foreign Policy after the Cold War: Superpower without a Mission*. London: Pinter.

–. 2003. "The Empire's Back in Town: Or America's Imperial Temptation – Again." *Millennium: Journal of International Studies* 32 (1): 1-27.

–. 2004. "Empire, Imperialism and the Bush Doctrine." *Review of International Studies* 30 (4): 585–608. http://dx.doi.org/10.1017/S0260210504006242.

Cox, M., and D. Stokes, eds. 2012. *US Foreign Policy*. Oxford: Oxford University Press.

Cox, R.W. 1993. "Gramsci, Hegemony, and International Relations: An Essay in Method." In *Gramsci, Historical Materialism, and International Relations*, ed. S. Gill, 49–66. New York: Cambridge University Press. http://dx.doi.org/10.1017/CBO9780511558993.003.

–, ed. 2012. *Corporate Power and Globalization in US Foreign Policy*. New York: Routledge.

Cozens, C. 2005. "CBS Cameraman Shot by US Troops." *Guardian*, April 8. http://guardian.co.uk/Iraq/Story/0,2763,1454559,00.html.

Cramer, G., and U. Prutsch. 2006. "Nelson A. Rockefeller's Office of Inter-American Affairs (1940–1946) and Record Group 229." *Hispanic American Historical Review* 86 (4): 785–806. http://dx.doi.org/10.1215/00182168-2006-050.

Creel, G. 1920. *How We Advertised America: The First Telling of the Amazing Story of the Committee on Public Information that Carried the Gospel of Americanism to Every Corner of the Globe*. New York: Harper & Brothers.

Cull, N.J. 2008. *The Cold War and the United States Information Agency: American Propaganda and Public Diplomacy, 1945–1989*. Cambridge: Cambridge University Press. http://dx.doi.org/10.1017/CBO9780511817151.

Cumings, B. 1992. *War and Television*. London: Verso.

Curran, J. 2002. *Media and Power*. New York: Routledge.

Curtin, M. 2003. "Media Capital: Towards the Study of Spatial Flows." *International Journal of Cultural Studies* 6 (2): 202–28. http://dx.doi.org/10.1177/13678779030062004.

Daily Mail Reporter. 2010. "Wikileaks: *Desperate Housewives* Does More to Combat Jihad than US Propaganda." *Mail Online*, December 8. http://www.dailymail.co.uk/news/article-1336778/Wikileaks-Desperate-Housewives-does-combat-jihad-US-propaganda.html

Dalby, S. 2008. "Imperialism, Domination, Culture: The Continued Relevance of Critical Geopolitics." *Geopolitics* 13 (3): 413–36. http://dx.doi.org/10.1080/14650040802203679.

Dale, H.C. 2009. "Public Diplomacy 2.0: Where the US Government Meets 'New Media.'" *Backgrounder* 2346 (2). http://www.heritage.org/research/reports/2009/12/public-diplomacy-2-0-where-the-us-government-meets-new-media

Dao, J. 2001. "Ads Now See Recruits for 'an Army of One.'" *New York Times*, January 10. http://www.nytimes.com/2001/01/10/us/ads-now-seek-recruits-for-an-army-of-one.html.

Dao, J., and E. Schmitt. 2002. "Pentagon Readies Efforts to Sway Sentiment Abroad." *New York Times*, February 19 http://www.nytimes.com/2002/02/19/world/nation-challenged-hearts-minds-pentagon-readies-efforts-sway-sentiment-abroad.html.

Dardis, F.E. 2006. "Marginalization Devices in US Press Coverage of Iraq War Protest: A Content Analysis." *Mass Communication & Society* 9 (2): 117–35. http://dx.doi.org/10.1207/s15327825mcs0902_1.

Davis, A. 2013. *Promotional Cultures*. Malden, MA: Polity Press.
DDB Worldwide. 2002. *America and Cultural Imperialism: A Small Step toward Understanding*. DDB Worldwide Communications Group, January 20. Thought Paper. https://www.utexas.edu/courses/kincaid/AI/readings/Cultural%20Imperialism.pdf"
de Grazia, V. 2005. *Irresistable Empire: America's Advance through 20th Century Europe*. Cambridge, MA: Harvard University Press.
de Matos, Xav. 2011. "Activision Reveals Sales Figures for *Black Ops* and *Modern Warfare 2*." *Shack News*, August 3. http://www.shacknews.com/article/69577/activision-reveals-sales-figures-black-ops-and-modern-warfare-2.
De Rooij, P. 2003. "The Hydra's New Head: Propagandists and Selling the US-Iraq War." CounterPunch, May 14. http://www.counterpunch.org/2003/05/13/the-hydra-s-new-head/.
DeCarlo, S. 2013. "Forbes Global 2000: The World's Biggest Public Companies. *Forbes*, April 17. http://www.forbes.com/sites/scottdecarlo/2013/04/17/the-worlds-biggest-companies-2/.
Dehart, C. 2013. "Hurricane 'Z' Makes Landfall; Max Brooks Joins Army North's Hurricane Rehearsal." US Army, www.army.mil, April 11. http://www.army.mil/article/100871/Hurricane__Z__makes_landfall__Max_Brooks_joins_Army_North_s_hurricane_rehearsal/.
Democracy Now! 2013. "The World Is a Battlefield: Jeremy Scahill on 'Dirty Wars' and Obama's Expanding Drone Attacks." Interview with Nermeen Shaikh and Jeremy Scahill, April 24. http://www.democracynow.org/2013/4/24/the_world_is_a_battlefield_jeremy
Der Derian, J. 2001. *Virtuous War: Mapping the Military Industrial-Media-Entertainment Network*. Boulder, CO: Westview Press.
Derene, G. 2008. "Wii All You Can Be? Why the Military Needs the Gaming Industry." *Popular Mechanics*, May 29. http://www.popularmechanics.com/technology/military/robots/4266106.
Dewey, J. 1985. *The Public and Its Problems*. Chicago: Ohio University Press.
Diamond, E., and S. Bates. 1996. "The Ancient History of the Internet." *American Studies Journal* 39: 1–4.
Dickenson, B. 2006. *Hollywood's New Radicalism: War, Globalization and the Movies from Reagan to George W. Bush*. New York: I.B. Taurus.
Dilanian, K., and R. Keegan. 2012. "Hollywood a Longtime Friend of the CIA." *Los Angeles Times*, March 26. http://articles.latimes.com/2012/may/26/nation/la-na-cia-hollywood-20120527.
Dittmer, J. 2010. *Popular Culture, Geopolitics and Identity*. New York: Rowman & Littlefield.
Dizard, W.P. 1961. *Strategy of Truth*. Washington, DC: Public Affairs Press.
—. 2001. *Digital Diplomacy: US Foreign Policy in the Information Age*. Westport: Praeger.
—. 2004. *Inventing Public Diplomacy: The Story of the US Information Agency*. Boulder, CO: Lynne Rienner.
Djerejian, E.P. 2003. *Changing Minds, Winning Peace: A New Strategic Direction for US Public Diplomacy in the Arab and Muslim World*. Report of the US Advisory Group on Public Diplomacy in the Arab and Muslim World, October 1. US Department of State. http://www.state.gov/documents/organization/24882.pdf.

Dodds, K. 2008. "Screening Terror: Hollywood, the United States and the Construction of Danger." *Critical Studies on Terrorism* 1 (2): 227–43. http://dx.doi.org/10.1080/17539150802184629.

Doherty, T. 1993. *Projections of War: Hollywood, American Culture and World War II*. Berkeley: University of California Press.

–. 2004. "The New War Movies as Moral Rearmament: *Black Hawk Down* and *We Were Soldiers*." In *The War Film*, ed. R. Eberwein, 214–22. New Brunswick, NJ: Rutgers University Press.

Domhoff, W.G. 2013. *Who Rules America? The Triumph of the Corporate Rich*. New York: McGraw-Hill.

Dorfman, A., and A. Mattelart. 1975. *How to Read Donald Duck: Imperialist Ideology in the Disney Comic*. New York: International General Editions.

Dorrien, G. 2004. *Imperial Designs: Neoconservatism and the New Pax Americana*. New York: Routledge. http://dx.doi.org/10.4324/9780203324806.

Douglas, A. 2012. "Here Are the 10 Highest Grossing Video Games Ever." June 13. http://www.businessinsider.com/here-are-the-top-10-highest-grossing-video-games-of-all-time-2012-6?op=1.

Downing, J.H. 2011. "Media Ownership, Concentration, and Control: The Evolution of Debate." In *The Handbook of Political Economy of Communications*, ed. J. Wasko, G. Murdock, and H. Sousa L., 140–68. Malden, MA: Blackwell. http://dx.doi.org/10.1002/9781444395402.ch7.

Doyle, G. 2012. *Audio-Visual Services: International Trade and Cultural Policy*. ABDI Working Paper 355. Tokyo: Asian Development Bank Institute; http://www.adbi.org/working-paper/2012/04/17/5049.audiovisual.srvc.intl.trade.cultural.policy/.

Drennan, J. 2014. "*Call of Duty*: Star Video Game Director Takes Unusual Think Tank Job." *Foreign Policy*, September 22. http://foreignpolicy.com/2014/09/22/call-of-duty-star-video-game-director-takes-unusual-think-tank-job/.

Dreyfuss, R. 2002. "Tinker, Banker, NeoCon, Spy." *American Prospect* 13 (21). http://prospect.org/article/tinker-banker-neocon-spy.

Eberhard, J. 2004. "Liberal Bias in Hollywood." Simply Search 4 It! March 5. http://www.simplysearch4it.com/article/34012.html.

Economist. 2002. "Think Local: Cultural Imperialism Doesn't Sell." April 11. http://www.economist.com/node/1066620.

–. 2007. "The Hobbled Hegemon." June 30. http://www.economist.com/node/9401945.

–. 2011. "Hollywood Goes Global." February 17. http://www.economist.com/node/18178291.

Elder, R.E. 1968. *The Information Machine: The United States Information Agency and American Foreign Policy*. New York: Syracuse University Press.

Elmer, G. 2002. "The Trouble with the Canadian 'Body Double': Runaway Productions and Foreign Location Shooting." *Screen* 43 (4): 423–31. http://dx.doi.org/10.1093/screen/43.4.423.

Elteren, M. V. 2006. "Rethinking Americanization Abroad: Toward a Critical Alternative to Prevailing Paradigms." *Journal of American Culture* 29 (3): 345–67.

eMarketer. 2014. "North America Holds Tight to World's Largest Ad Spending Share." *eMarketer*, September 30. http://www.emarketer.com/Article/North-America-Holds-Tight-Worlds-Largest-Ad-Spending-Share/1011243#sthash.FCDOgXsf.dpuf.

Enda, J. 2011. "Retreating from the World." *AJR* (December–January). http://ajrarchive.org/Article.asp?id=4985.
England, R., ed. 1984. *The Grenada Mission: Crisis Editorializing in the* New York Times, Wall Street Journal, Washington Post *and* Washington Times. Washington, DC: Ethics and Public Policy Center.
Engelhardt, T. 2010. *The American Way of War: How Bush's Wars Became Obama's*. Chicago: Haymarket Books.
—. 1994. "The Gulf War as Total Television." In *Seeing through the Media*, ed. S. Jeffords and L. Rabinovitz, 81–95. New Brunswick, NJ: Rutgers University Press.
Enloe, C. 1989. *Bananas, Beaches and Bases: Making Feminist Sense of International Politics*. Los Angeles: University of California. Press.
ESA (Entertainment Software Association). 2015. "Essential Facts about the Computer and Video Game Industry." http://www.theesa.com/wp-content/uploads/2015/04/ESA-Essential-Facts-2015.pdf.
—. 2014. *About*. http://www.theesa.com/about-esa/.
Entman, R.M. 1993. "Framing: Toward Clarification of a Fractured Paradigm." *Journal of Communication* 43 (4): 51–58. http://dx.doi.org/10.1111/j.1460-2466.1993.tb01304.x.
—. 2003. *Projections of Power: Framing News, Public Opinion and US Foreign Policy*. Chicago: University of Chicago Press. http://dx.doi.org/10.7208/chicago/9780226210735.001.0001.
Ewen, S. 1996. *PR! A Social History of Spin*. New York: Basic Books.
—. 2001. *Captains of Consciousness: Advertising and the Social Roots of the Consumer Culture*. New York: Basic Books.
FAIR. 2002. "The Office of Strategic Influence Is Gone, But Are Its Programs in Place?" Nov. 27. http://fair.org/press-release/the-office-of-strategic-influence-is-gone-but-are-its-programs-in-place/.
Falk, S.L. 1964. "The National Security Council under Truman, Eisenhower and Kennedy." *Political Science Quarterly* 79 (September): 403-34.
Farrier, D. 2010. "*Call of Duty: Black Ops* 'As Real as It Gets.'" 3 News, November 5. http://www.3news.co.nz/entertainment/call-of-duty-black-ops-as-real-as-it-gets-2010110517#axzz3P6bwwTVY.
Ferguson, N. 2005. *Colossus: The Rise and Fall of the American Empire*. New York: Penguin Books.
Fisher, L. 2004. *Presidential War Power*. Lawrence, KS: University Press of Kansas.
Fitzgerald, S.W. 2012. *Corporations and Cultural Industries: Time Warner, Bertelsmann, and News Corporation*. Lanham: Rowman & Littlefield.
Fleming, M. 2012. "Toldja! Relativity Closes Big Acquisition Deal for Navy Seal Movie *Act of Valor*." Deadline, June 11. http://www.deadline.com/2011/06/relativity-media-near-whopping-acquisition-deal-for-navy-seal-pic-act-of-valor/.
Flew, T. 2007. *Understanding Global Media*. New York: Palgrave Macmillan.
Foer, F. 2005. "The Source of the Trouble." *New York Magazine*, May 21. http://nymag.com/nymetro/news/media/features/9226/#.
Foley, M. 2012. "The Foreign Policy Process: Executive, Congress, Intelligence." In *US Foreign Policy*, ed. M. Cox and D. Stokes, 107–28. New York: Oxford University Press.
Forbes. 2014. "US Passes China to Become Most Favored Destination for Foreign Investment, But Washington Could Imperil That." February 2. http://www.forbes.

com/sites/beltway/2014/02/04/u-s-passes-china-to-become-most-favored-destination-for-foreign-investment-but-washington-could-imperil-that/.

Foreign Policy. 2013. "The Power Issue." http://www.foreignpolicy.com/the_power_issue.

Forsyth, S. 2005. "Hollywood Reloaded: The Film as Imperial Commodity." In *Socialist Register 2005: The Empire Re-Loaded*, ed. L. Panitch and C. Leys, 165–78. London: Merlin Press.

Fox News. 2003. "Transcript: Janeane Garofalo on Fox News Sunday." February 24. http://www.foxnews.com/story/2003/02/24/transcript-janeane-garofalo-on-fox-news-sunday/.

Frankel, C. 1965. *The Neglected Aspect of Foreign Affairs: American Educational and Cultural Policy Abroad*. Washington, DC: The Brookings Institute.

Fraser, M. 2003. *Weapons of Mass Distraction: American Empire and Soft Power*. Toronto: Key Porter Books.

Freedman, D. 2003. "Who Wants to Be a Millionaire? The Politics of Television Exports." *Information Communication and Society* 6 (1): 24–41. http://dx.doi.org/10.1080/1369118032000068787.

–. 2008. *The Politics of Media Policy*. Cambridge: Polity Press.

–. 2009. "'Smooth Operator?' The Propaganda Model and Moments of Crisis." *Westminster Papers in Communication and Culture* 6 (2): 59–72.

–. 2014. "Media Policy Research and the Media Industries." *Media Industries Journal* 1 (1): 11–15.

Friedman, T. 1999. "Manifesto for the Fast World." *New York Times*, March 28. http://www.nytimes.com/1999/03/28/magazine/a-manifesto-for-the-fast-world.html?pagewanted=all&src=pm.

Frontline. 2009. "Digital Nation: Waging War, A New Generation." http://www.pbs.org/wgbh/pages/frontline/digitalnation/waging-war/a-new-generation/the-army-experience-center.html.

Fukuyama, F. 1991. *The End of History and the Last Man*. New York: Free Press.

Fulbright, J.W. 1967. *The Arrogance of Power*. New York: Random House.

–. 1970. *The Pentagon Propaganda Machine*. New York: Liveright.

Gabbatt, A. 2010. "*Call of Duty: Black Ops* Upsets Cuba with Castro Mission." *Guardian*, November 11. http://www.theguardian.com/technology/2010/nov/11/call-of-duty-black-ops-cuba-castro.

Gale Encyclopedia of US Economic History. 2014. "Lee, Ivy Ledbetter." Encyclopedia.com, May 10, 2014. http://www.encyclopedia.com/doc/1G2-3406400522.html.

Garrison, A. 2004. "Defining Terrorism: Philosophy of the Bomb, Propaganda by Deed and Change through Fear and Violence." *Criminal Justice Studies* 17 (3): 259–79. http://dx.doi.org/10.1080/1478601042000281105.

Gaudiosi, J. 2011a. "Norway Suspect Used *Call of Duty* to Train for Massacre." *Forbes*, July 24. http://www.forbes.com/sites/johngaudiosi/2011/07/24/norway-suspect-used-activisions-call-of-duty-to-train-for-massacre/

–. 2011b. "Blackwater Founder Erik Prince Enters Video Game Business." CNN, September 12. http://www.cnn.com/2011/TECH/gaming.gadgets/09/12/erik.prince.interview/.

Gelb, L.H., and J. Zelmati. 2009. "Mission Unaccomplished." *Democracy: A Journal of Ideas* 13 (Summer): 10-24. http://www.democracyjournal.org/13/6686.php?page=all.

German, K. 1990. "Frank Capra's *Why We Fight* Series and the American Audience." *Western Journal of Speech Communication* 54 (2): 237–48. http://dx.doi.org/10.1080/10570319009374338.

Ghosh, P. 2013. "Bollywood at 100: How Big Is India's Mammoth Film Industry?" *International Business Times*. May 3. http://www.ibtimes.com/bollywood-100-how-big-indias-mammoth-film-industry-1236299.

Gilboa, E. 2005. "The CNN Effect: The Search for a Communication Theory of International Relations." *Political Communication* 22 (1): 27–44. http://dx.doi.org/10.1080/10584600590908429.

Gilens, M. 2012. *Affluence and Influence: Economic Inequality and Political Power in America*. Princeton, NJ: Princeton University Press.

Gilens, M., and B.I. Page. 2014. "Testing Theories of American Politics: Elites, Interest Groups, and Average Citizens." *Perspectives on Politics* 12 (3): 564–81. http://dx.doi.org/10.1017/S1537592714001595.

Gill, S., ed. 1993. *Gramsci, Historical Materialism, and International Relations*. New York: Cambridge University Press. http://dx.doi.org/10.1017/CBO9780511558993.

Gilson, D. 2011. "Only Little People Pay Taxes." *Mother Jones*. April 18. http://www.motherjones.com/politics/2011/04/taxes-richest-americans-charts-graph.

Gitlin, T. 2001. *Media Unlimited: How the Torrent of Images and Sounds Overwhelms Our Lives*. New York: Metropolitan Books.

Glassman, J.K. 2008. "Public Diplomacy 2.0: A New Approach to Global Engagement." Remarks to the New America Foundation. US Department of State. http://2001-2009.state.gov/r/us/2008/112605.htm.

Glassner, S.B. 2003. "Media and Military Try Experiment in Openness." *Washington Post*, March 7. A14.

Global Viewpoint. 2001. "Hollywood and the War against Terror." *New Perspectives Quarterly*, November 19. http://www.digitalnpq.org/global_services/global%20viewpoint/11-19-01 valenti.html.

Golloway, S. 2012. "How Hollywood Conquered the World (All Over Again)." *Foreign Policy*, February 23. http://foreignpolicy.com/2012/02/24/how-hollywood-conquered-the-world-all-over-again/

Goodman, A. 2003. "US Attacks Kill Three Journalists." CNN.com, April 8. http://www.cnn.com/2003/WORLD/meast/04/08/sprj.irq.hotel/.

Gottron, F. 2007. "Project Bioshield: Appropriations, Acquisitions, and Policy Implementation Issues for Congress." CRS Report for Congress, June 11. http://fas.org/sgp/crs/terror/RL33907.pdf.

Gould, E. 2012. *Among the Powers of the Earth: The American Revolution and the Making of a New World Empire*. Cambridge, MA: Harvard University Press.

Gowan, P. 1997. *The Global Gamble*. New York: Verso.

Graber, D. 2011. "Terrorism, Censorship, and the First Amendment." In *Media Power in Politics*, ed. D. Graber, 407–20. Washington, DC: QC Press.

Graffy, C. 2009. "The Rise of Public Diplomacy 2.0 in Revitalizing Public Diplomacy." *Journal of International Security Affairs* (Fall): 47–53.

Graham, R. 2008. "An Offer They Couldn't Refuse." *Guardian*, November 14. http://www.theguardian.com/film/2008/nov/14/thriller-ridley-scott.

Gramsci, A. 1971. *Selections from the Prison Notebooks*. New York: International Publishers.

Grandin, G. 2006. *Empire's Workshop: Latin America, the United States and the Rise of the New Imperialism*. New York: Holt.

Grant, P.S., and C. Wood. 2004. *Blockbusters and Trade Wars: Popular Culture in a Globalized World*. Vancouver: Douglas and McIntyre.

Greenslade, R. 2003. "Their Master's Voice." *Guardian*, February 17. http://www.guardian.co.uk/media/2003/feb/17/mondaymediasection.iraq.

Greenwald, G. 2012a. "Obama: A GOP President Should Have Rules Limiting the Kill Lists." *Guardian*, November 26. http://www.guardian.co.uk/commentisfree/2012/nov/26/obama-drones-kill-list-framework.

–. 2012b. "*Zero Dark Thirty*: CIA Hagiography, Pernicious Propaganda." *Guardian*, December 14. http://www.guardian.co.uk/commentisfree/2012/dec/14/zero-dark-thirty-cia-propaganda.

–. 2013. "Washington Gets Explicit: Its 'War on Terror' Is Permanent." *Guardian*, May 17. http://www.guardian.co.uk/commentisfree/2013/may/17/endless-war-on-terror-obama.

Griffin, B., M. Capassa, and J. Cukier. 2013. "FCC Clarifies Rule Governing Foreign Ownership of Broadcasting Stations." Mintz Levin, Communications, November 14. http://www.mintz.com/newsletter/2013/Advisories/3557-1213-NAT-COM/index.html.

Grondin, D. 2011. "The Other Spaces of War: War Beyond the Battlefield in the War on Terror." *Geopolitics* 16 (2): 253–79. http://dx.doi.org/10.1080/14650045.2010.538877.

–. D. 2014. "Publicizing the US National Security State through Entertainment." E-International Relations, August 6. http://www.e-ir.info/2014/08/06/publicizing-the-us-national-security-state-through-entertainment/.

Haiken, M. 2013. "Suicide Rate among Vets and Active Duty Military Jumps – Now 22 a Day." *Forbes*, February 5. http://www.forbes.com/sites/melaniehaiken/2013/02/05/22-the-number-of-veterans-who-now-commitsuicide-every-day/.

Hallin, D.C. 1989. *The Uncensored War: The Media and Vietnam*. Oakland: University of California Press.

–. 1997. "The Media and War." In *International Media Research: A Critical Survey*, ed. J. Corner, P. Schlesinger, and R. Silverstone, 208–30. London and New York: Routledge.

Hallward, P. 2010. *Damming the Flood: Haiti and the Politics of Containment*. New York: Verso.

Halper, S., and J. Clarke. 2004. *America Alone: The Neoconservatives and the Global Order*. Cambridge: Cambridge University Press. http://dx.doi.org/10.1017/CBO9780511509773.

Halpern, S. 2008. "Virtual Iraq." *The New Yorker*, May 19. http://www.newyorker.com/magazine/2008/05/19/virtual-iraq.

Halter, E. 2006. *From Sun Tzu to Xbox: War and Video Games*. New York: Thunder Mouth Press.

Hamel, M. 2014. "Netflix Bets on International Expansion to Keep Growing." CNBC, March 13. http://www.cnbc.com/id/101487231.

Hammond, W.H. 2000. *Reporting Vietnam: Media and Military at War*. Lawrence: University Press of Kansas.

Hansen, A.C. 1984. *USIA: Public Diplomacy in the Computer Age*. New York: Praeger.

Hardt, H. 1988. "Comparative Media Research: The World According to America." *Critical Studies in Mass Communication* 5 (10): 129–46.

Hardt, M., and A. Negri. 2000. *Empire*. Cambridge, MA: Harvard University Press.

Harmon, A. 2003. "More than Just a Game, But How Close to Reality?" *New York Times*, April 3. http://www.nytimes.com/2003/04/03/technology/more-than-just-a-game-but-how-close-to-reality.html.

Harris, M. 2014. *Five Came Back: A Story of Hollywood and the Second World War*. New York: Penguin Press.

Harvey, D. 2003. *The New Imperialism*. New York: Oxford.

–. 2005. *A Brief History of Neoliberalism*. New York: Oxford.

Hassner, P. 2002. "The United States: The Empire of Force or the Force of Empire?" Chaillot Papers 54. Paris: European Union ISS. Institute of Security Studies. http://www.iss.europa.eu/publications/detail/article/the-united-states-the-empire-of-force-or-the-force-of-empire/.

Hastings, M. 2013. "*Zero Dark Thirty* and the CIA's Hollywood Coup." Buzzfeed, January 8. http://www.buzzfeed.com/mhastings/the-cias-hollywood-coup.

Hayes, D., and M. Guardino. 2010. "Whose Views Made the News? Media Coverage and the March to War in Iraq." *Political Communication* 27 (1): 59–87. http://dx.doi.org/10.1080/10584600903502615.

Herman, E., and N. Chomsky. 1988. *Manufacturing Consent: The Political Economy of the Mass Media*. New York: Pantheon Books.

Herman, E., and R. McChesney. 1997. *The Global Media: The New Missionaries of Global Capitalism*. London, Washington: Continuum.

Hersh, S. 2003. "Selective Intelligence." *New Yorker*, May 12. http://www.newyorker.com/magazine/2003/05/12/selective-intelligence.

Herz, J.C. 1997. *Joystick Nation: How Videogames Ate Our Quarters, Won Our Hearts, and Rewired Our Minds*. Boston: Little, Brown.

Herz, J.C., and M. Macedonia. 2002. "Computer Games and the Military: Two Views." *Defense Horizons* 11 (1). Center for Technology and National Security Policy, National Defense University. http://www.isn.ethz.ch/Digital-Library/Publications/Detail/?ots591=0c54e3b3-1e9c-be1e-2c24-a6a8c7060233&lng=en&id=135079.

Hiebert, R.E. 1966. *Courtier to the Crowd: The Story of Ivy Lee and the Development of Public Relations*. Ames: Iowa State University Press.

Hills, J. 2002. *The Struggle for Control of Global Communication: The Formative Century*. Chicago: University of Illinois Press.

–. 2007. *Tele-Communications and Empire*. Chicago: University of Illinois Press.

Hind, D. 2010. *The Return of the Public*. New York: Verso.

Hoad, P. 2013. "Hollywood's Hold over Global Box Office: 63% and Falling." *Guardian*, April 2. http://www.theguardian.com/film/filmblog/2013/apr/02/hollywood-hold-global-box-office.

Hodes, J., and E. Ruby-Sachs. 2002 "*America's Army* Targets Youth." *The Nation*, August 23.http://www.thenation.com/article/americas-army-targets-youth.

Hollywood Tonight. 2007. "About the Production." http://www.hollywoodtonight.com/wbpictures/iamlegend/notes005.html.

Holsti, K.J. 2011. "Exceptionalism in American Foreign Policy: Is It Exceptional?" *European Journal of International Relations* 17 (3): 381–404. http://dx.doi.org/10.1177/1354066110377674.

Holsti, O.R. 2004. *Public Opinion and American Foreign Policy.* Ann Arbor, MI: University of Michigan.

Horkheimer, M., and T. Adorno. 1995. *The Culture Industry: Enlightenment as Mass Deception. The Dialectic of the Enlightenment.* New York: Continuum.

Horne, G. 2001. *Class Struggles in Hollywood, 1930–1950: Moguls, Mobsters, Stars, Reds and Trade Unionists.* Austin: University of Texas Press.

Hosenball, M. 2007. "Myth Making." MSNBC, *Newsweek*, April 28. http://web.archive.org/web/20070501100844/http://www.msnbc.msn.com/id/18368821/site/newsweek/.

Houpt, S. 2013. "Ken Taylor Sets the Record Straight about *Argo*'s Take on the 'Canadian Caper.'" *Globe and Mail*, February 25. http://www.theglobeandmail.com/arts/awards-and-festivals/film-awards/ken-taylor-sets-the-record-straight-about-argos-take-on-the-canadian-caper/article9044112/.

Howell, C.D. 1987. "War, Television and Public Opinion." *Military Review* 67 (2): 71–79.

Hudson, J. 2007. "Disney Video Launch *Welcome–Portraits of America*." Dipnote (US Department of State blog), October 25. https://blogs.state.gov/stories/2007/10/26/disney-video-launch-welcome-portraits-america.

–. 2013. "US Spends $24 Million on 'Propaganda Plane' Few Can See or Hear." *Foreign Policy*, July 28. http://foreignpolicy.com/2013/07/28/u-s-spends-24-million-on-propaganda-plane-few-can-see-or-hear/.

Huntemann, N., and M.T. Payne. 2010. Introduction. In *Joystick Soldiers: The Politics of Play in Military Video Games*, 1–19. New York: Routledge.

Hurdle, J. 2009. "US Army Recruiting at the Mall with Video Games." Reuters, January 9. http://www.reuters.com/article/2009/01/10/us-usa-army-recruiting-idUSTRE50819H20090110.

IGN. 2008. "Topware Entertains the Troops." IGN.com, September 19. http://ca.ign.com/articles/2008/09/19/topware-entertains-the-troops.

Ignatieff, M. 2003. "The Burden." *New York Times*, January 5. http://www.nytimes.com/2003/01/05/magazine/the-american-empire-the-burden.html?pagewanted=all&src=pm.

Innis, H.A. 1950. *The Bias of Communication.* Toronto: University of Toronto Press.

–. 1995. "Great Britain, the United States, and Canada." In *Staples, Markets and Cultural Change: Harold A. Innis, Selected Essays*, ed. D. Drache, 271–89. Montreal/Kingston: McGill-Queen's University Press.

–. 2007. *Empire and Communications.* Toronto: Dundurn Press.

IIPA (International Intellectual Property Alliance). 2013. *About IIPA.* http://www.iipa.com/aboutiipa.html.

Internet Association. 2013. *About Internet Association.* http://internetassociation.org/.

Ismi, A. 2014. "BRICS and the SCO Challenge US Global Dominance." Canadian Centre for Policy Alternatives, November 1. https://www.policyalternatives.ca/publications/monitor/brics-and-sco-challenge-us-global-dominance.

Jacobs, A. 2003. "My Week at Embed Boot Camp." *New York Times*, March 2. http://www.nytimes.com/2003/03/02/magazine/02PROCESS.html?pagewanted=all12.

Jacobs, L. and B. Page. 2005. "Who Influences U.S. Foreignolicy?" *American Political Science Review* 99 (1): 107–23.

Jamail, D. 2007. "Another Casualty: Coverage of the Iraq War." *Foreign Policy in Focus*, March 23. http://www.fpif.org/fpiftxt/4105.

James, M. 2013. "Global Spending for Media and Entertainment to Rise Steadily." *Lost Angeles Times*, June 5. http://www.latimes.com/entertainment/envelope/cotown/la-fi-ct-media-pwc-20130605-story.html.

Jenkins, T. 2009. "How the Central Intelligence Agency Works with Hollywood: An Interview with Paul Barry, the CIA's New Entertainment Industry Liaison." *Media Culture and Society* 31 (3): 489–95. http://dx.doi.org/10.1177/0163443709102721.

—. 2012. *The CIA in Hollywood: How the Agency Shapes Film and Television*. Austin, TX: University of Texas Press.

Jin, D.Y. 2005. "The Telecom Crisis and Beyond: Restructuring of the Global Telecommunications System." *Gazette: The International Journal for Communication Studies* 67 (3): 289–304. http://dx.doi.org/10.1177/0016549205052232.

—. 2007. "Reinterpretation of Cultural Imperialism: Emerging Domestic Market vs. Continuing US Dominance." *Media Culture and Society* 29 (5): 753–71. http://dx.doi.org/10.1177/0163443707080535.

—. 2008. "Neoliberal Restructuring of the Global Communication System: Mergers and Acquisitions." *Media Culture and Society* 30 (3): 357–73. http://dx.doi.org/10.1177/0163443708088792.

—. 2011. "A Critical Analysis of US Cultural Policy in the Global Film Market: Nation-States and FTAs." *International Communication Gazette* 73 (8): 651–69. http://dx.doi.org/10.1177/1748048511420092.

—. 2012. "Transforming the Global Film Industries: Horizontal Integration and Vertical Concentration amid Neoliberal Globalization." *International Communication Gazette* 74 (5): 405–22. http://dx.doi.org/10.1177/1748048512445149.

—. 2013. "The Construction of Platform Imperialism in the Globalization Era." *TripleC* 11 (1): 145–72.

Jinks, D., and D. Sloss. 2004. "Is the President Bound by the Geneva Conventions?" *Cornell Law Review* 90 (1): 96–202.

Johnson, C. 2004. *The Sorrows of Empire: Militarism, Secrecy, and the End of the Republic*. New York: Metropolitan Books.

—. 2010. *Dismantling the Empire: America's Last Best Hope*. New York: Metropolitan Books.

Johnson, L.B. 1965. "Intensified and Expanded PSYOPS Activities in Vietnam." *National Security Action Memorandum 330*, April 9. Washington, DC.

Johnston, W. 2010. "War Games Lure Recruits for 'Real Thing.'" *NPR*, July 31. http://www.npr.org/2010/07/31/128875936/war-games-lure-recruits-for-real-thing.

JCS (Joint Chiefs of Staff). 1996. *Joint Vision 2010*. Washington, DC: Government Printing Press.

—. 2007. *Department of Defense Dictionary of Military and Associated Terms, Joint Publication 1–02*. March. Washington, DC: Department of Defense.

Julian, G. 2007. "Transforming the Department of Defense Strategic Communication." In *Information as Power: An Anthology of US Army War College Student Papers*, ed. D. Murphy, J. Groah, D. Smith, and C. Ayers, 53–58. Carlisle, PA: US Army War College.

—. 2011. "Hollywood Tries a New Battle Plan." *Wall Street Journal*, August 26. http://www.wsj.com/articles/SB10001424053111904787404576528293606172306.

Kaldor, M. 2007. *New and Old Wars: Organized Violence in a Global Era*. Stanford: Stanford University Press.

Kamiya, G. 2005. "Iraq's Unseen War: The Photos Washington Doesn't Want You to See." Spiegel Online International, August 25. http://www.spiegel.de/international/iraq-s-unseen-war-the-photos-washington-doesn-t-want-you-to-see-a-371411.html.

—. 2007. "Iraq: Why the Media Failed." Salon, April 10. http://www.salon.com/2007/04/10/media_failure/.

Kampfner, J. 2008. "The Truth about Jessica." *Guardian*, May 15. http://www.theguardian.com/world/2003/may/15/iraq.usa2.

Kaplan, A. 2002. *The Anarchy of Empire in the Making of US Culture*. Cambridge, MA: Harvard University Press.

Kaplan, R. 2014. "In Defense of Empire." *The Atlantic*, March 14. http://www.theatlantic.com/magazine/archive/2014/04/in-defense-of-empire/358645/.

Karl, J. 2008. "The Pentagon's Propaganda Machine?" ABC News, April 21. http://abcnews.go.com/Blotter/story?id=4696120&page=1#.TweG59RSS_g.

Keane, M. 2006. "Once Were Peripheral: Creating Media Capacity in East Asia." *Media Culture and Society* 28 (6): 835–55. http://dx.doi.org/10.1177/0163443706068712.

Kellerhals, M.D., Jr. 2009. "State's McHale to Spearhead US Global Public Engagement." IIP Digital, June 2. http://iipdigital.usembassy.gov/st/english/article/2009/06/20090602083933dmslahrellek0.6198542.html#axzz2aCOM3gc5.

Kellman, S.G. 2005. "Winning the Next War at the Multiplex." High Beam Research, February 4. http://www.highbeam.com/doc/1P3-831126521.html.

Kellner, D. 1992. *The Persian Gulf TV War*. Boulder, CO: Westview Press.

Kennedy, P. 1987. *The Rise and Fall of Great Powers*. New York: Random House.

Kennedy, W.V. 1993. *Media and the Military: Why the Press Cannot Be Trusted to Cover a War*. Westport: Praeger.

Keohane, R. 1984. *After Hegemony: Corporation and Discord in the World Political Economy*. Princeton, NJ: Princeton University Press.

Khanfar, W. 2005. "Why Did You Want to Bomb Me, Mr. Bush and Mr. Blair?" *Guardian*, December 1. http://www.theguardian.com/world/2005/dec/01/iraq.usa.

King, G. 2007. "Play, Modality and Claims of Realism in *Full Spectrum Warrior*." In *Videogame, Player, Text*, ed. B. Atkins and T. Krzywinska, 52–65. Manchester and New York: Manchester University Press.

Kispal-Kovacs, J. 2010. *Film, Television and American Society: Lectures on the Media and on Empire*. Dubuque, IA: Kendall Hunt.

Klein, N. 2007. *The Shock Doctrine: The Rise of Disaster Capitalism*. Toronto: Alfred A. Knopf.

Klindo, M., and R. Phillips. 2005. "Military Interference in American Film Production." World Socialist Web Site, March 14. http://www.wsws.org/en/articles/2005/03/holl-m14.html.

Kline, S., N. Dyer-Witherford, and G. De Peuter. 2003. *Digital Play: the Interaction of Technology, Culture and Marketing*. Montreal and Kingston: McGill-Queen's University Press.

Knightley, P. 1975. *The First Casualty: From the Crimea to Vietnam, the War Correspondent as Hero, Propaganda and Myth Maker*. New York: Harcourt Brace.

—. 2003. "History or Bunkum?" *British Journalism Review* 14 (2): 7–14. http://dx.doi.org/10.1177/09564748030142002.

Kocieniewski, D. 2011. "Rich Tax Breaks Bolster Makers of Video Games." *New York Times*, September 10. http://www.nytimes.com/2011/09/11/technology/rich-tax-breaks-bolster-video-game-makers.html.

Koppes, C.R., and G.D. Black. 1977. "What to Show the World: The Office of War Information and Hollywood, 1942–1945." *Journal of American History* 64 (1): 87–105. http://dx.doi.org/10.2307/1888275.

Korolov, M. 2013. "15 Most Powerful Big Data Companies." Network World, August 12. http://www.networkworld.com/article/2288276/big-data-business-intelligence/114134-15-most-powerful-Big-Data-companies.html.

Kozlov, V. 2013 "*Stalingrad* Tops Russia's Box Office for 2013." Hollywood Reporter, December 27. http://www.hollywoodreporter.com/news/stalingrad-tops-russias-box-office-667735.

Kraidy, M.M. 2005. *Hybridity, or, The Cultural Logic of Globalization*. Philadelphia: Temple University Press.

Kremer, J., M. Stigset, and S. Treloar. 2011. "Norway Shooting Suspect Breivik Is Ordered into Isolation for Four Weeks." Bloomberg, July 25. http://www.bloomberg.com/news/articles/2011-07-24/norway-killing-suspect-may-explain-motives.

Krugman, P. 2015. "Errors and Lies." *New York Times*, May 18. http://www.nytimes.com/2015/05/18/opinion/paul-krugman-errors-and-lies.html?_r=0.

Krulak, C.C. 1997. "Military Thinking and Decision Making Exercises." *Marine Corps Order 1500.55*, Department of the Navy, April 12. http://www.marines.mil/Portals/59/Publications/MCO%201500.55.pdf.

Kruzel, J.J. 2007. "Service Members Get Sneak Preview of *Transformers*." US Department of Defense, June 29. http://www.defense.gov/news/newsarticle.aspx?id=46591.

Kumar, D. 2006. "Media, War and Propaganda: Strategies of Information Management During the 2003 Iraq War." *Critical Studies in Media Communication* 3 (1): 46–69.

Kumar, D., and D. Kundnani. 2014. "Imagining National Security: The CIA, Hollywood, and the War on Terror." *Democratic Communiqué* 26 (2): 72–83.

Kumar, P. 2011. "Shrinking Foreign Coverage." *American Journalism Review*, December–January. http://ajrarchive.org/article.asp?id=4998.

Kurtz, H. 2003. "For Media after Iraq, a Case of Shell Shock." *Washington Post*, April 28. http://www.washingtonpost.com.

LaFeber, W. 1975. *The New Empire: An Interpretation of American Expansion, 1860–1898*. Ithaca, NY: Cornell University Press.

—. 1994. *The American Age: US Foreign Policy at Home and Abroad 1750 to the Present*. New York: W.W. Norton.

—. 1999. "The Tension between Democracy and Capitalism during the American Century." In *The Ambiguous Legacy: US Foreign Relations in the 'American Century,'* ed. M.J. Hogan, 152–82. New York: Cambridge University Press. http://dx.doi.org/10.1017/CBO9780511625954.008.

Lamar, J.V. 1986. "The Pentagon Goes Hollywood." *Time Magazine*, November 24. http://content.time.com/time/magazine/article/0,9171,962933,00.html.

LaRocque, G. 1997. *The Military in the Movies: Transcript of a Program from America's Defense Monitor*. Washington, DC: Center for Defense Information.

Larson, C. 1948. "The Domestic Motion Picture Work of the Office of War Information." *Hollywood Quarterly* 3 (4): 434–43. http://dx.doi.org/10.2307/1209318.

Lasswell, H. 1970. "Must Science Serve Political Power?" *American Psychologist* 25 (2): 117–23. http://dx.doi.org/10.1037/h0029372.

Latham, M.E. 2000. *Modernization as Ideology: American Social Science and 'Nation Building' in the Kennedy Era*. Chapel Hill: University of North Carolina Press.

Layne, C. 1993. "The Unipolar Illusion: Why New Great Powers Will Rise." *International Security* 17 (4): 5–51. http://dx.doi.org/10.2307/2539020.

–. 2012. "US Decline." In *US Foreign Policy*, ed. M. Cox and D. Stokes, 410–27. New York: Oxford University Press.

Lee, K. 2008. "'The Little State Department': Hollywood and the MPAA's Influence on US Trade Relations." *Northwestern Journal of International Law and Business* 28 (2): 371–97.

Lee, T. 2014. "How the Revolving Door Lets Hollywood Shape Obama's Agenda." Vox, April 22. http://www.vox.com/2014/4/22/5636466/hollywood-just-hired-another-white-house-trade-official.

Lenoir, T. 2000. "All But War Is Simulation: The Military-Entertainment Complex." *Configurations* 8 (3): 289–335. http://dx.doi.org/10.1353/con.2000.0022.

–. 2003. "Programming Theaters of War: Gamemakers as Soldiers." In *Bombs and Bandwidth: The Emerging Relationship between Information Technology and Security*, ed. R. Latham, 175–99. New York and London: The New Press.

Lenoir, T., and H. Lowood. 2002. *Theaters of War: The Military-Entertainment Complex*. Stanford University. http://www.stanford.edu/dept/HPST/TimLenoir/Publications/Lenoir-Lowood_TheatersOfWar.pdf.

Lessig, L. 2012. *Republic, Lost: How Money Corrupts Congress – And a Plan to Stop It*. New York: Twelve.

Lewis, A. 2012. "'Game of Thrones' Most Pirated Show of 2012." *The Hollywood Reporter*, December 27. http://www.hollywoodreporter.com/live-feed/game-thrones-2012s-top-10-406420.

Lewis, J., and R. Brookes. 2004. "How British Television News Represented the Case for War." In *Reporting War*, ed. S. Allan and B. Zelizer, 283–300. New York: Routledge.

Lewis, J., and T. Miller, eds. *Critical Cultural Policy Studies: A Reader*. Malden, MA: Blackwell Publishing.

Lewis, M., and Reading-Smith, M. 2008. "False Pretenses." The Center for Public Integrity, January 23. http://www.publicintegrity.org/2008/01/23/5641/false-pretenses.

Lexington. 2012. "Not Bluffing." *Economist*, March 2. http://www.economist.com/blogs/lexington/2012/03/obama-iran.

Liebes, T., and E. Katz. 1990. *The Export of Meaning: Cross-Cultural Readings of Dallas*. Oxford: Oxford University Press.

Lindorff, D. 2012. "Are US Troops Targeting Journalists?" CounterPunch, November 26. http://www.counterpunch.org/2012/11/26/are-us-troops-targeting-journalists/.

Linkins, J. 2009. "Ralph Peters Calls for Military Killing of War Journalists." *Huff Post Media*, June 26. http://www.huffingtonpost.com/2009/05/26/ralph-peters-calls-for-mi_n_207719.html.

Lippmann, W. 1920. *Liberty and the News*. New York: Harcourt and Brace.

–. 1922. *Public Opinion*. New York: Free Press.

–. 1955. *Essays in the Public Philosophy*. Boston: Little, Brown.

Lord, C. 1989. "The Psychological Dimension in National Security." In *Political Warfare and Psychological Operations: Rethinking the US Approach*, ed. F.B. Barnett and C. Lord, 13–37. Washington, DC: National Defense University Press.
Louw, E. 2005. *The Media and Political Process*. London: Sage.
Louw, P.E. 2003. "The 'War against Terrorism': A Public Relations Challenge for the Pentagon." *Gazette: International Journal for Communication Studies* 65 (3): 211–30. http://dx.doi.org/10.1177/0016549203065003001.
Lubin, G. 2011. "Hillary Clinton Says Al Jazeera Is Putting American Media to Shame." Business Insider, March 2. http://www.businessinsider.com/hillary-clinton-Al Jazeera-2011-3.
Lublin, J.S. 2010. "The Year's Top 10 Highest Paid CEOs." *Wall Street Journal*, November 14. http://www.wsj.com/articles/SB10001424052748704393604575614852198144276.
Luce, H.R. 1941. "The American Century." *Life* (Chicago) February 17, 61–65.
Lucas, J. 2007. "Deaths in Other Nations since WW II Due to US Interventions." Countercurrents, April 24. http://www.countercurrents.org/lucas240407.htm.
Lundestad, G. 1998. *Empire by Integration: The United States and European Integration, 1945–1997*. New York: Oxford University Press.
Lyman, R. 2001. "White House Sets Meeting with Film Executives to Discuss War on Terrorism." *New York Times*, November 8. http://www.nytimes.com/2001/11/08/national/08HOLL.html.
MacKay, N. 2003. "Revealed: The Secret Cabal which Spun for Blair." *Sunday Herald*, June 8. http://globalresearch.ca/articles/MAC308A.html.
Maddaus, G. 2014. "Here Are the Winners and Losers in California's $330 Million Film Tax Subsidy." *LA Weekly*, August 28. http://www.laweekly.com/news/here-are-the-winners-and-losers-in-californias-330-million-film-tax-subsidy-5036475.
Mail Today Reporter. 2012. "CSI the Most Watched Show in the World." *Mail Online India*, June 12. http://www.dailymail.co.uk/indiahome/indianews/article-2160093/CSI-watched-world.html.
Mallaby, S. 2002. "The Reluctant Imperialist: Terrorism, Failed States and the Case for American Empire." *Foreign Affairs* 81 (2): 2–7. http://dx.doi.org/10.2307/20033079.
Malone, G.D. 1988. *Political Advocacy and Cultural Communication: Organizing the Nation's Public Diplomacy*. Lanham, MD: University Press of America.
Mandel, E. 1999. *Late Capitalism*. New York: Verso.
Marchand, R. 1986. *Advertising the American Dream: Making Way for Modernity, 1920–1940*. Oakland: University of California Press.
Mariscal, J. 2007. "The Poverty Draft: Do Military Recruiters Disproportionately Target Communities of Color and the Poor?" The Free Library, June 1. http://www.thefreelibrary.com.
Martin, A., and T. Lin. 2011. "Keyboards First. Then Grenades." *New York Times*, May 1. http://www.nytimes.com/2011/05/02/technology/02wargames.html.
Martin, D. 2012. "7 Navy SEALs Disciplined for Role with Video Game." CBS News, November 8. http://www.cbsnews.com/news/7-navy-seals-disciplined-for-role-with-video-game/.
Mattelart, A. 2002. "An Archaeology of the Global Era: Constructing a Belief." *Media Culture and Society* 24 (5): 591–612. http://dx.doi.org/10.1177/016344370202400502.

Matthews, L.J., and T. Pavri, eds. 1999. *Population Diversity and the US Army*. Strategic Studies Institute. Carlisle, PA: US Army War College.

Maxwell, R. 2001. "Remembering Herbert I. Schiller." *Television and New Media* 2 (1): 3–6. http://dx.doi.org/10.1177/152747640100200101.

—. 2003. *Herbert Schiller*. New York: Rowman & Littlefield.

McChesney, R.W. 1999. *Rich Media, Poor Democracy: Communication Politics in Dubious Times*. New York: The New Press.

—. 2004. *The Problem of the Media: US Communication Politics in the 21st Century*. New York: Monthly Review Press.

—. 2008. *The Political Economy of Media: Enduring Issues, Emerging Dilemmas*. New York: Monthly Review Press.

—. 2014a. *Blowing the Roof Off the Twenty-First Century*. New York: Monthly Review Press.

—. 2014b. "Sharp Left Turn for the Media Reform Movement." *Monthly Review* 65 (9). http://monthlyreview.org/2014/02/01/sharp-left-turn-media-reform-movement/.

McChesney, R.W., and J. Nichols. 2010. *The Death and Life of American Journalism: The Media Revolution that Will Begin the World Again*. Philadelphia: Nation Books.

—. 2012. "This Isn't What Democracy Looks Like." *Monthly Review* (New York) 64 (6): 1. http://dx.doi.org/10.14452/MR-064-06-2012-10_1 http://monthlyreview.org/2012/11/01/this-isnt-what-democracy-looks-like.

—. 2002. *Our Media, Not Theirs: The Democratic Struggle against Corporate Media*. New York: Seven Stories Press.

McDowell, S.D. 2003. "Theory and Research in International Communication: A Historical and Institutional Account." In *International and Development Communication: A 21st Century Perspective*, ed. B. Mody, 5–18. London: Sage Publications. http://dx.doi.org/10.4135/9781452229737.n2.

McGinnis, J. 1988. *The Selling of the President*. New York: Penguin.

McHugh, P. 2011. "Navy SEAL Risks, Rewards Captured in Feature Film." *San Francisco Chronicle*, June 7. http://www.sfgate.com/news/article/Navy-SEAL-risks-rewards-captured-in-feature-film-2368341.php.

McIntyre, J. 2003. "Lynch: Military Played Up Rescue Too Much." CNN.com, November 7. http://www.cnn.com/2003/US/11/07/lynch.interview/index.html?_s=PM:US.

McLaughlin, S. 2009. "US Army Expands Use of Video Games for Training." *World Politics Review*, May 8. http://www.worldpoliticsreview.com/articles/3724/u-s-army-expands-use-of-video-games-for-training.

McLeroy, C. 2008. "Army Experience Center Opens in Philadelphia." US Army, www.army.mil, September 2. http://www.army.mil/article/12072/army-experience-center-opens-in-philadelphia/.

McLuhan, M. 1997. *Understanding Media: The Extensions of Man*. Cambridge, MA: MIT Press.

Medved, M. 2006. "War Films, Hollywood and Popular Culture." TownHall.com, May 19. http://townhall.com/columnists/michaelmedved/2006/05/19/war_films,_hollywood_and_popular_culture/page/full/.

Meier, B., and A. Martin. 2012. "Real and Virtual Firearms Nurture a Marketing Link." *New York Times*, December 24. http://www.nytimes.com/2012/12/25/business/real-and-virtual-firearms-nurture-marketing-link.html.

Mermin, J. 1997. "Television News and American Intervention in Somalia: The Myth of a Media-Driven Foreign Policy." *Political Science Quarterly* 112 (3): 385–403. http://dx.doi.org/10.2307/2657563.

–. 1999. *Debating War and Peace: Media Coverage of US Intervention in the Post-Vietnam Era*. Princeton, NJ: Princeton University Press. http://dx.doi.org/10.1515/9781400823321.

Meserve, J. 2008. "Biological Terror Attack Likely by 2013, Panel Says." CNN.com, December 2. http://www.cnn.com/2008/US/12/02/terror.report/.

Metz, T., M. Garrett, J. Hutton, and T. Bush. 2006. "Massing Effects in the Information Domain: A Case Study in Aggressive Information Operations." *Military Review* 86 (3): 2–12.

Mezoff, L. 2009. "*America's Army* Game Sets Five Guinness World Records." US Army, www.army.mil, February 10. http://www.army.mil/article/16678/americas-army-game-sets-five-guinness-world-records/.

Milbank, D. 2003. "Curtains Ordered for Media Coverage of Returning Coffins." *Washington Post*, October 21. http://www.informationclearinghouse.info/article6078.htm.

Miles, D. 2007. "Movie Makers Team with Military to Create Realism." US Department of State, June 21. http://www.defense.gov/news/newsarticle.aspx?id=46352.

Millar, L. 2002. "Critics Disturbed by Hollywood, Defence Relationship." ABC News, July 7. http://www.abc.net.au/correspondents/s600389.htm.

Miller, C.J. 2006. "The 'B' Move Goes to War in Hitler, *The Beast of Berlin*." *Film History* 36 (1): 58–64.

Miller, J. 2012. "Global Nollywood: The Nigerian Movie Industry and Alternative Global Networks in Production and Distribution." *Global Media and Communication* 8 (2): 117–33. http://dx.doi.org/10.1177/1742766512444340.

Miller, P. 2009. "G.I. Joystick: New Video Games Train Today's Troops." *PC World*. http://www.pcworld.com/article/169229/military_training_by_gaming.html.

Miller, T., N. Govil, J. McMurria, R. Maxwell, and T. Wang. 2005. *Global Hollywood 2*. London: British Film Institute.

Miracle, T. 2003. "The Army and Embedded Media." *Military Review*, September-October 41–45.

Mirrlees, T. 2009. "Digital Militainment by Design: Producing and Playing SOCOM Navy Seals." *International Journal of Media and Cultural Politics* 5 (3): 161–81.

–. 2013a. *Global Entertainment Media: Between Cultural Imperialism and Cultural Globalization*. New York: Routledge.

–. 2013b. "How to Read *Iron Man*." *Cineaction*, 4–11.

–. 2014. "*Medal of Honor: Operation Anaconda*; Playing the War in Afghanistan." *Democratic Communiqué* 26 (2): 84–106.

Mooers, C., ed. 2006. *The New Imperialists: Ideologies of Empire*. Oxford: One World Press.

Moran, A. 2009. "Global Franchising, Local Customizing: The Cultural Economy of TV Program Formats." *Continuum* (Perth) 23 (2): 115–25. http://dx.doi.org/10.1080/10304310802706932.

Morgenthau, H.J. 1978. *Politics among Nations*. New York: Knopf.

Morris, N. 2002. "The Myth of Unadulterated Culture Meets the Threat of Imported Media." *Media Culture and Society* 24 (2): 278–89. http://dx.doi.org/10.1177/016344370202400208.

Morwood, N. 2014. "War Crimes, Cognitive Dissonance and the Abject: An Analysis of the Anti-War Wargame *Spec Ops: The Line*." *Democratic Communiqué* 26 (2): 107–21.

Mosco, V. 2009. *The Political Economy of Communication*. London: Sage Publications. http://dx.doi.org/10.4135/9781446279946.

MPAA (Motion Picture Association of America). 2014a. "Policy Focus and Positions." MPAA, Policy. http://www.mpaa.org/policy-focus-mpaa-blog/.

–. 2014a. "MPAA, Our Story." http://www.mpaa.org/our-story/.

–. 2014b. "Access to Global Markets." http://www.mpaa.org/access-to-global-markets/.

–. 2014c. "MPAA Annual Trade Barrier Report Filing to USTR." http://www.mpaa.org/wp-content/uploads/2014/10/MPAA-Foreign-Trade-Barriers-Report.pdf.

Mount, M. 2009. "Ban Lifted, Media Witness Solemn Return of Fallen Service Member. CNN, April 6. http://edition.cnn.com/2009/POLITICS/04/06/photo.ban.lifted/.

Mowry, L. 2012. "Team Edwards Supports Warner Brothers' *Man of Steel*." Edwards Air Force Base, July 2. http://www.edwards.af.mil/news/story.asp?id=123289052.

Mullen, A. 2009. "The Propaganda Model after 20 Years: Interview with Edward S. Herman and Noam Chomsky." *Westminster Papers in Communication and Culture* 6 (2): 12–22.

Munro, R. 1990. "Good-Bye to Hollywood." Delivered to Town Hall of California, February 14. Los Angeles, California. http://connection.ebscohost.com/c/speeches/9007160489/good-bye-hollywood.

Murdock, G. 2006a. "Cosmopolitans and Conquistadors: Empires, Nations and Networks." In *Communications Media, Globalization and Empire*, ed. O. Boyd-Barrett, 17–32. Eastleigh: John Libbey.

–. 2006b. "Notes from the Number One Country." *International Journal of Cultural Policy* 12 (2): 209–27. http://dx.doi.org/10.1080/10286630600813727.

Murse, T. 2012. "How Much US Debt Does China Really Own?" About.com, February 14. http://usgovinfo.about.com/od/moneymatters/ss/How-Much-US-Debt-Does-China-Own.htm.

Musser, C. 1990. *The American of Cinema: The American Screen to 1907*. Berkeley: University of California Press.

Nakamura, K., and Weed, M.C. 2009. "US Public Diplomacy: Background and Current Issues." Congressional Research Service, December 18. https://fas.org/sgp/crs/row/R40989.pdf.

Napoli, P. M. 2008. "Bridging Cultural Policy and Media Policy." *Journal of Arts Management, Law and Society* 37(4): 311–32.

Nash, G.D. 1985. *The American West Transformed: The Impact of the Second World War*. Bloomington: Indiana University Press.

NAB (National Association of Broadcasters). 2012. NAB, About. http://www.nab.org/about/default.asp.

National Commission on Terrorist Attacks upon the United States. 2004. *The 9/11 Commission Report*. New York: Claitor's Law Books and Publishing.

National Security Council. 1947. NSC-4A: Psychological Operations. December 9. http://fas.org/irp/offdocs/nsc-hst/nsc-4.htm.

–. 1954, January 25. *Responsibilities and Principles Governing the Conduct of the Foreign Information Program and Psychological Warfare*. Washington, DC: National Security Council.

–. 1958. "Wartime Organization for Overseas Psychological Operations." National Security Council Memorandum 5812/1, June 4. Washington, DC: NSC.

–. 1983. "Management of Public Diplomacy Relative to National Security (NSC-77)." Washington, DC: NSC.

Neil, D. 2009. "Where Men Win Glory: The Odyssey of Pat Tillman by Job Krakauer." *LA Times*, September 11. http://www.latimes.com/world/afghanistan-pakistan/la-et-book11-2009sep11-story.html#page=1.

Neocleous, M. 2007. "Security, Liberty and the Myth of Balance: Towards a Critique of Security Politics." *Contemporary Political Theory* 6 (1): 131–49.

Neuman, J. 2001. "Public Diplomacy Is Shaped in President's Ornate War Room." *Los Angeles Times*, December 22. http://articles.latimes.com/2001/dec/22/news/mn-17270.

Newscorpwatch. 2008. "Military Analysts Named in Times Expose Appeared or Were Quoted More than 4,500 Times on Broadcast Nets, Cables, NPR." Newscorpwatch, May 13. http://newscorpwatch.org/research/200805130001.

New York Times. 2015. "Highest Paid Chiefs in 2014." *New York Times*, May 16. http://www.nytimes.com/interactive/2015/05/14/business/executive-compensation.html.

NewZoo. 2014. "Top 100 Countries Represent 99.8% of 81% In Global Games Market." NewZoo Games Market Research, May 23. http://www.newzoo.com/insights/top-100-countries-represent-99-6-81-5bn-global-games-market/.

Nichols, J., and R.W. McChesney. 2013. *Dollarocracy: How the Money and the Media Election Complex Is Destroying America*. New York: Nation Books.

Ninkovich, F. 2001. *The United States and Imperialism*. Oxford: Blackwell.

Noam, E.M. 2009. *Media Ownership and Concentration in America*. New York: Oxford University Press. http://dx.doi.org/10.1093/acprof:oso/9780195188523.001.0001.

Nordenstreng, K. 2013. "How the New World Order and Imperialism Challenge Media Studies." *TripleC* 11 (2): 348–58.

Nowak, P. 2010. "Taliban Pulled from *Medal of Honor* Game." CBC News, Technology and Science, October 1. http://www.cbc.ca/news/technology/taliban-pulled-from-medal-of-honor-game-1.944482.

NTSA (National Training and Simulation Association). 2011. "A Primer on Modeling and Simulation: The World of M&S." http://www.corporatepress.com/clientfiles/ntsa/.

Nye, J. 2004. *Soft Power: The Means to Success in World Politics*. Toronto: HarperCollins.

–. 2009. "The US Can Reclaim 'Smart Power.'" *Los Angeles Times*, January 21. http://www.latimes.com/la-oe-nye21-2009jan21-story.html.

O'Donnell, M. 2004. "Bring It On: The Apocalypse of George W. Bush." *Media International Australia Incorporated* 113: 10–22.

Oba, G., and S. Chan-Olmsted. 2007. "Video Strategy of Transnational Media Corporations: A Resource-Based Examination of Global Alliances and Patterns." *Journal of Media Business Studies* 4 (2): 1–25.

Office of the Federal Register National Archives and Records Administration. 2013. *Title 22: Foreign Relations*. Washington, DC: US Superintendent of Documents.

Office of the United States Trade Representative. 2014. *Special 301 Report*. https://ustr.gov/sites/default/files/USTR%202014%20Special%20301%20Report%20to%20Congress%20FINAL.pdf.

Open Secrets. 2014. "Revolving Door." OpenSecrets.org., Influence and Lobbying. https://www.opensecrets.org/revolving/
Ornstein, J.J., and T.E. Mann. 2006. "When Congress Checks Out." *Foreign Affairs*. http://www.foreignaffairs.com/articles/62091/norman-j-ornstein-and-thomas-e-mann/when-congress-checks-out.
Orriss, B. 1984. *When Hollywood Ruled the Skies: The Aviation Film Classics of World War II*. Hawthorne: Aero Associates Inc.
Paddock, A.H. 2002. *US Army Special Warfare: Its Origins*. Lawrence, KS: University Press of Kansas.
Page, B.I., and M.M. Bouton. 2011. *The Foreign Policy Disconnect*. Chicago, IL: Chicago University Press.
Panitch, L. 1996. "Rethinking the Role of the State." In *Globalization: Critical Reflections*, ed. J. Mittelman, 83–113. Boulder, CO: Lynne Rienner.
Panitch, L., and S. Gindin. 2004. "Global Capitalism and American Empire." In *The New Imperial Challenge: Socialist Register 2004*, ed. L. Panitch and C. Leys, 1–45. London: Merlin Press.
–. 2012. *The Making of Global Capitalism: The Political Economy of American Empire*. New York: Verso.
Parenti, M. 2004. *Superpatriotism*. San Francisco: City Lights Books.
Park, Y., and H. Schwarz. 2005. "Editorial: Extending American Hegemony beyond Empire." *Interventions* 7 (2): 153–61. http://dx.doi.org/10.1080/13698010500146633.
Parry-Giles, S. 2002. *The Rhetorical Presidency, Propaganda, and the Cold War, 1945–1955*. London: Praeger.
Paschall, W. 2002. "Submarine Sailors Get Games from Game Industry." US Navy, December 18. http://www.navy.mil/submit/display.asp?story_id=5115.
Patel, Sital S. 2014. "Highest-Paid CEOs Concentrated in Media and Entertainment Businesses." MarketWatch, May 27. http://blogs.marketwatch.com/thetell/2014/05/27/highest-paid-ceos-concentrated-in-media-and-entertainment-businesses/.
Paterson, C. 2005. "When the Global Media Don't 'Play Ball': The Exportation of Coercion." *International Journal of Media and Cultural Politics* 1 (1): 53–58. http://dx.doi.org/10.1386/macp.1.1.53/3.
–. 2011. "Government Intervention in the Iraq War Media Narrative through Direct Coercion." *Global Media and Communication* 7 (3): 181–86. http://dx.doi.org/10.1177/1742766511427446.
–. 2014. *War Reporters under Threat: The United States and Media Freedom*. London: Pluto Press.
Patterson, J. 2007. "Shame of a Nation." *Guardian*, August 24. http://www.theguardian.com/film/2007/aug/24/3.
Payne, M. 2009. "Manufacturing Militainment: Video Game Producers and Military Brand Games." In *War Isn't Hell, It's Entertainment: Essays on Visual Media and the Representation of Conflict*, ed. R. Schubart, F. Virchow, D. White-Stanley, and T. Thomas, 238–55. Jefferson, NC: McFarland.
–. 2014. "WarBytes: The Critique of Militainment in *Spec Ops: The Line*." *Critical Studies in Media Communication* 31 (4): 265–82. http://dx.doi.org/10.1080/15295036.2014.881518.
Pecency, M. 1999. *Democracy at the Point of Bayonets*. University Park: Pennsylvania State University Press.

Peck, M. 2012. "Since When Does Brookings Make Video Games?" *Foreign Policy*, http://foreignpolicy.com/2012/05/08/since-when-does-brookings-make-video-games/.

Perkins, J. 2009. *The Secret History of the American Empire: The Truth about Economic Hit Men, Jackals, and How to Change the World*. New York: Plume.

Perlez, Jane. 2002. "Muslim-as-Apple-Pie Videos Greeted with Skepticism." Global Issues, October 30. http://www.globalissues.org/article/384/muslim-as-apple-pie-videos-are-greeted-with-skepticism.

Peterson, K. 2005. "Sony Considers Zipper Great Fit." *Seattle Times*, March 19. http://www.seattletimes.com/business/sony-considers-zipper-great-fit/.

Peterson, P.G. 2002. "Public Diplomacy and the War on Terrorism." http://dx.doi.org/10.2307/20033270.

—. 2003. "Views of a Changing World 2003: War with Iraq Further Divides Global Politics." Pew Research Center, US Politics and Polity, June 3. http://www.people-press.org/2003/06/03/views-of-a-changing-world-2003/.

—. 2013. "America's Global Image Remains More Positive than China's." Pew Research Centre Global Attitudes & Trends, July 18. http://www.pewglobal.org/2013/07/18/americas-global-image-remains-more-positive-than-chinas/.

Phillips, J., and N. Gardiner. 2004. "Kofi Annan's Iraq Blunder." Fox News, October 12. http://www.foxnews.com/story/2004/10/12/kofi-annan-iraq-blunder/.

Phillips, T. 2011. "Norway Stores Pull Violent Video Games Including *Call of Duty* after Massacre." Metro, August 2. http://metro.co.uk/2011/08/02/norway-stores-pull-violent-video-games-including-call-of-duty-99567/.

Pickard, V. 2014. *America's Battle for Media Democracy: The Triumph of Corporate Libertarianism and the Future of Media Reform*. Cambridge, MA: Harvard University Press.

Pidd, H. 2012. "Anders Breivik 'Trained' for Shooting Attacks by Playing *Call of Duty*." *Guardian*, April 19. http://www.guardian.co.uk/world/2012/apr/19/anders-breivik-call-of-duty.

Piketty, T. 2014. *Capital in the Twenty-First Century*. Cambridge, MA: Harvard University Press.

Pincus, W. 2014. "Islamic State Fight Is a War, Not a Video Game." Washington Post, October 13. http://www.washingtonpost.com/world/national-security/islamic-state-fight-is-a-war-not-a-video-game/2014/10/13/ecdd1a24-4ff3-11e4-babe-e91da079cb8a_story.html.

Plotz, D. 2003. "Iraq: The Computer Game, What 'Virtual World' Games Can Teach the Real World about Reconstructing Iraq." *Slate*, June 19. http://www.slate.com/articles/news_and_politics/iraqs_progress/2003/06/iraq_the_computer_game.html.

Pollack, K. 2002. *The Threatening Storm: The Case For Invading Iraq*. New York: Random House.

Power, M. 2007. "Digitized Virtuosity: Video War Games and Post-9/11 Cyber-Deterrence." *Security Dialogue* 38 (2): 271–88.

Preston, W., E.S. Herman, and H.I. Schiller. 1989. *Hope and Folly: The United States and UNESCO, 1945–1985*. Minneapolis: University of Minnesota Press.

Price, G. 2014. "Super Bowl 2014 Ratings." *International Business Times*, January 30. http://www.ibtimes.com/super-bowl-2014-ratings-how-many-countries-will-watch-american-football-game-1551791.

PricewaterhouseCoopers. 2013. *Global Entertainment and Media Outlook, 2013–2017*. http://www.pwc.ru/en/entertainment-media/publications/outlook-2013.jhtml.

Puppis, M. 2008. "National Media Regulation in the Era of Free Trade: The Role of Global Media Governance." *European Journal of Communication* 23 (4): 405–24. http://dx.doi.org/10.1177/0267323108096992.

Rachman, G. 2011. "Think Again: American Decline." *Foreign Policy*, January 3. http://foreignpolicy.com/2011/01/03/think-again-american-decline/.

Rainey, J. 2005. "Unseen Pictures, Untold Stories." *Los Angeles Times*, May 21. http://www.latimes.com/nation/la-na-iraqphoto21may21-story.html.

Rampton, S. 2007. "Shared Values Revisited." *PR Watch*, October 17. http://www.prwatch.org/news/2007/10/6465/shared-values-revisited.

RAND Corporation. 1996. *Military Recruiting Outlook*. Santa Monica, CA: RAND.

Rauschenberger, E. 2003. "It's Only a Movie – Right? Deconstructing Cultural Imperialism." Paper for Department of Politics, New York University. http://politics.as.nyu.edu/admin/staging/IO/4600/rauschenberger_thesis.pdf.

Reagan, M.B. 2008. "US Military Recruits Children." Truth Out, July 23. http://www.truth-out.org/archive/article/us-military-recruits-children.

Reagan, R. 1984. "US International Information Policy." National Security Decision Directive Number 130. Washington, DC: White House.

RIAA (Recording Industry Association of America). 2013. About. http://www.riaa.com/aboutus.php.

Reed, C. 2009. "Journalists' Recent Work Examined before Embeds." *Stars and Stripes*, August 24. http://www.stripes.com/news/journalists-recent-work-examined-before-embeds-1.94239.

Reed, C., K. Baron, and L. Shane. 2009. "Files Prove Pentagon Is Profiling Reporters." Stars and Stripes, August 29. http://www.stripes.com/news/files-prove-pentagon-is-profiling-reporters-1.94248.

Reich, R.B. 2010. *Aftershock: The Next Economy and America's Future*. New York: Knopf.

Renda, M.A. 2001. *Taking Haiti: Military Occupation and the Culture of US Imperialism, 1915–1940*. Chapel Hill: University of North Carolina Press.

Rendall, S., and T. Broughel. 2003. "Amplifying Officials, Squelching Dissent." *Extra!* http://fair.org/extra-online-articles/amplifying-officials-squelching-dissent/.

Reporters Without Borders. 2005. *Reporters Without Borders Annual Report 2005 – Iraq*. http://www.refworld.org/docid/46e690e323.html.

Retort (I. Boal, T.J. Clark, J. Matthews, and M. Watts). 2004. "Afflicted Powers: The State, Spectacle and September 11." *New Left Review* 27: 5–21.

Rice, C. 2005. "Karen Hughes Appointed." USC Annenberg, Center on Public Diplomacy, March 15. http://uscpublicdiplomacy.org/pdin_monitor_article/karen_hughes_appointment_as_undersecretary_of_state_for_public_diplomacy.

Riddell, R. 1997. "*Doom* Goes to War." *Wired* 5 (4). http://archive.wired.com/wired/archive/5.04/ff_doom.html.

Risen, C. 2005. "Branding Nations." *New York Times*, December 11. http://www.nytimes.com/2005/12/11/magazine/11ideas1-5.html?_r=0.

Risen, J. 2014. *Pay Any Price: Greed, Power and Endless War*. New York: Harcourt.

Roach, C. 1997. "Cultural Imperialism and Resistance in Media Theory and Literary Theory." *Media Culture and Society* 19 (1): 47–66. http://dx.doi.org/10.1177/016344397019001004.

Robb, D. 2002. "To the Shores of Hollywood: Marine Corps Fights to Polish Image in *Windtalkers*." *Washington Post*, June 15.

—. 2004. *Operation Hollywood: How the Pentagon Shapes and Censors the Movies*. New York: Prometheus Books.

Roberts, J. 2004. "Pentagon: Families Want Photo Ban." CBSNews.com, April 23. http://www.cbsnews.com/news/pentagon-families-want-photo-ban/.

Robinson, P. 2005. "The CNN Effect Revisited." *Critical Studies in Media Communication* 22 (4): 344–49. http://dx.doi.org/10.1080/07393180500288519.

Robson, S. 2008. "Not Playing Around: Army to Invest $50 Million in Combat Training Games." Stars and Stripes, November 23. http://www.stripes.com/news/not-playing-around-army-to-invest-50m-in-combat-training-games-1.85595.

Rodriguez, J.L. 2004. "Embedding Success into the Military-Media Relationship." In *Perspectives on Embedding Media*, ed. M. Pasquarett, 57–84. US Army War College. http://www.dtic.mil/cgi-bin/GetTRDoc?AD=ada423760.

Rollins, P. 1996. "Frank Capra's *Why We Fight* Film Series and Our American Dream." *Journal of American Culture* 19 (4): 81–86. http://dx.doi.org/10.1111/j.1542-734X.1996.1904_81.x.

Root, E. 1922. "A Requisite for the Success of Popular Diplomacy." *Foreign Affairs* 1 (1): 3. http://dx.doi.org/10.2307/20028194.

Rosen, K. 2014. "America Spends More on Military than Other Top 10 Countries Combined." World Mic, February 3. http://www.mic.com/articles/79673/america-spends-more-on-military-than-the-other-top-10-countries-combined.

Rosenberg, E.S. 1982. *Spreading the American Dream: American Economic and Cultural Expansion 1890–1945*. New York: Hill and Wang.

Ross, B., and J. Rackmill. 2005. "Full Spectrum Failure? Army Video Game Draws Fire: Military Wasted Millions on Training Project, Critics Charge." ABCnews.com, May 25, http://abcnews.go.com/WNT/print?id=787575.

Ross, S.J. 2011. *Hollywood Left and Right: How Movie Stars Shaped American Politics*. New York: Oxford University Press.

Rothkopf, D. 1997. "In Praise of Cultural Imperialism?" *Foreign Policy* 107 (Summer): 38–53.

—. 2005. *Running the World: The Inside Story of the National Security Council*. New York: Perseus Books.

Rutenberg, J. 2001. "A Nation Challenged: Entertainment; Hollywood Seeks Role in the War." *New York Times*, October 20. http://www.nytimes.com/2001/10/20/us/a-nation-challenged-entertainment-hollywood-seeks-role-in-the-war.html.

—. 2003. "Cable's War Coverage Suggests a New 'Fox Effect' on Television." *New York Times*, April 16. http://www.nytimes.com/2003/04/16/us/nation-war-media-cable-s-war-coverage-suggests-new-fox-effect-television.html.

Rutherford, P. 2000. *Endless Propaganda: The Advertising of Public Goods*. Toronto: Toronto University Press.

—. 2004. *Weapons of Mass Persuasion: Marketing the War against Iraq*. Toronto: University of Toronto Press.

Ryan, M. 1998. *Knowledge Diplomacy: Global Competition and the Politics of Intellectual Property*. Washington, DC: Brookings Institute.

Rycroft, M. 2005. "The Secret Downing Street Memo." May 1. Internet Way Back Machine (London, UK). http://web.archive.org/web/20110723222004/http://www.timesonline.co.uk/tol/news/uk/article387374.ece.

Rydell, R., and R. Kroes. 2005. *Buffalo Bill in Bologna. The Americanization of the World, 1869–1922*. Chicago and London: Chicago University Press. http://dx.doi.org/10.7208/chicago/9780226732343.001.0001.

Said, E. 1993. *Culture and Imperialism*. New York: Vintage.

Sanders, K. 2006. "Venezuela Targets Mercenaries." IGN, May 25. http://ca.ign.com/articles/2006/05/25/venezuela-targets-mercenaries.

—. 2010. "Obama to 'Aggressively Protect' Intellectual Property." CNN News, March 12. http://www.cnet.com/news/obama-to-aggressively-protect-intellectual-property/.

Scahill, J. 2013. *Dirty Wars: The World Is a Battlefield*. New York: Nation Books.

Scarry, E. 1985. *The Body in Pain*. New York: Oxford University Press.

Schiesel, S. 2005. "On Maneuvers with the Army's Game Squad." *New York Times*, February 17. http://www.nytimes.com/2005/02/17/technology/circuits/17army.html?_r=0.

Schiller, D. 2007. *How to Think about Information*. Champaign: University of Illinois Press.

—. 2008a. "Review of *Media Policy and Globalization*, by Paula Chakravarty and Katherine Sarikakis." *Political Communication* 25 (1): 99–100. http://dx.doi.org/10.1080/10584600701808057.

—. 2008b. "The Militarization of US Communications." *Communication, Culture and Critique* 1 (1): 126–38. doi:10.1111/j.1753-9137.2007.00013.x

Schiller, H.I. 1969. *Mass Communication and American Empire*. Boston: Beacon Press.

—. 1973. *The Mind Managers*. Boston: Beacon Press.

—. 1976. *Communication and Cultural Domination*. Armonk, NY: M.E. Sharpe.

—. 1984. *Information and the Crisis Economy*. Norwood, NJ: Ablex.

—. 1989. *Culture Inc.: The Corporate Takeover of Public Expression*. New York: Oxford University Press.

—. 1991. "Not Yet the Post-Imperialist Era." *Critical Studies in Mass Communication* 8 (1): 13–28. http://dx.doi.org/10.1080/15295039109366777.

—. 1992. *Mass Communication and American Empire*. New York: August M. Kelley.

—. 2000. *Living in the Number One Country: Reflections of a Critic of American Empire*. New York: Seven Stories Press.

Schlesinger, A.M. 1973. *The Imperial Presidency*. Boston: Houghton Mifflin.

Schlesinger, R. 2011. "Obama Has Mentioned 'American Exceptionalism' More than Bush." US News, January 31. http://www.usnews.com/opinion/blogs/robert-schlesinger/2011/01/31/obama-has-mentioned-american-exceptionalism-more-than-bush.

Schlesinger, S., S. Kinzer, J. Coatsworth, and R. Nuccio. 2006. *Bitter Fruit: The Story of the American Coup in Guatemala*. Cambridge, MA: David Rockefeller Center for Latin American Studies.

Schmitt, E., and J. Dao. 2002. "A Damaged Information Office Is Declared Closed by Rumsfeld." *New York Times*, February 27. http://www.nytimes.com/2002/02/27/international/27MILI.html.

Schneider, B.R. 2009. "Obama Begins Repairing America's Image Abroad." CNN, February 19. http://www.cnn.com/2009/POLITICS/02/19/obama.image/index.html.

Schorr, D. 1991. "Ten Days that Shook the White House." *Columbia Journalism Review* 1 (2): 21–23.

Schroeder, P. 2003. "Is the US an Empire?" History News Network, October 2. http://historynewsnetwork.org/article/1237.

Scott, A.J. 2005. *On Hollywood: The Place, the Industry*. Princeton, NJ: Princeton University Press.

Scott, A.J., and N.E. Pope. 2007. "Hollywood, Vancouver, and the World: Employment Relocation and the Emergence of Satellite Production Centers in the Motion Picture Industry." *Environment and Planning A* 39 (6): 1364–81. http://dx.doi.org/10.1068/a38215.

Seaver, B.M. 1998. "The Public Dimension of Foreign Policy." *Harvard International Journal of Press/Politics* 3 (1): 65–91. http://dx.doi.org/10.1177/1081180X98003001006.

Sessions, D. 2008. "Onward, T.V. Soldiers." *Slate*, April 20. http://www.slate.com/articles/news_and_politics/todays_papers/2008/04/onward_tv_soldiers.html.

Shachtman, N. 2008. "Army Builds Fantasy Island in *Second Life*." December 3. http://www.wired.com/2008/12/the-armys-new-f/.

Shaheen, J.G. 2003. "Reel Bad Arabs: How Hollywood Vilifies a People." *Annals* 588:171–97.

Shaw, Scott A. 2013. "Rally Point for Leaders: Building an Organization's Mission Command Culture." *Infantry* 102 (4): 20–25. http://usacac.army.mil/cac2/IPO/repository/Infantry%20Magazine%20OCT-DEC13.pdf.

Shaw, T. 2007. *Hollywood's Cold War*. Amherst: University of Massachusetts Press. http://dx.doi.org/10.3366/edinburgh/9780748625239.001.0001.

Shohat, E., and R. Stam. 1994. *Unthinking Eurocentrism: Multiculturalism and the Media*. New York: Routledge.

–. 2007. "Imperialism and the Fantasies of Democracy." *Rethinking Marxism* 19 (3): 298–305. http://dx.doi.org/10.1080/08935690701412687.

Short, K.R.M. 1985. "Hollywood: An Essential War Industry." *Historical Journal of Film, Radio, and Television* 5 (1): 90–99.

Simpson, C. 1994. *Science of Coercion: Communication Research and Psychological Warfare, 1945–1960*. Oxford: Oxford University Press.

Sinclair, B. 2009. "*America's Army* Bill: $32.8 million." GameSpot, December 9. http://www.gamespot.com/articles/americas-army-bill-328-million/1100-6242635/.

–. 2010. "Meet the Sims ... and Shoot Them." *Foreign Policy*, February 11. http://foreignpolicy.com/2010/02/11/meet-the-sims-and-shoot-them/.

Sirota, D. 2011a. "Why Can't We Say "Empire"? *Salon*, October 24. http://www.salon.com/2011/10/24/why_cant_we_say_empire/.

–. 2011b. "25 Years Later, How *Top Gun* Made America Love War." *Washington Post*, August 26. http://www.washingtonpost.com/opinions.

Sklar, R. 1975. *Movie-Made America: A Cultural History of American Movies*. New York: Vintage Books.

Slagle, M. 2003. "Pentagon and CIA Enlist Video Games." Science on NBCNews.com, October 3. http://www.nbcnews.com/id/3131181/ns/technology_and_science-science/t/pentagon-cia-enlist-video-games/.

Smith, S.D. 2006. "Hollywood, Military Cooperation Often Mutually Beneficial." US Department of Defense, August 21. http://www.defense.gov/news/newsarticle.aspx?id=516.

Smythe, D.W. 1981. *Dependency Road: Communications, Capitalism, Consciousness, and Canada*. Norwood, NJ: Ablex.

—. 2001. "On the Audience Commodity and Its Work." In *Media and Cultural Studies: Keyworks*, ed. M. Durham and D. Kellner, 253–79. Malden, MA: Blackwell.

Snider, M. 2004. "War Game Launch All Out Sales Assault." *USA Today*, June 9, http://usatoday30.usatoday.com/life/lifestyle/2004-06-09-war-video-games_x.htm.

—. 2010. "Taliban Label Discharged from *Medal of Honor* Multiplayer Mode." *USA Today*, Game Hunters, October. 1. http://content.usatoday.com/communities/gamehunters/post/2010/09/taliban-label-out-of-medal-of-honor-/1.

Snow, N. 1998. "The Smith-Mundt Act of 1948." *Peace Review* 10 (4): 619–24. http://dx.doi.org/10.1080/10402659808426214.

—. 2003. *Propaganda Inc.: Selling America's Culture to the World*. New York: Seven Stories.

—. 2008. "International Exchanges and the US Image." *Annals of the American Academy of Political and Social Science* 616 (1): 198–222. http://dx.doi.org/10.1177/0002716207311864.

Snow, N., and P.M. Taylor. 2006. "The Revival of the Propaganda State: US Propaganda at Home and Abroad since 9/11." *International Communication Gazette* 68 (5–6): 389–407. http://dx.doi.org/10.1177/1748048506068718.

Solomon, N. 2004. "They Shoot Journalists, Don't They?" *Counterpunch*, March 11. http://www.counterpunch.org/2004/03/11/they-shoot-journalists-don-t-they/.

Solomon, W.S. 1992. "News Frames and Media Packages Covering El Salvador." *Critical Studies in Mass Communication* 9 (1): 56–74. http://dx.doi.org/10.1080/15295039209366815.

Sorenson, T. 1968. *The Word War: The Story of American Propaganda*. New York, London: Harper and Row.

Sowards, S.K. 2003. "MTV Asia: Localizing the Global Media." In *The Globalization of Corporate Media Hegemony*, ed. L. Artz and Y.R. Kamalipour, 229–43. New York: State University of New York Press.

Sparks, C. 2007a. "Extending and Refining the Propaganda Model." *Westminster Papers in Communication and Culture* 4 (2): 68–84.

—. 2007b. *Globalization, Development and the Mass Media*. Los Angeles: Sage Publications.

—. 2012. "Media and Cultural Imperialism Reconsidered." *Chinese Journal of Communication* 5 (3): 281–99. http://dx.doi.org/10.1080/17544750.2012.701417.

—. 2014. "Deconstructing the BRICS." *International Journal of Communication* 8 (1): 392–418.

Springer, C. 1991. "Military Propaganda: Defense Department Films from World War II and Vietnam." In *The Vietnam War and American Culture*, ed. J.C. Rowe and R. Berg, 95–114. New York: Columbia University Press.

Sproule, J.M. 1997. *Propaganda and Democracy: The American Experience of Media and Mass Persuasion*. Cambridge: Cambridge University Press.

Stahl, R. 2006. "Have You Played the War on Terror?" *Critical Studies in Media Communication* 23 (2): 112–30. http://dx.doi.org/10.1080/07393180600714489.

—. 2010. *Militainment, Inc*. New York: Routledge.

Stainburn, S. 1997. "Feds on Film." Government Executive, April 1. http://www.govexec.com/magazine/1997/04/feds-on-film/246/.

Starr, A. 2001. "The War on Terror: Charlotte Beers' Toughest Sell." *Business Week*, December 17, 56.

Starr, P. 2009. "Goodbye to the Age of Newspapers (Hello to a New Era of Corruption)." *New Republic*: 27–35. http://www.newrepublic.com/article/goodbye-the-age-newspapers-hello-new-era-corruption.

Starrs, S. 2014. "The Chimera of Global Convergence." *New Left Review* 87 (1): 81–96.

–. 2015. "Making the World Safe for Big Business." *Jacobin*, May 13. https://www.jacobinmag.com/2015/05/trans-pacific-parternship-china-united-states-asia/.

Stauber, J. 2002. "Telling Stories to Sell War." *PRWatch*, December 26. http://www.prwatch.org/spin/2002/12/1639/telling-stories-sell-war.

Stauber, J., and S. Rampton. 1995. *Toxic Sludge Is Good for You*. Monroe, ME: Common Courage Press.

Statista. 2014. "Revenue of the Largest Computer and Video Game Publishers Worldwide in 2013" (in Billion Euros). http://www.statista.com/statistics/273838/revenue-of-the-largest-video-game-publishers-worldwide/.

Stech, F.J. 1994. "Winning CNN Wars." *Parameters* (Autumn): 37–56. http://strategicstudiesinstitute.army.mil/pubs/parameters/Articles/1994/stech.htm.

Steele, R.W. 1984. "The Great Debate: Roosevelt, the Media, and the Coming of War, 1940–1941." *Journal of American History* 71 (1): 69–92. http://dx.doi.org/10.2307/1899834.

Stein, J., and T. Dickinson. 2006. "Lie by Lie: A Timeline of How We Got into Iraq." *Mother Jones*, September/October. http://www.motherjones.com/politics/2011/12/leadup-iraq-war-timeline.

Steinmetz, G. 2005. "Return to Empire: The New Imperialism in Comparative Historical Perspective." *Sociological Theory* 23 (4): 339–67. http://dx.doi.org/10.1111/j.0735-2751.2005.00258.x.

Stewart, J.B. 2013. "High Income, Low Taxes and Never a Bad Year." *New York Times*, November 1. http://www.nytimes.com/2013/11/02/business/high-earnings-low-taxes-and-never-a-bad-year.html?ref=business&_r=0.

Steyn, M. 2007. "Hollywood Shoots Itself in the Foot." *Maclean's*, November 15. http://www.freerepublic.com/focus/news/1928388/posts?page=71.

Stiglitz, J.E. 2011. "Of the 1%, by the 1%, for the 1%." *Vanity Fair*, http://www.vanityfair.com/news/2011/05/top-one-percent-201105.

Stiglitz, J.E., and L.J. Bilmes. 2008. *The Three Trillion Dollar War*. New York: W.W. Norton.

Stinson, S. 2010. "Soldiers Trained to Kill, But Never 'Untrained.'" *National Post*, Full Comment, http://news.nationalpost.com/full-comment/scott-stinson-solders-trained-to-kill-but-never-untrained.

Stokes, D. 2005. "The Heart of Empire? Theorizing US Empire in an Era of Transnational Capitalism." *Third World Quarterly* 26 (2): 217–36. http://dx.doi.org/10.1080/0143659042000339092.

Stoner Saunders, F. 1999. *The Cultural Cold War: The CIA and the World of Arts and Letters*. New York: The New Press.

Story, L., T. Fehr, and D. Watkins. 2012. "United States of Subsidies: Explore the Data." *New York Times*, December 1. http://www.nytimes.com/interactive/2012/12/01/us/government-incentives.html.

Straubhaar, J. 1991. "Beyond Media Imperialism: Asymmetrical Interdependence and Cultural Proximity." *Critical Studies in Mass Communication* 8 (1): 39–59. http://dx.doi.org/10.1080/15295039109366779.

Strauss, B. 2013. "China Now World's Second-Largest Film Market." *Morning Sun*, May 27. http://www.themorningsun.com/article/20130527/NEWS05/130529616/china-now-world-8217-s-second-largest-film-market.
Street, P. 2010. *The Empire's New Clothes: Barack Obama in the Real World of Power*. New York: Paradigm.
Suid, L. 2001. "Pearl Harbor: More or Less." *Air Power History* 48 (1): 38–43.
–. 2002. *Guts and Glory: The Making of the American Military Image in Film*. Lexington: University Press of Kentucky.
Sulzberger, A.G. 2010, September 9. "Combat Games Go Too Far for Military." New York Times, http://www.nytimes.com/2010/09/10/us/10military.html.
Summers, R.E., ed. 1972. *America's Weapons of Psychological Warfare*. New York: Arno Press.
Sutter, J.D. 2012. "Norway Mass-Shooting Trial Reopens Debate on Violent Video Games." CNN, April 20. http://www.cnn.com/2012/04/19/tech/gaming-gadgets/games-violence-norway-react/index.html.
Sweeney, M.S. 2006. *The Military and the Press: An Uneasy Truce*. Evanston, IL: Northwestern University Press.
Swofford, A. 2005. *Jarhead: A Marine's Chronicle of the Gulf War and Other Battle*s. New York: Scribner.
Synovitz, R. 2002. "Afghanistan: Report Says Pentagon Restricted Journalists' Access to War Sites." Radio Free Europe/Radio Liberty, August 5. http://www.rferl.org/content/article/1100453.html.
Tapper, J. 2003. "Would You Buy a US Foreign Policy from This Man?" *Salon*, April 25. http://www.salon.com/2003/04/25/propaganda_10/.
Tassi, P. 2013. "The Ten Best Selling Games of the 2012 – Industry Down 22%." *Forbes*, November 1. http://www.forbes.com/sites/insertcoin/2013/01/11/the-ten-best-selling-games-of-the-2012-industry-down-22/.
Taylor, P.M. 1992. *War and the Media: Propaganda and Persuasion in the Gulf War*. Manchester: Manchester University Press.
–. 1997. *Global Communications, International Affairs, and the Media since 1945*. London, New York: Routledge. http://dx.doi.org/10.4324/9780203429624.
Teinowitz, I. 2002. "Charlotte Beers and the Selling of America." *Advertising Age*, September 23. http://adage.com/article/news/charlotte-beers-selling-america/35830/.
Telotte, J.P. 2007. "Crossing Borders and Opening Boxes: Disney and Hybrid Animation." *Quarterly Review of Film and Video* 24 (2): 107–16. http://dx.doi.org/10.1080/10509200500486155.
Tharoor, I. 2011. "Clinton Applauds Al Jazeera, Rolls Eyes at US Media." *Time*, March 3. http://world.time.com/2011/03/03/clinton-applauds-al-jazeera-rolls-eyes-at-u-s-media/.
"The Yes Men." 2009. *The New York Times*, July 4. http://nytimes-se.com/todays-paper/NYTimes-SE.pdf.
Thompson, D. 2005. "Pentagon Propaganda Program Orders." Global Policy Forum, December 29. https://www.globalpolicy.org/component/content/article/168/36674.html.
Thompson, L. 2014. "Five Reasons China Won't Be a Big Threat to America's Global Power." *Forbes*, June 6. http://www.forbes.com/sites/lorenthompson/2014/06/06/five-reasons-china-wont-be-a-big-threat-to-americas-global-power/June 6.

Thompson, M. 2008. "Killing in the Name Of: The US Army and Video Games." Ars Technica, Opposable Thumbs/Gaming and Entertainment, December 7. http://arstechnica.com/gaming/2008/12/army-video-games/.

Thomson, C. 2004. "The Making of an Xbox Warrior." *New York Times*, August 22. http://www.nytimes.com/2004/08/22/magazine/the-making-of-an-x-box-warrior.html.

Thomson, C., and W.H.C. Laves. 1963. *Cultural Relations and US Foreign Policy*. Bloomington: Indiana University Press.

Thompson, F. 2002. *Texas Hollywood: Filmmaking in San Antonio since 1910*. San Antonio: Maverick Publishing.

Thrall, T. 2000. *War in the Media Age*. New Jersey: Hampton Press.

Throsby, D. 2010. *The Economics of Cultural Policy*. New York: Cambridge University Press.

Thussu, D.K. 2006. *International Communication: Continuity and Change*. London: Arnold Press.

–, ed. 2007. *Media on the Move: Global Flow and Contra-Flow*. New York: Routledge.

Tomb, R. 2011. "Retired FBI Employee Who Helped Crew in J. *Edgar* Reflects on Movie and Power of Hollywood." *Ticklethewire*, November 23. http://www.ticklethewire.com/tag/rex-tomb/.

Tomlinson, J. 1991. *Cultural Imperialism*. Baltimore: John Hopkins University Press.

Transnational Institute. 2013. "State of Power 2013." http://www.tni.org/briefing/state-power-2013.

Trento, J., C. Waltemeyer, and B. Gaskill. 2013. "The Selling of the Pentagon 2013." DC Bureau, September 30. http://www.dcbureau.org/201309309080/national-security-news-service/the-selling-of-the-pentagon-2013.html.

Trivedi, B.P. 2001. "US Buys Up Afghanistan Images from Top Satellite." National Geographic News, October 25. http://news.nationalgeographic.com/news/2001/10/1025_TVikonos.html.

Truman, H.S. 1950. "Address on Foreign Policy at a Luncheon of the American Society of Newspaper Editors." http://www.trumanlibrary.org/publicpapers/index.php?pid=715.

Tsui, C. 2013. "Foreign Films Overtake Domestic Productions at 2012 Chinese Box Office." *Hollywood Reporter*, January 1. http://www.hollywoodreporter.com/news/foreign-films-overtake-domestic-productions-407387.

Tunstall, J. 2008. *The Media Were American: US Mass Media in Decline*. New York: Oxford University Press.

Turse, N. 2003a. "Bringing the War Home: The New Military-Industrial-Entertainment Complex at War and Play." *Insider Daily*, October 17. http://www.nickturse.com/articles/tom_warhome.html.

–. 2003b. "The Military-Industrial-Entertainment Complex Takes Training over 'There.'" *Dissident Voice*, November 6. www.dissidentvoice.org/Articles9/Turse_Over-There.htm.

–. 2008. *The Complex: How the Military Invades Our Everyday Lives*. New York: Metropolitan Books.

–. 2012. *The Changing Face of Empire: Special Ops, Drones, Spies, Proxy Fighters, Secret Bases and Cyber Warfare*. Chicago: Haymarket Books.

Tutwiler, M.B. 2003. "Confirmation Hearing, Testimony before the Senate Foreign Relations Committee." US Department of State, October 29. http://2001-2009.state.gov/r/us/27372.htm.

—. 2004a. "Public Diplomacy Activities and Programs." Testimony before the House Committee on Government Reform Subcommittee on National Security, Emerging Threats and International Relations. US Department of State, February 10. http://2001-2009.state.gov/r/us/2004/29251.htm.

—. 2004b. "Public Diplomacy: Reaching beyond Traditional Audiences." US Department of State. http://2001-2009.state.gov/r/us/2004/29111.htm.

Tyrrell, I., and J. Sexton, eds. 2015. *Empire's Twin: U.S. Anti-Imperialism from the Founding Era to the Age of Terrorism*. Ithaca/London: Cornell University Press.

Urwand, B. 2013. *The Collaboration: Hollywood's Pact with Hitler*. New York: Belknap Press.

US Army. 2010. *Information Operations Primer*. http://www.iwar.org.uk/iwar/resources/primer/info-ops-primer.pdf.

USCAnnenberg. 2008. Hollywood and Soft Power. YouTube video, 54.57. July 24, 2009. https://www.youtube.com/watch?v=ZVEEoeREAB0.

US Congress. 2001a. *The Message Is America: Rethinking Public Diplomacy; Hearing before the Committee on International Relations, House of Representatives*. 107th Cong., 2nd sess. Remarks of the Honorable Henry Hyde.

—. 2001b. *The Role of Public Diplomacy in Support of the Anti-Terrorism Campaign; Hearings before the Committee on International Relations*. 107th Cong., 2nd Sess. Remarks of the Honorable Charlotte Beers.

US Congress, Subcommittee on International Organizations and Movements of the Committee on Foreign Affairs, Ideological Operations and Foreign Policy. 1964. Rep. No. 2, "Winning the Cold War: The US Ideological Offensive." House Report No. 1352, 88th Congress, 2nd Session.

DOD (US Department of Defense). 1952. "Organization, Office of Psychological Policy." Department of Defense Directive C-5132.1 (April 21).

—. 1988. Directive 5410.16, "Department of Defense Assistance to Non-Government, Entertainment-Oriented Motion Picture, Television and Video Productions" (January 26). http://www.dtic.mil/whs/directives/corres/pdf/541016p.pdf.

—. 2001a. *Report of the Defense Science Board Task Force on Managed Information Dissemination*. Office of the Under Secretary of Defense for Acquisition, Technology, Logistics (October). Washington, DC: DOD.

—. 2003a. "Public Affairs Guidance on Embedding Media." http://www.defense.gov/news/Feb2003/d20030228pag.pdf.

—. 2003b. *Information Operations Roadmap*. http://www.information-retrieval.info/docs/info_ops_roadmap.pdf.

—. 2003c. *FM 3–13, Information Operations: Doctrine, Tactics, Techniques, and Procedures. Information* Operations. http://fas.org/irp/doddir/army/fm3-13-2003.pdf.

—. 2010. "Active Duty Military Personnel Strengths by Regional Area and by Country." http://www.globalsecurity.org/military/library/report/2011/hst1103.pdf.

—. 2012. *Information Operations: Joint Publication 3-13*. Defense Innovation Marketplace, November 27. http://www.defenseinnovationmarketplace.mil/resources/12102012_io1.pdf.

References 295

—. 2014. Assistant Secretary of Defense for Public Affairs. http://www.defense.gov/pubs/almanac/asdpa.aspx.
—. 2014. "About the Office of Public Affairs." August 19. http://www.dhs.gov/about-office-public-affairs.
US Department of Homeland Security and US Department of State, prods. 2007. *Welcome: Portraits of America*. In partnership with Walt Disney Parks and Resorts. YouTube video, 7:24. October 28. https://www.youtube.com/watch?v=2NpHwYrIXWY.
US Department of State. 2001. *Office of the Spokesman: Remarks of Secretary of State Colin Powell at NetDiplomacy Conference*. Washington, DC.
—. 2007. "Private Sector Summit on Public Diplomacy: Models for Action." January 9. http://2001-2009.state.gov/documents/organization/82818.pdf.
—. 2014. "Under Secretary for Public Diplomacy and Public Affairs." February 14. http://www.state.gov/r/.
USC ICT (Institute for Creative Technologies). 2011. "USC Institute for Creative Technologies Receives $135 Million Contract Extension From U.S. Army." September 1. http://ict.usc.edu/news/usc-institute-for-creative-technologies-receives-135-million-contract-extension-from-u-s-army/.
USITC (United States International Trade Commission). 2014. "Recent Trends in US Services Trade: 2014 Annual Report." http://www.usitc.gov/publications/332/pub4463.pdf.
USTR (United States Trade Representative). 2015. *2015 Special 301 Report*. April. https://ustr.gov/sites/default/files/2015-Special-301-Report-FINAL.pdf.
van der Graaf, S., and D.B. Nieborg. 2003. "Together We Brand: *America's Army*." In *Level Up: Digital Games Research Conference*, ed. Marinka Copier and Joost Racssens, 324–38. Utrecht: Utrecht University.
Vargas, J.A. 2006. "Virtual Reality Prepares Soldiers for Real War." *Washington Post*, February 14. http://www.washingtonpost.com/wp-dyn/content/article/2006/02/13/AR2006021302437.html.
Vine, D. 2012. "How US Taxpayers Are Paying the Pentagon to Occupy the Planet." Al Jazeera, December 14. http://www.aljazeera.com/indepth/opinion/2012/12/20121213122226666895.html.
Wagenleitner, R. 1994. *Coca-Colonization and the Cold War*. Chapel Hill and London: University of North Carolina Press.
Walker, T.W. 1991. *Revolution and Counterrevolution in Nicaragua*. Boulder, CO: Westview.
Wallerstein, I. 2003. *The Decline of American Power*. New York: New Press.
Walsh, D. 2002. "US Actor Sean Penn Visits Baghdad." World Socialist Website, December 20. https://www.wsws.org/en/articles/2002/12/penn-d20.html.
Walt, S.M. 2011. "The End of the American Era." *National Interest*, October 25. http://nationalinterest.org/article/the-end-the-american-era-6037.
Warner, K. 2012. "Katy Perry 'Sore and Exhausted' after 'Part of Me' Video." MTV, March 21. http://www.mtv.com/news/1681555/katy-perry-part-of-me-training/.
Warren, M. 2012. "Anti-Hollywood 'Act of Valor' a Soldier's Soldiering Film about the SEALs." *Washington Times*, February 23. http://www.washingtontimes.com/news/2012/feb/23/act-of-valor-soldiers-soldiering-film-seals/?page=all.
Wasko, J., G. Murdock, and H. Sousa. 2011. "Introduction: The Political Economy of Communications—Core Concerns and Issues." In *The Handbook of*

Political Economy of Communications, 1–10. Blackwell. http://dx.doi.org/10.1002/9781444395402.ch.

Wattenberg, B. 1991. *The First Universal Nation: Leading Indicators and Ideas about the Surge of America in the 1990s*. New York: Free Press.

Weiner, J. 2002. "Quiet in Hollywood." *The Nation*, December 16. http://www.thenation.com/docprint.mhtml?i=20021216&s=wiener.

Weinraub, B. 2011. "After the Attacks: Hollywood; For Now, Film Industry Scratches Violence in Favor of Family Fare and Patriotism." *New York Times*, September 16. http://www.nytimes.com/2001/09/16/us/after-attacks-hollywood-for-now-film-industry-scratches-violence-favor-family.html.

Weissman, S. 2005. "Dead Messengers: How the US Military Threatens Journalists." *Truthout*, March 7. http://truth-out.org/archive/component/k2/item/52806:to-investigation-steve-weissman--part-iv-but-what-about-aljazeera.

—. 2013. "The Return of the Monopoly: An Infographic." *The Atlantic*, March 20. http://www.theatlantic.com/magazine/archive/2013/04/the-chartist/309271/.

Wellemeyer, J. 2006. "Hollywood and the Spread of Anti-Americanism." NPR, December 20. http://www.npr.org/templates/story/story.php?storyId=6625002.

Wentz, L. 2003. "Executive Order 13283: Establishing the Office of Global Communications." http://fas.org/irp/offdocs/eo/eo-13283.htm.

—. 2008. "An Instant Overhaul for Tainted Brand America." *Advertising Age*, November 10. http://adage.com/article/news/obama-win-offers-instant-overhaul-tainted-brand-america/132352/.

—. 2009. *Statement by the President on the White House Organization for Homeland Security and Counterterrorism*. Office of the Press Secretary, May 26. http://www.whitehouse.gov/the-press-office/statement-president-white-house-organization-homeland-security-and-counterterrorism.

—. 2013. *Remarks by President Obama in Address to the United Nations General Assembly*. September 24. http://www.whitehouse.gov/the-press-office/2013/09/24/remarks-president-obama-address-united-nations-general-assembly.

Whitman, B. 2003. "Interview with BBC TV, US Department of Defense Transcript." US Department of Defense, April 18. http://www.defense.gov/Transcripts/Transcript.aspx?TranscriptID=2471.

Willens, M. 2015. "NBCUniversal to Produce American TV Shows for European Broadcasters." *International Business Times*, April 14. http://www.ibtimes.com/nbcuniversal-produce-american-tv-shows-european-broadcasters-1881835.

Williams, C. 2012. "MPs Call for Violent Video Game Ban after Breivik Claims that He 'Trained' on *Call of Duty: Modern Warfare*." http://www.telegraph.co.uk/technology/video-games/9272774/MPs-call-for-violent-video-game-ban-after-Breivik-claims-that-he-trained-on-Call-of-Duty-Modern-Warfare.html.

Williams, K. 1993. "The Light at the End of the Tunnel: The Mass Media, Public Opinion and the Vietnam War." In *Getting the Message: News, Truth and Power*, ed. John Eldridge, 305–30. New York: Routledge.

Williams, W.A. 1955. "The Frontier Thesis and American Foreign Policy." *Pacific Historical Review* 24 (10): 379–95.

—. 1980. *Empire as a Way of Life*. New York: Oxford University Press.

Wilson, J. 2003. "US Troops 'Crazy' in Killing of Cameraman Jamie Wilson in Baghdad." *Guardian*, August 19. http://www.theguardian.com/media/2003/aug/19/iraqandthemedia.iraq.

Wilson, M. 2002. "Thousands at Central Park Rally Oppose an Iraq War." *New York Times*, October 7. http://www.nytimes.com/2002/10/07/nyregion/thousands-at-central-park-rally-oppose-an-iraq-war.html.

Wilson Center. 2011. *Congress' Influence on Foreign Policy: For Better or Worse?* Panelists: Former Sen. J.E. Sununu (R-N.H.), senior policy adviser, A. Gump; D. McKean, public policy scholar, Woodrow Wilson Center; J.M. Lindsay, senior vice-president, Council on Foreign Relations; G.R. Chaddock, congressional correspondent. October 17. http://www.wilsoncenter.org/event/congress%E2%80%99-influence-foreign-policy-for-better-or-worse.

Winseck, D. 2008. "The State of Media Ownership and Media Markets: Competition or Concentration and Why Should We Care?" *Social Compass* 2 (1): 34–47. http://dx.doi.org/10.1111/j.1751-9020.2007.00061.x.

Winseck, D., and D.Y. Jin, eds. 2011. *The Political Economies of Media: The Transformation of the Global Media Industries*. London, New York: Bloomsbury Academic. http://dx.doi.org/10.5040/9781849664264.

Winseck, D., and R.M. Pike. 2007. *Communication and Empire: Media, Markets and Globalization, 1860–1930*. Durham: Duke University Press. http://dx.doi.org/10.1215/9780822389996.

Wittkopf, E.R., C.M. Jones, and C.W. Kegley. 2003. *American Foreign Policy: Pattern and Process*. Belmont, CA: Thomson Higher Education.

Wolf, J. 2003. "Al Jazeera Defends Images, Won't Censor War Horror." *Reuters*, March 30. http://www.reuters.com/news.

Wolfe, P. 2006. "Settler Colonialism and the Elimination of the Native." *Journal of Genocide Research* 8 (4): 387–409. http://dx.doi.org/10.1080/14623520601056240.

Women's Media Center. 2014. *The Status of Women in the U.S. Media 2014*. http://wmc.3cdn.net/6dd3de8ca65852dbd4_fjm6yck9o.pdf.

Wood, E.M. 2003. *Empire of Capital*. New York: Verso.

Wright, R. 2004. "US Struggles to Win Hearts, Minds in the Muslim World." *Washington Post*, August 20. http://www.washingtonpost.com/wp-dyn/articles/A17134-2004Aug19.html.

WTO (World Trade Organization). 2010. "Audiovisual Services: Background Note by the Secretariat." January 12. http://www.oecd.org/tad/servicestrade/47559464.pdf.

Wyant, C. 2012. "Who's Joining the US Military? Poor, Women and Minorities Targeted." *Mint Press News*, December 18. http://www.mintpressnews.com/whos-joining-the-us-military-poor-women-and-minorities-targeted/43418/.

Wylie, D. 2010. "Minister Gives War Video Game Thumbs Down." Canada.com. August 25. http://www2.canada.com/news/minister+gives+video+game+thumbs+down/3445730/story.html?id=3445730.

Yahr, E. 2012. "'Stars Earn Stripes' Military Operatives Respond to Show Criticism: 'We're Not Glorifying War.'" *Washington Post*, August 24. http://www.washingtonpost.com/blogs/tv-column/post/stars-earn-stripes-military-operatives-respond-to-show-criticism-were-not-glorifying-war/2012/08/24/7b8ce6e8-ee33-11e1-afd8-097e90f99d05_blog.html.

Young, M.B. 2003. "In the Combat Zone." *Radical History Review* 85 (1): 253–64.

Young, R.C. 2001. *Postcolonialism: An Historical Introduction*. Malden, MA: Blackwell.

Zakaria, F. 2008. *The Post-American World*. New York: W.W. Norton.

–. 2011. "Are America's Best Days Behind Us?" *Time*, March 3. http://content.time.com/time/magazine/article/0,9171,2056723,00.html.

Zewe, C. 2004. "Infoganda in Uniform: the Bush Administration Creates Media Outlets to Tell Its Story." Nieman Foundation. http://www.nieman.harvard.edu/reports/article/100788/Infoganda-in-Uniform.aspx.

Ziezulewicz, G. 2009. "Military Uses Virtual Therapy to Help Troops Heal Wounds." *Stars and Stripes*, June 29. http://www.stripes.com/news/military-uses-virtual-therapy-to-help-troops-heal-wounds-1.92986.

Zoroya, G. 2003. "Return of US War Dead Kept Solemn, Secret. *USA Today*, December 31. http://usatoday30.usatoday.com/news/nation/2003-12-31-casket-usat_x.htm.

Zyda, M. 1997. *Modeling and Simulation: Linking Entertainment and Defense*. National Academies Press. PDF e-book. http://www.nap.edu/openbook.php?record_id=5830.

Index

Abu Ghraib prison, 97, 155
academy: denial of US Empire by, 30–31; discourse after 9/11, 31–32; engineering of consent by, 16–17; and military-industrial complex, 23–24; political economy approach by, 16–17
Act of Valor (film), 187–88
Activision Blizzard, 104, 109, 202, 229
Adobe Systems, 108, 120
Adorno, Theodore, 103–4
advertising industry: branding campaigns, xii, 91–92, 95, 213; and consumerism, 115–16; and culture industries, 114–16, 186–87; glocalization, 114–15; historical background, 64–65, 71, 76–77, 80; major corporations, 107; news media revenue from, 158–59; product placement by, 186–87; in War on Terror, 91–93. *See also* media conglomerates
Afghanistan, US invasion: censorship and coercion after, 140–41, 226–28; cultural exchanges before, 94–95; digital games on, 218–20, 224–28; film/TV industry on, 178–80; historical background, 90; news media on, 139–40; propaganda, 140–41
Africa, 3, 60, 105, 179
Agency, The (TV series), 180, 190, 198
Agency for International Development, US, 6
Air Force, US, 5, 187. *See also* military
Al Jazeera, 92–93, 96, 154–55, 242, 247
al-Qaeda: in cultural products, 5, 163, 192–93; terrorist attacks by, 89–90, 143–45. *See also* bin Laden, Osama; September 11 terrorist attacks
Alamo, The (film), 173
Alhurra TV network (OPD), 96
Alias (TV series), 163, 190
Amazon, 108, 118, 120, 239
AMC Entertainment, 120
America's Army (digital games), 213–15, 217–18, 229, 243
American Civil Liberties Union (ACLU), 243
American Economy (film), 86
Animal Farm (film), 188
Anthony, Dave, 62

anti-Americanism: and culture industry, 248–49; and Iraq War, 154; US elitist view of non-US publics, 101; and War on Terror, 90–91, 95, 97–98
anti-imperialists, 25–27, 244–45, 247–49
anti-war movement. *See* peace movements
Apocalypse Now (film), 194–95
Apple, 107–8, 120, 213, 239
Arabic-language broadcasting, 92–94, 96, 154–55, 242, 247
Argo (film), 163, 191–93
Army, US: *America's Army* (digital games), 213–15, 217–18, 229, 243; branding campaign, xii, 213. *See also* military
Army Experience Center (AEC), 217
Association of American Publishers (AAP), 116
Atari, 205–6
Attack! (film), 194
Away All Boats (film), 171

Bad Company (film), 185, 190
Band of Brothers (TV series), 176, 184
Baruch, Donald, 170, 172
Battle: Los Angeles (film), 185
Battlefield (digital game), 61, 229–31
Battleship (film), 185
Battlezone (digital game), 206
BBG (Broadcasting Board of Governors), 7, 88, 94, 96–97, 99
BDA (Business for Diplomatic Action), 91
BECA (Bureau of Educational and Cultural Affairs), 82, 94–96, 99
Beers, Charlotte, 91–95
Beggs, John, 81
Behind Enemy Lines (films), 179, 185
Bernays, Edward, 21, 67–68, 82
bin Laden, Osama: digital games on, 61, 219, 222–23; films and TV shows on, 163–64, 192–93, 198
Biological Weapons Convention, 256–57
Birth of a Nation, The (film), 165

Black Hawk Down (film), 179, 185, 193, 198
Blackwater (digital game), 225
BMP (Bureau of Motion Pictures), 77, 167–68
book publishers. *See* publishing industry
Bourne trilogy (films), 200
Bowling for Columbine (film), 196
Brazil, 51–52, 117, 237
Breivik, Anders, 201–3
BRICS nations, 51–54, 116, 237
Bridges at Toko-Ri, The (film), 171
Britain. *See* United Kingdom
Broadcasting Board of Governors (BBG), 7, 88, 94, 96–97, 99
Brothers in Arms (digital game), 223
BSA/Software Alliance, 117–18
Bureau of Educational and Cultural Affairs (BECA), 82, 94–96, 99
Bureau of Information, 82
Bureau of International Information Programs, 56, 94, 99
Bureau of Motion Pictures (BMP), 77, 167–68
Bureau of Public Affairs, 56, 94, 99
Burnett, Mark, 5, 114
Bush, George H.W., 83, 87, 137. *See also* Gulf War
Bush, George W., 30, 49, 151, 179; administration, 42–43, 90, 96, 143–44, 151. *See also* Iraq War (2003–); War on Terror (2001–9)
Business for Diplomatic Action (BDA), 91

Caine Mutiny, The (film), 171
Call of Duty: Advanced Warfare, 104; *Black Ops*, 225, 235; *Black Ops II*, 3–4, 6, 62; franchise, 61, 62, 104, 202–3, 230, 243; *Modern Warfare*, 229, 230; *Modern Warfare 2*, 60, 202, 243
Canada, 123, 124, 249
capitalism: and culture industries, 4, 10, 55–56, 109–13; and economic crises, 53; and film/TV industry, 197–98; historical background, 38–43, 123–24; political economy

Index 301

approach to, 13–17; telecom industry, 123–24; and wealth inequality, 19
capitalist imperialism: about, 33–34, 38–39; and cultural imperialism, 19–21; and cultural products, 24–25; historical background, 36–43; and neoliberalism, 41–43; and non-territorial colonialism, 35; resistance to, 37–38; and war, 36–37, 42. *See also* cultural imperialism; Empire, US; media conglomerates
Capra, Frank, 166, 168, 169
Captain Newman, M.D. (film), 172
Captain Phillips (film), 185
Carter, James "Jimmy," 83
Casablanca (film), 168
Catch-22 (film), 195
CBS Corporation, 106, 107, 120, 157, 158–59, 177, 239
censorship and coercion: about, 132, 200, 241–42; consent to, 148–49, 160–61, 166, 198, 200, 248; digital games industry, 225–28, 233; economic incentives, 200, 247–48; film/TV industry, 72–73, 77–78, 166, 169, 178, 200, 242; film/TV script control, 167–68, 170–74, 181–84, 186–87, 189–90, 194–95, 242, 255; Hollywood Red Scare, 170–71; lack of transparency of, 200; and news media, 132, 160–61, 241; non-aligned journalists, 57, 154–56; pacifist views, 166, 194, 199; satellite images, 140; speakers' programs, 75; war casualties, 78, 152–54; war and embedded journalists, 146–49
censorship and coercion, historical background: Afghanistan, 140–41, 226–28; the Cold War, 170–71; the Iraq War, 146–49, 151–56, 178; the Vietnam War, 134–35, 173–74; WWI, 72–73, 165–66; WWII, 76, 77–78, 167–69

Center for Strategic Counterterrorism Communications, 56
Central Intelligence Agency (CIA): in *Argo* and *Zero Dark Thirty*, 190–93; black ops and torture, 42, 50, 190, 192–93, 200; in the Cold War, 79, 81, 188–90; film/TV industry relations, 188–95, 199–200; in film/TV productions, 163–64, 190–93; historical background, 42, 79, 190; and Iraq War, 144–45; liaison office, 189–90; NSC's direction of, 45; public relations, 56–57, 190; script control, 181–84, 189–90, 194–95, 198–200; subsidies from, 195, 199–200
Cheney, Dick, 48
China: advertising industry, 116; censorship, 127; comparison with US, 51–54, 116; culture industry, 105, 109, 117, 127; in digital games, 61; economic rise of, 51–54, 237; film market in, 3, 5, 198; historical background, 39; protection of culture, 127
Chomsky, Noam, ix–x, 12, 199
Chrome Specforce (digital game), 209
CIA. *See* Central Intelligence Agency (CIA)
Cisco Systems, 108, 120, 239
civil society and special interest groups: about, 46–47; influence on decision-making, 46; influence in war, 69–70; lobbying by, 46–47, 118–19. *See also* democracy; lobbyists
Clarke, Victoria, 145, 146
class. *See* social class
Clinton, Bill, 87–89
Clinton, Hillary, 15, 129–30
Clooney, George, 59–60
Close Combat (digital game), 231
CNN, 3, 96, 107, 139, 142, 158–59. *See also* news media
coercion of culture industry. *See* censorship and coercion

Cold War (1946–91): CIA and culture industry, 188–93; cultural exchanges, 82; culture industry, 78, 104, 122; digital games on, 225; film/TV industry, 86–87, 169–76, 188–93; historical background, 40–41, 78–87; impact of *Top Gun* on military during, 175–76; Korean War, 80, 133, 171, 173; news, 83–84, 136–37; psy-ops, 16, 136–37; public diplomacy, 78–87, 100–1; radio, 85–86; USIA during, 81–84. *See also* Vietnam War

Collateral Damage (film), 198

colonialism: and hegemony, 36; historical background, 34–35; territorial vs non-territorial, 31, 34–35; US as post-colonial empire, 17–18, 31–32. *See also* Empire, US

Combat Elite (digital game), 223

Comcast-NBC Universal, 3, 106, 107, 108, 119, 120, 239

comic books. *See* publishing industry

Committee to Protect Journalists (CPJ), 155

Committee on Public Information (CPI), 68–73, 133, 165–66

communications and political economy, 13–17

communications technology. *See* information and communications technology (ICT) industry

computer games. *See* digital games

Conflict franchise (digital games), 203, 223–24

Congress, US, 45–46

Congress for Cultural Freedom, 188

console games. *See* digital games

Constitution, US, 44–45, 117, 199, 242, 247

consumerism: and advertising industry, 115–16; and cultural imperialism, 20–21, 115; and cultural products, 24–25; film portrayals of, 71–72, 86; and government policies, 239–40; historical background, 41, 64–65, 68, 71–72, 76–77; and US Empire, 18. *See also* capitalism

copyright. *See* intellectual property rights

corporations, US: about, 55–56; against anti-Americanism, 90–91; corporate vs democratic values, 55, 250–51; ex-military consultants, 184–85; historical background, 64–66; lobbying by, 46–47, 117–19; military-industrial complex, 20, 23–24, 53–54, 184–85; and public relations, 65–66; weapons industry, 5, 23–24. *See also* consumerism; media conglomerates; power elites

Cox, Michael, 38, 41

CPI (Committee on Public Information), 68–73, 133, 165–66

CPJ (Committee to Protect Journalists), 155

Creel, George, 69–71, 73, 238

CSI (TV series), 3

Cuba, 6, 86–88, 99, 164, 190, 224, 235

Cuba Waits (film), 86

cultural exchanges: historical background, 74, 82, 88; and public diplomacy, 239; recent programs, 94–97, 99

cultural imperialism: about, 10–11, 19–20, 26–29, 238, 244; and capitalism, 55–56; centre-periphery model, 27; defined, 19–20; democratization of, 247, 251–52; engineering of consent, 16–17; and glocalization, 114–15; and power elites, 237–38; recent theories, 26–29; resistance to, 125–26; telecom industry, 125–26. *See also* capitalist imperialism; Empire, US; globalization; media conglomerates; power elites

cultural products: about, 115, 244, 249; cross-border productions, 110–11; and cultural imperialism, 24–25, 115; defined, 24; exceptionalism themes, 24–25, 255–57; future

Index

threats portrayed in, 61–62; glocalization of, 74, 93, 114–15, 126–27, 239; and national identity, 58–59; transnational products, 25, 104, 113–15, 127–28, 239, 254. *See also* digital games; films; radio; television shows

culture industry: about, xii, 7–9, 103–6, 238, 249, 257; and capitalism, 4, 55–56, 109–15, 126–27, 248–49; cross-border productions, 110–11; democratization of, 247–52; economic power, 3–4, 22–23, 126–28; and engineering of consent, 12–13; free flow doctrine, 23, 122–23, 124; global audiences, 113–16; historical background, 64–65, 103–4, 122–23; myth of liberal dominance of, 180, 188, 196–97, 248–49; and national identity, 58–59; and neoliberalism, 125–26, 127; and non-US industries, 22–23, 105–6, 109–13, 128–29; political economy approach, 13–17; reality vs representation, 244; reform movements, 251–52; trends, 105, 109, 126–30. *See also* war and culture industry; *and specific sectors*

culture industry and DOD. *See* censorship and coercion; digital games industry and DOD; film/TV industry and DOD; media conglomerates and DOD; news media and DOD; war and culture industry

culture industry and government policy: about, 116–17, 239–40, 257; agencies, 249–50; democratic values, 55, 250–51; deregulation and privatization, 123–26; intellectual property rights, 119–20; licensing agreements, 112–13; and lobbyists, 117–19, 239–40; reform movements, 251–52; subsidies for, 57, 120–21; trade liberalization, 122–23. *See also* intellectual property rights; war and culture industry

Darfur genocide, 60
Dark Knight, The (films), 3, 113
DARWARS Ambush! (digital game), 218
Debt of Honour (Clancy), 62
Deer Hunter (film), 194–95
Defense Department. *See* Department of Defense (DOD)
Defense.gov News, 57
Dell Computers, 107–8, 120
democracy: and anti-imperialism, 25–26; and capitalism, 19, 22, 46; civil society groups, 46–47, 69–70, 118–19; CNN-effect theory, 139; corporate vs democratic values, 55, 250–51; and cultural policy, 249–51; decision-making hierarchies, 43–44, 237–38; democratization of culture industries, 247–48, 251–52; democratization of government, 245–47; elections, 46–48, 98–99; elitist theory of public opinion, 21–22, 48; ideal vs actual democracy, 16, 18–19, 244–45; meaningful participation, 44, 66; media democracy groups, 118, 241–42, 245, 251; and military-industrial complex, 23–24; news media's watchdog role, 132, 161–62, 241–42; political economy approach to, 13–17; public broadcasting, 23, 55, 124, 251–52; Schiller on, 19, 25–26; special interest groups, 46–47. *See also* elections, US; government, US; power elites
Democracy Now!, 242, 245
Department of Defense (DOD): and cultural policy, 249; information operations, 141–43; military-industrial complex, 20, 23–24, 53–54, 257; news media, 57, 149–50; NSC's role, 45; pseudo-events,

150–51, 241; public affairs office, 56–57; statistics on, 54. *See also* information operations (IO); military; military, recruitment; psychological operations (PSY-OPS)
Department of Defense (DOD) and culture industry. *See* censorship and coercion; digital games industry and DOD; film/TV industry and DOD; media conglomerates and DOD; news media and DOD
Department of Defense Special Assistant for Entertainment Media (DODSAEM), 180–82
Department of Homeland Security, 45, 56, 252, 256
Department of State, 45, 56, 89, 116, 249. *See also* Office of Public Diplomacy (OPD)
digital games: actual war vs digital war, 131, 203, 215, 230, 234–35; anti-war games, 235; bestsellers, 3–4, 104, 202, 203, 215, 230; cultural sensitivity training, 219; enemy play options, 226–28; free games, 209, 214; markets for, 202–3, 214–15; and masculinity, 231; online games, 205–7, 214–15, 226; peace option omission, 60, 224, 233; procedural logic in, 232–33; realism, 229–33; therapy for soldiers, 202, 222–23, 228–29, 234, 235; violence issues, 202–3, 227–28, 230; war crimes and black ops, 224–25, 230; war as fun, 220–21, 243. See also *America's Army* (digital games); *Call of Duty*, franchise
digital games industry: about, 5–6, 108–9, 202–4, 233–35; democratization of, 234; economic power of, 3–4, 108–9, 233; historical background, 204–9; lobbying by, 118, 209; and non-US industries, 109, 207, 218; public relations, 222–28; virtual worlds, 204–5, 209

digital games industry and DOD: about, 13, 203–4, 210–12, 233–35, 240–41, 243; agencies of DOD, 210–12, 243; budgets, 211, 213–14; censorship and coercion, 225–28, 233; consultants, 5, 215, 229; culture industry relations, 57–58; DOD's liaison offices, 57; historical background, 204–9; online games, 205–7, 214–15, 226; realism of games, 229–33; recruitment of military, 206, 212–18, 243; rehabilitation of military, 228–30; research and development, 204–6, 208–12, 233, 243; simulation networks, 205–9; subsidies for industry, 57, 120–21, 203, 206, 207, 243; symbiotic relationship, 207–12, 220–21, 233; training, 202, 204–12, 218–22, 243
DirecTV, 106, 239
Dirty Dozen (film), *The*, 172
Dish Network, 106, 239
Disney. *See* Walt Disney Company, The
Dive Bomber (film), 167
DOD. *See* Department of Defense (DOD)
DoD News Channel, 149–50
DODSAEM (Department of Defense Special Assistant for Entertainment Media), 180–82
Doom (digital game), 208
Dr. Strangelove (film), 195
draft, military, 166–67, 212. *See also* military, recruitment

EA. *See* Electronic Arts (EA)
eBay, 108, 118, 120, 239
economy, US: about, 51–53; advertising industry, 116; CEO salaries, 107; culture industry, 3–4, 22–23, 126–28; decline of, 51–54; deregulation and privatization, 123–26; financial crisis of 2008, 51–52; historical background, 40; media conglomerates, 3, 10, 55–56,

106–7, 109, 128; neoliberalism, 123–26; news media downsizing, 157–58; oligopolistic markets, 106. *See also* capitalism
educational exchanges. *See* cultural exchanges
Egypt, 94–95
EILO (Entertainment Industry Liaison Office), 189–90
Eisenhower, Dwight D., 23–24, 81–82, 133–34
elections, US, 46–48, 98–99
Electronic Arts (EA), 5, 109, 120, 207, 210, 223–24, 225–27, 229
elites, power. *See* power elites
Empire, US: about, 9–10, 17–18, 30–33, 236–38; basic elements of empires, 32–33; and capitalism, 10, 18, 33–34; and culture industry, 7–9; decision-making hierarchies, 33, 43–48, 237–38; decline of, 51–54, 237; denial of, 30–31; discourse after 9/11, 31–32; exceptionalist ideology, 49–51; expansionism, 33, 35; hegemony of, 33, 36–38; historical background, 34–37, 38–43, 50; ideal vs actuality, 244–45; instability of, 35–36; negative effects of, 244–45; political economy approach to, 13–17; resistance to hegemony, 25–26, 37–38; soft vs hard power, 16–17, 30, 36–38; territorial vs non-territorial rule, 34–35; and war, 36–37. *See also* capitalist imperialism; cultural imperialism; exceptionalism
Ender's Game (film), 62
Enemy at the Gates (film), 185
engineering of consent: black vs white propaganda, 140–41; and culture industry, 12–13, 238, 242; by DOD, 24, 241; elitist theory of public opinion, 21–22, 48; flacking of dissenters, 12, 154–56, 160–61; H. Clinton on, 15; historical background, 65–66; Lippmann's theory of, 21–22, 48, 66–68; political economy approach to, 16–17; propaganda model, 12; psy-ops, 133–34, 141; and public diplomacy, 15, 239; and public relations, 222. *See also* psychological operations (PSY-OPS)
England. *See* United Kingdom
Entertainment Industry Liaison Office (EILO), 189–90
Entertainment Software Association (ESA), 118
Escape to Freedom (film), 86
Europe, 77, 88, 127
EverQuest (digital game), 206–7
exceptionalism: about, 33, 49–51, 237; in cultural products, 24–25, 255–57; defined, 237; and film/TV industry, 197–98, 255–57; historical background, 34, 50; ideology of, 49–50; and news media, 161; in non-US countries, 49; Obama on, 9, 49; and power elites, 48; Schiller on, 24–25; and security threats, 50–51; superiority of US, 33, 49; of US Empire, 33, 51
exchange programs. *See* cultural exchanges
executive branch, US, 44–46, 101. *See also* National Security Council (NSC); president, US

Facebook, 6, 120
Fahrenheit 9/11 (film), 200
Federal Communications Commission (FCC), 116, 121
film/TV industry: and celebrity power, 196–97; CIA relations, 188–94; economic power of, 3, 105, 127–28; and exceptionalism, 197–98, 255–57; film distribution, 110; lobbying by, 46–47, 117–19; media conglomerates, 195–96; non-US industries, 105, 109–13, 127,

128–29; private military consultants to, 184–85; product placement, 186–87; Red Scare in 1950s, 170–71; time between actual war vs reel war, 178–79; trends, 105, 109, 128–30. *See also* media conglomerates

film/TV industry, historical background: Afghanistan, 179–80; the Cold War, 86–87, 169–76; the Iraq War, 178–80; Spanish-American War, 164–65; the Vietnam War, 134–35, 173–74; the War on Terror, 177–80; WWI, 71–73, 165–66; WWII, 74, 76, 77–78, 166–69

film/TV industry and DOD: about, 163–64, 193–98, 240, 242; actual war vs media war, 135–36, 174–75; censorship and coercion, 72–74, 77–78, 166–69, 178, 242; culture industry relations, 57–58; influence on *Transformers* series, 186–87; initiation of projects by DOD, 187–88; liaison offices, 57, 169–73, 175–76, 180–88, 242; myth of liberal dominance of, 180, 188, 196–97, 248–49; pacifist vs militarized views, 73, 194–95, 199, 242; script control, 167–68, 170–74, 181–84, 186–87, 189–90, 194–95, 199–200, 242, 255; subsidies for industry, 57, 120–21, 171–72, 175–76, 182–83, 193–94, 199–200, 242, 255; technical assistance, 166, 169–70, 171, 181–83, 184–86; transparency of relationship, 200. *See also* censorship and coercion

films: about, 113–14; blockbusters, 104, 113–15, 185–86, 253–57; CIA in *Argo* and *Zero Dark Thirty*, 190–93; future threats portrayed in, 62, 176; global audiences, 104, 113–15; highest-grossing films, 104, 113–14, 127; *I Am Legend* blockbuster, 253–57; markets for, 3–5, 128–30, 197–98; pro-military vs pacifist views, 170–71; product placement in, 186–87; *Transformers* franchise, 4, 104, 113–14, 179, 185–87; transnational films, 25, 104, 113–14, 239, 254; *Welcome* campaign, 252–57

financial crisis of 2008, 51–52

Firefight (simulator), 205

First Amendment rights, 117, 199, 242, 247. *See also* Constitution, US

First World War: censorship, 72–73, 165–66; culture industry, 70–72, 165–66; digital games on, 230; historical background, 39; interwar years, 73–74, 166; psy-ops practices, 16, 133; public relations, 68–73, 133, 165–66

Fiserv, 108, 120

The Flying Leathernecks (film), 171

FM 3-13 (DOD), 142–43

foreign countries. *See* non-US countries

foreign policy. *See* international relations

Fox, Liam, 226

Fox News, 107, 157–59

Fraser, Matthew, 16–17

Free Press, 118, 241–42, 251

Friedman, Thomas, 41–42

From Here to Eternity (film), 171

Fugitive Hunter (digital game), 203, 222–23

Fulbright scholarship program, 12, 82, 88, 94, 95, 99

Full Metal Jacket (film), 195

Full Spectrum Warrior (digital game), 203, 221–22

Game of Thrones (TV series), 4

games. *See* digital games

Gathering of Eagles, A (film), 172

gender issues: masculinity and militarism, 231; media conglomerates, 106–7; women-friendly military, 4

Germany, 86, 166

Ghost Recon (digital game), 221, 231

Gindin, Sam, xiii

Glassman, James, 99–100
global financial crisis of 2008, 51–52
global media. *See* media conglomerates
global War on Terror. *See* War on Terror (2001–9)
globalization: about, xii-xiii, 27, 32; compared with imperialism, xiii, 9; theory of cultural imperialism, 27–29; transnational cultural products, 25, 104, 113–14, 127–28, 239, 254
glocalization of cultural products, 74, 93, 114–15, 126–27, 239
Goodrich, Greg, 225, 227
Google, 55, 91, 108, 118, 120, 239
government, US: division of powers, 44–45; elections, 47–48; executive branch, 44–46, 101; myth of social neutrality, 18–19; power elites, 48. *See also* Constitution, US; culture industry and government policy; military; president, US
Grand Theft Auto (digital game), 228
Great Britain. *See* United Kingdom
Great Recession. *See* global financial crisis of 2008
Green Berets, The (film), 173–74
Guantanamo Bay prison, 97
Gulf War, 137–39, 207, 223

Harvey, David, xiii, 33–34
hegemony, defined, 36. *See also* Empire, US
Herman, E., 12, 199
Hewlett-Packard, 107, 108, 120
Hi (OPD magazine), 93
High Noon (film), 173
historiography: political economy approach, 13–17; and US Empire, 30–31, 33
Hollywood film/TV industry. *See* film/TV industry
Holsti, O.R., 246–47
Homeland (TV series), 163
Hong Kong, 105
Horkheimer, Max, 103–4

Hughes, Karen, 97–98, 254
Hussein, Saddam, 41, 143–45, 151, 154, 203, 223
Huston, John, 169

I Am Legend (film), 253–57
I Wanted Wings (film), 167, 168
IBM, 108, 120, 166, 239
ICT. *See* information and communications technology (ICT) industry
ICT (digital games). *See* Institute for Creative Technologies (ICT)
Ignatieff, Michael, 31–32
IMF (International Monetary Fund), 40, 41, 125, 240
IMG (Information Media Guarantee), 84–85
imperialism, 9, 17–18, 31. *See also* capitalist imperialism; cultural imperialism; Empire, US; media conglomerates
In the Valley of Elah (film), 195
India, 51–52, 105, 116–17, 124, 237
industries. *See* corporations, US
industries, culture. *See* culture industry; digital games industry; film/TV industry; information and communications technology (ICT) industry; media conglomerates; news media
Information Agency, US (USIA), 81–87, 99, 134
information and communications technology (ICT) industry: about, 107–8, 239–40; "big data" firms, 108; and cultural imperialism, 20–21; lobbying by, 117–18; major corporations, 107–8, 239; military-industrial-communications complex, 12, 23–24, 240, 257; and non-US industries, 109–13, 128; subsidies for, 120–21. *See also* media conglomerates
Information and Educational Exchange Act, US, 79

Information Media Guarantee (IMG), 84–85
information operations (IO): about, 57–58, 141–43, 241; information centres, 149; strategies, 142–45; war casualties, 152–54. See also news media and DOD
Information Operations Roadmap (DOD), 58, 142
Institute for Creative Technologies (ICT), 62, 177, 210–11, 221, 228–29, 243
Integration (film), 86
intellectual property rights: about, 119–21, 240; copyright, 118–20; and culture industry, 119–20, 127; digital games, 205, 211, 221; film/TV industry, 111–13; licensing agreements, 112–13; lobbying for, 117–18; US law as world law, 125
Interactive Digital Software Association, 209
International Broadcasting Bureau, 88
International Communications Agency, US (ICA), 83
International Criminal Court, 42, 50, 60
International Intellectual Property Alliance, 118
International Monetary Fund (IMF), 40, 41, 125, 240
international relations: about, 18; Congress's role, 45–46; denial of US Empire, 30–31; electorate's influence on, 47–48; historical background, 34–37, 38–43; liberal developmentalism (pre-1945), 36–38; lobbying for, 47; NSC direction of, 44–45; and power elites, 48; Schiller on, 18. See also Empire, US; National Security Council (NSC); public diplomacy abroad
International Telecommunications Union, 124, 240
Internet games. See digital games
Internet industries. See information and communications technology (ICT) industry

interwar years, 73–74, 166
IO. See information operations (IO)
IPR. See intellectual property rights
Iran: in *Argo*, 191–93; in digital games, 61, 230–31; US broadcasts into, 88, 94
Iraq Veterans Against the War, 243
Iraq War (1990–91). See Gulf War
Iraq War (2003–): about, 143–45, 156; censorship and coercion, 151–56; digital games industry, xii, 203, 218–20, 229–30; false pretexts for, x, xii, 143–44, 223; film/TV industry, 178–80, 196, 200; financial costs of, 52; increase in anti-Americanism, 97–98; journalists, 57, 144, 154–56, 160–61; news media, 6–7, 145–51, 156–61; peace movement, x–xii, 144–45, 160; public diplomacy, 97; rehabilitation of soldiers, 228–30; torture, 50, 97. See also Hussein, Saddam
Iron Man (films), 185

Japan, 3, 109, 123–24, 207
JFK (film), 190
John F. Kennedy (film), 86
Johnson, Lyndon B., 83, 119, 134, 173
Joint Hometown News Service (JHNS), 6–7
Joint Vision (DOD), 58, 141
journalists: actual war vs media war, 131, 135–36, 161; downsizing of news media, 157–58; embedded vs non-embedded, 146–49; flacking of, 154–56; foreign news services, 70–71; in the Gulf War, 138; in Iraq War, 57, 144, 154–56, 160–61; non-aligned journalists, 57, 154–56; professionalism and sources, 159–60; self-censorship, 148–49, 160–61, 166, 198; 24-hour 7-day cycle, 139–40, 141; in Vietnam War, 135; war casualties, 57, 154–55, 241; in WWI, 70–71

journals. *See* publishing industry
Just Cause (digital game), 224

Kennedy, John F., 51, 82–83, 86, 134, 173
Kennedy, Paul, 51
Kingdom, The (film), 163, 179
Kony 2012 (digital game), 60
Korean War, 80, 133, 171, 173
Krugman, Paul, 143
Kuma/War (digital game), 61, 230–31
Kuwait War. *See* Gulf War

Latin America: in cultural products, 61, 86; historical background, 39, 73–74, 76; psy-ops, 134, 137
Law and Order (TV series), 198
Lebanon, 94–95
Lee, Ivy Ledbetter, 65–66
liberals. *See* progressives and liberals
Liberty Global, 106
Lippmann, Walter, 21–22, 48, 66–69
lobbyists: about, 46–47, 118–19, 239–40; civil society groups, 46–47, 118–19; and culture industries, 117–19; historical background, 165; myth of neutral government, 18–19. *See also* power elites
localized cultural products (glocalization), 74, 93, 114–15, 126–27, 239
Longest Day, The (film), 171–72
Lord of War (film), 200
Luce, Henry, 103–4
Luraschi, Luigi, 188–89
Lynch, Jessica, 150–51

MacKay, Peter, 226
Madden NFL 13, 4
magazine publishers. *See* publishing industry
Man of Steel (film), 4–5, 185
manufacture of consent, 66–67. *See also* engineering of consent
Marine Corps, US: and digital games industry, 208, 218, 230, 231; film censorship, 199; liaison office, 203;

recruitment, 4, 208, 217. *See also* military
Maze Wars (digital game), 205
McCann-Erickson, 92
McChesney, Robert W., 14, 245, 251
McLuhan, Marshall, 57
Medal of Honor (digital game), xii, 5, 223–28, 230
media conglomerates: about, 7, 10, 22–23, 55–56, 106–9, 239–40; and capitalism, 55–56, 128, 156–57, 247; CEO salaries, 107; and cultural imperialism, 20–22; economic power of, 3, 10, 55–56, 106–7, 109, 128; historical background, 55–56, 123; lobbying by, 46–47, 117–19; major corporations, 55, 106–7, 239; media consolidation, 121; and non-US industries, 109–13, 124, 128, 239–40; and public diplomacy, 101; regulation and privatization, 121, 123–26, 195; subsidies for, 57, 120–21, 145, 249–51; transnational cultural products, 25, 104, 113–14, 127–28, 239, 254; trends, 109, 157–58. *See also* culture industry; film/TV industry; news media
media conglomerates and DOD: about, 12–13, 156, 240–41; culture industry relations, 57–58; leadership by power elite, 106–7, 156–57, 195–96; and military-industrial-complex, 20, 23–24, 53–54, 257; and news downsizing, 157–58; ownership and editorial policy, 156–57; profit motive, 156–57, 257. *See also* censorship and coercion
Medved, Michael, 248
Mercenaries (digital games), 224–25, 235
Microsoft, 107–8, 109, 120, 239
Middle East: cultural exchanges, 94–95; in digital games, 235; US broadcasts into, 88, 93–94, 96. *See also specific countries*
Midway Games, 120

militainment products, 199–200, 240–41. *See also* cultural products; digital games; films; television shows
military: branding of, 213; Bush Doctrine, 42; comparative strength of, 54; experience centers, 217; and imperialist capitalism, 42; military-industrial-communications complex, 12, 24, 240, 257; military-industrial complex, 20, 23–24, 53–54, 257; rehabilitation after trauma, 228–29, 230; soft vs hard power of, 36–37; suicide prevention by, 228–29; training, 204–12, 218–22. *See also* Department of Defense (DOD); war; *and specific wars*
military, recruitment: branding of military, xii, 4; digital games, 206, 212–18, 243; DOD public affairs office, 56–57; draft, 166–67, 212; films initiated for, 187–88; historical background, 71, 166–67; human rights of children, 243; impact of *Top Gun*, 175–76; post-Cold War period, 176–77; race and class, 212–13, 217–18; virtual worlds, 6
military and culture industries. *See* censorship and coercion; digital games industry and DOD; film/TV industry and DOD; media conglomerates and DOD; news media and DOD
Miller, Judith, xii, 144
Missing in Action (film), 175
Modeling, Virtual Environments and Simulation Institute (MOVES), 207, 210, 211, 213, 243
Modern Warfare (digital game), 229
MOH. See *Medal of Honor* (digital game)
Moonves, Leslie, 107, 177
Moore, Michael, 196, 199
Motion Picture Association of America (MPAA), 11, 46–47, 116, 119, 125, 195–96
Motion Picture Production Office (MPPO), 170–73

motion pictures. *See* film/TV industry
MPAA. *See* Motion Picture Association of America (MPAA)
MPPO. *See* Motion Picture Production Office (MPPO)
MSNBC, 159
MTV Networks, 115. *See also* Viacom
Munro, Richard, 10
Murdoch, Rupert, 107, 157
MUSA Military Entertainment Consulting, 184–85
music industry, 4, 85–86, 117. *See also* media conglomerates
Muslim Life in America (OPD), 93
Muslims: and anti-Americanism, 95, 97–98; cultural exchanges, 94–96; digital games on, 221–22; portrayals of, 92–95, 180; US broadcasts abroad to, 93–94, 96; in War on Terror, 92–94

9/11 terrorist attacks. *See* September 11 terrorist attacks
1984 (film), 188
nation-states: branding of, 91–92, 95; BRICS nations, 51–54, 116, 237; and capitalism, 10; hierarchy of, 236–37; political economy approach, 13–17. *See also* Empire, US; non-US countries
National Association of Broadcasters (NAB), 116
national identity: and culture industry, 58–59, 129–30; and patriotism, 11–12; and war dissent, 157; and war support, 11–12, 160–61, 195–96, 198
national security: biological weapons, 256–57; and capitalism, 34; democratization of, 245–47; future threats portrayed in cultural products, 61–62; and imagination training, 61–63; and immigration, 256; as justification for undemocratic actions, 15; NSC's role in defining, 45; and public opinion, 139

National Security Council (NSC): about, 44–45, 79; direction of USIA, 81; historical background, 40, 79, 99, 134; psy-ops, 134; public diplomacy, 45, 79, 89, 99. *See also* president, US
NATO, 40, 43, 54, 62, 139, 226–27
Navy, US: films and TV shows, 5, 187–88; SEALS in digital games, 215–17, 222–23, 229. *See also* military
NBCUniversal, 3, 55, 106, 107, 110, 157, 158–59, 239
neoliberalism: and capitalist imperialism, 41–43; under Clinton, 87–88; and culture industry, 10, 126–27, 247; and democratization, 247; deregulation and privatization, 123–26; and telecom industry, 123–24
Netflix, 108
New World Information and Communication Order (NWICO), 125–26
New Zealand, 124
News Corporation, 3, 55, 106, 107, 110, 119, 195, 239, 247
news media: about, 131–33, 241; actual war vs media war, 131, 135–36, 161; advertising revenue of, 158–59; CNN-effect theory, 139; democratization of, 55, 132, 241–42, 251–52; downsizing of, 157–58; global media events, xi, 90, 104, 201–2; major corporations, 107; niche markets, 160; and non-US industries, 109–13; ownership and editorial policy, 156–57; public broadcasting, 23, 55, 124, 251–52; 24-hour 7-day cycle, 139–40, 141; watchdog role of, 131–32, 161–62, 241. *See also* journalists; media conglomerates; newspapers; radio; sourcing of news; television industry
news media and DOD: about, 131–33, 156, 161–62, 240–42; culture industry relations, 57–58; editorial policy, 157–59; historical background, 70–72, 76; information operations, 57–58, 141–43; in Vietnam War, 134–36, 139. *See also* censorship and coercion; information operations (IO); sourcing of news
news media and DOD strategies: about, 57–58, 156, 241; advertising, 71; cable TV channel, 241; embeds with troops, 146–49, 241; experts, 145–46; historical background, 70–71; hometown news services, 6–7; information centres, 149, 241; information operations, 57–58, 142–45; information war rooms, 139–40; news releases, 149–50, 152–53, 241; non-aligned journalists, 57, 154–56; pseudo-events, 150–51, 241; psy-ops, 133–34, 141; sourcing, defined, 12; war casualties, 57, 152–54. *See also* sourcing of news
newspapers: advertising, 116; downsizing of, 157–58; editorial independence, 76, 156–57; foreign news, 70–71, 157–58; media conglomeration, 121–22; Operation Iraqi Freedom, 148, 150–53, 157–59; in WWI, 70–71. *See also* news media; sourcing of news
Nigeria, 105
Night of the Dragon (film), 173
Nintendo, 207
Nixon, Richard, 83, 134, 135
non-commercial broadcasting, 23, 55, 124, 251–52
non-US countries: about, 128, 240; BRICS countries, 51–54, 116, 237; culture industries of, 22–23, 105–6, 109–13, 128–29; digital games, 109, 207, 218; exceptionalism, 49; film/TV industry, 105, 109–13, 127, 128–29; free flow doctrine, 23, 122–23, 124; media conglomerates,

109–10, 124, 128, 239–40; and neoliberalism, 42; power relations with US, 22–23; protection of culture, 23, 27, 59, 102, 125–29, 240, 249; relationships of US and non-US industries, 109–13; resistance to US Empire, 37–38; theory of cultural imperialism, 27; unequal cultural mixing, 128–29; US elitist view of non-US publics, 101; and US hegemony, 36–38. *See also* war

North Korea, 224

Norway massacre, 201–3

NSC. *See* National Security Council (NSC)

NWICO. *See* New World Information and Communication Order (NWICO)

Nye, Joseph, 16–17, 30, 36

Obama, Barack, 9, 30, 49; administration, xiv, 43–44, 98–100

OCIAA. *See* Office of the Coordinator of Inter-American Affairs (OCIAA)

Office of the Coordinator of Inter-American Affairs (OCIAA), 73, 76, 78

Office of Global Communications (OGC), 141

Office of International Information and Cultural Affairs, 78

Office of Public Diplomacy (OPD): about, 56–57, 91–100; branding campaign, 91–92, 95; focus on Muslims, 92–94; under G. Bush, 91–99; under Obama, 99–100; Shared Values campaign, 92–95

Office of Research and Media Reaction, 82

Office of Strategic Influence (OSI), 140–41

Office of War Information (OWI), 75–78, 85, 133, 167–69

online games. *See* digital games

OPD. *See* Office of Public Diplomacy (OPD)

Operation Enduring Freedom (film), 178

Operation Iraqi Freedom. *See* Iraq War (2003–)

Oracle, 108, 120

Orwell, George, 188

OSI. *See* Office of Strategic Influence (OSI)

OWI. *See* Office of War Information (OWI)

Pacific, The (TV series), 184

pacifism. *See* peace movements

Panitch, Leo, xiii

Paterson, Chris, 154, 156

patriotism. *See* national identity

Patton (film), 174

peace movements: censorship of, 166, 194, 199; and Cold War, 170–71; and Iraq War, x–xii, 144–45, 160; portrayals during war, 73, 78, 133, 158, 160, 166; power elites vs pacifists, 246; pro-military vs pacifist views, 73, 170–71, 194–95, 199, 242; and Vietnam War, 135–36

Pearl Harbor, attacks, 61, 75, 76, 171, 179

Pearl Harbor (film), 61, 179, 185

Pentagon, attacks. *See* September 11 terrorist attacks

Pentagon Channel, 149–50

Periscope (digital game), 205

Perry, Katy, 4

Persian Gulf War, 137–39, 207, 223

Platoon (film), 194–95

PlayStation, 3–4, 215, 217, 219, 220

political economy approach, 13–17. *See also* Schiller, Herbert I.

Pong (digital game), 205

post, telegraphy, and telecommunications (PTT) apparatus, 123

post–Cold War period: cultural exchanges, 88; culture industry, 104, 176–77; political economy

Index

approach to, 16–17; public diplomacy, 87–89
poverty. *See* social class; wealth inequality
Powell, Colin, xii, 91, 144, 154
power elites: about, 18–19, 48, 237–38; decision-making hierarchies, 43–48, 237–38; and democracy, 19, 48, 250–51; and exceptionalism, 48; historical background, 65–66; Lippmann's theory of public opinion, 21–22, 48, 66–68; lobbying by, 46–47, 117–19; in media conglomerates, 106–7, 156–57, 195–96; myth of neutral government, 18–19; and national security, 246–47; and neoliberalism, 42; wealth of, 53
praxis and political economy approach, 13–17
president, US: about, ix, 44–46; campaign finances, 47; democratization of, ix, 48, 245; public diplomacy, 101. *See also* Bush, George W.; Clinton, Bill; National Security Council (NSC); Obama, Barack; Reagan, Ronald
press. *See* news media; newspapers
Program Executive Office for Simulation, Training and Instrumentation (PEO STRI), 210, 243
progressives and liberals: as anti-imperialists, 245; and democratization, 245–47; myth of culture industry dominance, 180, 188, 196–97, 248–49
propaganda. *See* engineering of consent; psychological operations (PSY-OPS)
psychological operations (PSY-OPS): about, 58, 133–34, 141–43; black vs white propaganda, 140–41; CNN effect, 139; and culture industry, 140–41; in film/TV productions, 163–64; shift to information operations, 141–43. *See also* information operations (IO)
psychological operations (PSY-OPS), historical background: in Afghanistan and Iraq War, 139–41; the Cold War, 79, 81, 86, 134–37; the Gulf War, 137–39; the Vietnam War, 134–36, 139; WWI and WWII, 133. *See also* information operations (IO)
public broadcasting, 23, 55, 124, 251–52
public diplomacy abroad: about, 22, 100–2, 238–39; cultural sovereignty of non-US countries, 102; dissent from, 101, 238–39; and engineering of consent, 15, 239; ethnocentric views, 101–2; goals of, 90, 238–39; H. Clinton on, 15; nations as brands, 91–92, 95; public affairs agencies of DOD, 24, 56–58, 238, 240; shift to information operations, 141–43. *See also* engineering of consent; information operations (IO); Office of Public Diplomacy (OPD)
public diplomacy abroad, historical background: the Cold War, 78–87, 134–37; Obama's administration, 98–100; the post-Cold War period, 87–89; War on Terror, 89–98; WWI, 68–73; WWII, 73–78
public opinion: about, 59–60; CNN-effect theory, 139; elitist theory of, 21–22, 48; Lippmann's theories, 66–68; research in the Cold War, 82; research in the War on Terror, 95, 97–98
public relations at home: about, 56–57; defined, 67; and digital games industry, 222–28; and election campaigns, 98–99; major agencies, 107; theories of, 21–22, 66–68. *See also* engineering of consent
public relations at home, historical background: the Gulf War, 137–39; before WWI, 65–66; WWI, 68–73,

133, 165–66; the War on Terror, 97–98
publishing industry: in the Cold War, 84–85; future threats portrayed by, 62; globalization of, 84–85; lobbying by, 117; in Obama's administration, 99; OPD's focus on US Muslims, 93; subsidies for, 84–85, 120; in WWII, 76–77. *See also* media conglomerates

Quiet American, The (film), 198

racial issues: censorship in WWII, 78, 168; digital games, 221–22; film/TV industry, 86, 165, 180, 188–89; media conglomerates, 106–7; military recruitment, 212–13; power elites, 106–7
radio: BBG's promotion of, 7; in the Cold War, 85–86; deregulation and privatization of, 123–24; lobbying by, 117; in Obama's administration, 99; public broadcasters, 23, 55, 124, 251–52; Voice of America, 7, 76, 78, 85–86, 88, 99; in War on Terror, 94; in WWII, 74–76, 78. *See also* media conglomerates
Radio Free Europe/Radio Liberty, 7, 86, 88, 99
Radio Sawa, 94
Reagan, Ronald, 83, 123, 125, 136–37, 168–69, 197, 206
Real News, The, 241–42
Real War (digital games), 222
Rebuilding Afghanistan (film), xii
recording industry. *See* music industry
Recording Industry Association of America (RIAA), 117
recruitment, military. *See* military, recruitment
Redacted (film), 200
resistance to Empire. *See* anti-imperialists
Rice, Condoleezza, 97–98, 144, 256
Roosevelt, Franklin D., 39, 73–75
Rothkopf, David, 16, 48

Rove, Karl, 178, 180
Rumsfeld, Donald, xii, 58, 141–42, 144, 146, 154
Run Silent, Run Deep (film), 171
Russia: in digital games, 60, 61; economic rise of, 51–52, 237; film/TV industry, 105, 109, 117, 127, 242; ICT corporations, 109; military strength, 54; post-Cold War period, 88

Sahara (film), 168
Saludos Amigos (film), 74
Saving Jessica Lynch (film), 150–51
Saving Private Ryan (film), 176, 184, 193
Scahill, Jeremy, 245
Schiller, Dan, 27–28
Schiller, Herbert I., 17–29; anti-imperialism, 25–26; capitalism's impact on democracy, 19; cultural imperialism, 19–22; cultural products, 24–25; media conglomerates, 22–23; permanent war, 23–24; power elites, 18–19; PR campaigns, 21–22; theory of cultural imperialism, 26–29; US as post-colonial empire, 17–18
SEALS. *See* Navy, US
Searchers, The (film), 173
Second Life (virtual worlds), 6
Second World War: about, 78; censorship and coercion, 75–78, 167–69; culture industry, 103, 122; digital games, xii, 223–24; films/TV series, 77–78, 166–69, 171–74, 176, 179; historical background, 39–40, 73–78; interwar years, 73–74, 166; news, 75, 84; public relations (OCIAA), 73–75, 78; public relations (OWI), 75–78, 85, 133, 167–69; publishing industry, 76–77; radio, 74–76; recruitment and draft, 166–67; rejection of territorial imperialism, 35; time between actual war vs reel war, 178–79
Sega, 207

September 11 terrorist attacks: about, 89–90, 143–44; discourse after, 31–32; in films and TV series, 61, 192–93, 198; impact on digital games industry, 222–23; impact on film/TV industry, 177–80, 198, 200. *See also* Afghanistan, US invasion; Iraq War (2003–); War on Terror (2001–9)
Sesame Street (TV series), 93
Sex and the City (TV series), 198
Shane (film), 173
Siege, The (film), 61, 176
SIMnet, 206–7, 215
Simulation and Training Technology Center (STTC), 210, 243
Since You Went Away (film), 168
Six Days in Fallujah (digital game), 230
social class: censorship in WWII, 168; and military recruitment, 212–13, 217–18; Schiller on, 18–19; wealth inequality, 65, 250, 256. *See also* power elites
social media, 6, 100, 108, 118, 120
SOCOM franchise (digital games), 215–17, 229
software industry. *See* information and communications technology (ICT) industry
Sony, 5, 109, 127, 195, 207, 215, 216–17, 221
sourcing of news: about, 6–7, 12, 241; in the Cold War, 84, 136–37; defined, 12; dissenting voices, 160; DOD's public affairs office, 56–57; and downsizing of news media, 157–58; economic incentives, 149–50; embedded vs non-embedded journalists, 146–49; experts, 145–46; in the Gulf War, 137–38; information centres, 149; information operations, 141–43; in the Iraq War, 6–7, 142, 145–51, 156–61; news releases, 149–50; and professionalism, 159–60. *See also* news media and DOD strategies

South Africa, 51–52, 237
Soviet Union, 40–41, 49, 51. *See also* Cold War (1946–91); Russia
SpaceWar! (digital game), 204–5
Spanish-American War, 164–65
Sparks, Colin, 19–21, 28, 54
speakers' programs: censorship of, 75; in Obama's administration, 99; in wartime, 69–70, 75
special interest groups, US, 46–47. *See also* civil society and special interest groups; lobbyists
Special Ops (digital game), 235
Spider-Man (films), 113–14, 127
Spirit of America, The (film), 178
Stalingrad (film), 105
Stars Earn Stripes (TV show), 5
the state. *See* nation-states
State Department. *See* Department of State
Sudan, 60
Swofford, Anthony, 174

24 (TV series), xii, 163, 180, 190
Take-Two Interactive, 109
Tears of the Sun (film), xii
technology industry. *See* information and communications technology (ICT) industry
technology industry and games. *See* digital games industry
telecommunications industry, 123–26. *See also* media conglomerates
television industry: coverage of Iraq War, 159–60; coverage of Vietnam War, 135–36; deregulation and privatization, 123–24; economic power of, 3, 127–28; lobbying by, 117; portrayals of Muslims, 180; public broadcasters, 23, 55, 124, 251–52; US broadcasts into Muslim countries, 96. *See also* film/TV industry; media conglomerates; news media
television shows: glocalization of, 93, 114–15; markets, 3, 127–28;

military reality shows, 5; OPD shows on US Muslims, 92–93; pirated shows, 4; transnational shows, 25, 114–15, 127–28, 239; and War on Terror, 92–93
terrorism: digital games industry, 203, 222–25; in film/TV productions, xii, 163–64, 176–77; Norway massacre, 201–3; as permanent threat, 230–31, 234; post-Cold War period, 176–77. *See also* September 11 terrorist attacks; War on Terror (2001–9)
Thin Red Line, The (film), 195
Third World War in digital games, 61, 230
This Is the Army (film), 168–69
This War of Mine (digital game), 235
Thompson, Mike, 232
Three Caballeros, The (film), 74
Three Days of the Condor (film), 190
Time Warner, 10, 107, 110, 119, 120–21, 195–96, 253–57
Tio, Federico, 254
Tom Clancy franchise (digital game), 203, 218, 224
Top Gun (film), 175–76
Top Model (TV), 114
trade relations: about, 122–26; BRICS agreements, 51–52; under Clinton administration, 87–88; copyright protection, 118–20; free flow doctrine, 23, 122–23, 124; historical background, 40, 41, 122–23; international organizations, 41, 124–25, 240; interwar years, 166; neoliberalism, 124–25; regulation of commerce, 121; US dominance in cultural industries, 127–28
Transformers (films), 4, 104, 113–14, 179, 185–87
transnational corporations. *See* media conglomerates
transnational cultural products, 25, 104, 113–14, 127–28, 239, 254. *See also* cultural products
Truman, Harry S., 79–81

Tutwiler, Margaret, 95–97
TV. *See* film/TV industry; television industry
Twitter, 6, 100, 120

U-571 (film), 176
Uncommon Valor (film), 175
Under Siege (film), 176
United 93 (film), 179
United Kingdom: digital games, 202, 226; exceptionalism, 49; film/TV industry, 127, 188; media industry, 109, 123, 126; neoliberalism, 123
United Nations: free flow ideal, 122; historical background, 39–40; UNESCO and cultural diversity, 125–26
University of Southern California, ICT. *See* Institute for Creative Technologies (ICT)
UrbanSim (digital game), 219
USIA (US Information Agency), 81–87, 99, 134

Valenti, Jack, 119, 173, 195–96
Venezuela, digital war games, 235
Verizon, 108, 120
Viacom, 3, 106, 107, 110, 115, 239
Victors, The (film), 194
video games. *See* digital games
video-sharing websites, and DOD, 6
Vietnam War: actual war vs media war, 135–36, 174–75; anti-war views, 135–36, 174; censorship and coercion, 134–35, 173–74; digital games, 224; film/TV industry, 86, 173–75, 194–95; media coverage, 135–36, 139; psy-ops, 134–35, 139
Virtual Iraq (digital game), 228–29
Viy 3D (film), 127
Voice of America (VOA), 7, 76, 78, 85–86, 88, 99
voters. *See* elections, US

Walt Disney Company, The, 74, 107, 110, 117, 119, 168, 178, 252–57

war: about, 11–12, 23–24, 36–37, 131–32; anti-war views, 135–36, 174, 235; Bush Doctrine, 42; child soldiers, 60; Darfur genocide, 60; and exceptionalism, 51; as first solution to problems, 11–12; as fun, 220–21, 234, 243; as glamorous, 138, 174–75; historical background, 36–37; military-industrial complex, 20, 23–24, 53–54, 257; as normal way of life, 132, 138; as permanent state, 23, 36–37, 50–51, 60, 230–31, 234; powers of Congress under Constitution, 45–46; universalization of threats, 50–51; and US Empire, 36–37; veterans, 174, 228–29. *See also specific wars*
war and culture industry: about, 11–13, 23–24, 57–58; actual war vs media war, 131, 135–36, 161, 174–75, 180, 187, 203, 230, 234–35; aestheticization of war in film, 187, 199–200; digital games, 60, 203, 243; DOD's liaison offices, 57; film allegories of, 179; future threats portrayed by, 61–62; McLuhan's hot vs cold wars, 57; mediascapes, 60–62; militainment products, 199–200, 240–41; pro-military vs pacifist views, 73, 170–71, 194–95, 199, 242; public opinion on war, 59–60; time between actual war vs reel war, 178–79
War Hunt (film), 194
War Lover, The (film), 194
War on Terror (2001–9): about, 42, 89–90; anti-Americanism, 90–91; branding of, xii; Bush Doctrine, 42, 90; Bush's administration, ix, 90, 139–40, 177–79, 180; cultural exchanges, 94–96; digital games, 203, 222–23; digital games industry, 209; engineering of consent, 16–17, 90, 139–41; film/TV industry, 177–80, 195–96; in films and TV series, 200; information operations, 141–43; Obama's administration, 43–44, 98–102; public diplomacy, 89–102; US broadcasts into Muslim countries, 93–94, 96. *See also* Afghanistan, US invasion; Iraq War (2003–)
Warner Brothers, 5, 77, 107, 166–67, 168, 177, 255
Warriors, Inc., 184
Wayne, John, 173, 188
wealth inequality, 19, 65, 250, 256. *See also* social class
weapons industry, 5, 23–24. *See also* war
Welcome (media campaign), 252–57
Why Vietnam? (DOD film), 173
Why We Fight (film series), 168, 169
Wilkinson, Jim, 139–40, 150–51
Wilson, Woodrow, 39, 68–69, 165
Windtalkers (film), 185, 199
Wings (film), 166
wireless communications, 84, 88
World Bank, 40, 41, 125
World Trade Center, attacks, 92, 179, 192, 198. *See also* September 11 terrorist attacks
World Trade Center (film), 179
World Trade Organization (WTO), 41, 124–25, 240
World War I. *See* First World War
World War II. *See* Second World War
World War Z (film), 62
World of Warcraft (digital game), 207

Yahoo, 120, 229
Yes Men, The, 243
YouTube, 6

Zabel, Bryce, 177
Zanuck, Darryl, 171–72, 188
Zero Dark Thirty (film), 163, 192–93
Zipper Interactive, 215–17
ZunZuneo (social media), 6
Zyda, Michael, 207–9

Printed and bound in Canada by Friesens

Set in Futura Condensed and Warnock by Apex CoVantage, LLC

Copy editor: Stephanie VanderMeulen

Proofreader: Dallas Harrison

Indexer: Judy Dunlop